WAR IN PEACETIME

THE HISTORY AND LESSONS OF KOREA

DS918
C62

WAR IN PEACETIME

THE HISTORY AND LESSONS OF KOREA

BY J. LAWTON COLLINS

ILLUSTRATED WITH
PHOTOGRAPHS AND MAPS

1969

HOUGHTON MIFFLIN COMPANY BOSTON

JUN 10 1970

151608

THE MAPS FOR THIS BOOK
WERE DRAWN BY THEODORE R. MILLER
FROM SKETCHES BY B. C. MOSSMAN

First Printing c

Copyright © 1969 by J. Lawton Collins

*All rights reserved. No part of this work may be
reproduced or transmitted in any form by any means,
electronic or mechanical, including photocopying and record-
ing, or by any information storage or retrieval system,
without permission in writing from the publisher.*

Library of Congress Catalog Card Number: 69–15008
Printed in the United States of America

TO THE GALLANT MEN OF ALL NATIONS

WHO FOUGHT IN KOREA UNDER

THE UNITED NATIONS COMMAND

PREFACE

THE KOREAN WAR was the first large-scale war in American history that began and ended without a declaration of war by the Congress of the United States. It was also the first, and possibly will be the last war to be fought under the aegis of the United Nations. It had far more than the normal complement of political, military, economic and social problems that mark any international conflict.

I was the Chief of Staff of the United States Army and a member of the Joint Chiefs of Staff, the senior military advisory body to the President and the Secretary of Defense, throughout the Korean war. In addition, as Executive Agent for the JCS, I had the responsibility of transmitting instructions from the Joint Chiefs to the United Nations Command, monitoring reports to and from the U.N. Command, and initiating appropriate recommendations for JCS studies or actions. In order to have firsthand evaluations of the combat situation during critical periods, I made a number of trips to Japan and Korea for consultations with General MacArthur and his successors and visited commanders of the United States Eighth Army and the Korean army in the field.

In carrying out these duties I often found myself in the center of conflicting political-military considerations which influenced the JCS in its recommendations to the Secretary of Defense and the President. It is important to note that the Joint Chiefs made *recommendations,* not decisions, though their recommendations properly carried considerable weight with the President, and with the Secretaries of State and Defense and the National Security Council who constitute the principal overall advisers to the President on the conduct of war.

A number of books have been written about the Korean war, but none by a member of the JCS as then constituted, of which the Chairman, General of the Army Omar N. Bradley, and I are the only members still living who served with the Chiefs throughout the war. While I have no mandate to speak for the other Chiefs, I feel a certain obligation to present the story of the unique Korean struggle primarily from the viewpoint of the Joint Chiefs of Staff. I have done this solely on my own responsibility.

I have relied extensively for the essential narrative on the excellent official histories prepared under the direction of Brigadier General Hal C. Pattison, Chief of Military History, Department of the Army, and his Chief Historian, Dr. Stetson Conn, by Roy E. Appleman, James F. Schnabel, Dr. W. G. Hermes, and B. C. Mossman. I am grateful also to my old friend, Rear Admiral Ernest M. Eller, U.S. Navy, Director of Naval History; to the members of the U.S. Marine Corps who prepared the history, *U.S. Marine Operations in Korea, 1950–53;* to James A. Field, Jr. for his *History of United States Naval Operations in Korea;* and to Robert F. Futrell for his *United States Air Forces in Korea.*

I am especially indebted to Thomas C. Hohman, Lois Aldridge, and Hazel Ward of the World War II Division, National Archives and Records Service; to Dr. R. A. Winnacker, Paul N. Kearney, and Richard R. Day of the Defense Department; to Evelyn Robinson of the Army Library, and to Donna H. Traxler of the U.S. Army Photographic Agency for their invaluable documentary research assistance; to my long-time friend and associate, General Charles L. Bolté, who carefully proofread the manuscript; to my former secretary Betty Covert, who expertly transcribed my longhand manuscript into finished type; and to B. C. Mossman who prepared the base maps.

Finally, I am happy to acknowledge my constant gratitude to my wife, Gladys Easterbrook Collins, whose encouragement, sound judgment, and wise counsel contributed greatly to the writing of this book.

J. LAWTON COLLINS

CONTENTS

ILLUSTRATIONS

(following page 128)

U.S. Joint Chiefs of Staff at beginning of Korean war

A South Korean soldier relaxes on a hillside overlooking railroad yards in Pusan, Korea

General Collins presents the United Nations flag to General MacArthur atop MacArthur's headquarters in Tokyo

General Collins talks with wounded Corporal Ralph E. Hargrove

Korean refugees moving along the road to Taegu

Korean refugees jamming aboard trains at a railroad station

Korean refugees preparing to board a vessel for evacuation from the fighting area north of Pusan

Major General O. P. Smith, USMC, confers with Vice Admiral J. H. Doyle, USN, aboard the USS *Rochester* prior to Inchon invasion. *Official U.S. Navy Photograph*

U.S. Marines approaching Blue Beach, Inchon

One bulldozer pulls another along the muddy shore of Walmido as equipment is unloaded from LST's

Men of the 5th Regiment, 1st Cavalry Division, use a shallow boat to cross the Naktong River west of Taegu

Aerial view of the Chosin Reservoir area

Major General Edward H. Almond, Commanding General X Corps, and Vice Admiral Arthur D. Struble, Commander Seventh Fleet, converse aboard the U.S. battleship *Missouri*

Korean refugees crowded aboard fishing boats to evacuate Hungnam. *Official U.S. Navy Photograph.*

Men of the 8th Cavalry Regiment, 1st Cavalry Division, supported by tanks, move up to assault positions in North Korea

A Korean carries his aged father across the icy Han River southeast of Seoul in their flight south

(following page 272)

Secretary of the Army Frank Pace, Jr., and General Collins present the first Korean service ribbons to three wounded veterans

Men of the 187th Airborne Regimental Combat Team, U.S. Eighth Army, charge over the top of Hill 299, through Chinese Communist fire

Members of the 1st Battalion, 24th Infantry Regiment, 25th Division, trudge up the rocky mountainside ten miles south of Chorwon

Helicopter pilot prepares to take off for the 1st Mobile Army Surgical Hospital, Korea, with a wounded man

Paratroopers of the 187th Airborne Regimental Combat Team float earthward from C-119 planes to cut off retreating Communist units, south of Munsan

Tanks of the 72d Tank Battalion attached to the 2d U.S. Infantry Division move into position to support infantry of the ROK 8th Division in the Central Highlands, North Korea

Admiral Forrest P. Sherman, Chief of Naval Operations, and Lieutenant General Edward H. Almond, Commanding General U.S. X Corps, prepare to leave Corps airstrip to visit 1st Marine Division in Korea

Pfc. Robert V. Lombardi and Pfc. Floyd R. Turberville, Company M, 23d Regiment, U.S. 2d Infantry Division, fire their mortar at Chinese Communist positions on Heartbreak Ridge

General Collins stands with other Army generals after his arrival at the X Corps airstrip to begin an inspection tour of the Corps area

Chief of Naval Operations Admiral William M. Fechteler, escorted by Captain W. R. Smedberg III, inspecting United States Marines aboard the USS *Iowa. Courtesy Commander Frank A. McQuade, USNRR*

Riflemen of Company L, 21st Regiment, 24th U.S. Infantry Division, return to their bunkers along the reverse slope of the ridge line commanding the heights of Kumsong

Major General William K. Harrison attends a meeting of the Military

Armistice Commission at the United Nations base camp, Munsan-ni. *Signal Corps Photograph*

Chinese Communist forces in one of the thirty compounds of the United Nations prisoner of war camp on Kojo-do

Major General William F. Dean, after being presented Korea's highest award, the Taeguk Medal with Gold Star, by President Syngman Rhee. Looking on is General Mark W. Clark, Commander-in-Chief, U.N. Command

(Unless otherwise credited the photographs are reproduced through the courtesy of the U.S. Army)

MAPS

WAR IN PEACETIME

THE HISTORY AND LESSONS OF KOREA

I

THE DIE IS CAST

INSISTENT POUNDING on the door of our cottage on the Chesapeake Bay woke us from a sound sleep. My wife Gladys and I had driven from our quarters at Fort Lesley J. McNair in Washington on Friday for a weekend rest. Now the sun was barely over the rim of the broad bay, and I wondered what could be so urgent on such a bright Sunday morning. It was Sergeant Ed Davis, my trusted driver, with the startling news: "General, the North Koreans have attacked, and you have to get to the Pentagon as fast as you can." The date was June 25, 1950.

We had built the cottage six months earlier, shortly after I had become Army Chief of Staff. Realizing that in this new position we would be subjected to a busy schedule, both social and official, Gladys had wisely urged that we find a haven to which we could escape occasionally from the fascinating, but tiring, cocktail-dinner circuit of Washington.

We finally found an ideal spot at Scientists' Cliffs in near-by Maryland, where among unspoiled woods of holly, dogwood, and towering tulip poplars on the cliffs of Calvert County we built our cottage directly above a sandy beach. One of our daughters named the retreat "Jayhawk Rest" after the telephone code call, "Jayhawk Forward," of my VII Corps command post in Europe. Here on weekends we busied ourselves planting shrubs and a lawn, fishing, and collecting ancient sea shells and shark teeth that washed down from marine deposits of the Miocene era, which can still be seen clearly high up on the cliffs above the present level of the bay.

The Korean war, to which we awoke so abruptly that Sunday morning, was to interrupt the frequency and peacefulness of our visits to the Chesapeake during the trying three years that followed.

Gladys was up at Sergeant Davis's report, and by the time I was dressed she had a pot of coffee ready for me. In a few minutes Sergeant Davis and I were on our way, leaving Gladys to close up the cottage.

As we whirred north through the rolling tobacco fields of Maryland, my mind went back to another Sunday morning, when I had heard over the radio word of the Japanese attack on Pearl Harbor. I was serving then in Birmingham, Alabama, as Chief of Staff to Major General Robert C. Richardson, Jr., commander of the VII Corps, United States Army, which was supervising the training of three National Guard divisions. Three days after the Japanese attack VII Corps Headquarters was ordered to California to organize the defenses of that state against possible submarine attack. I had kissed my wife and three children good-bye and promised to find a new home and school in California, and then I did not see the family again for a period of two years, during which I served in Hawaii and in the South Pacific against the Japanese. After a brief visit home at Christmas of 1943 I was switched to the European theater, where I rejoined the VII Corps, this time as its commander, for the Normandy invasion and the drive across Europe to a meeting with the Russians on the Elbe fifty miles from Berlin.

Back in Washington after the war, I had served as Chief of Staff of the Army Field Forces, Army Chief of Information, Deputy Chief of Staff to General Eisenhower, and Vice Chief to General Bradley before succeeding Bradley, on October 1, 1949, as Chief of Staff of the United States Army.

When the Japanese bombed Pearl Harbor on December 7, 1941, I was outraged, as were all Americans, and shocked at the dreadful loss of American lives. At the same time I had a sense of relief that at last we would be doing our part in a war from which I had felt we could not escape and for which we had been preparing for more than a year. I was convinced also that with this stupid attack the German-Japanese alliance was doomed to defeat. My reactions now to the attack from North Korea were far more sober and uncertain.

I had followed closely the United States' military actions in the Pacific leading to the Japanese offer to surrender on August 10, 1945, within a few days after the atomic attack on Hiroshima, but I knew nothing of the Yalta agreements, which offered territorial concessions to Russia in return for her promise to enter the war against Japan after Germany's defeat. When the Russians finally declared war on August 8, 1945, I had commented to my wife that the war with Japan would be over in a week.* The Russians had moved promptly to stake out a claim to the spoils of war by attacking Japanese forces in Manchuria and Korea and had received the surrender of most of those forces. The terms of surrender, supplemented by later agreements, had provided for joint Allied occupation of Korea, to be followed at an indefinite later date by independence. The 38th Parallel had been established as the southern boundary of the Russian zone of occupation (Map 1). The Russians had quickly sealed off this boundary, cutting interzonal communications and establishing military posts armed with machine guns, covering all approaches from the south. During the next five years they had thwarted repeated efforts of the United States and the United Nations to create a unified and independent Korea, which had been pledged by Roosevelt, Churchill, and Chiang Kai-shek in the Cairo Declaration of November, 1943, and agreed to by Stalin at Teheran, November 28–December 1.

Now, on June 25, 1950, the North Korean Army, which the Russians had trained and equipped for just such an offensive operation, was attacking South Korea in flagrant violation of the Cairo Declaration. It was not clear at the time, but this attack was

---

* While stationed in the Philippine Islands from 1933 to 1936 I had traveled fairly extensively in Japan. Then, as an instructor at the Army War College just prior to World War II, I had monitored the student studies of a possible war with Japan. I knew Japan's vulnerability to aerial bombing and sea blockade. Even before the Hiroshima bombing I was convinced that, once the Germans had been defeated, we could concentrate our tremendous sea and air power against Japan and force her surrender without an invasion and without any help from Russia. I had made this prediction to Alexander P. de Seversky, when the famous advocate of air power visited my VII Corps command post near Aachen in World War II.

to prove to be one of the first in a series of "wars of liberation." This one was designed to unite Korea, not as an independent nation, but as a satellite of the Soviet Union.

Before leaving our cottage that morning, as I had hurriedly downed my coffee, Gladys, evidently thinking back to Pearl Harbor, had asked quietly, "Does this again mean war?" I could not say.

This time, unlike 1941, the United States was not being attacked directly; we had no troops under fire in Korea and no commitment to come to the aid of South Korea in the event of attack. Nonetheless, I felt certain that we would not stand idly by in the face of this naked aggression against a country we had helped to liberate in World War II from Japanese domination.

As Sergeant Davis and I rolled on toward Washington, I thought how fortunate it was for us that the Soviets had picked for this venture the one area in the world where the United States military forces of all arms were well positioned if we should decide to intervene. We had in Korea only a training mission, the Korean military Advisory Group, advisory to the newly created army of the Republic of Korea, but in near-by Japan our Eighth Army, on occupation duty, had four infantry divisions, with eighteen fighter squadrons, a light-bomber wing, and a troop-carrier wing of the Air Force available for support. Our Navy ships in the Far East consisted of one cruiser, four destroyers, and a number of amphibious and cargo vessels. We had also in the western Pacific the more powerful Seventh Fleet, including the aircraft carrier *Valley Forge*, a heavy cruiser, and a number of destroyers, submarines, and auxiliary vessels. All these forces except the Seventh Fleet were under command of General Douglas MacArthur, Commander in Chief, Far East, with headquarters in Tokyo. Nowhere else abroad did we have such forces of all arms immediately available for employment.

One week after I had become Chief of Staff of the United States Army, in October of 1949, I had flown out to Japan to pay my respects to General MacArthur and to inspect the troops of the Eighth Army. Prior to my visit none of the Joint Chiefs of Staff (JCS) (that is, the chiefs of the Army, Navy, and Air Force) who are the principal military advisers to the President and the Secretary of Defense had visited General MacArthur's headquarters since General Eisenhower's trip in 1946. I had sensed that General MacArthur, still provoked by the relatively greater importance given the European theater than the Pacific area, might be somewhat put out by this seeming slight.*

As a young captain after the First World War I had been an instructor at the United States Military Academy at West Point during part of the time that General MacArthur was Superintendent. The general maintained an aloof position then, and we junior officers saw little of him. Later, in 1935, when he went to the Philippines as Military Adviser to President Manuel Quezon, I was stationed there as the Operations Officer of the U.S. Army's Philippine Division. Even then I had few direct contacts with him but did have frequent dealings with Colonel Dwight D. Eisenhower, who was a member of his staff.

My only other previous association with General MacArthur was even more vicarious. During my Christmas visit home from the South Pacific in 1943 I called on General George C. Marshall, the Army Chief of Staff. Some years before I had served under General Marshall as an instructor at the Infantry School and on the Secretariat of his War Department staff. When, in 1943, I saw the general in his office, he had just returned from a trip to MacArthur's command in the Southwest Pacific. He told me that while talking to MacArthur in Australia he had mentioned that he was considering me for command of a corps. He went on to say, with a rare twinkle in his eyes, that MacArthur had replied, "But Collins is too young!"

It was only a few days later that General Eisenhower informed me I would command the VII Corps for the Normandy invasion.

On the occasion of my visit to Tokyo General MacArthur received me most cordially, emphasizing his welcome with a magnificent military review in my honor on the broad parade grounds in

* My sensing of General MacArthur's feelings was confirmed by Senator H. Alexander Smith in a statement at the Congressional inquiry following the relief of MacArthur which became known as the MacArthur Hearings (page 1033 of the Hearings report).

front of the Japanese Emperor's palace. At the reviewing stand
I saw Senator H. Alexander Smith, a member of the Senate Armed
Services Committee, sitting there with other guests. I promptly
invited him to take the review with me; thereby, on impulse, gaining a firm friend.

In my subsequent inspection visits to the troops it was evident
that the recent emphasis on training, inaugurated by General
Walton H. Walker, the commander of the Eighth Army in Japan,
had reached only the battalion level and had not overcome the
inevitable slackness that results from occupation duty. On my
return to Washington I had reported to Secretary of the Army
Frank Pace that given time, deficiencies in combat readiness could
be corrected. Now it appeared there would not be time.

*

After establishment of the Department of Defense (DOD) in
1947, the Secretary of Defense approved continuation of the
practice of designating one of the Chiefs of Staff, Army, Navy or
Air Force, as Executive Agent for the JCS for each potential
theater of operations around the world. I, as Army Chief of Staff,
was Executive Agent for the JCS for military operations in the
Far East, including Korea. While no formal instructions were
issued charging the Department of the Army with responsibility
for administrative support of the Far East theater, this was *de
facto* the case. Under the Army Organization Act of 1950, the
sole authority within the Department of the Army for such
matters resides in the Secretary of the Army. This allocation of
responsibilities between the Secretary for administrative support
and the Chief of Staff for military operations under the Joint
Chiefs of Staff called for more than mere cooperation between
the Secretary and his Chief of Staff. It demanded full understanding, mutual confidence and respect. I was fortunate during
the Korean war in having just such a relationship with our fine
Secretary, Frank Pace, Jr.

Before succeeding General Omar N. Bradley as Chief of Staff
I had served as his Deputy. The increasing commitments of the
Army abroad were forcing him to devote an ever-increasing part of

his attention to the JCS, leaving little time for his responsibilities to the Secretary of the Army in the daily management of the military aspects of the service. The Chief needed additional top assistants, and under instructions from him I studied the organization of the upper echelons of the General Staff. Bradley and the Secretary approved my recommendations for the establishment of the offices of a Vice Chief of Staff and two Deputy Chiefs, one for Operations and Administration and the other for Plans. These were later approved by the Congress. I became the alter ego of the Chief, working closely with the Secretary in the day-in and day-out business of the army, and, in the absence of the Chief, representing him on the JCS.

I continued this organization after I succeeded Bradley. For my Vice Chief I chose General Wade H. Haislip, an exceptionally able executive, with whom I had served in Germany after World War I. He was a tower of strength to me during most of the Korean war, freeing me to make numerous trips of inspection to the Far Eastern and European theaters, for both of which I was Executive Agent. When Ham Haislip retired on July 1, 1951, another outstanding officer, General John E. Hull, was picked to succeed him. The two Deputies also were exceptional men: General Matthew B. Ridgway, for Operations and Administration, and General Alfred M. Gruenther, for Plans. They were later succeeded by Generals Maxwell D. Taylor and Charles L. Bolté, both top-flight. With such able assistants my tasks as Chief were greatly lightened.

In addition to the Deputy Chiefs of Staff, the longstanding organization of the General Staff of the Army, which I did not change, provided four Assistant Chiefs of Staff, each in charge of a major sphere of staff responsibility. Their official designation was as follows:

> Assistant Chief of Staff, Operations, G-1
> Assistant Chief of Staff, Intelligence, G-2
> Assistant Chief of Staff, Operations, G-3
> Assistant Chief of Staff, Logistics, G-4

For the sake of brevity they were frequently referred to simply

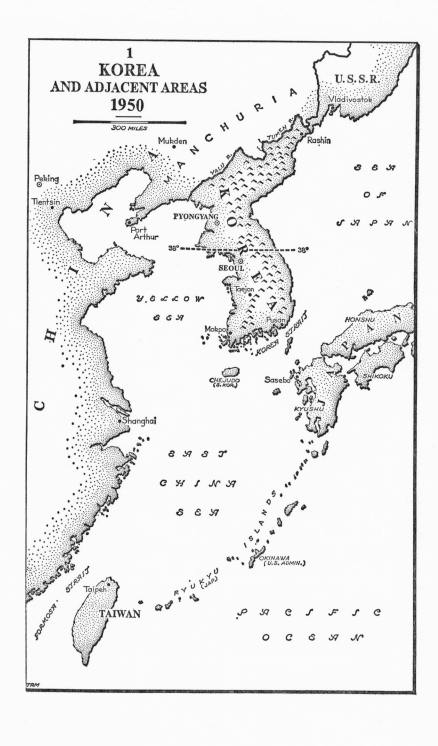

1
KOREA
AND ADJACENT AREAS
1950

300 MILES

MANCHURIA

U.S.S.R.

Vladivostok

Mukden

Rashin

Peking

Tientsin

Port
Arthur

PYONGYANG

38°   38°

SEOUL

Taejon

YELLOW
SEA

Mokpo

Pusan

SEA

OF

JAPAN

HONSHU

KOREA STRAIT

CHEJUDO
(S. KOR.)

Sasebo

KYUSHU

SHIKOKU

JAPAN

Shanghai

EAST

CHINA

SEA

ISLANDS

OKINAWA
(U.S. ADMIN.)

CHINA

FORMOSA STRAIT

Taipeh

TAIWAN

RYUKYU
(JAP.)

PACIFIC

OCEAN

TRM

by their G designations. G-3 actually was responsible for the preparation of plans for operations, and the monitoring of their execution.

＊

On this Sunday morning, as Sergeant Davis and I neared Washington, I realized that I would need all the help the staff could muster. I had run over in my mind the various steps that should be initiated at once, if they had not already been taken by the army staff and the joint staff of the JCS. No time was left for further thought as Sergeant Davis wheeled the car across the 14th Street bridge over the Potomac and on to the Pentagon.

There I learned that the first official word of the attack had been received from the Army Military Attaché in Seoul at 9:25 P.M. the night before. The attack had been launched almost nine hours earlier, at 4:00 A.M., Sunday, June 25, Korean time (Korean time is fifteen hours ahead of Washington Daylight Saving Time). (See Maps 1 and 2.)

Messages flooded in thereafter. Army duty officers had notified appropriate senior staff members, the other services, and the State Department, which had just received a cable from the U.S. Ambassador to Korea, John J. Muccio. Secretary Pace happened to be with Assistant Secretary of State Dean Rusk when the State Department called Rusk to inform him of the attack. Pace accompanied Rusk to the State Department at once and later went to his office in the Pentagon. My competent staff apparently decided that they could handle all preliminary actions without bothering me and probably figured, correctly, that I would soon need all the sleep I could get. A special map room and message center had been established, and a teletype conference with Major General Charles A. Willoughby, MacArthur's Intelligence Officer, G-2, had provided further information confirming the scale of the North Korean attack.

Secretary of State Dean Acheson had telephoned President Truman Saturday night at the President's home in Independence, Missouri. They had agreed to request an emergency meeting of

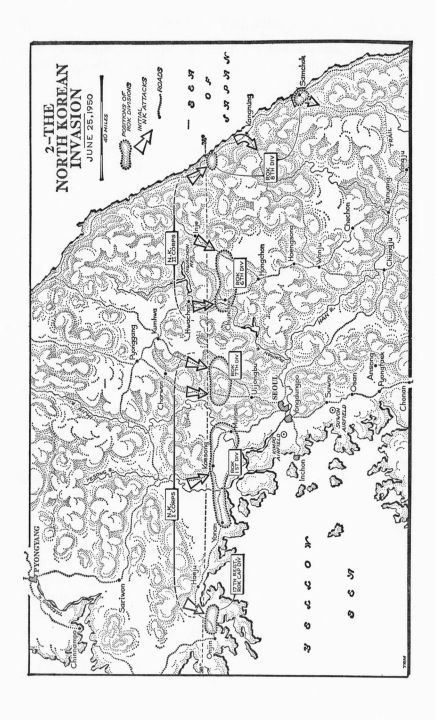

2—THE
NORTH KOREAN
INVASION
JUNE 25, 1950

40 MILES

POSITIONS OF
ROK DIVISIONS

INITIAL
NK ATTACKS

ROADS

the U.N. Security Council to consider the threat to peace. This request was made near midnight. Acheson called the President again on Sunday morning, bringing him up to date on the worsening situation. The President said he would return at once to Washington and requested Acheson to develop in conjunction with the service Secretaries and the JCS some plans for his consideration on arrival. En route by air the President radioed Secretary Acheson to arrange a dinner conference that evening with his principal advisers from the State and Defense Departments.

Before noon on Sunday staff representatives of the two departments met at the State Department to finish arrangements for the emergency meeting of the United Nations Security Council and to develop tentative courses of action for consideration by the President. Secretary Pace and I joined this group after the discussion had started.

Secretary of Defense Louis A. Johnson and General Omar N. Bradley, then Chairman of the JCS, had returned only the night before from the Far East, where they had had a number of conferences with General MacArthur and his staff. Secretary Johnson stated later that they had received no intimation of an imminent attack by the North Koreans. Johnson had been advised of the reported attack shortly before midnight on Saturday, but on Sunday morning he and Bradley had decided to meet a long-standing commitment to participate in a military conference at Norfolk, only an hour's flight from Washington. They returned later in the day but too late for the staff meeting at the State Department.

The available records at present are insufficient and do not make clear everything that transpired at this staff meeting. It was agreed that General MacArthur's headquarters should be advised of certain possible courses of action. These included the shipment of supplies and equipment to the army of the Republic of Korea — which, in fact, MacArthur had already initiated — and the possibility of assigning to MacArthur operational control of all United States military activities in Korea. The latter would include action by sea and air forces to ensure safe evacuation of

American nationals via ports and airfields in the Seoul-Kimpo-Inchon area. If the United Nations should call on member countries to intervene in Korea, MacArthur would be prepared to use elements of his forces and the Seventh Fleet, which would be made available to him, to stabilize the situation and, if possible, to re-establish the 38th Parallel boundary.

These tentative plans were transmitted in the afternoon by army telecon (teleconference) to MacArthur's Chief of Staff, Major General Edward M. Almond, and his G-2, General Willoughby.

While these matters were being cleared, I reviewed with my Assistant Chief of Staff for Operations, G-3, General Bolté, the existing instructions and documents applicable to the Korean situation. These included the missions assigned General Mac-Arthur as Commander in Chief, Far East, which, after the withdrawal of the United States occupation forces in June, 1949, excluded any direct responsibility for Korea except logistical support of the U.S. Embassy and of the training mission, the Korean Military Advisory Group. We received also the duties of the latter, the military-aid agreement with the Republic of Korea, and the strength and dispositions of United States and Soviet military forces in the Far East. At 3:00 P.M. I briefed the Secretaries of Army, Navy, and Air Force on these items.

At 2:00 P.M. of this fast-moving day, June 25, the U.N. Security Council met to consider the Korean situation. The Russian delegate was absent, having abstained from all Council meetings since January 10, 1950, when the Council had refused to unseat Nationalist China. The Russians thereby missed the opportunity to veto a resolution submitted by the United States delegate, Ernest A. Gross. Except for Yugoslavia, the only Communist country then a member of the Council, abstaining, the Council unanimously approved the resolution condemning the North Korean attack, demanding the withdrawal of the North Korean forces to north of the 38th Parallel, and calling on "all members to render every assistance to the United Nations in the execution of this resolution and to refrain from giving assistance to the North Korean authorities."

The President arrived back in Washington late in the afternoon. He was met at the airport by Secretaries Acheson and Johnson, who rode with him to the Blair House, across Pennsylvania Avenue from the White House, where the President was residing while the White House was being renovated. En route they gave Mr. Truman the latest information.

Little time remained before the President's dinner guests assembled at seven-thirty. Present were Secretary of State Dean Acheson, Secretary of Defense Louis A. Johnson, Army Secretary Frank Pace, Jr., Secretary of the Navy Francis P. Matthews, Air Force Secretary Thomas K. Finletter, Chairman of JCS General Omar N. Bradley, the service Chiefs, Collins, Chief of Staff of the Army, Admiral Forrest Sherman, Chief of Naval Operations and Hoyt S. Vandenberg, Chief of Staff of the Air Force, Under Secretary of State James E. Webb, Assistant Secretaries of State Dean Rusk and John D. Hickerson, and Ambassador-at-Large Philip Jessup.

While awaiting the arrival of one of the guests Secretary Acheson outlined his activities during the day and the action taken by the United Nations. Secretary Johnson interjected that he wished to have General Bradley read a memorandum from General MacArthur in regard to Formosa, since he thought it was of great importance. The President allowed Bradley to complete his reading; then, perhaps sensing that the question of Formosa was a diversion from the main topic of the evening, he announced that there would be no further discussion of the Far East until after dinner.

When the servants had cleared the table and left the dining-room, Acheson initiated the talk by summarizing the series of messages from Ambassador Muccio. Johnson in his testimony at the MacArthur hearings a year later referred to a brisk argument he remembered having with Acheson at this point: he wished to have the possibility of a Communist attack on Formosa discussed before considering the Korean situation, but the President vetoed his suggestion.

Acheson reported the United Nations resolution condemning the North Korean attack. He then gave his recommendations for immediate action based on the meeting between the State and Defense departments earlier in the day, advance word of which had been transmitted to MacArthur's staff by army telecon. A general discussion followed, the President asking each participant for any comment he wished to make. No one demurred from Acheson's recommendations. I gave the gist of the latest telecon on the military situation and spelled out the location and strength of United States and Soviet forces in the Far East. Sherman and Vandenberg felt that air and sea action alone might suffice to halt the North Koreans, but I stated that if the army of the Republic of Korea (ROK) was badly hurt, United States ground forces would be needed. I suggested that MacArthur be authorized to send a survey party to Korea to determine the actual situation and the condition of the ROK Army.

The President doubted that the Communists would heed any warning from the United Nations and said he regarded the North Korean attack as a further testing of our determination to prevent the spread of their areas of domination, like their tests in Iran, Turkey, Greece, and Berlin. Bradley said that a firm line had to be drawn somewhere and this was it. The President agreed. He directed the service Chiefs to issue the necessary orders to implement the agreed recommendations, including the movement of the Seventh Fleet and additional air units to the Far East and authorizing MacArthur to send a survey party to Korea.

This was the first of a number of conferences conducted by President Truman that I attended in the next two years. Increasingly I came to have tremendous admiration for this remarkable man. Perhaps it was because he had had little experience in foreign affairs before becoming president that he developed a rare talent for listening to his advisers in this field and quickly getting to the root of a problem. He was ever ready to hear both sides of a proposition and would balance them objectively and finally come up with a clear-cut, fearless decision. Once a decision was taken, he rarely deviated from it and always accepted full responsibility for the outcome, good or bad. Now he was about to take a firm stand against Communist imperialism in the Far East, as he had done earlier in the face of Russian threats to Iran, Turkey, Greece, and Berlin.

As soon as possible after dinner the Joint Chiefs arranged a teleconference with General MacArthur. Secretaries Pace and Finletter sat in on this conference in the army's communications center in the Pentagon. MacArthur was advised that the shipment of arms and equipment needed by the ROK Army to hold the capital city Seoul, the Kimpo airfield just across the Han River from Seoul, and the near-by port of Inchon, was to be protected by sufficient air and naval power to ensure its safe arrival. (See Map 2.) He was directed to employ such naval and air forces needed south of the 38th Parallel to prevent the overrunning of the Seoul-Kimpo-Inchon area and to ensure the safe evacuation of American dependents and other American noncombatants. Finally, he was told to send to Korea a survey party of selected officers to check and report back on the military situation and how best to assist the forces of the Republic of Korea. MacArthur was informed that the Seventh Fleet had been ordered from the Philippines and Okinawa to Sasebo, Japan (Map 1), where it would pass to operational control of the Commander, U.S. Naval Forces, Far East. In this telecon MacArthur was not made responsible for all operations in Korea. The United States Military Training Mission (Korean Military Advisory Group [KMAG]) and the actual evacuation were still being supervised by Ambassador Muccio, acting under instructions from the State Department. General MacArthur was not placed in command of military activities in Korea until June 27.

Reports from Korea on Monday, June 26, continued to picture a deteriorating situation, forecasting the early fall of Seoul. The President of the Republic of Korea, Syngman Rhee, sent a personal and urgent appeal to President Truman for help. That evening Mr. Truman called to Blair House his State and Defense advisers, most of whom had been present Sunday night. General Bradley briefed the gathering on the latest information.

It was apparent to all that ROK resistance would not be able to protect Seoul and Inchon and the Kimpo airfield, from which Americans were being evacuated by sea and air. Secretary Acheson recommended that the mission assigned the day before to United States air and naval forces be broadened to authorize combat operations below the 38th Parallel in support of ROK forces and to protect the port of Pusan and the Kimpo airfield. In view of growing concern that the Communists might take advantage of the situation to launch an attack on Formosa he also recommended that the Seventh Fleet be ordered to Formosan waters, its mission being to forestall any Chinese Communist attempt to invade Formosa and, concurrently, to dissuade Chiang Kai-shek from launching an attack against mainland China. No objection was raised to these proposals, and Mr. Truman promptly approved them.

Shortly after the meeting the JCS sent the necessary instructions by telecon to MacArthur to implement these decisions.

The next day, June 27, the Republic of Korea appealed to the United Nations for assistance. At the urging of Warren Austin, the United States Representative on the Security Council, the Council condemned the continuing attack by the North Koreans as a breach of the peace, demanded an immediate end to the fighting, and called on members of the United Nations to furnish assistance to the Republic of Korea to repel the attack and restore peace and security. This important resolution, again voted in the absence of the Russian representative, confirmed actions already taken by the United States and laid the groundwork for subsequent United States moves and the later active participation of other member countries. Again the Russians had missed an opportunity to veto essential U.N. Security Council action.

That afternoon the Secretaries of State and Defense, the service Secretaries, and the Joint Chiefs attended a meeting with the President and senior congressional leaders of both parties at the White House. Secretary Acheson briefed the group on developments in Korea, and the President read a statement, later made public, outlining the actions taken by the United States in support of the United Nations resolution. Various questions about military dispositions were answered by the Chiefs, and a number of political questions by the President and Acheson. Of the latter the most significant was a query by Congressman Charles A. Eaton, New Jersey, concerning whether the United States was now committed to the defense of South Korea. President Truman replied to the effect that with the adoption of the U.N. resolution, the United Nations had assumed responsibility for the defense of South Korea. The United States shared that responsibility with the other member countries of the United Nations.

Out in the Far East MacArthur's survey group, headed by Brigadier General John H. Church, had flown to Korea that morning and immediately begun its evaluation. By then MacArthur had received JCS instructions placing him in command of all military operations in Korea. Church was directed to coordinate our assistance to the ROK Army, to assume control of the Korean Military Advisory Group with that army, and to set up an American Advance Command Post.

General Church, an able and dynamic officer, established a temporary office in Suwon, south of Inchon. The survey group was soon almost inundated by ROK forces fleeing in disorder from Seoul. This flight was halted by General Chae, Chief of Staff of the ROK Army, with the assistance of officers from the advisory group and the advance command post, and some semblance of order was established in scattered positions along the Han River south of Seoul. The failure of the ROK Army to stand and fight was a great disappointment to the officers of the advisory group. Unfortunately, the Japanese army in its long occupation of Korea had suppressed the development of native leaders, and the United States, fearful that the fiery Syngman Rhee might try unilaterally to unite Korea by force, had failed to give adequate support to the fledgling ROK Army. The latter had only recently been created from a constabulary force that had been organized for internal police duty. By contrast, the Army of North Korea had been trained by the Russians for offensive warfare and equipped with tanks, medium artillery, and supporting aircraft. Included in it were many tough and experienced individuals and some units made up of Korean veterans who had served in the Chinese Communist armies. The near collapse of the ROK Army under the attack of this powerful force was another example of the result of American unwillingness in peacetime to face up to costly and unpleasant military facts until too late.

North Korean troops broke through the last organized resistance on the northern outskirts of Seoul on the morning of June 28. By nightfall Church was convinced that, although the Han River might be held for a while by the ROK Army, the 38th Parallel could be regained only by the introduction of U.S. Army or other ground forces. He radioed this opinion to General MacArthur.

After receiving Church's alarming report General MacArthur made a dramatic and essential move of the type for which he was justly famous. On Thursday morning, June 29, he flew to Korea in order personally to judge the military situation and to bolster the sagging ROK Army morale. He was accompanied by five key members of his staff and four newsmen from Tokyo.

En route he made another characteristically bold decision. He had received reports of Russian-built Yak fighter bombers operating from airfields in North Korea in support of the attack. One of the accompanying newsmen, Roy McCartney, later wrote:

> On the way to Korea, MacArthur resumed pacing while weighing aloud how he could "take out" the airfields from which the North Korean fighters were operating. "Where's the President's directive?" he asked his intelligence chief, General Willoughby. "How can I bomb north of the 38th Parallel without Washington hanging me?" It turned out that Willoughby, usually a meticulous man, had left Truman's directive in Tokyo. A half-hour later MacArthur emerged from his private cabin and remarked almost casually, "I've decided to bomb north of the 38th Parallel. The B-29's will be out tomorrow. The order has gone to Okinawa."

MacArthur had dictated to Lieutenant General George E. Stratemeyer, his Far East Air Force Commander, who was aboard, an order which Colonel Story, MacArthur's pilot, said was sent by the plane's radio at 0800 (Korean time), June 29, 1950, to Stratemeyer's headquarters in Tokyo: "Partridge from Stratemeyer. Take out North Korean airfields immediately. No publicity. MacArthur approves." This was sent twenty-four hours before the Joint Chiefs of Staff, with the President's approval, had rescinded the earlier Presidential limitations on bombing north of the 38th Parallel in Korea.

General MacArthur's decision to bomb airfields in the north was undoubtedly warranted from a strictly military viewpoint. However, in retrospect, this action, contrary to the President's instructions and unknown to him, was the precursor of later actions and attitudes that led to MacArthur's relief from command.

Some warrant for MacArthur's decision was given graphically as his plane came in to land at Suwon airfield: two Yak fighters bombed one end of the runway. His party landed safely and unperturbed. They were met by General Church and were soon joined by President Rhee, Ambassador Muccio, and General Chae.

Church and Muccio gave the party their latest information, which President Rhee was said to have summarized as "We are in a hell of a fix." So they were, but to judge for himself MacArthur drove with his party, past groups of smiling Korean stragglers still carrying arms and ammunition and saluting smartly, to the south bank of the Han River, opposite Seoul. Some firing was going on, but it was obvious that through lack of leadership or will to fight the ROK Army alone would not be able to stop the swarming attack of the North Koreans.

Meanwhile reports reaching the JCS direct from the Far East were so threatening that Secretary Johnson, who kept in touch with the situation, advised the President that further United States action might be necessary. At a high-level conference of the "Blair House Group" that afternoon the President approved a new directive (JCS 84631) to MacArthur, which had been recommended by the Secretary of Defense and the JCS, authorizing MacArthur to (1) employ U.S. Army service troops to maintain communications and other essential services in South Korea, (2) employ U.S. Army combat troops to secure a port and air base in the Pusan-Chinhae area (Map 2) at the southern tip of Korea, (3) employ naval and air forces in North Korea well clear of the frontiers of Manchuria and the Soviet Union, (4) by naval and air action secure Formosa from invasion by Chinese Communists and likewise prevent any invasion of mainland China from Formosa, and (5) continue to send supplies and ammunition from Japan to the ROK Army and furnish an estimate of additional requirements. Furthermore, the Seventh Fleet was assigned to his operational control, and he was advised that naval commanders in the Pacific would render him all practicable support. The President added a precautionary statement that these instructions did "not constitute a decision to engage in war with the Soviet Union if Soviet forces intervene in Korea." In such event our troops were to defend themselves and report the situation to Washington.

Authorization for the employment of U.S. Army combat troops was limited to the Pusan area and would not be available for defense of the Han River.

This dispatch, authorizing bombardment of military targets in North Korea, was not received by General MacArthur until the day after his return to Tokyo from Korea.

Even while returning to Japan General MacArthur had started to draft a report to the JCS, and it was sent off shortly after his arrival in Tokyo. This dispatch painted a gloomy but realistic picture of the Korean situation. He doubted whether the critical Han River line would be held. General MacArthur concluded:

> The only assurance for the holding of the present line, and the ability to regain later the lost ground, is through the introduction of U.S. ground combat forces into the Korean battle area. To continue to utilize the forces of our Air and Navy without an effective ground element cannot be decisive.
>
> If authorized, it is my intention immediately to move a U.S. regimental combat team to the reinforcement of the vital area discussed and to provide for a possible build-up to a two division strength from the troops in Japan for an early counteroffensive.

I received this message, number C56942, about midnight June 29–30, Washington time. I was so concerned by the critical situation it depicted and the urgency of MacArthur's request that I arranged for a teleconference with General MacArthur at about 3:00 A.M. Washington time, June 30 (5:00 P.M., Tokyo time).

The telecon actually started at 3:40 A.M. Present with MacArthur at his headquarters in Tokyo were his Chief of Staff, General Almond, and five of his principal staff officers. With me in the communications room in the Pentagon were General

Gruenther and the heads of the Army General Staff Divisions. The State Department, which had been advised of General Mac-Arthur's report and our plans for the telecon, was represented by the Assistant Secretary for Far Eastern Affairs, Dean Rusk, and the Korean Desk Officer, Neil W. Bond.

A teleconference is conducted by flashing questions and answers between the participants on screens at each end of a communications line, much as stock market information is relayed by ticker tape. In a telecon each series of questions and answers appears in full on the screens at both ends and remains visible while the conferees consider the content. Teletyped copies of the questions and answers are immediately available as the conference progresses. As initiator of the conference, I had worked out with the staff a series of questions dealing with the situation in Korea.

There was an eerie quality about this telecon that makes it stand out sharply in my memory. The air was fraught with tension as we assembled in the middle of the night in the Army's darkened telecon room in the Pentagon. All of the men present, though outwardly calm, realized the critical importance of the impending discussions between conferees on opposite sides of the world. We instinctively spoke with hushed voices as the questions, numbered serially, were flashed on the screen, and we pictured in our minds the gathering in Tokyo where answers were being framed that would vitally affect our participation in this strange new war.

The more important items were as follows:

DA-1 [Department of the Army No. 1]

Authorization proposed in your C56942 will require Presidential decision which will take several hours for consideration. Meanwhile, you are authorized in accordance with Par. 2B, JCS 84631, to move one RCT [Regimental Combat Team] immediately to Pusan base area. This will be amplified in our telecon scheduled for 30080Z.

FECOM-1 [Far East Command No. 1]

Your authorization, while establishing basic principle that U.S. ground combat troops may be used in Korea, does not give sufficient latitude for efficient operation in present situation. It does not satisfy the basic requirement contained in my message C56942. Time is of the essence and a clear-cut decision without delay is imperative.

DA-2

I was present at White House conference late afternoon June 29 when decision was made to authorize action covered in JCS 84631. Tenor of decision clearly indicated to me that the President would wish carefully to consider with his top advisers authorizing introduction of American combat forces into battle area. Will not authorization given you in DA-1 permit initiation of movement? Prior to completion of this movement we should be able to obtain definite decision on your proposal. Does this meet your requirement for the present?

No reply was received to DA-2. We took this to mean that General MacArthur stood by his emphatic plea for a decision "without delay." After discussing this conclusion with the staff members and State Department representatives present I sent:

DA-9 Ref FEC-1.

I will proceed immediately through Secretary of the Army to request Presidential approval your proposal to move one RCT into forward combat area. Will advise you soon as possible, perhaps within half hour.

No acknowledgment of DA-9 was received. Since time was critical, I did not attempt to secure the concurrence of the other members of the JCS. I stepped from the conference room, while the staff continued the telecon with items of less importance, and called Secretary Pace at his home. I gave him the gist of General MacArthur's report and his urgent request at the telecon. I recommended that approval for dispatch of a regimental combat team to the Korean battle area be secured from the President at once. Secretary Pace agreed and woke President Truman by a call to his bedside phone. A few minutes later Pace telephoned me that the President did not hesitate in giving his approval to the movement of the team.

In less than an hour from the receipt of the telecon item FEC-1 and before the telecon was concluded I sent this message:

DA-10

Your recommendation to move one Regimental Combat Team to combat area is approved. You will be advised later as to further build-up.

General MacArthur replied at once:

FEC Item 8 Reur DA-10

Acknowledged. Is there anything further now?

The telecon was concluded by DA-11:

Everyone here delighted your prompt action in personally securing firsthand view of situation. Congratulations and best wishes. We have full confidence in you and your command.

Nothing further here. End DA-11.

At 8:30 that morning President Truman assembled almost the same group of advisers which had met on June 25 at the Blair House. The President informed the group of his early morning decision and then called for advice on the additional troops to be employed. It was quickly agreed that General MacArthur's request for two divisions should be approved. On Admiral Sherman's recommendation President Truman approved a naval blockade of North Korea.

Immediately after this meeting the JCS informed MacArthur of these decisions.

By dark on July 1 a small advance force of two reinforced rifle companies of the 1st Battalion, 21st Infantry, 24th Infantry Division, landed at Pusan, having been turned south by bad weather in the Suwon area, and General MacArthur had issued orders for the follow-up movement of the remainder of the 24th Division.

The die had been cast, and for the first time in history the United States was involved, in a far Asian country that few Americans had ever heard of before, in a war in peacetime that began and ended without a congressional declaration of war.*

* Among earlier incidents involving U.S. military forces without declarations of war were naval engagements against French vessels during President John Adams' administration in 1797; the Boxer Rebellion, 1900–1901; seizure of Vera Cruz in 1914 under President Wilson; and General Pershing's Punitive Expedition into Mexico in 1916. All were limited operations that did not lead to war.

II

POLITICAL-MILITARY BACKGROUND

Korea: Satellite or Independent?

KOREA HAD BEEN a recognized political entity long before the discovery of America. Its recorded history dates back to 57 B.C., though references to the area antedate the Christian era by two thousand years. It was at various times subservient to the Chinese empire, but at the end of the Sino-Japanese War of 1894–95 China and Japan recognized the complete independence of Korea. Conflicting interests of Russia and Japan in Korea and in the Vladivostok area of the Maritime Province of Siberia led to the Russo-Japanese War of 1904–05, which was settled through the mediation of President Theodore Roosevelt. The Treaty of Portsmouth permitted Japanese occupation of Korea, which was followed in 1910 by the forcible annexation and incorporation of Korea into the Japanese empire.

At the Cairo Conference in 1943 it was agreed by President Franklin D. Roosevelt, Prime Minister Churchill, and Generalissimo Chiang Kai-shek that Korea was eventually to be "free and independent." However, at Potsdam in July, 1945, as part of the arrangements for Russia's projected entry into the war against Japan, President Truman, Churchill, and Stalin agreed on a joint American-Russian occupation of Korea following the surrender of Japanese forces there, with the 38th Parallel as a temporary dividing line between the occupying forces.* Russian troops entered

---

* About midnight, August 10–11, 1945, Colonel Charles H. Bonesteel and Major Dean Rusk, then a Reserve Officer on active duty with the Operations Division of the War Department General Staff, began drafting part of a General Order that would define the zones to be occupied in Korea by American and Russian forces. They were given thirty minutes to complete their draft, which a State-War-Navy

Korea on August 10, 1945, four days before Japan offered to surrender. American troops arrived on September 8.

Under urging from the United States the foreign ministers of the United States, Great Britain, and the Soviet Union at a conference in Moscow in December, 1945, agreed on a plan for a joint trusteeship for Korea. This plan created a U.S.-U.S.S.R. Joint Commission which, after discussions with representatives of Korean political parties and social organizations, was expected to submit to the governments of the United States, Great Britain, the Soviet Union, and China recommendations for the formation of a provisional government for a unified Korea. Then, after consultation between the Joint Commission and the provisional government, the Commission was to present to the four powers proposals for a four-power trusteeship of Korea to last "up to five years." South Korean nationalists, led by Syngman Rhee, who demanded immediate independence, protested violently against the proposed trusteeship. Communist minority groups in the south promptly announced acceptance of the trustee proposal.

Riots that broke out in the American zone played into the hands of the Russians, who refused to consider any integration of the two zones. They had already constructed barriers across all lines of communications at the 38th Parallel and covered these obstructions with machine guns facing south.

Efforts made by Lieutenant General John R. Hodge, the com-

Coordinating Committee was waiting for. The State Department wished the dividing line to be as far north as possible, while the military departments, knowing that the Russians could overrun all of Korea before any American troops could land there, were more cautious. Bonesteel and Rusk wanted to follow local provincial boundary lines north of Seoul, which would violate political divisions as little as possible and would place the capital city in the American zone. The only map immediately available was a small-scale wall map of the Far East, and time was pressing. Bonesteel noted that the 38th Parallel passed north of Seoul and almost divided Korea into two equal parts. He seized on it as the proposed zonal boundary. It was approved by the President and accepted later by the Russians.

Though Bonesteel and Rusk did not know it at the time, they had hit on the same parallel that had been proposed to the Russians by the Japanese General Yamagata in 1896 to divide Japanese and Russian spheres of influence, Japan getting the southern zone. The Russian negotiator, Alexis Lobanov-Rostovskii, refused because "Korea's destiny as a component part of the Russian empire . . . had been foreordained for us to fulfill." From *Russia in Manchuria* (1892–1906), by B. A. Romanov, translated by Susan Wilbur Jones.

mander of the American occupation forces, to iron out differences with his Russian opposite number proved futile, as did the meetings of the U.S.-U.S.S.R. Joint Commission, which convened in Seoul on March 20, 1946. The Russians insisted that only Koreans who supported the Moscow agreement on trusteeship were eligible for membership in the provisional government. The Americans opposed this stand.

After two years of negotiations, which foundered repeatedly on this fundamental issue, the United States placed the matter before the General Assembly of the United Nations on September 23, 1947. The United States recommended that both occupation zones hold elections under observation of the United Nations, after which a U.N. Temporary Commission would supervise the formation of a national government.

The Russian Representative protested that the United Nations had no jurisdiction in Korea and, after the U.N. General Assembly voted support of the United States' proposal, Russia refused to take any part in the Temporary Commission. When this commission was constituted despite Soviet objections, the Russians cut off half of the electric power being sent to South Korea from the hydroelectric dams in North Korea.

Elections for a National Assembly were held in the south under observation of the Temporary Commission on May 10, 1948. North Korea did not participate, the Commission was barred from the area north of the 38th Parallel, and the results of the election were not recognized by the puppet government that the Soviet Union had set up there under Communist control. Four days later the Russians cut off all power to South Korea. The Commission reported that the election results were "a valid expression of the free will of the electorate in those parts of Korea which were accessible to the Commission and in which the inhabitants constituted approximately two thirds of the people of all Korea."

The new assembly of the Republic of Korea convened on May 31, 1948. After considerable debate it adopted a constitution in July and appointed Syngman Rhee as its president.

The Republic was formally proclaimed by General MacArthur at gala ceremonies in Seoul on August 15, 1948. Three weeks later the puppet government in North Korea, the so-called Democratic Peoples' Republic of Korea,* claimed sovereignty over all Korea. It was recognized at once by the Soviet Union and by its satellites in eastern Europe and Outer Mongolia. Russia's determination not to permit a peaceful union of Korea was now out in the open.

Having formalized the set-up of its new satellite, backed by a full-fledged North Korean military force of all arms, Russia's next move was to announce that its own forces would be withdrawn by the end of the year and to demand that the United States do likewise. The United States replied that withdrawal was only part of the entire Korean situation, which should be discussed at the U.N. General Assembly. The Soviets completed their withdrawal in December. On motion of the Soviet Union, the U.N. General Assembly on December 12 called for complete withdrawal of American forces. President Rhee had meanwhile made a direct appeal to President Truman to retain an occupation force and establish a military and naval mission until the defense forces of the Republic of Korea should become capable of dealing with any threat from without or within the country.

On January 19, 1949, the Joint Chiefs of Staff asked General MacArthur for his recommendation on the possible effects of withdrawal and on appropriate timing. MacArthur replied that it was not feasible within the resources available to the Far East Command to establish a ROK Army capable of repelling an all-out North Korean attack. He concluded, "It should be recognized that in the event of any serious threat to the security of Korea, strategic and military considerations will force abandonment of any pretense of military support." He suggested May 10, 1949, the anniversary of South Korea's general election, as a suitable date to complete our withdrawal.

On March 22, 1949, the U.S. National Security Council, with State Department and JCS agreement, recommended to the President that all United States combat forces be out of Korea by June 30, 1949. President Truman approved.

---

* This name will not be used herein; "The Republic" always refers to the Republic of Korea ("ROK"). "The North Koreans" ("NK") will signify the people of the puppet government.

General MacArthur's concurrence with our withdrawal from Korea was fully warranted in light of the world situation at that time and the relative weakness of the forces assigned to his command in comparison with the Russians in the Far East. Starting April 1, 1948, the Soviet Union had gradually clamped a railway and highway blockade on Berlin, which was broken by the allied airlift at midnight, May 11–12, 1949, only after almost thirteen months of tense confrontation. The menace of Russian direct intervention in Korea, with attendant danger to Japan, was ever present. The Soviets maintained powerful forces of all arms in the Vladivostok area within 600 nautical miles of Tokyo. Furthermore, the potential Russian threat to Japan had been increased by the Soviet acquisition of South Sakhalin, the Kurile Islands, and two small islands just off the coast of Hokkaido, the northernmost of the Japanese Islands. General MacArthur's principal mission was the defense of Japan. Hence, in the event of a major war his strategic plans called for complete withdrawal from Korea, which was to be neutralized as a base for possible enemy operations as far as possible by sea and air power.

These plans were in consonance with a policy, approved by President Truman on April 4, 1948, and based on recommendations of the Joint Chiefs of Staff, which stated: "The United States should not become so irrevocably involved in the Korean situation that an action taken by any faction in Korea or by any other power in Korea could be considered a 'casus belli' for the United States."

On June 20, 1949, ten days before the scheduled date of withdrawal, General Bradley, then Chief of Staff of the Army, questioned our national policy in reference to Korea and the decision to withdraw our occupation forces. He submitted a memorandum to the JCS, stating his fears that complete withdrawal might result in an invasion from the north. He recommended that in such event United States nationals be evacuated and the aggression be reported to the U.N. Security Council as a threat to international peace. Depending on the action of the United Nations Security Council, a composite United Nations force might be introduced to check the aggression.

The other members of the Joint Chiefs of Staff felt the matter should not be reopened with the U.S. National Security Council. Their majority view stated: "From the strategic viewpoint, the position of the Joint Chiefs of Staff regarding Korea, summarized briefly, is that Korea is of little strategic value to the United States and that any commitment to United States use of military force in Korea would be ill-advised and impracticable in view of the potentialities of the over-all world situation and of our heavy international obligations as compared with our current military strength."

In accordance with the March 22 decision of the National Security Council, as approved by the President, the last United States combat troops were withdrawn from Korea to Japan on June 30, 1949.

Our national policy toward Korea was revealed publicly for the first time on January 12, 1950, by Secretary of State Dean Acheson in a speech before the National Press Club in Washington. After pointing out that the United States was committed to the defense of Japan, Acheson described our line of defense in the Far East:

> This defensive perimeter runs along the Aleutians to Japan and then goes to the Ryukyus. We hold important defensive positions in the Ryukyu Islands (including Okinawa) and these we will continue to hold. . . .
> The defensive perimeter runs from the Ryukyus to the Philippine Islands. . . . It is hardly necessary for me to say that an attack on the Philippines could not and would not be tolerated by the United States. . . .
> So far as the military security of other areas of the Pacific is concerned, it must be clear that no person can guarantee these areas against military attack. But it must also be clear that such a guaranty is hardly sensible or necessary within the realm of practical relationship.
> Should such an attack occur — one hesitates to say where such an armed attack could come from — the initial reliance must be on the people attacked to resist it and then upon the

commitments of the entire civilized world under the Charter of the United Nations which so far has not proved a weak reed to lean on by any people who are determined to protect their independence against outside aggression.

This statement has long been interpreted by many people as having signalled to the Communists that the United States would not defend Korea in the event of an attack. No one will ever know what effect, if any, the statement had on the Russians and their North Korean puppets. In fairness to Secretary Acheson it should be noted that his statement was in accord with the views of the Joint Chiefs of Staff and of General MacArthur, the responsible commander in the field. Moreover, the implication in his statement was reasonably clear that, while the United States was disclaiming any unilateral responsibility for Korean defense, we would respond, in conjunction with other members of the United Nations, to any call for help made to the United Nations by the Republic of Korea. Why the Secretary of State felt impelled to make this disclaimer publicly, I have never understood. I imagine that, like a batter swinging at a bad ball, he later would have liked to have had that swing back again.

In any event, the North Koreans had begun probing attacks across the 38th Parallel in May, 1949, just before the American withdrawal from Korea. Hundreds of such probes followed in the next year. While the ROK Army threw back all these minor attacks, the North Korean troops were gaining offensive experience and detailed knowledge of South Korean dispositions. By June of 1950 the North Korean Army was ready for the real push.

Undeclared War or Police Action?

In authorizing the dispatch of United States armed forces to Korea following the NK Army attack of June 25, 1950, President Truman had acted under his constitutional authority as Commander in Chief of the Army and Navy and under the general powers of the President to conduct the foreign relations of the United States.

The President had not asked Congress for a declaration of war. A year later, during the MacArthur Hearings, in answer to a question from Senator Leverett Saltonstall whether it would not have been better if the President had asked for such a declaration, Secretary of State Acheson replied in part:

> If you ask me whether it would have been better, all I can say is to recite the facts of the situation. I doubt whether it would have made any difference.
>
> The facts were that action had to be taken with the utmost speed and action was taken, beginning on a Sunday and going through until the latter part of the week.
>
> . . . If there had been a lot of time here, then it might possibly have been desirable to take it to Congress.
>
> But certainly I do not believe the President would have gone to Congress for the purpose of asking for a declaration of war against anybody, because this was an action of the United Nations to repel an aggression and was not a question of a war against any other country.

Acheson might have added that this action was directed against only a part of Korea, called North Korea, the legal existence of which as an independent country had not been recognized by either the United Nations or the United States. The United States would scarcely have declared war on a legally nonexisting country.

There were many precedents for Mr. Truman's use of troops in police actions abroad without congressional approval, notably President McKinley's reaction to the Boxer Rebellion in China in 1900: he sent five thousand troops to join other foreign contingents to relieve the Chinese siege of the foreign sector in Peking and re-establish the treaty status of foreign missions there.

On the other hand, as eminent a lawyer as Senator Robert Taft stated on June 28, 1950:*

> I shall discuss later the question of whether the President is usurping his powers as Commander-in-Chief. It is my own

* For a thorough analysis of the President's authority to repel the attack in Korea see Memorandum of July 3, 1950, prepared by the Department of State, *House Report 2495*, 81st Congress, pp. 61–68.

opinion that he is doing so, but I may say that if a joint resolution were introduced asking for approval of the use of our armed forces already sent to Korea and full support of them in their present venture, I would vote in favor of it.

The lack of a congressional declaration of war was of less practical importance than the fact that the decision to enter the conflict was part of an international act of the United Nations rather than a unilateral act of the United States. True, the initial moves to protect the evacuation of United States nationals from Seoul were solely American emergency measures. However, after the Korean National Assembly had appealed to the United Nations, the U.N. Security Council on June 27, 1950, adopted a resolution recommending that:

> . . . the Members of the United Nations furnish such assistance to the Republic of Korea as may be necessary to repel the armed attack and to restore international peace and security in the area.

In response to this resolution the United Kingdom, Australia, New Zealand, Canada, the Netherlands, and Nationalist China offered military forces.

It should be noted that the June 27 resolution was adopted prior to any United States action to move troops to Korea and prior to the June 29 authorization to MacArthur to employ naval and air forces north of the 38th Parallel.*

Then on July 7, 1950, the U.N. Security Council adopted a

---

* *The U.N. Security Council resolution of June 25, 1950* (see Chapter 1, page 12) had determined that "a breach of the peace" had occurred and demanded the withdrawal of the North Korean forces. It called on all member nations "to render every assistance to the United Nations in the execution of this resolution." The United States decisions of June 25–26 to employ United States air and naval forces south of the 38th Parallel were made pursuant to the June 25 United Nations resolution. Some critics of the United States actions taken prior to June 27 have claimed that the United Nations resolution of June 27, which specifically called on member nations to furnish assistance to "repel the armed attack and to restore international peace and security to the area," was an entirely new resolution. The United States regarded the June 27 resolution as merely a clarification of the June 25 resolution and the July 7 resolution as a summary of the two June resolutions with an added provision for the establishment of the United Nations Command.

resolution that set the legal status and objectives in Korea for all
United Nations forces, including those of the United States. On
the basis of reports of the U.N. Temporary Commission in Korea
the Council had determined that the North Korean attack was a
breach of the peace and had noted that a number of member
nations had made offers of assistance to the Republic of Korea.
The resolution stated these observations and then continued:

> 3. Recommends that all members providing military forces
> and other assistance pursuant to the aforesaid Security Council
> resolutions (of June 25 and 27) make such forces and other
> assistance available to a unified command under the United
> States.
> 4. Requests the United States to designate the commander of
> such forces.
> 5. Authorizes the unified command at its discretion to use the
> United Nations flag in the course of operations against North
> Korean forces concurrently with the flags of the various nations
> participating.

Prior to the adoption of the July 7 resolution the U.N. Secretary
General, Trygve Lie, had circulated a proposal to members of the
Security Council providing for a "Committee on Coordination of
Assistance for Korea" to supervise the military action in Korea.
When asked by the State Department to comment on this proposal, the Joint Chiefs of Staff offered strong objections. We
pointed out that to place a United Nations committee in the chain
of command could seriously interfere with the strategic and
tactical control of operations by General MacArthur and his commanders of army, navy and air forces in the field. We favored a
command arrangement somewhat comparable to our own execu-
tive-agency system, that is, one in which the United States would
act as executive agent for the United Nations, with no one inter-
posed between MacArthur and the United Nations. Our suggestions were followed. The resolution as adopted by the Security
Council called simply for periodic reports from the United Nations commander.

In consonance with the July 7 resolution the Joint Chiefs of

Staff made the obvious recommendation to the President that General MacArthur be designated Commander in Chief, United Nations Command; on July 8, 1950, he was so named by President Truman. On July 14 President Syngman Rhee placed all his Republic's forces under MacArthur's command. The same date President Truman designated the U.S. Joint Chiefs of Staff his military agents for Korea.

Accordingly, the JCS issued detailed instructions to General MacArthur. He was cautioned to avoid any appearance of unilateral American action: "For world-wide political reasons it is important to emphasize repeatedly the fact that our operations are in support of the United Nations Security Council."

In the subsequent military operations in Korea the fact was often lost sight of that American forces there were acting for the United Nations, under authority delegated to the United States by the United Nations, and with an objective set by the United Nations: "to repel the armed attack and to restore international peace and security in the area." The President, the State Department, and the JCS were acutely conscious that, even though the American forces constituted the bulk of the U.N. Command, other than troops of the Republic, and paid practically all costs, we did not have complete freedom of action. The legitimate aspirations of the Republic of Korea, as expressed by the volatile, often cantankerous Syngman Rhee, and also the frequently divergent views of our other allies, had to be considered in every major operational decision.

In this situation I was often reminded of an admonition given ruefully to my class at the Army War College in 1938 by General Fox Connor, Pershing's able operations officer in World War I: "If you have to go to war, for God's sake do it without allies!"

We had learned in two world wars some of the disadvantages of allies, however essential they were. The fact that we were operating in Korea under the aegis of the United Nations was a great political asset in combatting Communist propaganda and consolidating free-world support, but no one could foretell the complications it would introduce into the fighting against Communist armed forces as this strange war in peacetime developed.

As we shall later see, many of these complications fell on General MacArthur as U.N. Commander and on the JCS.

The Joint Chiefs of Staff

The Joint Chiefs of Staff was a relatively new agency in the United States Government. It had its genesis in World War II when, with the approval of President Roosevelt, General George C. Marshall, Chief of Staff of the Army, General Henry H. Arnold, head of the Army Air Forces, Admiral Ernest J. King, Chief of Naval Operations, and Admiral William D. Leahy, the President's personal Chief of Staff, constituted an informal body to coordinate the plans and operations of our armed forces. The National Security Act of 1947 legalized the JCS as the principal military advisers of the President and the Secretary of Defense. Under this act, as later amended in 1949, the Joint Chiefs consisted of a nonvoting Chairman, the Chiefs of Staff of the Army, Navy, and Air Force, and, since 1952, the Commandant of the Marine Corps when matters directly affecting the U.S. Marine Corps are being considered. In 1950 the newly constituted JCS was called upon to operate under war conditions for the first time.

Fortunately, each of the Chiefs had had extensive wartime experience as commanders of large combat units and as senior staff officers in World War II.

I had become a member of the JCS on October 1, 1949, when I succeeded General Bradley as Chief of Staff of the Army; Bradley then became the first Chairman of the JCS.

Omar N. Bradley, like General Eisenhower and most senior U.S. Army commanders of World War II, had never commanded a combat unit larger than a battalion when General Marshall assigned him to command of the II Corps of General Patton's Seventh Army in North Africa. He did such an effective job there, and in the Sicily campaign, that he was selected to head the U.S. First Army for the Normandy invasion. After the breakout west of Saint-Lô Bradley activated the Twelfth Army Group, consisting of the First and Third Armies, later joined by the Ninth Army, which raised the Twelfth Army Group to a strength of over a million men. General Bradley thus commanded more men in action than any other leader in all our military history. After World War II and before succeeding General Eisenhower as Chief of Staff he took over the Veterans Administration at a critical period. He demonstrated executive ability and rare courage in preventing undue political influence from dominating the organization and the locations of veterans' hospitals. Calm and level-headed, with excellent judgment of men and affairs and a simple honesty that radiated from his rough-hewn face, he was well fitted to serve as Chairman of the JCS.

Admiral Forrest Sherman, a graduate of the Naval Academy, had been a naval aviator. Prior to World War II he had been in the War Plans division of the office of the Chief of Naval Operations. After the outbreak of war, he commanded the aircraft carrier *Wasp* until it was sunk by a Japanese submarine in the Solomon Islands campaign in September of 1942. He later became Deputy Chief of Staff to the Commander in Chief in the Pacific, Admiral Chester W. Nimitz. Admiral Sherman had represented the U.S. Navy at the initial conference with the Japanese in August 1945 in Manila before the Japanese surrender. He returned to Washington with Admiral Nimitz when the latter became Chief of Naval Operations, serving as Nimitz's Deputy for Operations. After a tour as Commander of the U.S. Sixth Fleet in the Mediterranean he succeeded Admiral Louis Denfeld as Chief of Naval Operations in 1949.

General Hoyt S. Vandenberg, the youngest of the Chiefs, had served as Chief of Operations for General Arnold in the early days of World War II. He was sent to England to help prepare plans for the invasion of North Africa, where he landed on D Day, November 8, 1942. Shortly thereafter he became Deputy Commander of the Northwest Strategic Air Forces in Africa. He next went to Moscow as air adviser to Ambassador Harriman in the winter of 1943. During the preparations for Normandy he was Deputy Air Commander of the Allied Air Forces in England. After the Normandy landings he commanded the Ninth Tactical Air Force, furnishing medium and fighter bomber support for the Twelfth Army Group until the end of the war. After returning home he had served successively as one of General Arnold's principal assistants, as Intelligence Officer, G-2, of the Army under General Eisenhower, as Vice Chief of Staff of the Air Force, and then as Chief of Staff. Between these assignments he had served a tour as head of the Central Intelligence Agency.

Bradley, Vandenberg, and I had a common background of training at West Point and the additional bond of service together in combat in Europe, where Vandenberg's bombers frequently furnished air support for Bradley's First Army, of which my VII Corps was a part. Brad and I had been tactical instructors together under General Marshall at the Infantry School at Fort Benning and had served on the Secretariat of the War Department General Staff. I had played softball and squash with Vandenberg while he was a student and I an instructor at the Army War College just before World War II.

I had met Admiral Sherman during my service in the Pacific but did not get to know him well until after the war. This was while I was acting as spokesman for the War Department in presenting to the Congress the first plan for unification of the armed services. Sherman had been one of the leaders of the Navy's opposition to the plan. Though disagreeing with him, I came to respect him as an opponent. Later, in the fight on unification, Sherman demonstrated skill as a negotiator for the Navy in reaching agreements with General Lauris Norstad, then head of the War Plans Division of the War Department, particularly in regard to the roles of naval and military aviation, which alleviated Navy objections to unification. Once the Unification Act was passed, Sherman faithfully accepted it and was a loyal and cooperative member of the Joint Chiefs of Staff. We were never intimate friends, but I had great respect for him as a man and as a naval expert.

The Joint Chiefs of Staff of 1950 had been struggling to reverse the trend of reductions in all of our military services, which had set in immediately after the victory over Germany and Japan. The mighty forces which the United States had raised and equipped during World War II had been wrecked in our rush to demobilize once victory was achieved. While the Russians were maintaining much of their war strength and beginning their stranglehold on Eastern Europe and North Korea, public and congressional pressure in the United States to "bring the boys home" would brook no delay.

I shall never forget the day in 1946 when I accompanied General Eisenhower, then Army Chief of Staff, to Capitol Hill to explain to an impatient House Military Affairs Committee what the War Department was doing in order to speed demobilization. The Chairman, Representative J. Parnell Thomas, invited Eisenhower to step into his office for a moment before opening the hearings. As we entered, Eisenhower was confronted with a group of women arranged around a table on which was stacked a pile of baby shoes. The resultant picture, which had been thoughtfully provided for, of a smug politician and a furious Eisenhower glaring in surprised dismay, was one of the "great" pictures of this hectic period. It was blown up and featured at the next meeting of the managing editors of one of the major news services.

As a consequence of such political maneuvers, which unquestionably gratified the Communists, hundreds of ships and planes were "moth-balled," and tanks, artillery, trucks, and other Army equipment were left in open fields and beaches all over the world as the troops were marched or flown to the nearest ports for rapid transport home. And the personnel strength of the military services was cut and cut with each annual congressional appropriation.

In this atmosphere of retrenchment the JCS during the period of 1947 to 1950 had to re-evaluate and revise their strategic estimates of our commitments and capabilities around the world. This evaluation revived many of the divergencies in views which had existed within the JCS during World War II.

These had to do principally with the relative importance given to the European and Pacific areas. General Marshall and the War Department had acted as executive agents for the European area; Admiral King and the Navy Department, for the Pacific. There was an inevitable tendency of the Navy to regard the war in the Pacific as its war and entitled to greater support, not only because of the Navy's assignment as executive agent, but because the vast ocean was the locus of conflict and its islands could then be reached only from the sea. The Army regarded Germany as a far more powerful and dangerous enemy than Japan and a greater threat to our economy, our system of government, and our basic concepts of freedom. Hitler and Naziism had to be defeated first, while we held Japan in check and gradually whittled down her strength. Despite President Roosevelt's bias toward the Navy,* stemming from his earlier service as Assistant Secretary of the Navy, he and his chief political advisers usually supported General Marshall. Consequently, our European forces and their allies generally received priority in the allocation of men and supplies.

Many of these differences carried over into the postwar period, the Russian-Chinese alliance and Communism replacing Germany and Naziism as a threat to peace and international security. The JCS continued to be torn between its military responsibilities, on the one hand to Europe and on the other to the Far East. Initially the Army troops and supporting air and naval forces remaining on occupation duties in foreign lands favored the Far East, there being four divisions in Japan and only the equivalent of two divisions in Germany, Austria, and Trieste. As Russia increased its pressure on the nations of Eastern Europe, and one by one they fell under Communist domination, Washington's concern for the freedom of Europe and, indeed, of the entire free world grew apace. In 1947 the Truman Doctrine, designed to check further Communist expansion, was announced, and the Marshall Plan, to assist in the economic rehabilitation of Europe, was initiated. Finally, the "suicide" death of Jan Masaryk, Foreign Minister of Czechoslovakia, and the overthrow in 1948 of President Eduard Beneš galvanized Europe and the United States into defensive preparations. On April 4, 1949, the United States joined NATO, the North Atlantic Treaty Organization, the first military alliance outside the western hemisphere in our peacetime history. Under NATO we pledged in advance, subject to our constitutional pro-

* General Marshall once gave me an example of his difficulty in securing support from President Roosevelt for the Army's personnel requirements, which greatly exceeded the Navy's. Whenever he presented to the President a list of recommendations for promotion to general officer, Roosevelt would ask, "Where is the Navy's list?" The President wished to make an admiral whenever an army or air corps general was selected.

cesses, American military support to any member country in the event of external attack. This immediately placed a new and increased burden on the military forces of the United States, planning for which fell on the JCS.

It was, therefore, with considerable misgiving that the JCS faced the new situation in the Far East precipitated by the North Korean attack in June 1950.

Why the Change in United States Policy Toward Involvement in Korea?

Considering how firmly United States policy was committed against our becoming involved in any kind of war in Korea, the question naturally arises: how and why the sudden change in this policy in less than one week between the North Korean attack on June 25, 1950, and the dispatch of U.S. Army troops to Pusan on June 30?

First of all, I believe our political and military leaders were surprised and deeply shocked by the bald actuality of the North Korean attack. In spite of many advance warnings from President Rhee, General Hodge, and intelligence sources, apparently we could not believe that such a small puppet state as North Korea would blatantly defy the United States and the United Nations. Our prestige in Asia and that of the United Nations were suddenly at stake, and we reacted accordingly.

We received a second shock when it became quickly evident that the ROK Army's capacity to stop the attack had been grossly exaggerated. General MacArthur had been skeptical that the United States would or should devote the resources of manpower and materiel to develop its capacity. In 1948 he had reported to the JCS that he did not have the resources of men or materiel to establish an effective ROK Army. He advocated, instead, a strengthening of the constabulary that had been created in 1946. With the assumption by the State Department of responsibility for American interests in Korea in August 1948 neither the Department of the Army nor General MacArthur had any direct responsibility for the security of Korea. The State Department and the JCS — the latter in its role as military advisers to the President — had to depend for their estimates of the ROK Army's defensive ability on the evaluations of Brigadier General William L. Roberts, head of the Korean Military Advisory Group, which operated under Ambassador Muccio in Korea. Drawing his conclusions from General Roberts' reports, Major General Bolté had just testified in June 1949 at a congressional hearing on Korean aid, defending the withdrawal of American troops: "We feel that the [native] forces in Korea now are better equipped than the North Korean troops . . . the Army as the Executive agent for the Joint Chiefs of Staff for the Far East is not only agreeable to the withdrawal of the tactical formations from Korea, but is heartily in favor of it as they [sic] feel that the point has been reached in the development of South Korean forces and in the supplying of material aid to the South Korean forces that it has reached a point [sic] where the tactical units can and should be withdrawn."

In the same vein on June 13, 1950, only two weeks before the North Korean attack, William C. Foster, then Deputy Administrator of the Economic Cooperation Administration, had testified before the Senate Appropriations Committee: "The rigorous training program has built up a well-disciplined army of 100,000 soldiers, one that is prepared to meet any challenge by the North Korean forces, and one that has cleaned out the guerilla bands in South Korea in one area after another." Foster had made this statement on the basis of undisclosed "official sources."

When I had gone out to see General MacArthur in October, 1949, right after becoming Chief of Staff, I had intended to visit Korea to check on our training mission there. Unfortunately, before this was possible I was called back to Washington to testify before the House Armed Forces Committee in the squabble between the Air Force and the Navy over the B-36, which was the chief Washington interest of that time. As far as I have been able to determine, no member of the Chiefs of Staff nor its Joint Strategic Survey Committee had visited Korea from 1946 until I went there on July 14, 1950, shortly after the fighting began.

I realized then that the Army staff, the Joint Chiefs, and the

Economic Cooperation Administration had been led astray by the faulty estimates of General Roberts. The ROK Army had a long way to go before it could reach the professional competence that had been instilled into the North Korean forces by the Russians. Roberts retired for age ten days before the North Korean attack. He was succeeded by Brigadier General Francis W. Farrell on July 24.

In sharp contrast to these optimistic statements was the warning given the Senate Armed Services Committee by Ambassador Muccio on June 6, 1950: ". . . the undeniable materiel superiority of the North Korean forces would provide North Korea with the margin of victory in the event of a full-scale invasion of the Republic, particularly in the matter of heavy infantry support weapons, tanks and combat aircraft which the USSR has supplied and continues to supply."

The fact that neither Ambassador Muccio nor General Roberts reported to General MacArthur probably accounts for the failure of MacArthur's headquarters to pick up the differences in their estimates of the relative capacities of the two opposing forces. The intelligence agencies of the Defense and Army Departments in Washington should have noted these divergencies, including the contrast between Muccio's and Foster's estimates. Apparently they did not.

There seems to be little question from the evidence now available that prior to 1950 the JCS, along with the State Department, counted on the ROK Army forces to check and delay any attack by the North Koreans long enough to allow pressure from the United Nations to force a halt. It was expected that, if the Russians then entered the fight, it would mean a major war, in which event all Americans would be evacuated at once. It was hoped that, if Russia did not step in, reliance would be placed, as Secretary Acheson phrased it, "on the people attacked to resist it and then upon the commitments of the entire civilized world under the Charter of the United Nations."

The second shock had come when it was evident from the first days of action in Korea, confirmed by General MacArthur personally, that the ROK Army would not hold long enough for a broadly based United Nations force to be assembled. It was also obvious that with an overwhelming victory in sight the North Koreans would pay no attention to mere political pressure from the United Nations. The United States was the only member country with forces immediately available for intervention. If we did not interpose at once, South Korea would be overrun.

The third shock was the conviction in the minds of the President and his principal State and Defense advisers, who were assembled at the three Blair House conferences following the North Korean attack, that it was the Soviet Union, not merely a Communist puppet, that was challenging the United States and the United Nations. The Soviet Union having been checked in its program of imperialist expansion in Iran in 1946, in Greece from 1947 to 1949, and in Berlin in 1949, had unquestionably shifted its probings for weakness to the Far East. Ho Chi Minh was relentlessly pressing the French in Indo-China, whom we were then supporting with military aid. If South Korea were to fall to Communism, Indo-China and, probably, Indonesia would follow, and the whole balance of power in the Far East would be upset. Such an upset would be a direct threat, not only to Japan, but also to the United States and to the whole concept of international peace under the Charter of the United Nations.

The President and his advisers during June 25 to 27, 1950, were faced with the realities of a situation menacingly different from the situation that had existed when our policy of not becoming involved in a war in Korea was formulated.

Consideration of this changed situation was compressed into a period of five days while Ambassador Muccio in Seoul and General MacArthur, the two responsible officials in the field, were urging immediate action on the part of the United States. President Truman made the decision to support their recommendations. He never vacillated on this sound decision.

III

TOO LITTLE AND ALMOST TOO LATE

Task Force Smith

ON THE EVENING OF June 30 Lieutenant Colonel Charles B. Smith, Commanding Officer of the 1st Battalion, 21st Infantry, 24th Division, was aroused from sleep shortly after he had turned in. He had been up all the previous night because of a precautionary alert at Camp Wood, where the battalion was stationed, on the Japanese island of Kyushu. But he jumped out of bed when he learned that his regimental commander, Colonel Richard W. Stephens, was on the phone. Stephens was brief: "The lid has blown off. Get on your clothes and report to the CP [command post]."

Brad Smith, class of 1939 at West Point, had served under my command in the 25th Infantry Division in the South Pacific in World War II. He had come to my attention then as a bright young officer who showed great promise. Now matured and with combat experience back of him, he was well qualified to lead the first American army troops to fight in the Korean war.

At the regimental command post Smith learned that the task force he was to command would consist essentially of his 1st Battalion less two companies. It was limited in size by the number of available C-54 planes that were to fly it to Korea from Itazuke, the U.S. Air Force base nearest Korea. Rounded out by part of the Battalion Headquarters Company, a communications section, and a composite platoon of 75mm recoilless rifles and 4.2-inch mortars, the task force added up to 406 officers and men. It was scarcely a formidable body for checking even the leading elements of the NK divisions driving south from Seoul toward

Taejon, the new seat of the ROK government. Loaded into trucks for the 75-mile drive from Camp Wood to Itazuke, Task Force Smith at 3:00 A.M. on July 1 started its historic movement inauspiciously in a downpour of rain.

After a jostling drive of five hours the convoy arrived at the air base at 8:05 A.M., July 1. The 24th Division commander, Major General William F. Dean, was there with a word of good cheer. His instructions to Smith were short but adequate:

> When you get to Pusan, head for Taejon. We want to stop the North Koreans as far from Pusan as we can. Block the main road as far north as possible. Contact General Church. If you can't locate him, go to Taejon and beyond if you can. Sorry I can't give you more information. That's all I've got. Good luck to you, and God bless you and your men.

The small airstrip near Pusan was socked in with fog as the transport planes approached. The first two had to turn back to Japan; it was 11:00 A.M. before one of them landed, and the other, with Smith aboard, did not arrive until about 2:30 P.M. The battalion moved by truck through Pusan to the railway station, where it was to board a train for Taejon. Crowds of Koreans in holiday mood, oblivious to, or ignorant of, the critical situation farther north, cheered the Americans on their way. Flags, banners, and streamers waved gaily, and bands blared, as the crowded train chugged off at 8:00 P.M.

Another fatiguing overnight ride brought Task Force Smith to Taejon. Smith reported there to General Church, who had moved down to Taejon from Suwon the day before. Church gave Smith the latest information he had and indicated that the battalion would be railed to the vicinity of Pyongtaek* south of Suwon to meet the oncoming NK invaders (Map 2). Smith wisely suggested that he be permitted to go forward to become familiar with

---

* The spelling of Korean place names varies on different local maps, and such names are frequently divided by apostrophes, e.g., P'yongt'aek. In some instances the final group of letters is the Korean word for some geographical feature, e.g., *do* in Wolmi-do means island. For uniformity I have followed the spelling used by the Historical Division of the U.S. Army, but have eliminated all apostrophes.

the terrain and reconnoiter for delaying positions while his men got some rest. Accordingly, while the troops moved into bivouac, Smith and his principal staff officers and unit commanders drove off in jeeps over the potholed road leading north to Osan. They had to pick their way through swarms of refugees and ROK soldiers plodding south.

A few miles north of Osan he found what he was looking for. An irregular line of hills stretched across the main road and the railway to the east, with commanding observation covering the lower ground to the north, over which the enemy would have to approach. Smith issued oral orders for the organization of the position, after which the party headed back for Taejon, arriving there well after dark. Shortly thereafter the task force received orders from General Church to reload the train and proceed north to Pyongtaek.

There the task force was joined on July 4 by a detachment of the 52d Field Artillery Battalion under command of Lieutenant Colonel Miller O. Perry. This detachment included Battery A, equipped with six 105mm howitzers. Later that day Brigadier General George B. Barth, commanding the artillery of the 25th Division on loan to the 24th Division, was sent forward to Pyongtaek by General Dean. Dean and Barth had flown over to Taejon after MacArthur had received word from the JCS that President Truman had approved the employment of two American divisions in Korea. MacArthur had placed Dean in command of all United States Army Forces in Korea, into which the Korean Military Advisory Group was merged. Dean appointed Church Deputy Commander.

One of the great assets of long service in the Regular Army is that most senior officers get to know each other. Bill Dean, like Hoyt Vandenberg, had been a student at the Army War College during my tour as an instructor there. We had played on opposing softball teams. Bill had once been ragged by his teammates for "red-appling" an instructor when, in one game, I had hit three home runs over his head while he was playing too shallow in center field. John Church and I had served together in the Philippines, and our families had made a trip together to Peking in

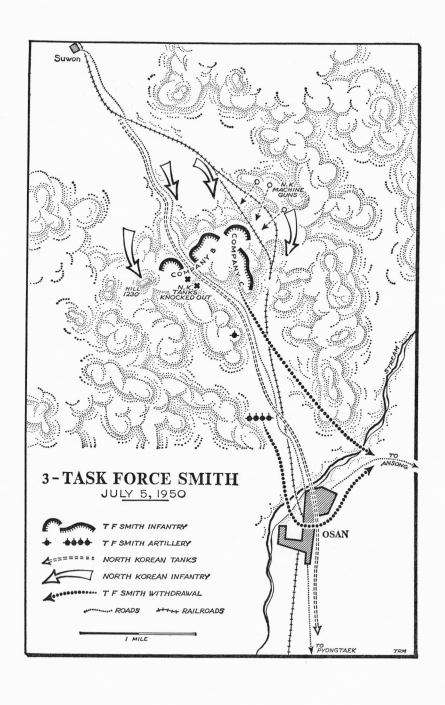

Suwon

N.K. MACHINE GUNS

COMPANY B

COMPANY C

HILL 1230

N.K. TANKS KNOCKED OUT

STREAM

TO ANSONG

OSAN

3 - TASK FORCE SMITH
JULY 5, 1950

T F SMITH INFANTRY

T F SMITH ARTILLERY

NORTH KOREAN TANKS

NORTH KOREAN INFANTRY

T F SMITH WITHDRAWAL

ROADS   RAILROADS

1 MILE

TO PYONGTAEK

TRM

1934. Bittman Barth had served under my command in Company K of the 8th Infantry in the Army of Occupation in Coblenz, Germany, after World War I. Our paths had crossed again during the Cherbourg campaign of World War II. I had selected him to command a regiment in the 90th Division, which needed front-line leadership, and Barth had done an outstanding job until he was seriously wounded while leading his regiment. These three men — Dean, Church, and Barth — and many others who served in positions of high responsibility in Korea were well known to me. Most of them had been tested under fire in World War II and had met that test.

Barth relayed to Smith instructions from Church to occupy the position Smith had selected near Osan. Once again Task Force Smith moved out about midnight, this time in commandeered Korean trucks and miscellaneous vehicles. The Korean drivers fled as soon as they realized they were moving back north. Smith replaced them with soldiers. Progress was slow. With little or no information about the location of the NK forces Smith had the column moving without lights. It was about 3:00 A.M. on July 5 when the selected position was reached. By daylight heavy weapons and the artillery battery were in place, and the riflemen dug in.

As indicated on Map 3, Smith had deployed his two rifle companies astride the main road and east of it to cover the railroad. The frontage of a mile was extensive for his small force, yet the position could be outflanked easily by a strong attacker. Smith's greatest weaknesses, however, were his lack of a reserve and the inadequacy of his supporting heavy weapons and artillery. A complete infantry battalion comprised three rifle companies, one of which would normally be held in reserve, and a heavy-weapons company of mortars and machine guns.

Four howitzers of Battery A were emplaced just off the road in a concealed position 2000 yards back of the infantry. A single 105mm howitzer was placed nearer the front in position to enfilade the road where it cut through Company B's position.

Unfortunately, there was no way to make up for the shortage of effective antitank ammunition. After World War II a special "high-explosive antitank" ammunition, known as HEAT, had been developed for our field artillery and infantry antitank bazookas and mortars. This new ammunition was in limited supply in the Far Eastern Command. The supply officer of the 52d Field Artillery Battalion had been able to obtain only eighteen rounds of HEAT ammunition for the battalion before it sailed from Japan. Battery A was allotted its share, six rounds. These were placed with the lone forward howitzer. There were no antitank or personnel mines.

As seems usual in war, it was raining when dawn broke. Since no North Koreans were in sight, Smith had his machine guns, mortars, and artillery do registration fire on key terrain features to the front. The brave little force was as well prepared as it could be, when at 7:00 A.M. Smith picked up through field glasses an enemy column emerging from Suwon.

As the column drew nearer, eight tanks were noted at its head. When they came within range, an artillery forward observer called for a concentration on the leading tanks. The first American artillery fire fell at 8:16 A.M. on July 5, 1950. The observer quickly adjusted the fire, and high-explosive shells began landing squarely among the oncoming tanks. But with hatches closed the Russian-built T-34 tanks were impervious to normal 105mm shells and, staying in column on the road, they rumbled steadily ahead as Smith's infantrymen watched in amazement.

The American recoilless riflemen held their fire until the tanks had closed to within 700 yards. They scored several direct hits, but the T-34's frontal armor shed these blows, and the tanks fired back with their 85mm cannon and heavy machine guns. The tanks clanked uphill and passed right through Company B, spraying the infantry intrenchments on either side. Second Lieutenant Ollie V. Connor, manning a 2.36-inch bazooka in a roadside ditch, waited as the tanks went by without spotting him. Then he pumped round after round into the more vulnerable rear ends of the T-34's without any visible effect. They moved on until the leading pair went over the high point in the pass, where they came under direct fire of the lone forward howitzer. The first two were stopped at once, probably by HEAT rounds. They pulled to the side to let the others pass, one of them bursting into flames. But the six HEAT shells were quickly expended, and the remaining high explosives could not pierce heavy armor even at point blank range. The single howitzer was knocked out by a direct hit from one of the tank's 85mm cannons.

Behind the leading echelon of eight tanks others followed at intervals in groups of four, their hatches tightly "buttoned up." They could have raised havoc with the infantry but, except for bursts of machine-gun fire, they paid little attention to the dough-boys as they drove through the pass. Even when they came under direct fire from Battery A, they made no real effort to knock out the battery, which the tank crews apparently had difficulty in locating. Pausing only briefly in an area defiladed from direct fire, they charged downhill, one or two at a time, their turret guns firing wildly, past Battery A and on down the road toward Osan. Five bazooka teams of artillerymen, one led by the batta-lion's commander, Miller Perry, joined the ineffectual effort to destroy the T-34's. In a brush with one of these Perry was wounded in the leg. Refusing evacuation, he continued to direct operations as succeeding batches of tanks appeared. Two more tanks were disabled, and their crews were killed. Thirty-three enemy tanks passed through Task Force Smith.

When it became apparent that enemy tanks would break through Smith's delaying position, General Barth started back by jeep to Pyongtaek to alert the 1st Battalion, 34th Infantry of the 24th Division, which was expected to arrive there from Pusan that evening.

Strangely, NK infantry did not follow the tank column closely. A lull fell over the battlefield, during which Smith surveyed his losses. Approximately twenty infantrymen had been killed or wounded. Wire communications to Battery A had been destroyed, and so had most of the trucks and jeeps that had been parked back of the front-line positions. Brad Smith had cause for con-cern as he searched with his glasses for enemy infantry, which he knew was bound to come. While his men waited in a steady rain, they deepened their foxholes, patched communications, and checked their weapons.

Smith picked up the first signs of further enemy movement near Suwon about 11:00 A.M., perhaps an hour after the tanks had passed through. It proved to be a long column of trucks led by three tanks and followed by several miles of marching men. At sight of this powerful force, a chill of apprehension must have run through Smith's little force, already somewhat shaken by the knowledge that an enemy tank column was operating somewhere in its rear.

The only thing Smith's force had in its favor was that the North Koreans apparently were not aware of the Americans' presence and for the moment were "sitting ducks," as Smith's men waited unseen until the trucks were only 1000 yards away. The opening salvos of artillery and mortars landed smack among the trucks, many of which burst into flame or overturned, spilling men and equipment on all sides, while 50-caliber machine guns swept the column. Back of the burning vehicles a battalion or more of men poured from their trucks and deployed in the open fields. Farther back, beyond range, other infantry units remained aboard trucks and waited for the enemy to flee — as the ill-equipped ROK forces had so often done.

Up front the three NK tanks moved within a few hundred yards of the American lines and raked them with cannon and machine-gun fire. With some protection from this fire enemy infantry began moving up on either side of the road. Accurate American fire broke up all efforts to advance frontally but could not stop flanking movements under cover. Within an hour a strong enemy force had occupied Hill 1230, west of the road, and began pouring fire into the separate platoon of Company B on the knoll below. Smith was forced to withdraw this platoon to join Company B's main position east of the road. His 4.2-inch mortars were moved up closer, along with all available ammunition, into a tighter defensive perimeter on the high ground east of the road. The battalion was now lacking effective artillery support because the enemy tanks had cut wire communications to Battery A.

Increasing amounts of enemy mortar and artillery fire were hitting both Companies B and C, and by 2:00 P.M. the NK machine guns were firing into the American positions from high ground east of Company C. Every effort to lay new wire lines from

Battery A to the infantry was thwarted by this directly observed fire.

From his command post within the perimeter Smith followed the action with growing concern. Rifle ammunition was down to less than twenty rounds per man. He feared that the tanks had destroyed Battery A's howitzers, from which he was now receiving no fire support. He had no information on where the T-34's were or what they were up to in his rear. It was only a question of time before both flanks of his position would be turned, and he had no reserve with which to meet the threat of encirclement. No American aviation was available to hold off the powerful enemy force to his front, waiting to pounce for the kill. Clearly it was time to withdraw, if his task force was to be saved from destruction. He could not afford to wait for darkness to screen the movement.

About 2:00 P.M. Smith issued instructions for the rearward movement. Each platoon as it withdrew was to be covered by the fire of another unit to the front. The route was to be down the ridge between the railroad and the highway and thence along the road and stream valley toward Osan.

A daylight withdrawal under fire is always a tough maneuver to execute. Task Force Smith suffered its heaviest casualties as the North Koreans poured direct machine-gun fire into the retreating groups of Americans. One platoon of Company B, the last off the hill, never received the word to withdraw and was cut off. Weapons groups had to abandon machine guns and mortars too heavy to move any distance by hand. The dead and twenty-five or more wounded on litters had to be left behind. An unidentified medical sergeant volunteered to stay with these litter cases. The wounded able to walk tried to keep up with their units, but many fell by the wayside.

Colonel Smith stayed at his command post until Company B was ready to pull out. He and his small party headed back to check on the artillery. They were surprised to find intact the four-gun battery, which had not yet come under infantry attack. There was no time to call up the artillery trucks from Osan, where they had been parked under cover, so sights and breech blocks were removed from the guns and carried off in the few available jeeps,

along with all fire-control equipment. Smith, Perry, and the gun-
ners walked back to Osan. There they found the artillery trucks
where they had been hidden. The artillerymen and Smith's
headquarters party mounted the trucks and moved east through
Osan toward Ansong. The convoy soon picked up groups of men
from Companies B and C straggling back over the hills and
through the rice paddies. Unfortunately, not knowing where the
enemy tanks were, Smith had not designated any rear assembly
position. Infantrymen moving individually or in small parties under their officers and noncoms drifted south to the area between
Pyongtaek and Ansong.

Luckily there was no pursuit. Smith's convoy, with about 100
infantrymen, arrived safely at Ansong after dark the same day,
July 5. The next morning Smith and his infantrymen continued on
to Chonan, south of Pyongtaek, where he hoped to reconstitute
his battalion. Actually, the reconstitution was not effected until
July 11, at Chochiwon, where Companies B and C, brought to
strength with replacements, rejoined the 21st Regiment, newly
arrived from Pusan. Perry and the men of Battery A, 52d Field
Artillery, drove to Pyongtaek, where Perry reported to General
Barth the fate of Task Force Smith.

Back at Chonan Brad Smith counted his losses. They totalled
about 150 officers and men — killed, wounded, or missing. Additional survivors straggled back to the American lines during the
next several days. All of the artillery forward observers and
the members of Battery A's machine gun and bazooka teams were
lost.

Thus ended the gallant but relatively futile action of Task
Force Smith. It fought bravely while it lasted, but it was up
against overwhelming odds.* Hastily assembled in Japan — as it
had to be — limited in strength by the few air transports available
to fly it to Korea, and having practically no means of stopping
T-34 tanks and no combat support aviation, it proved inadequate

* The above narrative of the actions of Task Force Smith is based on the
thoroughly researched account in the United States Army's official history, *South
to the Naktong, North to the Yalu,* by Roy E. Appleman. The narrative has been
checked for accuracy by the task force commander, who retired in 1966 as a
Brigadier General.

to do more than serve as a first check against the North Korean invaders pouring south from captured Seoul. General MacArthur later gave the task force perhaps exaggerated credit for preventing the North Koreans from driving all the way to Pusan within the first week. He probably meant to give this credit not only to Task Force Smith but to the entire 24th Infantry Division, which followed the task force to Korea as rapidly as the division could be moved.

The 24th Division's Ordeal

The account of Task Force Smith's operations has been given in some detail, not only because the task force was the first American army unit in action in the Korean War, but because its experience was fairly typical of those of successive elements of the 24th Division.* These units had to be thrown into action piecemeal as they moved up to the front from Pusan.

The 1st Battalion, 34th Infantry, fought at Pyongtaek on July 5–6 but was outflanked and driven back with heavy losses. The same happened to the 3d Battalion, 34th Infantry, at Chonan on July 7 to 8 and to the 21st Infantry, which Brad Smith's reconstituted 1st Battalion had joined, at Chonui-Chochiwon, 12 miles south of Chonan, from July 8 to July 12. The 3d Regiment of the 24th Division, the 19th Infantry, had its baptism by fire on the Kum River from July 13 to July 16.

It was not until the 19th Infantry arrived in the vicinity of Taejon on July 11–12 that General Dean was able to establish some semblance of a division position. This he did along the Kum River, the first large stream south of the Han River. The Kum is a formidable natural barrier sweeping in an irregular arc around the important road and rail center of Taejon, from the Sobaek Mountains to the China Sea. Unfortunately, the 24th Division, with two of its regiments badly battered, was not in good enough

---

* Combat divisions of the United States Army, depending on the nature of their troops, are designated as Infantry, Cavalry, Airborne or Armored divisions, with numerical prefixes, e.g., 24th Infantry Division. Each division consists normally of three regiments which are designated by a number, e.g., 8th Cavalry Regiment or 8th Cavalry. The numbering of divisions and regiments no longer follows consecutively, but has traditional or historical significance.

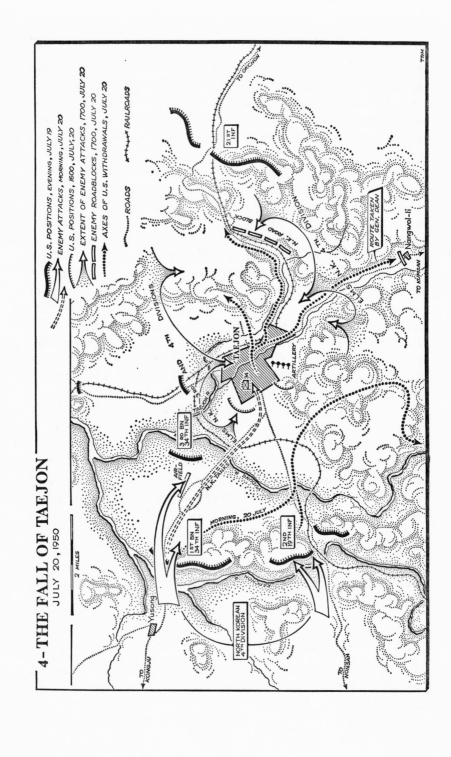

4- THE FALL OF TAEJON
JULY 20, 1950

U.S. POSITIONS, EVENING, JULY 19
ENEMY ATTACKS, MORNING, JULY 20
U.S. POSITIONS, 1600, JULY 20
EXTENT OF ENEMY ATTACKS, 1700, JULY 20
ENEMY ROADBLOCKS, 1700, JULY 20
AXES OF U.S. WITHDRAWALS, JULY 20
ROADS
RAILROADS

2 MILES

TO OKCHON

21ST INF

7TH DIVISION

N.K. ROAD BLOCK

3RD DIVISION

ROK GEN. TAKEN BY GEN. DEAN

Nangwol-li

TO KUMSAN

TAEJON

ARTILLERY

AID

4TH DIVISION

KUM RIVER

3RD BN 34TH INF

N.K. ROAD

AIR FIELD

N.K. ROAD

1ST BN 34TH INF

MORNING, 20 JULY

2ND 19TH INF

NORTH KOREAN 4TH DIVISION

Yusong

TO KONGJU

TO NONSAN

7RM

shape to hold even such a strong position. In order to cover the main approaches to the city, Dean had to dispose the 34th and 19th Infantry Regiments from west to east on a front of 18 miles — too great a front for these understrength units. The 21st Regiment, now at little more than battalion strength, was in reserve southeast of Taejon.

The 3d and 4th North Korean Divisions, which had also suffered heavy casualties in action and from bombers, were still far stronger than the U.S. 24th Division and had the advantage of choice of time, place, and direction of attack. Their attack was launched under cover of darkness early on July 14 and was concentrated first on the left flank of Dean's 34th Infantry Regiment, which gave way without much of a fight; this exposed the west flank and rear of the 19th Infantry. Following their usual tactic, the North Koreans, while pinning down the front-line units, turned both flanks of the 19th Infantry and established strong roadblocks to its rear. After two days of tough fighting, during which the regimental commander, Colonel Guy S. Meloy, Jr., was wounded and one of two battalion commanders was killed, the 19th Infantry was forced to withdraw to the vicinity of Taejon with great losses of men and materiel. The regiment and attached units and supporting artillery lost 650 officers and men, almost 20 percent of their initial strength.

Once again, this regiment, like the 21st and 34th Infantry Regiments, paid the penalty of having to try to hold overextended frontages with only two understrength battalions instead of three. Air support, which still had to come largely from Japan, was scanty and poorly coordinated, partly from lack of training and partly from inadequate communications equipment. And our soldiers, in contrast to the toughened North Koreans, were not conditioned to the burning sun, steep hills, and rugged terrain of Korea.

Taejon (See May 4)

As General Dean appraised the situation on the evening of July 16, he undoubtedly realized that the 24th Division, which he commanded, was now a division in name only. Each of his regiments was down in strength to the equivalent of a battalion. The 19th and 34th had new commanders. Colonel Meloy of the 19th had been evacuated wounded. Colonel Charles E. Beauchamp, who had just arrived from Japan to assume command of the 34th Infantry, was its fourth commander since the regiment had arrived in Korea two weeks before. The morale of men in all units was low, affected by frequent changes of command and the succession of defeats in their first experiences in combat. General Dean, tough, fine soldier that he was, had not spared himself in the ordeal through which the division had passed. He was nearing the limit of his endurance.

The mission assigned him by General MacArthur had been to achieve the maximal delay of the NK forces as far north of Pusan as possible, pending arrival of reinforcements. Prior to the Kum River battle he had selected his next delaying position on a high ridge back of the Kapchon River 3 miles west of Taejon.

General Dean had planned to withdraw from Taejon on July 19 after forcing the North Koreans to deploy and prepare their attack, but this was changed by a visit from Lieutenant General Walton H. Walker, commander of the Eighth Army, who flew into Taejon that morning from his command post at Taegu. General MacArthur had sent Walker over to take command in Korea on July 13 in anticipation of the arrival of the 25th Infantry Division and other reinforcing units of the Eighth Army. The 25th Division was already committed north of Taegu to back up the hard-pressed ROK Army, which had been operating east of the 24th Division. The 1st Cavalry Division had started to land that day at Pohang-dong on the Korean southeast coast. Walker planned to move it overland to reinforce the 24th Division in the mountain passes southeast of Taejon. He hoped that with the Eighth Army and the ROK Army he would be able to stabilize the front from the upper reaches of the Naktong River to Yongdok on the east coast, until he could pass to the counteroffensive.

Walker told Dean that to get the 1st Cavalry Division into position he would need two days' delay at Taejon. He also told Dean that he had confidence in Dean's judgment and that, if it became necessary to abandon Taejon earlier, Dean should do so. After Walker left, Dean informed Colonel Stephens, commanding the 21st Infantry, that the scheduled withdrawal would be delayed twenty-four hours. He then drove to Yongdong, 28 miles southeast of Taejon, where his headquarters had already been established. There he decided to move the 2d Battalion, 19th Infantry, back up to Taejon to bolster Colonel Beauchamp's 34th Infantry south flank. He also directed his staff to issue orders attaching the division Reconnaissance Company to the 34th Infantry. In placing this company directly under control of the 34th Dean wished to ensure that it would furnish to Beauchamp immediate information of any enemy move against the 34th's exposed left flank. He later said he had not intended to move the Reconnaissance Company to Taejon from Kumsan, 20 miles south of Taejon, where it was fairly well placed for performing its mission; however, the order as issued directed the move to Taejon. In giving up control of the Reconnaissance Company Dean, like General Lee with Jeb Stuart at Gettysburg, lost his "eyes and ears," which could have kept him informed about what was happening on the division's south flank. Dean subsequently said this was one of his greatest mistakes in the Taejon battle.

Division headquarters at Yongdong was too far back to control any action at Taejon, so Dean went back to Taejon for the night, taking with him only an aide, First Lieutenant Arthur M. Clarke, and two assistant staff officers.

The North Korean's attack on Taejon began the morning of July 19 with a succession of small bombing and machine-gun raids. This was their first attack by air against an American position. It was not effective. The U.S. Air Force countered with attacks against known and suspected enemy concentration points north and west of Taejon. These attacks could not be sustained because there were only two small fighter strips capable of handling American fighter bombers within the Eighth Army and ROK lines.

More serious than these air strikes were the attacks of the NK 4th Division, which were skillfully directed against the 34th Infantry. The latter held off the North Koreans during daylight hours, though its 1st Battalion and the 2d Battalion, 19th Infantry, were fully engaged, and heavy concentrations of artillery were pounding the airstrip area and the infantry positions. After dark there was growing evidence that the enemy was infiltrating in the mile-wide gap between these two battalions and around the south flank. Lieutenant Colonel Harold B. Ayers, commanding officer of the 1st Battalion, 34th Infantry, recommended to Beauchamp that the regiment withdraw, a suggestion he had made also in the afternoon. However, Beauchamp felt he could hold the city another day and, presumably, General Dean agreed. During the night the enemy, following his standard tactic, was quietly blockading the Kumsan and Okchon roads close to Taejon. Patrols from the Reconnaissance Company in the city timidly probed at these blocks but apparently failed to report their location or strength to Colonel Beauchamp or General Dean.

The main NK attack was launched about 3:00 A.M. on July 20. The 1st Battalion, 34th Infantry, was quickly outflanked and penetrated by enemy tanks and infantry, and wire communication lines between battalion headquarters and its rifle companies were cut. Colonel Ayers got a message through to Colonel Beauchamp that his position was being overrun by tanks, which were on the way to Taejon. Then the telephone line to the battalion went out. Beauchamp tried to reach Ayers' command post by jeep but in the darkness was almost run over by an enemy tank at a road junction on the western outskirts of the city. He was slightly wounded and the jeep set afire. The colonel scrambled back until he found a bazooka team, which was equipped with one of the newly arrived 3.5-inch rocket launchers. He led this team back to the road junction, where its rockets set the T-34 afire. Later this team and another from the Reconnaissance Company destroyed two other enemy tanks approaching from the airstrip. These were the first T-34's known definitely to have been destroyed in Korea by 3.5-inch rocket HEAT ammunition.

Shortly after daylight Colonel Beauchamp, out of communication with his 1st Battalion, had ordered the 3d Battalion to attack in the gap between the 1st Battalion, 34th Infantry, and the 2d Battalion, 19th Infantry. The leading company soon ran into an enemy force, estimated to be a battalion with six T-34 tanks, on the road to the airstrip. The company was dispersed, and the battalion, making no further effort, returned to its original position east of the airfield. It stayed there the rest of the morning, unmolested by enemy action except for occasional mortar and artillery fire, but it apparently remained out of touch with regimental headquarters, which failed to check on the outcome of the action.

Soon after this abortive attack three NK tanks, their decks crowded with soldiers, entered Taejon from the northwest. They drove without opposition to the central square, where the soldiers scattered into buildings, from which they delivered sniping fire throughout the day. The tanks then turned on a large compound, where the Service Company and 1st Battalion motor pools and kitchen trucks were located. About 150 men were in the compound when the tank cannon opened fire. A number of men were killed, some vehicles were destroyed, and an ammunition truck was set afire. Not until after the tanks had rumbled away did anyone in the compound find a 3.5-inch bazooka. Then, to add to the confusion, someone fired a 3.5-inch rocket at snipers in a building, setting it on fire. The fire jumped to near-by thatched-roofed houses and soon spread over a large section of the city.

Eight or ten T-34 tanks penetrated the city during the day, moving either singly or in pairs without supporting infantry. They did considerable damage but caused no panic, and all were ultimately destroyed, mostly by 3.5-inch rockets. General Dean personally led some of the bazooka teams in a successful effort to convince the men that their new weapon was a tank killer. But the personal involvement of a senior commander in the combat of small units or in one small segment of an action tends to divert his mind from larger issues. And possibly the presence of the division commander in and about the regimental command post, even though General Dean did not interfere, caused Colonel Beauchamp, new to the regiment and to North Korean tactics, to hold back from taking vigorous action to determine the actual status of his units and the enemy.

For, while these random tank encounters were occurring in Taejon, unbeknownst to either Dean or Beauchamp, the enemy was continuing his encircling movements on the south and east and establishing roadblocks along all roads out of the city. For some time there had been no telephone or radio contact with the 1st Battalion, 34th Infantry, or the 2d Battalion, 19th Infantry, and runners had not been able to reach them. Apparently this information was not relayed to Beauchamp. At noon, Dean and Beauchamp had a quiet lunch together at the command post, completely unaware that the two battalions they assumed were still in position along the Kapchon River had actually disappeared into the hills. Perhaps sensing something forboding in the relative quiet in the city itself, Dean, after lunch, directed Beauchamp to initiate a daylight withdrawal instead of waiting until dark. It was already too late.

It has been difficult for military historians to piece together, from interviews and correspondence with survivors and from the location of destroyed vehicles discovered later when Taejon was retaken, just what happened in the last agonizing hours of the 34th Infantry's attempts at withdrawal from Taejon. Shortly after noon enemy troops west and northwest of the city began putting pressure on the few antitank and combat engineer units guarding the city entrances. Mortar and artillery salvos increased, starting numerous fires, which hung a pall of smoke over the doomed city. In some instances enemy forces moving to the attack were mistaken for friendly troops falling back and were not engaged. By mid-afternoon enemy groups began penetrating the city.

About 3:00 P.M. Colonel Beauchamp left his command post to check on the movement of the first convoy going out by way of the Okchon road. He never got back. While endeavoring to turn around four fleeing light tanks of the 24th Reconnaissance Company he and the tanks were caught by enemy fire. Realizing he was cut off from Taejon, Beauchamp decided to employ the tanks to establish a delaying position at a pass four miles to the east. He added some passing antiaircraft vehicles with multiple machine-gun mounts but was unable to flag down an infantry company driving wildly past. Seeing that the road was undergoing increasing fire, Beauchamp telephoned the Assistant Division Commander, Brigadier General Pearson Menoher, at the 21st Infantry regimental command post in Okchon. Menoher told him to come on in to Okchon for a full report.

After lunch General Dean had also left the 34th Infantry command post to check on preparations for, and progress of, the withdrawal. It was not until late afternoon that he learned that Colonel Beauchamp had not returned. By this time he knew also of the ambuscades on the Okchon road, and he could both see and hear the increasing firing within the city. After filing a message, to be radioed to the 24th Division headquarters in Yongdong, to send a column of tanks to open the Okchon road he ordered the regimental executive, Lieutenant Colonel Robert L. Wadlington, to close the command post and organize a convoy to break through to Okchon. Dean and Clarke took their places in the convoy as it started from the command post area about 6:00 P.M. Driving through the tortuous streets, the convoy was stopped by disabled vehicles at almost every intersection while being swept by murderous machine-gun fire. The convoy soon broke up into small groups, which tried to get around the blocked intersections by way of side streets and back alleys, some of which were aflame with burning houses. Turns were missed and directions lost. Those groups that succeeded in getting out of the city were either ambushed or trapped by the omnipresent roadblocks. Most had to destroy their vehicles and make their way by foot over the hills toward Kumsan or Yongdong.

General Dean's jeep and an escort sped past one flaming intersection and were well on the way toward Kumsan before his aide, Lieutenant Clarke, discovered that they had missed the road fork to Okchon. It was too late to turn back. Some distance out of town they came on a wrecked truck with several wounded men in it. Dean stopped, had these men loaded into the two jeeps, and waved them on. He and two or three other soldiers clambered aboard an escaping half-track vehicle and sped south. But not for long. A short distance ahead the jeeps and half-track were halted by an overturned truck which was covered by enemy machine-gun and rifle fire. The group, including the wounded, tumbled into the ditches. Dean and most of the party crawled off and hid in a garden on the banks of the Taejon River until black darkness fell.

According to Lieutenant Clarke's later account, they then crossed to the west of the river and began climbing a rugged mountain. General Dean and the able men took turns in helping the badly wounded. Frequent stops were made for rest, since everyone was exhausted. Some time after midnight Clarke, who was leading the group, suddenly realized that he was alone. He turned back and found several of the party asleep, but Dean was missing. One of the men said that the general had gone for water for the wounded. Figuring that Dean could make the round trip to the river in about an hour, Clarke decided to wait two hours. When Dean had not returned by 3:15 A.M., Clarke woke the sleeping men, and they climbed to the top of the mountain, which they reached by dawn. The group rested there all day, about 5 miles south of Taejon, waiting in vain for the general to return. After darkness fell, Clarke led his party back down the mountain and recrossed the river, but with no sign of General Dean. Heading east into the mountains and then south, the party eventually made its way into Yongdong on July 23.

More than three years passed before General Dean's final ordeal became known. In going down to the Taejon River for water he had tripped in the darkness, fallen down a steep slope, and been knocked unconscious. On regaining consciousness he found that he had a broken shoulder, a badly gashed head, and many bruises. The party was nowhere in sight, and he realized it had had to go on without him. For the next thirty-six days Dean moved south through the mountains trying to reach our lines. But the North Koreans were moving rapidly and with little opposition at this time, and Dean had to travel through rugged country to avoid detection. On August 25 two South Koreans, who pretended to be guiding him to safety, led him into a prearranged North Korean ambush. The emaciated general, almost starved, weighed only 130 pounds, sixty pounds under his normal 190. For the next three years he languished in a prison camp without being able to get any word to his family. He was finally released to American authorities at Panmunjom on September 4, 1953.

The 24th Division had succeeded in delaying the greatly superior North Korean forces for two and a half weeks, thereby gaining the precious time required to bring essential reinforcements from Japan and the United States. The division had accomplished its mission but at a dreadful price. When it was relieved by the 1st Cavalry Division at Yongdong on July 22 it mustered 8660 of its initial strength of 12,197, a loss of almost 30 percent. Equipment losses were estimated at 60 to 70 percent.

General Dean and units of the 24th Infantry Division made a number of mistakes at Taejon and in the earlier engagements, which Dean honestly admitted in his moving book *General Dean's Story*. But he and his division were less the victims of their own errors than of the disregard of the American people for the necessity, in peacetime, of being prepared for war.

IV

MILITARY PLANS AND BUDGETS

Why the Ordeal of the 24th Division?

THE CASUALTIES and humiliations suffered by the 24th Infantry Division stemmed from several causes, some military, some economic, and some political.

Peacetime occupation duty in a foreign land probably is the worst possible precondition for combat. Until April of 1949, when General MacArthur relinquished to Japanese authorities most of the police and administrative responsibilities of the occupation forces, divisions of the Far East Command had little time or incentive to engage in training. The emphasis was on orderliness, good conduct, and "lending a helping hand to a defeated foe." Even after military training was stressed in the new directives of the Eighth Army, there were severe physical limitations on field exercises. The islands of Japan are overcrowded, its arable land is at a premium, and almost every hillside is terraced for cultivation. In an effort to assist the Japanese in the production of essential food the firing ranges for artillery, tanks, mortars, and even small arms were strictly limited, and large-scale maneuver areas were nonexistent. When the Korean war broke, few units of the Eighth Army had reached a satisfactory level of battalion training, and combined training with air and naval support had just got under way. None of the four divisions had operated in the field as a division since World War II.

After World War II, as was pointed out earlier in this book, we dismantled the most powerful military forces the United States had ever created. The Army had been particularly hard hit, since it bore the heaviest manpower requirements for occupation duties in both Europe and the Far East and for training missions abroad. With the expiration of the draft and the failure of the Congress to pass a compulsory training bill the Army was forced to rely on relatively short enlistment terms and increasingly lowered mental and physical standards. At the outset of the Korean war 43 percent of Army enlisted men in the Far East Command were rated in Class IV or V, the lowest ratings on the Army General Classification Tests. Even more important, with each successive reduction in appropriations the Army was faced with almost equally undesirable alternatives: either to reduce the number of divisions and auxiliary combat units it maintained or partially to skeletonize them. By 1949 the eighty-nine divisions that were sent abroad in World War II were cut to fourteen (four of which were solely for training purposes); these were regarded as the irreducible minimum. Even this small number could not be kept at full strength. One battalion was cut from each regiment of infantry and one battery from each battalion of artillery, and similar reductions were made in other units. The lack of these elements in the early phases of the Korean war, especially the shortage of reserve battalions, resulted in the loss, not only of battles, but also of American soldiers' lives.

Comparable deficiencies existed in the quality and quantity of materiel and equipment and of the military service units responsible for their maintenance. Large stocks of supplies had been left all over the Pacific at the end of World War II. Much of this had been collected and was in process of being rehabilitated in Japan, but in the face of the mounting stockpile the Administration and Congress ignored the fact that much of this materiel was outmoded, and many critical new items, such as medium tanks, 4.2-inch mortars, and 3.5-inch recoilless rifles, were in short supply. Though HEAT, the special antitank "shaped charge" ammunition for recoilless rifles, rockets, and artillery, had been developed during the period of 1942 to 1948, only modest quantities had been manufactured. Little of it was made available to the Far East Command, which had a lower priority for such shells than the European theater. Consequently, the units of the 24th Division sent to Korea had little or no effective means of stopping the T-34 tanks that caused such havoc in the division's early engagements.

It would seem that proper planning and budgeting should have obviated these personnel and materiel shortages. However, military plans and budget limitations except in wartime have invariably been in conflict. The essence of military planning is to look ahead to the requirements of the next war; but this is antithetic to the common American hope that each war will be the last. While a war is on, Congress and the people have supported unstintingly the demands of the military services but, once the war is over, political and economic pressures relegate military planning to the background.

Prior to the passage of the 1949 Amendments to the National Security Act there was little scientific correlation of military budgets and appropriations with military planning. The Joint Chiefs of Staff of that day endeavored to keep up-to-date strategic plans for all likely areas of conflict. These plans assigned missions to the Army, Navy, Air Force, and Marine Corps. According to their assigned missions, the services calculated the forces they required. When finally agreed to by the JCS, the major plan or plans and these "force tabs" were submitted to the Secretary of Defense for approval.

By 1949 the Secretary of Defense had established guidelines for military budgeting, which embodied political and economic factors in consonance with the President's overall programs. The JCS and the Army, Navy, and Air Force were limited by these guidelines in calculating their requirements for personnel and materiel. Even after we had worked for months, trying to reconcile true military requirements with the guidelines and translating these requirements into dollars and cents, the day would always come when we would be told that the dollar ceiling for each service was such-and-such below our final requests.

Then would begin the agonizing readjustment of the planned force tabs to meet the hard dollar allocations. The Chief of a service, together with his Secretary, then had to decide whether to reduce the number of combat units and supporting logistical elements or to maintain them at reduced strengths, hoping to

have time in case of emergency to flesh them out with reservists.

Military Budgets of FY 1949 and FY 1950

The history of the military budgets for the fiscal years 1949 (1948–
1949) and 1950 (1949–1950) illustrates the attitudes of the Administration and the Congress just prior to the Korean war. World
War II had proven the tremendous importance of supporting
air power, without which no major land or naval operation can
succeed. The newly created U.S. Air Force had just won its
fight, largely with Army support, for its own department within
the Department of Defense and was vying with the older services
for a larger share of military appropriations. For fiscal year 1949,
commencing July 1, 1948, the President originally submitted a
combined budget of $5.7 billion for the Army and Air Force.
Before Congress could take action on these estimates, the worsening international situation, particularly in Europe, caused the
President to submit supplemental estimates to increase the Army
and Air Force to a combined strength of 1,250,000 men and their
combined budgets to $7.2 billion. The Congress, while authoriz-
ing the obligation of $9.04 billion for the Army and Air Force,
actually limited their cash expenditures to a combined total of
$6.69 billion, with a total cash expenditure for the entire Depart-
ment of Defense of $10.4 billion.

The skeptical attitude of Congress was well stated by the report
of the House Appropriations Committee:

> . . . the committee's careful scrutiny of the estimates of man-
> power, equipment, and missions to be performed leads to the
> conclusion that the estimates of funds required are out of pro-
> portion to the actual needs on the basis of the Army's predic-
> tions of requirements. While the committee does not propose to
> reduce the size of the Army below numbers estimated by the
> military authorities as requisite or the amounts of equipment
> and supplies necessary to maintain such an Army, it is well
> aware of the fact that it is the habit of the services to estimate
> their fund requirements generously in order that they may be

able to meet all contingencies. This is a sound policy to follow during actual warfare and the Congress at that time approved it but there is no sound reason why the Army cannot be administered in peacetime with more regard for dollars than apparently is their custom or intent.

The military budget for the fiscal year 1950 was the first prepared under the terms of the "Unification Act" and the first to include a substantially autonomous budget for the Department of the Air Force. The original estimates of the services totalled $30 billion. This astonishing sum for a peacetime budget resulted partly from an internal struggle for funds, principally between the Air Force and naval aviation. More importantly, it reflected the genuine concern of the Chiefs of Staff over our decreasing ability to meet increasing commitments abroad. The Secretary of Defense reduced the original JCS estimates and recommended to the Bureau of the Budget a figure of $16.9 billion. He later cut this to $14.5 billion. After the President had obtained "the considered advice of civilian and military leaders best qualified to evaluate the international, strategic and economic aspects of our national defense requirements," he set a ceiling of $14.2 billion. Congress voted cash and contract authorizations of $4.248 billion for the Army, $4.105 billion for the Navy, $4.678 billion for the Air Force, and $191 million for the office of the Secretary of Defense, making a total of $13.222 billion, which was essentially the same as for the fiscal year 1949.

Similar reductions had been made in the preparation of the budget for the fiscal year 1951, which began July 1, 1950, right after the North Korean attack of June 25, 1950. This was the first budget under my tenure as Army Chief of Staff. It must be remembered that congressional hearings on this budget had begun in January of 1950. The original estimates of the services totalled approximately $20 billion. General Eisenhower, who had retired, was asked by the President to assist in reviewing these original estimates. The JCS in consultation with General Eisenhower reduced this to a somewhat lower figure. The President, on the advice of the Bureau of the Budget, fixed a ceiling of $13 billion, almost $1 billion less than the actual appropriation for the fiscal year 1950.

General Bradley, then Chairman of the JCS, accepted and defended this figure in the Senate Appropriations Subcommittee Hearings on March 13, 1950:

> I emphasized in my statement — maybe I did not emphasize it sufficiently — that the eventual strength of our country depends upon its industrial capacity. We must not destroy that by spending too much from year to year. So if we came here and recommended to you a $30,000,000,000 or $40,000,000,000 budget for defense, I think we would be doing a disservice and that maybe you should get a new Chairman of the Joint Chiefs of Staff if I were the one that did that.

I, likewise, as Army Chief of Staff, defended the $13 billion budget before the same senate subcommittee. In answer to a question from the Chairman, Senator Elmer Thomas of Oklahoma, the following colloquy developed:

> *General Collins:* We feel that everything we do in a military way now ought to be aimed primarily at the prevention of a third world war, not merely the winning of it. However, we must do everything we can so that, if war does come on, we will win it.
>
> But everything we do, in my judgment — and I feel this very strongly — ought to be along the line of seeing what we can do to prevent the development of another war. And I can assure you that that is our general thought. That is why the military departments have supported such things as the Marshall plan, the North Atlantic Treaty, and the mutual defense-assistance program.
>
> We think that those three programs, linked together with a strong military position on the part of the United States, will go a long way — and we think they have gone a long way — toward the prevention of war up to now.
>
> *Senator Saltonstall:* May I add one expression?
>
> *General Collins:* Yes, sir.
>
> *Senator Saltonstall:* Within our economic strength.

General Collins: And I thoroughly agree with that qualification, that Senator Saltonstall has added. We realize that, if there is anything that gives any nation pause today with respect to starting a possible war, it is less the actual military strength of the United States than the tremendous industrial potential of this country. And that is why, as military men, when you ask us the question, "Are we satisfied with $13,000,000,000," we say "No military man will ever tell you that he couldn't use more money, but we believe that, on balance — remembering that there is something besides sheer military might that is a deterrent to war — the $13,000,000,000 is an excellent figure, but a minimum figure.

In commenting specifically on the strength of the Army that could be maintained under the Army's allocation of $4.018 billion, within the $13 billion ceiling for the Department of Defense, I said:

The 10 divisions provided by this budget do not constitute the force in being that the Army considers necessary. We have consistently believed that we should have in the Regular Army, under conditions existing today, 12 Regular Army divisions trained and equipped for immediate deployment in the event of an emergency. We can safely reduce to approximately this number only if we maintain a high state of readiness in our National Guard and Organized Reserve Corps.

However, we are supporting this budget that will provide only 10 divisions because we realize the necessity to integrate Army requirements with those of the other Services within our national budget. And we will do everything within our power to lessen the risk that such a reduction must by necessity entail.

Actual expenditures for the fiscal year 1951, beginning the day we entered the Korean war, totalled $19.8 billion, which almost exactly equalled the original estimates of the services. Three supplemental budgets, which included obligations for future deliveries of additional ammunition and other materiel and equipment, had to be submitted during the fiscal year 1951, as the war developed. These totaled almost three times the original estimates. The following year, at the height of the war, the President recommended military obligations for the fiscal year 1952 of $60 billion.

From this record it is clear that members of the JCS, including General Bradley and myself, shared with the President, the Administration, and the Congress the responsibility for reductions in JCS estimates of military requirements, which so hampered our conduct of the Korean war. It has sometimes been argued — as it was once argued with me by a member of the Senate Armed Services Committee — that the JCS should submit its estimates of military requirements without any consideration of their impact on the national economy. There may be some theoretical merit to this idea, but it is contrary to our American system and, in fact, contrary to the Budget and Accounting Act of 1921. This act requires that officers and employees of the executive branch of the government support the President's budget recommendations and offer "no request for an increase in an item . . . unless at the request of either House of Congress." The prescribed procedure in the Department of the Army in my day was that an Army witness was bound to present and support all budget items unless specifically asked by a Committee member for the witness' personal views. This was frequently done, in which case the witness was free to express his own views or not, according to his judgment.

I always believed that in loyalty to the President — who, as Commander in Chief, bears the ultimate responsibility for the defense of our country — an officer of the armed services should fully support the President's program once it has been determined. I am convinced that as a practical matter ordinarily more can be accomplished by sticking to the established procedure within a service. Arguments should be made through the civilian Secretaries and the Bureau of the Budget and not directly or surreptitiously to the Congress. A Chief of Staff is sometimes faced with the dilemma of resigning or of going directly to the President, over the head of the Secretary of Defense — which he is entitled by law to do — if he cannot, in all conscience as a responsible military man, accept the final budget limitations. By the time I became Chief of Staff in October 1949, four of our fourteen divisions had been relegated to training-center duties, and the ten remaining combat divisions were far below authorized strength. When Secretary of Defense Louis Johnson announced at an Armed Forces Policy Council meeting another cut in the Army budget for the fiscal year 1951, which would have resulted in a further reduction in the effective strength of the Army, I finally had to say to him, "Mr. Secretary, this is the last cut in the Army that I will be able to accept." Johnson demanded, "What did you say?" I repeated, "This is the last cut in the Army that I will be able to accept." Johnson glared at me, and I am afraid that I glared back. I feel certain that if the Korean war had not intervened, I would have been relieved or forced to resign.

Looking back, perhaps the JCS should have taken a firmer stand in defending its $30 billion estimate for the fiscal year 1950, even in the face of broad public concern for the mounting national debt, the lessening purchasing power of the dollar, and the insistent demands for economy in government by all candidates for public office. This probably would not have had much practical effect under Secretary Johnson, who was once referred to by one of his civilian colleagues as "Secretary of Economy, not Secretary of Defense."

Re-examination of United States Objectives

I may be unfair to Johnson, since he probably had been carrying out instructions from President Truman, who had the ultimate responsibility for the budgetary program of his administration. With the darkening world situation and the expected early development of a thermonuclear capacity in the Soviet Union the President on January 31, 1950, called on the Secretaries of State and Defense and the Chairman of the Atomic Energy Commission for a re-examination of our objectives in peace and war and the effect of these objectives on our strategic plans.

Secretary Johnson referred the President's request to the JCS for comments and recommendations concerning the effect of the Soviet thermonuclear capacity on our emergency and long-range strategic plans. The JCS designated their Joint Strategic Survey Committee to initiate the military study and to work with the State Department's Policy Planning Staff, headed by Paul Nitze, on the preparation of a joint State-Defense paper. Secretary Johnson named General James H. Burns, one of his assistants, to coordinate the actions and views of all interested Defense Department agencies, including the service Secretaries.

By April 1, 1950, a completed State-Defense report, with concurrences from the JCS, the Secretaries of Army, Navy, and Air Force, and General Burns, was approved by the Secretaries of State and Defense, who submitted it to the President a few days later. Shortly thereafter Mr. Truman directed the National Security Council to provide him with information about the implications of the State-Defense report of April 1, especially with respect to the programs envisaged and their costs. While this was being done, a paper was discussed and developed in the Security Council and finally approved by the President on April 25.

According to Cabell Phillips in his book *The Truman Presidency*, this study called for, in Phillips' words, ". . . the end of subordinating security needs to the traditional budgeting restrictions; of asking, 'How much security can we afford?' In other words, security must henceforth become the dominant element in the national budget, and other elements must be accommodated to it." As a member of the JCS I had access to the Security Council's study at the time, but it has not been declassified from its top security category. According to my memory it was not nearly as specific as Mr. Phillips indicates, though it did recommend rearmament and rehabilitation of our armed forces and increased help to our allies.

The study was transmitted to the Department of Defense for cost estimates, but too late to affect the initial budget for the fiscal year 1951. It should have come five years earlier, when we were wrecking our powerful World War II military forces, which now would have to be re-created.

More valid charges of military failures in the early phases of the Korean war — or, more accurately, failures of the established civilian-military *system* — can be made in the field of military intelligence. After the duty of overseeing American interests in Korea had been transferred in 1948 from General MacArthur to the Department of State, there was a hiatus of responsibility for intelligence. Korea was outside the geographical boundaries of the Far East Command, though the latter's Intelligence Officer, Major General Willoughby, maintained a surveillance detachment in Korea. Willoughby furnished several reports of rumored North Korean invasion plans to Washington in routine Daily Intelligence Summaries during the period of December 30, 1949, to May 25, 1950, but he discounted all of these reports. Similarly, a report from Ambassador Muccio to the Department of State in May 1950 stated that there seemed to be little likelihood that North Korean forces would attack the Republic of Korea in the near future. The Korean Military Advisory Group worked closely with ROK Army intelligence agencies and sent periodic reports to Ambassador Muccio. Copies of these reports ultimately reached the State Department and Army Intelligence in Washington. Perhaps it was because Korea had been regarded by both diplomatic and military leaders as an area of secondary interest to the United States that intelligence agencies throughout the government gave no concentrated or coordinated attention to the likelihood of an attack in that country.

Lack of Coordination of Intelligence

Major General Lyman L. Lemnitzer, on the staff of the Secretary of Defense, put his finger on the weakness of the lack of co-ordination within the intelligence community in Washington. In a memorandum to Secretary Johnson after the outbreak of the Korean war he wrote:

> I recommend that . . . a clear-cut inter-agency standing operating procedure be established now to insure that if (in the opinion of any intelligence agency, particularly CIA) an attack, or other noteworthy event, is impending, it is made a matter of special handling to insure that officials vitally concerned . . .

are promptly and personally informed thereof, in order that appropriate measures may be taken. This will prevent a repetition of the Korean situation and will insure, if there has been any vital intelligence data pointing to an imminent attack, that it will not be buried in a series of routine CIA intelligence reports.

But, as Colonel James F. Schnabel has pointed out in his excellent analysis of the Korean intelligence situation in 1950, any controversy over charges of intelligence failure are almost academic: "The United States had no plans to counter such an invasion, even had it forecast it to the very day. Its only planned reaction was to be the evacuation of U.S. nationals from Korea."

While there were some mitigating circumstances surrounding the failure of the intelligence community in Washington to take seriously the imminence of a North Korean invasion, it is difficult to understand the woeful underestimating by the Korean Military Advisory Group and the Far East Command of the leadership and fighting qualities of the North Korean Army. It was not until General MacArthur had received eyewitness reports from Generals Church and Dean, who had seen American troops — outnumbered though they were — badly mauled and skillfully outflanked by the North Koreans, that the extent of the task of saving Korea from being overrun began to be realized.

Far East Command Calls for Help

MacArthur relayed these reports to the Joint Chiefs of Staff in Washington, who were following the situation with increasing foreboding. By July 7 General MacArthur had more than doubled his original estimate of American strength that would be required to hold the North Koreans. He now estimated that he would need four or four and a half full-strength divisions plus an airborne regimental combat team and an armored group. He radioed the JCS that 30,000 officers and men would have to be sent from the United States at once. He warned the Joint Chiefs, "It is a minimum, without which success will be extremely doubtful."

Two days later, on July 9, General MacArthur nearly doubled his July 7 estimate. He radioed that the situation in Korea was critical. He expressed some doubt that with the forces available to him in the Far East Command he could hold even the southern tip of Korea. MacArthur concluded, "I strongly urge that, in addition to those forces already requisitioned, an army of at least four divisions, with all component services, be dispatched to this area without delay, and by every means available."

These and subsequent demands, all perfectly legitimate and warranted, placed a tremendous burden on the resources of the Defense Department, especially the Army which, as always, would have to do the bulk of the fighting and suffer the heaviest casualties. The JCS, and I personally as Army Chief of Staff, pledged to General MacArthur our full support. But it was impossible to meet promptly all his requests.

First of all, we did not have the wherewithal in the form of trained reserves of units or replacements and, second, we had to consider, not only the immediate danger in Korea, but also the much greater potential threat of a Communist attack against Berlin and Western Europe. Studies made in early July by the Joint Strategic Plans Committee, an agency of the JCS responsible for the preparation of strategic plans, pointed up the questions facing the JCS: Was the Communist action in Korea, in which for the first time the Russians were utilizing the forces of a satellite for external aggression, the beginning of a new phase of Communist action that would become world-wide? If so, how much of our existing military forces could we commit to Korea without seriously weakening our ability to meet emergencies elsewhere? And, finally, if we limited our commitments to Korea, would the United Nations forces be able to drive the North Koreans back across the 38th Parallel? The urgency of the situation in Korea prevented any orderly or conclusive evaluation of these questions before action had to be taken to prevent the complete overrunning of South Korea.

Individual replacements were in immediate demand, since all units in the Far East were under strength, and casualties added to the shortages from the first day of action. An airlift of 7350 replacements from the United States was initiated at once and built up as rapidly as transports and trained officers and soldiers could be made available. General MacArthur rightly demanded that replacements be trained men, ready to fight, since they would go directly into action to fill the ranks of depleted units of the 24th Division.

Here in the States the headquarters, depots, service installations, and even essential military schools were combed for qualified men. By the end of July, 7350 replacements had been flown to the Far East. But, counting combat losses and the number of men needed to bring the Far East Command's four divisions to authorized war strength, General MacArthur's requirement for replacements by September 1, 1950, totaled almost 82,000. This requirement simply could not be met on time, even though the President had authorized the recall of 25,000 members of the Enlisted Reserve Corps; these men would require some retraining, and most would have to go, initially at least, into the General Reserve.

In addition to individual replacements, General MacArthur submitted urgent pleas to the JCS for organized infantry battalions and artillery batteries for the four divisions of the Eighth Army. The infantry battalion and the division are the basic fighting units of the Army. The standard infantry division of World War II and the Korean war consisted principally of three infantry regiments and an artillery brigade. Each regiment was supposed to have three battalions. Normally, each infantry regiment was supported by an artillery battalion of three batteries of 105mm howitzers, but the infantry regiments in Japan had each been reduced by one battalion and the artillery battalions by one battery. Without its third battalion a regiment is vulnerable to enemy outflanking, a fact on which the North Koreans capitalized repeatedly. To bring the Eighth Army to proper organizational strength would require eleven additional battalions of infantry, eleven howitzer batteries, four medium-tank battalions, and twelve light-tank companies.

However, the General Reserve in the United States, on which the JCS relied to meet any unforeseen contingencies abroad, had a total of only eighteen infantry battalions, including those with the 82d Airborne Division and with our one Armored Division. The armored infantry battalions were not well suited for employment in Korea, and we had to keep the 82d Airborne Division intact for emergency use anywhere. By tapping units in Hawaii and Okinawa, besides the General Reserve, the best we could do was to earmark for Korea a total of eight full-strength infantry battalions and cadres for three more. Similarly, only by stripping batteries from Hawaii, Okinawa, and the General Reserve was the Army able to provide the requisite eleven batteries of 105mm howitzers. These units plus three medium-tank battalions and four antiaircraft battalions were approved for dispatch to the Far East Command. Somewhat later three of the five 155mm howitzer battalions in the General Reserve, the lone 8-inch howitzer battalion, the one 155mm gun battalion, an observation battalion, and the 5th Field Artillery Group Headquarters were cleared for shipment. In addition a number of ordnance ammunition and maintenance companies and signal, engineer, medical, quartermaster, and transportation units were required to build and operate ports, railroads, and supply depots and to provide the myriad services required of an army in the field. These also had to be taken from the General Reserve or called to active duty from the Organized Reserve or National Guard.

As Army Chief of Staff and Executive Agent for both the European theater and the Far East, I was perhaps more concerned than the other Chiefs with the strength and readiness for service of the General Reserve. Initially we would have to call on Regular Army units at home and abroad, but even these were far below authorized war strength and, when sent to the Far East, would have to be replaced in the General Reserve by National Guard or Organized Reserve units. Moreover, without a declaration of war or a national emergency declared by the President there were legal and technical difficulties in calling up individuals or units of the reserve components. It was not until June 30 that Congress gave the President this authority.

The withdrawal of most of the above-mentioned units from the General Reserve would so weaken our ability to react to any potential threat in theaters other than the Far East that the JCS felt that the risks it would entail should be brought to the attention of the Commander in Chief and his personal approval obtained. This was done through the Secretary of Defense, who concurred with the JCS recommendations. After considering the risks involved President Truman gave his approval.

The Visit of Vandenberg and Collins to the Far East Command

In order properly to weigh future requirements for men, materiel, and money, the President and his advisers needed more direct information. To this end the President on July 10 directed the JCS to send two of our members to the Far East for a firsthand estimate of the situation. General Vandenberg and I were designated. We were accompanied by Lieutenant Colonels Dickson and Denson of the Army Staff and by two officers from the Air Force Staff. We flew to Tokyo, arriving there in the early morning of July 13.

At 9:00 A.M. we met General MacArthur, Lieutenant General Walker, who had flown over from Korea, Major General Almond, who was MacArthur's Chief of Staff, and other key staff officers. Admiral Arthur Radford, the Commander in Chief of the Pacific Fleet, arrived during the conference.

MacArthur was cool and poised as always. He spoke with confidence and élan as he paced back and forth in his customary fashion. He always gave me the impression of addressing not just his immediate listeners but a larger audience unseen.

He gave a realistic appraisal of the situation, cautioning against underestimating the toughness, skill, and leadership of the North Koreans. He refused to guess where or exactly when the enemy advance would be halted but expressed confidence that the battlefront would be stabilized. This would be necessary before he could launch a counteroffensive. How soon it could be done and its ultimate success would depend directly on the speed with which we sent him replacements and the degree to which we met his requirement for additional troop units.

The General went on to say that he hoped to block off support to North Korea from Manchuria or China. He was sure that the Communists would try to reinforce the Koreans but was equally sure this could be prevented by medium-bomber attacks. He was convinced the Soviets would not go to war at this time but would make a maximal underground effort.

General MacArthur naturally was less concerned with the world situation beyond his sphere of responsibility than were the Joint Chiefs, though he assured us he was cognizant of our problems. He believed strongly that driving back the Communists in the *de facto* war in Korea would check Communist expansion everywhere and thus obviate the necessity of our being fully prepared to meet aggression elsewhere. In vigorous and colorful language he protested any delay or half-way measures. He urged immediate and maximal effort in support of the Far East Command from the start, rather than a gradual build-up. He wanted "to grab every ship in the Pacific and pour the support into the Far East," adding "To hell with the concept of business as usual." He said that admittedly the United States was playing a poor hand in the Far East, but long experience had convinced him that "it is how you play your poor hands rather than your good ones which counts in the long run."

Vandenberg and I agreed with the necessity for facing up to the immediate problem of halting the North Korean advance. I pointed out that to integrate the Command's requirements with the Administration's overall military program we needed to know when General MacArthur expected to be able to launch his major counteroffensive, what his requirements would be to re-establish the 38th Parallel position, and what strength he would need thereafter.

General MacArthur replied that it was impossible to say when he would be able to pass to the counteroffensive. He hoped to stop the NK advance when three American divisions were in action and then to launch an amphibious operation to cut the enemy lines of communications and routes of withdrawal. He would follow the amphibious maneuver with an overland pursuit of the withdrawing North Koreans. He said he meant to destroy the NK forces and not merely drive them back across the 38th Parallel. He said that in the aftermath of operations, the problem would be to "compose and unite Korea." He added that it might be necessary to occupy all of Korea, though this was speculative at that time. To do so a total of eight infantry divisions and an additional army headquarters would be required. In addition, the Japanese Police Force should be converted into a constabulary of four divisions, with American equipment to provide security for Japan.

General Vandenberg asked whether in the event of Chinese Communist reinforcements MacArthur visualized cutting them off at the North Korean border or by an advance into Manchuria? General MacArthur replied that he would cut them off in North Korea. He said he regarded Korea as a cul-de-sac. All routes into the country from Manchuria and Vladivostok have many tunnels and bridges. He saw a unique opportunity for the use of the atomic bomb to deal a crippling blow to these supply routes, which it would require six months to repair. This thought was not pursued, but MacArthur asked for an increase in supporting B-29 heavy bombers, saying that thirty daily bombing attacks would be sufficient to isolate Korea.

General Walker then reiterated the need for eleven battalions of infantry for the Eighth Army and urged that 3600 men be flown at once to Japan to fill out the 7th Division there, which had been stripped to reinforce the divisions fighting in Korea. General Almond ventured the hope that the front in Korea might be stabilized by mid-August or the first of September. Admiral Radford expressed agreement with the remarks of General Mac-Arthur.

MacArthur concluded the conference with the statement that the situation in the Far East should not be clouded with questions of priorities. "We win here or lose everywhere; if we win here, we improve the chances of winning everywhere."

After this conference General Vandenberg visited the head-quarters of the Far East Air Force for a discussion of Air Force requirements, while General Walker and I flew to Korea. I had never been to Korea before (though while in Peking I had applied for, and been refused, permission by the Japanese to go to Seoul in 1935), and I wanted to get some idea of the terrain and to discuss the situation on the ground with Generals Walker and Dean. After a six-hour flight in a DC-3 we landed at the forward echelon of Walker's headquarters at Taegu, 60 miles north of Pusan. There Walker again expressed accord with MacArthur's estimate of the combat situation and said that, barring unforeseen developments, he could hold a sizable bridgehead covering Pusan with the troops then in Korea and those en route from Japan.

Weather prevented our going on to the 24th Division's command post, then at Taejon, which had not yet been attacked. General Dean had come over earlier to Taegu to meet us. Everyone was calm and confident in Taegu, but it was evident that Bill Dean was tired and greatly worried over his losses. He said enemy tank penetrations were a problem but that the T-34's stuck to the roads and that, if the newly arrived 3.5-inch rockets were effective, they would help block the enemy advance. We promised him continued support.

It was necessary to get out of Taegu by dark, so we had only one hour on the ground, but the trip was worth while, not only as evidence of Washington's interest, but also because it gave me a better conception of the ruggedness of the Korean mountains and the problems our troops were facing in the field. We arrived back in Tokyo about 2:00 A.M. on July 14.

Later that morning in a simple ceremony atop the Dai Ichi Building I presented to General MacArthur the flag of the United Nations, which the U.N. Secretary General, Trygve Lie, had requested be flown over the headquarters of the Commander in Chief of the United Nations Command.

After this ceremony I met privately with General MacArthur. I briefly reviewed the situation as I saw it and gave him my personal judgment that he could count on the 2d Infantry Division, the 1st Marine Division, the 4th and 29th Regimental Combat Teams, and a regimental combat team from the 11th Airborne Division as reinforcements.

MacArthur again said he fully understood that we could not strip the General Reserve any further in the face of possible Russian moves in Europe or elsewhere and that he would make his plans for the counteroffensive on the basis of my estimate of the forces we could make available to him.

After this meeting I joined Lieutenant Colonels Dickson and Denson, who were conferring with General Almond and other members of MacArthur's staff on the details of troop requirements, particularly of service units, the organization of Japanese police forces, the development of the port of Pohang on the east coast, and preliminary plans for the amphibious operation. I questioned the feasibility of a landing at Inchon because of the high tides. Brigadier General Edwin K. Wright, Assistant Chief of Staff, Operations, G-3, in the Far East Command, pointed out possible alternative sites at Haeju and Chinampo. I emphasized the importance of pushing the construction of tactical airstrips in Korea to permit more continuous and effective time over targets in support of the infantry in combat.

General Vandenberg and I with our party left Tokyo at 2:00 P.M. local time and arrived in Washington at 8:00 A.M. Washington time the same date, July 14. We at once briefed the JCS and the Secretary of Defense and reported to the President. I stated my agreement with Generals MacArthur and Walker that the Eighth Army and the ROK Army would be able to hold a bridgehead covering Pusan, but I urged prompt reinforcements, as spelled out in staff papers, some of which had already been originated.

However, the North Koreans were offering no breathing spell, and rapid developments in Korea soon raised serious doubts whether the United Nations forces would be driven out of the country before reinforcements arrived.

V

THE EIGHTH ARMY STANDS AND FIGHTS

The Terrain of South Korea

THE MILITARY KEY to the defense of South Korea was the port of Pusan. There were several small fishing harbors south of the 38th Parallel, such as Pohang on the east coast and Mokpo and Kumsan on the Yellow Sea, but Pusan was the only port that had anything like the modern facilities and rail and highway connections adequate to handle the great mass of men, equipment, and supplies that would have to be brought to Korea to save it from being overrun. Pusan's four piers and intervening quays could berth two dozen or more ocean-going ships, and sheltered beaches provided space for fourteen LST's, large Navy landing ships. No other port approached its capacity for handling 45,000 measurement tons* daily. Fortunately for us, Pusan is located at the southeastern tip of the Korean peninsula, a little more than 100 miles from the chief southwest ports of Japan but about 575 miles from the Russian air and naval bases in the vicinity of Vladivostok.

The terrain of South Korea is not neatly compartmented, as a military man would like to have had it (Maps 1, 2, and 5), being a jumble of high mountains, steep hills, and tortuous valleys, but there are two principal ranges, the Taebaeks and Sobaeks, and two rivers of major importance. The high Taebaek Mountains parallel the east coast, their irregular crests 10 to 20 miles inland but with abrupt eastern spurs that almost crowd the coastal road into the Sea of Japan. Except for a break between Pohang and Taegu, the Taebaeks run all the way down to Pusan. The Sobaek Range extends out from the Taebaeks between Tanyang and Yongju and,

* A measurement ton is 40 cubic feet.

with many lateral offshoots, runs southwest through the central part of the country. The Naktong River and its tributaries drain the inner slopes of the two great ranges. The main stream rises in the Taebaeks and flows south to Andong and thence west for 20 miles before turning south again to snake its way to the Korean Strait just west of Pusan. The western slopes of the Sobaeks feed the upper reaches of the Kum River, which flows north, opposite in direction to the Naktong, for more than 100 miles, and then swings around Taejon to Kongju, where it turns southwest to the Yellow Sea at Kunsan.

Once the North Koreans had broken across the 38th Parallel, there were three principal routes south converging on Pusan: the main rail and highway from Seoul via Taejon and Taegu, which cuts diagonally across the Sobaek Range near Kumchon, the east coast road via Pohang, and the western highway leading south from Kongju to Kwanju and thence east via Chinju to Pusan. None of these roads was hard-surfaced, but the No. 1 highway, with its accompanying railway, had greater capacity than the others. It had the disadvantage of having to cross the Kum River twice, the difficult Sobaek Range, and then the broad Naktong before reaching Taegu. Not anticipating intervention by the Americans, the NK Army initially chose this route for its main drive on Pusan, using their 3d and 4th Divisions. Only the rapid deployment and successive delaying actions of the U.S. 24th Division had prevented what otherwise would have been an almost unimpeded drive to Pusan.

Meanwhile five NK divisions were committed to a slow and tortuous advance across the upper Sobaeks, opposed by remnants of the ROK Capital Division and the ROK 1st, 2d, 6th, and 8th Divisions. Only one NK division, the 5th, was directed along the east coast road, the shortest route to Pusan, which was guarded by the lone ROK 23d Regiment. The NK 5th Division dissipated some of its strength with needless incursions into the mountains instead of driving hard down to Pohang. From there it might have reached Pusan before American reinforcements, close air support, and gunfire from off-shore Navy vessels were able to bolster the faltering ROK 23d Regiment. The United States mili-

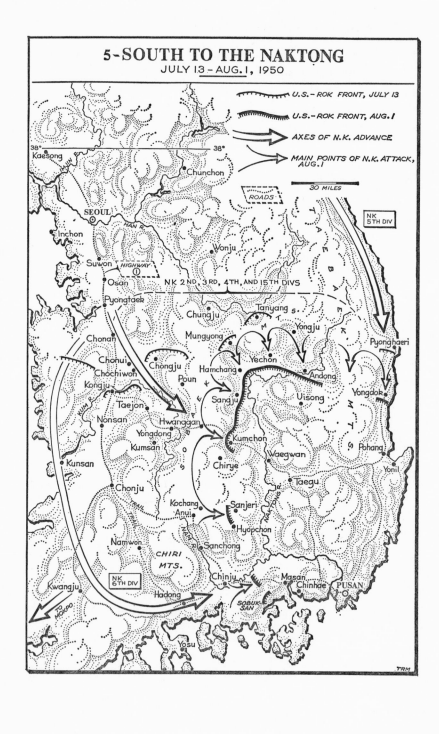

5-SOUTH TO THE NAKTONG
JULY 13 – AUG. 1, 1950

tary advisers, with the ROK 23d Regiment under Lieutenant
Colonel Rollins S. Emmerich, deserved much credit for rallying
the 23d Regiment on several occasions. In early July General
MacArthur had noted the threat to Pusan via the coastal road.
He had directed General Dean, even while Dean was trying desperately to hold the Kum River line north of Taejon, to send the
3d Battalion, 19th Infantry, to Pohang to protect that port and a
fighter strip being constructed at nearby Yonil.

General Walker Takes Command

No North Korean move in force down the western route from
Konju had developed when General Walker on July 13, 1950,
assumed command of the U.S. Army troops in Korea, with headquarters at Taegu. Four days later, after President Syngman Rhee
had assigned all ROK forces to the United Nations Command
under General MacArthur, Rhee directed the Chief of Staff of
the ROK Army, General Chung Il Kwon, to place himself under
command of the Eighth Army. Thereafter General Walker wisely
issued his instructions to the ROK Army in the form of requests
to the ROK Chief of Staff. General Kwon then gave his own
orders to ROK units, in conformity with the operations plans and
orders of the Eighth Army. This system worked well, with minimal friction, throughout the war.

General Walker, West Point class of 1912, was a chunky,
barrel-chested man with the lined face, if not the lean figure, of a
Texan. He had never lost the Texas twang to his voice nor the
toughness, drive, and determination characteristic of his native
state. He had led the XX Corps of General Patton's Third Army
in Europe with a gusto that rivaled that of his famous commander
and won for him the Distinguished Service Cross for gallantry
in action and the Distinguished Service Medal.

We had both been stationed at West Point after World War I,
and I had seen something of him in England before we jumped
off for Normandy in World War II, but I did not know Johnny
Walker well before Korea. I came to know and have great respect
for him during the trying days of the Pusan defenses, which

tested not only the tactical skill but the stout heart of this fine soldier.

The testing began at once. When Walker took command of the United Nations forces, they were strung out on a tenuous front extending from the Kum River across the foothills of the Sobaek Range, to the vicinity of Tonyang, and thence through the wilderness of the main Taebaek Mountains to Pyonghaeri on the east coast (Maps 2 and 5).

Walker's mission was to hold the NK advance as far from Pusan as possible, until MacArthur received the necessary reinforcements, shipping, and equipment from the States to launch a counteroffensive. With only three American divisions available — the depleted 24th, the newly arrived 25th, and the 1st Cavalry still en route from Japan — and a badly disorganized ROK Army, Walker was in for a rough time trying to block the three main approaches to Pusan. He would also have to ensure the retention of Taegu within the American-ROK lines. Taegu was the principal rail and highway center in the area and had the only fairly good airfield north of Pusan.

Walker's first concern was the positioning of my old division of World War II, the "Tropic Lightning" 25th Infantry Division, which landed at Pusan during July 10 to 15. Its commander, Major General William B. Kean, United States Military Academy class of 1919, was a sound, steady soldier with a quiet personality that had made him a valuable Chief of Staff to General Bradley in World War II. This was Kean's first experience in command of a unit in action, though he had seen considerable fighting in North Africa and Europe.

The battered ROK troops fighting to hold the passes across the Sobaek Range needed reinforcement to prevent the North Koreans from pouring down into the Naktong valley north of Taegu. On July 13 Walker ordered Kean to base his division on Sangju and to assist the ROK forces on the Yechon-Hamchan-Poun front. During the next two weeks the 24th and 35th Regiments fought delaying actions against the NK 2d Division, as they and ROK troops fell back on Sangju. In these actions elements of the 24th Infantry, the U.S. Army's last Negro regiment, broke on several occasions, a performance that was repeated until the regiment was desegregated on October 1, 1951.*

A critical situation developed on July 22 when ROK forces, falling back to the west of the 35th Infantry, left the Poun-Hwanggan road uncovered. Walker spotted this dangerous opening and promptly took an action that was to mark his uncanny skill in the handling of his scant reserves. The 27th Infantry, which had just been ordered to move up from Oisong to help out the ROK 8th Division at Andong, was turned around before reaching Andong and was moved to Hwanggan. From north of Hwanggan the 27th Infantry, under its brilliant young commander, Lieutenant Colonel John H. Michaelis, who was to distinguish himself later in the defense of Masan and Taegu, checked the NK 2d Division until relieved by the 1st Cavalry Division on July 29.

The third United States division to reach Korea was the 1st Cavalry Division — a misnomer, since the unit had been converted to infantry during World War II but had retained its cavalry designation for morale reasons. It was officered chiefly by former cavalrymen or armored tankers, who took pride in their cavalry heritage and instilled the same spirit in their men. Its commander was Major General Hobart R. Gay. He had been Chief of Staff to General George S. Patton, Jr., in the North Afri-

* The 24th Infantry Regiment was a holdover from the Civil War, having been retained as a Negro unit in the Regular Army as prescribed in the Revised Statutes of 1878. Near the end of World War II platoons of Negro volunteers had been attached to all white combat units in the European theater, including my VII Corps. Not only did they do well in action, but disciplinary problems, which had plagued many all-Negro units, particularly of a noncombat type, became negligible. I became convinced then that, on sound, military grounds, segregation in the Army should gradually be eliminated. The process would have to be gradual for many reasons, not the least of which was that it would take time for the country, especially the South, to adjust to complete integration. The Korean war proved without question that Negro soldiers, when properly trained and fully integrated with their white comrades, would fight as well and would readily be accepted as equals. Great credit is due General Ridgway for initiating and pushing for complete integration within the Eighth Army and the Far East Command. He was fully supported by Secretary Pace and by me. In fact, every step in the final desegregation of the Army took place during my tenure of office as Vice Chief or Chief of Staff and under the direction of two other Southerners, Secretaries Gordon Gray of North Carolina and Frank Pace of Arkansas.

For an account of integration in the Army see The Employment of Negro Troops by Ulysses Lee, Office of Chief of Military History, and Breakthrough on the Color Front by Lee Nichols, Random House.

can, Italian, and European campaigns of the Third Army and was imbued with Patton's hell-for-leather spirit. He was a skilled professional although, like Bill Kean, he was for the first time in independent command in action.

The First Cavalry Division landed at Pohang from July 18 to July 22. General MacArthur had hoped to employ this division in his contemplated amphibious counteroffensive, but the losses of the 24th Division had forced its early dispatch to bolster the front southeast of Taejon. By July 22 the 1st Cavalry had assumed responsibility for blocking the advance of the NK 3d Division along the vital Taejon-Taegu corridor. The 24th Division withdrew to Kumchon in Eighth Army reserve.

The enemy did not rest long after the fall of Taejon. On July 22 the NK 3d Division began its attack against the 1st Cavalry Division's position at Yongdong (Map 5). Using its tested flanking maneuver, this NK division turned the south flank of the cavalry position and by July 29 was threatening the 1st Cavalry's rear by way of Chirye. Walker again made a timely move by turning over to Major General Gay the 3d Battalion, 21st Infantry, 24th Division, which set up a blocking position north of Chirye. The same day Gay, whose division was not under severe direct pressure but could have been cut off from Taegu, ordered a withdrawal to new positions covering Kumchon, an important rail center 30 miles northwest of Taegu.

Apparently, there had been some confusion in the Eighth Army concerning the plans of the Army commander. On July 26 the Army headquarters had issued a warning order indicating that at some indeterminate date it would fall back to "prepared positions," which would be held until it could turn to the offensive. That same day Walker telephoned MacArthur's headquarters to request authority to move his advanced command post from Taegu to Pusan. General Almond took the call. Walker explained that there was a danger of loss or damage of his communications equipment, which was almost irreplaceable in the Far East, if the enemy got much closer to Taegu. Walker made no mention of moving any tactical units back toward Pusan. The positions referred to in the Army warning order actually had not been prepared and were well north of Taegu until the line crossed the Naktong above Kumchon. However, Almond felt that a move of the Army command post to Pusan might upset the ROK Army and cause rumors of possible evacuation of Korea. He said he would transmit the request to MacArthur. According to the account of a later interview that the military historian Roy E. Appleman had with Almond, Almond told MacArthur that he thought the situation in Korea was critical and required the personal attention of the Far East commander. MacArthur flew to Taegu the next morning, accompanied by Almond and a small staff. They were met by General Walker and Major General Earl E. Partridge, commanding the Fifth Air Force, whose advanced command post was also in Taegu. They went directly to Eighth Army headquarters, where MacArthur and Almond were closeted alone with Walker for an hour and a half. According to Appleman's account, MacArthur made no mention of Walker's request to move his command post, nor did he criticize Walker in any way, but he did emphasize the necessity of the Eighth Army's standing its ground. Later, in the presence of several Army staff members, General MacArthur said there would be no withdrawal from Korea, no repetition of Dunkirk.

It is not known what effect the visit of MacArthur had on the plans of Walker, an aggressive leader who normally needed no encouragement to stand and fight, but I have little doubt that the intervention of Almond, which led to MacArthur's visit, did nothing to ease the growing irritation between Walker and Almond, which had some influence on their later relationships.

In any event, the withdrawal of the 1st Cavalry Division to Kumchon on July 29, coupled with similar rearward movements of the 25th Infantry Division on the Sangju front, sometimes in panic and with little control in either division, raised the ire of Johnny Walker. He visited both division headquarters on that date, expressing his great disappointment and disapproval to both Gay and Kean. At the 25th Division command post he spoke vigorously to Kean and his staff. The Division Historian's notes paraphrase what General Walker said, in part, as follows:

General MacArthur was over here two days ago; he is thoroughly conversant with the situation. He knows where we are and what we have to fight with. He knows our needs and where the enemy is hitting the hardest. General MacArthur is doing everything possible to send reinforcements . . . We are fighting a battle against time. There will be no more retreating, withdrawal or readjustment of the lines or any other term you choose . . . There will be no Dunkirk, there will be no Bataan, a retreat to Pusan would be one of the greatest butcheries in history. We must fight until the end . . . If some of us must die, we will die fighting together. Any man who gives ground may be personally responsible for the death of thousands of his comrades.

I want you to put this out to all the men in the Division. I want everybody to understand that we are going to hold this line. We are going to win.

General Walker said much the same thing to General Gay the same afternoon when he visited Gay's command post in Kumchon. He questioned the withdrawal to Kumchon and directed that there be no more withdrawals.

Serious as these retreats were in the central area, Walker was soon to be faced with a situation in the southwest that threatened the entire position of the Eighth Army and, in fact, its very ability to maintain itself in Korea. While the NK 15th, 2d, 3d, and 4th Divisions were pushing back the 25th and 1st Cavalry Divisions on their front, the NK 6th Division was moving down a secondary road on the west coast to Kunsan and thence via Chonju toward Kwanju. The only friendly forces operating in this area were remnants of the ROK 7th Division and local police. Reports from these units were vague and infrequent but nonetheless alarming. Bad weather permitted only occasional reconnaissance flights until July 23. Flights then revealed that strong enemy forces were swinging east from Kwangju behind the southwest flank of the Eighth Army.

Walker at once asked that a major effort be made by the Fifth Air Force to block this movement and then called on his only available troops, the gallant but war-torn 24th Infantry Division, only one day out of the line after losing its commander, General Dean, and 1150 other men at Taejon. The new commander, General Church, was summoned to Eighth Army Headquarters on July 24. Johnny Walker told Church: "I'm sorry to have to do this, but the whole south flank is open, and reports indicate the Koreans are moving in. I want you to cover the area from Chinju (west of Masan) up to near Kumchon." Some idea of the task Walker perforce was assigning to Church's under-strength division may be gained from the fact that the frontage normally assigned a division in a defensive position does not exceed 10 or 12 miles; Kumchon and Chinju are 65 miles apart.

Chinju is the focal point of roads leading from the west to Pusan, 50 miles distant. General Church disposed his two available regiments to cover the approaches to Chinju from the north and northwest but could not stretch them to block the roads into Chinju from the west. General Walker's only recourse in filling this gap was to employ the two battalions of the 29th Infantry Regiment just arrived from Okinawa. The experience of these units again points up the dire straits of the Far East Command resulting from lack of preparation for war in peacetime. It also illustrates the bare margins of time and space under which Walker was working to meet succeeding crises. The Far East Command had promised the 29th Infantry that its two battalions would have at least six weeks of combat training before going to Korea. Instead, they embarked on short notice at Okinawa, after having been brought to full strength with raw recruits, and sailed direct to Pusan. There they were to have three days to draw equipment and test-fire weapons. Instead, the battalions were met at the docks with orders to proceed at once to Chinju, where they would be attached to the 19th Infantry Regiment of the 24th Division. At Chinju the battalions found themselves on the verge of combat in a land they had never seen before, with weapons they had not test-fired, and with new mortars and heavy machine guns from which the grease had been barely rubbed off.

It was no wonder that the 3d Battalion, 29th Infantry, the first to see action west of Chinju, suffered heavy casualties, including the battalion commander, the executive officer, and three company commanders. Severe losses were also sustained by the 1st Battalion, 29th Infantry.

By July 30 the NK 4th Division was attacking in force the 34th Infantry at Kochang, and the NK 6th Division was attacking at Chinju. The 34th Infantry, again faring badly, was driven from Kochang and fell back on Sanjeri along the road to Taegu. Fearful of a drive by the NK 4th Division on Taegu, General Walker had to make another emergency shift of his reserves. He brought the 1st Battalion, 21st Infantry, all the way from the Pohang-Yongdok area on the east coast to Hyopchon, where it took up a position backing up the 34th Infantry. And for the first time Walker called on the ROK Army for direct help. The 17th Regiment, one of the best ROK units, joined the American forces covering the approaches to the Naktong in the Hyopchon area.

The battalions of the 19th and 29th Infantry had delayed the enemy's advance on Masan, 30 miles west of Pusan, but did not end the threat to the Eighth Army's south flank. Walker was forced to move his last available reserve, Mike Michaelis' 27th Infantry, from Waegwan, where it had been out of action for only one day, to reinforce the area west of Masan. Once again Michaelis and the 27th proved their worth. The advance of the NK 6th Division was halted west of Masan by August 1, but the enemy was still too close for the safety of the vital port of Pusan. Weighing this danger and the overall situation, Walker made two bold decisions: to shift the 25th Division from the Taegu front to the Masan area and to withdraw the U.S. Eighth and the ROK Army back of the Naktong River.

The march of the 25th Division 150 miles by foot, motor, and rail from Sangju via Kumchon and Waegwan to Masan in a period of thirty-six hours was an amazing accomplishment and a tribute to the logistical and planning staffs of the Eighth Army and the 25th Division. At times columns of troops were moving parallel to the front and within 5 miles of the enemy. Lack of NK air power and the failure of the NK 2d and 3d Divisions to press their attack on the road center of Kumchon made the movement feasible.

But the North Koreans were still too close to Pusan for Walker to rest easily. Shortly after the arrival of the 25th Division in the Masan area Walker created a special task force under command of Major General Kean, consisting of that division (less the 27th Infantry back in Army reserve), the 5th Regimental Combat Team, and the 1st Marine Brigade under Brigadier General Edward A. Craig, just arrived from the States. Task Force Kean had the objective of securing the Chinju Pass and the south bank of the Nam River east thereof. The task force jumped off on the morning of August 7 in the first American counteroffensive of the war.

Unfortunately, Task Force Kean, made up of quickly assembled units operating together for the first time, proved ineffective against the tough North Koreans. Most of the units fought bravely, but by the end of the first day few initial objectives had been taken, and it became apparent on August 8 that the task force had run head on into a North Korean attack aimed at Pusan.

For the next five days the outcome swayed back and forth. Throughout, the enemy held tenaciously to an abandoned coal mine on the high Sobuk-san, from which it launched raids against supply lines and artillery positions. Two battalions of the 25th Division artillery were overrun with heavy losses of men and guns. The 5th Marines did succeed in bypassing the heaviest fighting in the central area and by noon on August 12 had come close to Chinju. That evening the Marine's brigade commander, Craig, received orders from Kean to withdraw his troops to Chindongni. Walker had even greater need for the brigade farther north, where an enemy penetration was threatening to disrupt the entire defenses of the Eighth Army.

General Walker was forced to call off the attack west of Masan and to disband Task Force Kean. Though the attack failed in its chief objectives, it did drive back the attack of the NK 6th Division on Pusan and provided valuable battle experience to the 25th Division and the 5th Regimental Combat Team.

JCS Plans for Reinforcements

While operations in Korea were increasing in intensity, the JCS in Washington were completing plans to develop reinforcements for NATO and the Far East, to reconstitute the General Reserve, and to increase procurement of ammunition and other materiel and supplies. By mid-July the commitment of the 2d Infantry Division, two infantry regimental combat teams, an airborne regimental combat team, and the 1st Marine Division to the Far East Command had reduced the General Reserve to the 82d Airborne Division and a regimental combat team as the only combat-ready ground troops in the States. On urgent recommendations of the JCS, approved by the Secretary of Defense, President Truman asked for and secured congressional approval for expanded budgetary appropriations and the removal of all ceilings on military personnel. On June 30, 1950, Congress also authorized the President to order units and individuals of the National Guard and the Organized Reserve Corps into federal service for a period of twenty-one months.

The other members of the JCS had been reluctant, as I was, to recommend a call-up of National Guard divisions until we had a clearer picture of the overall requirements for both Europe and Korea. Federalizing selected Guard units for long periods in peacetime is somewhat inequitable to the men of the units selected and to some extent is contrary to the basic concept of the National Guard, which is intended primarily for internal security within the States except in times of general mobilization. The alternative is the creation of additional units in the Regular Army. Congress usually is loathe to give such authorization because of the fear of committing itself to a larger standing army after the emergency is over. But with continuing North Korean advances in Korea and on the urging of General Bolté, my Operations Officer, G-3, on July 31 I proposed to the JCS the federalization of four National Guard divisions and two National Guard regimental combat teams. The JCS agreed, as did the Secretary of Defense, and President Truman approved the call-up, effective September 1, 1950. After balancing the training status and geographical locations of the best qualified Guard divisions, General Mark W. Clark, the Chief of the Army Field Forces, the top training man in the Army, recommended the selection of the 28th Division (Pennsylvania), the 40th (California), the 43d (Rhode Island and Connecticut), the 45th (Oklahoma), and two regimental combat teams, the 19th (South Dakota) and the 278th (Tennessee). These units were to be brought to war strength through Selective Service. They would not be ready for combat until the spring of 1951.

The demands, however, from the Far East for additional troops and replacements continued. Early in August I sent my Deputy Chief of Staff for Operations and Administration, Lieutenant General Matthew B. Ridgway, to the Far East to review the Korean situation with Generals MacArthur and Walker. Matt Ridgway and I had been classmates at West Point, and his 82d Airborne Division had fought brilliantly in my VII Corps in Normandy. I knew that I could depend on his ability to evaluate the situation in Korea and the further needs of the Far East Command. I knew also that he had the confidence of MacArthur, under whom he had served as Director of Athletics at West Point while MacArthur was Superintendent.

Ridgway met MacArthur in Tokyo and visited the Eighth Army in Korea. The main request he brought back from MacArthur was that the 3d Infantry Division, which had just been activated, be stationed in Japan until a military Japanese Police Force could be established. Other than the 82d Airborne Division this was the only combat division, untrained though it was, in the General Reserve. The JCS were reluctant to release it but finally did so, and President Truman again took the risk of authorizing its withdrawal from the General Reserve.

During this same period the need for two corps headquarters and supporting communications and service units to control and support the growing forces of the United Nations Command became mandatory. Two skeletonized corps headquarters, the I Corps under Major General John B. Coulter, who had com-

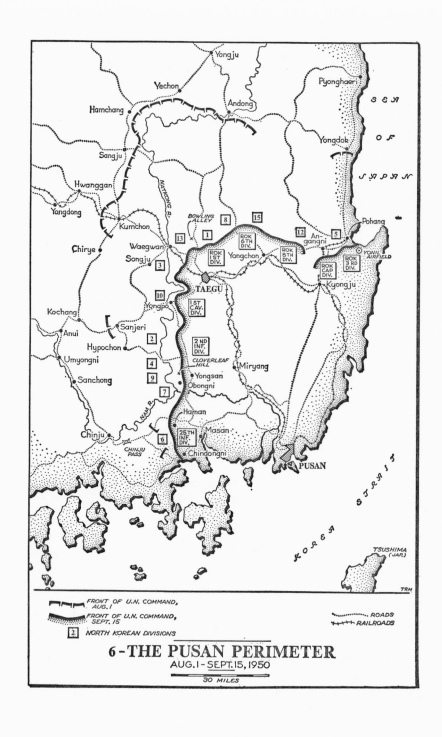

SEA
OF
JAPAN

Yongju

Pyonghae-ri

Yechon

Hamchang

Andong

Yongdok

Sangju

Hwanggan

Yongdong

Kumchon

BOWLING
ALLEY

8

15

12

Pohang

13

1

An-
gangni

5

YONIL
AIRFIELD

Chirye

Waegwan

ROK
6TH
DIV.

Songju

3

ROK
1ST
DIV.

Yongchon

ROK
8TH
DIV.

ROK
3RD
DIV.

Kyongju

ROK
CAP.
DIV.

NAKTONG R.

Kochang

10

Yongpo

TAEGU

1ST
CAV.
DIV.

Anui

Sanjeri

2

Hypochon

Umyongni

4

2ND
INF.
DIV.

CLOVERLEAF
HILL

Miryang

Sanchong

9

Yongsan
Obongni

7

NAM R.

Haman

Chinju

6

25TH
INF.
DIV.

Masan

CHINJU
PASS

Chindongni

PUSAN

KOREA
STRAIT

TSUSHIMA
(JAP.)

TRM

FRONT OF U.N. COMMAND,
AUG. 1

FRONT OF U.N. COMMAND,
SEPT. 15

2 NORTH KOREAN DIVISIONS

········· ROADS
+++++ RAILROADS

6–THE PUSAN PERIMETER
AUG. 1 – SEPT. 15, 1950

30 MILES

manded the 85th Infantry Division in Italy in World War II, and the IX Corps under Major General Frank W. Milburn, plus signal battalions and medical and military police units from the National Guard and Organized Reserve Corps, were promised for September and October. Corps artillery units would have to come later.

On August 24 General MacArthur took another important step to relieve General Walker of any residual responsibilities for service installations of the Eighth Army remaining in Japan by establishing the Japan Logistical Command, with Headquarters in Yokohama, under Major General Walter L. Weible, U.S. Army. It became the duty of this command to supply and support the Eighth Army in the field, freeing General Walker to devote himself solely to directing the operations of the American and ROK forces.

The Pusan Perimeter

General Walker's decision to shift the 25th Division from the Taegu front forced a concurrent decision to withdraw the Eighth and ROK armies back of the Naktong River. There is no record indicating that Walker cleared this move with MacArthur, though they may have discussed it when MacArthur visited the Eighth Army command post on July 27. Walker knew he would not have sufficient forces left on the central front to risk trying to hold west of the Naktong, with that formidable stream at his back. He decided rightly to put the Naktong in his front rather than have it in his rear.

The withdrawal order, effective August 1, established what became known as the Pusan Perimeter (Map 6), which enclosed a rectangular area 50 miles in width from the Naktong to the Sea of Japan and roughly 100 miles in depth. The Naktong valley, which bordered this area on the north and west, formed a deep protective moat along most of the front. The stream itself varied in width from a few hundred yards in front of the ROK Army to a half-mile or more in its lower reaches and had depths to six or eight feet. The river was fordable with difficulty in many places in the dry season, with sandy banks at the feet of the bordering hills. These rose steeply to commanding heights on both sides. The many snake-like coils of the Naktong added greatly to the actual length of the river and afforded the enemy opportunities for flanking attacks, to establish bridgeheads across the river in areas bound by these loops. One such area, which became known as the Naktong Bulge, was just north of the junction with the Nam River, where the Naktong makes a wide swing to the west. It later became the scene of bitter fighting.

General Walker disposed his two armies as shown on Map 6. The ROK Army had been reorganized into two corps under battle-proven leaders, with sectors as indicated. Both armies followed the standard American doctrine for a river-line defense. Key hills along the river overlooking likely points of crossing were lightly held, the stronger forces farther back being kept in reserve for counterattack. Artillery was registered on all known fords and ferries and along probable avenues of penetration. With their extended frontages neither the Eighth Army nor the ROK Army could be strong everywhere. The enemy was bound to be able to get across the river wherever he decided to concentrate his efforts. The big job of the Americans and the South Koreans would be to counterattack and drive the North Koreans back into the river with heavy losses of men and equipment. The success of this tactic would depend upon General Walker's ability to generate the necessary reserves from his still under-strength and weary forces and to use them at the right time and place. These forces would be strengthened during the course of the battle by the 2d Infantry Division from the States and late in August by the British 27th Infantry Brigade, the first United Nations reinforcements other than Americans. In addition, six United States medium-tank battalions, more than a match for the Russian T-34's, arrived during August, giving the Eighth Army a preponderance in armor of five to one over the North Koreans. The United Nations forces would also have the great advantage of control of the air, which was to become one of the determining factors in the ensuing battles.

On the west side of the Naktong the North Koreans readied

ten divisions for the assault on the allied positions. Despite their amazing success until then and the losses they had inflicted on the Americans, they had sustained heavy casualties, not only in the ground fighting, but also from increasing harassment by American air strikes. Forced to move only at night, they were still able to bring down adequate supplies of ammunition. The North Koreans seized rice, their staple food, from the local villages and impressed large numbers of the villagers as replacements. They knew that, with more Americans arriving daily, time was working against them. They initiated reconnaissance probes at once, and without waiting for full coordination they launched two major attacks across the Naktong on August 5, one on the front of the ROK Army north of Taegu and the other in the Naktong Bulge opposite Yongsan. These attacks opened the first phase of the great defensive battle of the Pusan Perimeter.

The First Battle of the Naktong Bulge

In pitch-black darkness elements of the NK 4th Division waded across the Naktong on the north loop of the river, slipped between front-line units of the 34th Infantry, 24th Division, and then fanned out and seized Cloverleaf Hill above the road to Yongsan. Local counterattacks of the 34th Infantry checked the advance, but in the next two days and nights the enemy increased its hold on Cloverleaf and adjacent Obongni in the center of the bulge. Realizing that the 24th Division was still less than 50 percent effective, General Walker turned over to General Church the 9th Infantry, the first regiment of the U.S. 2d Division to arrive in Korea. But the 9th, commanded by Colonel John G. Hill, like most American units in action in Korea for the first time, was unable to recapture the Cloverleaf hill mass, though it did stop an enemy attack launched on August 10 from Cloverleaf. To strengthen their attack the enemy had to get their artillery and heavy equipment across the river. Working at night, they constructed a number of "underwater bridges" made of rocks and logs covered with sandbags to within a foot of the surface. These improved fords were difficult to locate and relatively invulnerable to artillery and air bombardment. Trucks, artillery, some tanks, and heavy weapons crossed over them under cover of darkness. By dawn of August 12 the entire NK 4th Division was across the river and had begun to move to the southwest of Yongsan.

Alert to this danger, General Walker ordered the 2d Battalion, 27th Infantry, in army reserve at Masan, to attack north across the Nam River against the south flank of the North Koreans. By midnight the 2d Battalion had a bridgehead over the Nam. To ensure success of this key attack, General Walker attached the entire 27th Infantry to the 24th Division. The "Wolfhounds" pierced the enemy flank and seized the high ground north and east of Yongsan. There they were met by the 1st Battalion, 23d Infantry, the second regiment of the 2d Infantry Division that Walker had committed immediately on arrival from Pusan. Thus, by prompt and vigorous action, Walker had effectively sealed off the enemy penetration south of Yongsan.

Meanwhile, Colonel Hill, whom Church had placed in command of all troops in the center of the bulge, was attacking desperately to drive the enemy from the Cloverleaf hills, and the NK 4th Division was striving with equal fury to break out to the east. The severity of this fighting is illustrated by the case of Master Sergeant Warren H. Jordan of Company E, 9th Infantry. During one week Sergeant Jordan had to take command of the company five different times when all company officers had been killed or wounded or were out from heat exhaustion. On one occasion, as the action surged back and forth across the Cloverleaf, the 1st Battalion, 9th Infantry, lost sixty men who were killed or wounded in one hour. Finally on August 15, its last reserves exhausted, Task Force Hill suspended its attack and dug in.

Impatient as Walker was to drive the NK 4th Division back across the river, he realized that the 24th Division, which had been continuously engaged for more than two months, could not do so without further reinforcements. The only reserve he had available was the 1st Marine Brigade, which he had just withdrawn from Task Force Kean west of Masan. After scanning the rest of the front, including the area south of Waegwan, where Taegu was being threatened, and the east coast corridor, where the NK 5th Division had broken through south of Pohang and was menacing Pusan from the north, Walker decided to throw the Marine Brigade into the Naktong Bulge fight.

General Church assumed command of the combined Army-Marine attack. He planned a double penetration of the enemy front, the 19th and 34th Regiments attacking north of Cloverleaf and the 5th Marines attacking south of it. The 9th Infantry would make a holding attack against Cloverleaf in the center and would be pinched out after the flanks had been overrun. It was the first well-planned and coordinated American attack in Korea. It went off at 4:00 P.M., preceded by a concentrated artillery preparation with air-bursting shells over Cloverleaf. This preparation cut down the enemy defenders, and the 9th Infantry quickly overran Cloverleaf. The 9th was then able to support the attack on Obongni with flanking fire, enabling the Marines to gain a foothold on Obongni by dark. During this action the first tank encounter of the war occurred between T-34's and American Pershings in the draw between Cloverleaf and Obongni. Four T-34's were destroyed by the combined fires of two 3.5-inch rocket teams and three Pershing tanks. T-34 dominance of the battlefield was definitely at an end.

The American attack was renewed the next morning, August 18. It rolled forward, supported by effective air and artillery bombardment. Soon air reconnaissance and forward observers were reporting NK withdrawals all across the front. Fighter planes ravaged the North Koreans, now in full flight across the river, while artillery concentrations took their toll. By nightfall the Naktong Bulge was cleared of the enemy. The NK 4th Division lost practically all of its heavy equipment and weapons. More than 1200 NK soldiers were buried by the U.S. 24th Division. American casualties were also heavy, but our troops had proven again that they not only could stand and fight but could successfully counterattack.

General Walker had won his first battle but had little time to savor his victory; for other crises were developing near the east coast and in the Taegu sector.

The Pohang-Kyongju Corridor

While the Naktong Bulge fight was progressing, three NK divisions were attacking down the east coastal road toward Pohang and through the mountains via Angangni, opposed by the ROK 3d and Capital Divisions. By August 10 the ROK 3d Division had been trapped south of Yongdok by the NK 5th Division, which had cut the road in its rear and was nearing Pohang. A short distance west elements of the NK 12th Division had reached the important lateral Pohang-Taegu road near Angangni (Map 6).

When word of this situation reached General Walker, as the Naktong Bulge fight was hanging in the balance, he flew with General Partridge and General Farrell, Chief of the Korean Military Advisory Group, to the Yonil airfield, where he was met by Colonel Emmerich, military adviser to the ROK 3d Division. Emmerich had been flown in by helicopter from the cruiser *Helena,* which was giving the ROK Army gunfire support. Walker instructed Emmerich to have the ROK 3d Division hold in place and prevent the NK 5th Division tanks and artillery from approaching closer to Pohang. But to ensure that Yonil would not be lost General Walker again had to use part of his Eighth Army reserve, the 3d Battalion, 9th Infantry, even though the 9th Regimental Combat Team (less the 3d Battalion) was heavily engaged in the Naktong Bulge. A task force consisting of the 3d Battalion, 9th Infantry, a tank company, and other attachments, under command of Brigadier General Joseph S. Bradley, fought its way through two ambushes east of Angangni and set up a perimeter around the Yonil airstrip. Despite this fact, as NK forces neared Yonil, Far East Air Force Headquarters in Japan, fearful of losing planes from mortar fire, abandoned Yonil on August 13. The same day the ROK 3d Division, under air cover from the Fifth Air Force and gunfire support from United States naval vessels offshore, was evacuated by LST's to the vicinity of Yonil.

For the next several days the ROK I Corps, now consisting of the Capital Division and the 3d and 8th Divisions, supported by tanks and artillery from Task Force Bradley, engaged in a seesaw battle with the North Koreans along the front from Pohang to Angangni. Under improving leadership the ROK Army fought the enemy to a standstill and then drove him into the mountains. The important Pohang-Taegu lateral was cleared, and the NK threat to Pusan down the east coast–Kyongju corridor was ended for the present.

The Taegu Front

General Walker's concern for the defense of the Perimeter was not limited to the two flanks. Though the approach to Pusan by way of Taegu was longer than by way of Pohang or Masan, there was more maneuvering room for the enemy if he should be able to break through at Taegu, and he would have the advantage of a better road and rail net to support his advance. Furthermore, he had a preponderance of strength, five infantry divisions reinforced with armor, which were preparing to attack Taegu from the north and west.

During August 4 to 9 the enemy crossed the Naktong on the front of the ROK II Corps and the 1st Cavalry Division at several points. In the 1st Cavalry sector the NK 3d Division was repulsed with heavy losses by prompt counterattacks, spurred on by General Walker, who appeared at General Gay's command post on the morning of August 9.

But to the north of Taegu, though the ROK 1st Division under General Pak Sun Yup fought valiantly, the enemy was able to penetrate within artillery range of Taegu. The city was packed with refugees, who became panicky on August 18 when a few enemy shells landed near the railway station. President Syngman Rhee initiated the movement of his capital to Pusan, and the Korean Provincial Government ordered the evacuation of Taegu. Swarms of refugees began pouring out of the city on all roads to the south, threatening to block the movement of Michaelis' 27th Infantry, which Walker had again called upon, this time from the Naktong Bulge, to block the enemy advance along the Sangju-Taegu corridor.

Repercussions in Washington

The threatening situation in August around the Pusan Perimeter had repercussions all the way to Washington. Some news correspondents, although reporting accurately the successive withdrawals of the Eighth Army, had alarmed a number of our congressmen and a large segment of our people about whether we would be able to maintain a foothold in Korea. A member of the House Armed Services Committee had declared publicly in mid-July that the Eighth Army might have to evacuate Korea in seventy-two hours.

I had always felt that one of the main responsibilities of the Chief of Staff was to report to the Congress and the American people on the military situation, good or bad. This required me to gather as much first-hand information as time from duties in Washington permitted. The JCS had designated Admiral Sherman and me to go to the Far East in mid-August to consult with General MacArthur about plans for an amphibious landing at Inchon. I decided to take advantage of this trip to visit front-line units of the Eighth Army in order to make my own estimate of the situation.

We arrived in Tokyo on August 21 and were met at the airport by General MacArthur and members of his staff. As was always the case, Sherman and I stayed at the guest house within the compound of the General's residence, which prior to World War II was the residence of the United States ambassador. There we had dinner with the General and his lovely wife.

The following morning Admiral Sherman and myself, with Admirals Radford and Joy and Air Force Generals Stratemeyer, Edwards, and Weyland, flew to Korea for a briefing at General Walker's headquarters on the current situation of the Eighth Army. Tight as the situation was, I was gratified to find Walker fuming a bit, as usual, at having to give ground but fully confident that the Eighth Army and our ROK allies would hold the Pusan

Perimeter. After the briefing the party split up, the Navy and Air groups to tour activities of special interest to them and Walker and I to visit units of the Eighth Army.

We headed first for the critical front northwest of Taegu, where the NK 13th Division was almost knocking at the doors of the city. As we drove along we passed long lines of refugees moving south from the battle front. Once again I was saddened, as I had been in Belgium at the opening of the Battle of the Bulge in 1944, by the plight of refugees fleeing from their homes. The Korean peasants, trudging hopelessly on foot, women carrying frightened children in their arms, some obviously bearing others in their wombs, some dragging unwilling oxen pulling carts laden with their few earthly possessions, the old and the feeble falling fear-stricken behind — these were even more heart-moving than the Belgians of the Ardennes. I shall never forget one Korean man, no longer young, an A-frame on his back laden with two sacks of rice, atop which sat his wizened old mother. Though war may have its great moments of testing men in defense of freedom, its burden is misery and suffering.

Walker and I were on our way to see Mike Michaelis and his 27th Infantry. We found Michaelis at his command post in a large concrete culvert under a straight stretch of road that ran through a narrow valley 13 miles from Taegu. Our soldiers had dubbed this stretch of road the "Bowling Alley" because of the solid shells from enemy tanks at the head of the valley, which ricocheted down the road with thunderous reverberations. Michaelis was calm and cool in spite of the fact that he never knew when the road behind him might be cut by enemy infiltrating down from the ridges hemming in the narrow valley.* His regiment had beaten off repeated attacks, supported by T-34 tanks, the burned-out hulks of which marked the limit of enemy advance a few hundred yards from the command post. I was proud of this fine young commander and his 27th Infantry. Credit for saving Taegu in this critical period must go also to the sturdy ROK

* I learned later that the road back of Michaelis' command post had been shelled and cut by a small enemy force fifteen minutes after we had left the command post (*Washington Evening Star*, August 24, 1950, AP dispatch, Tokyo dated August 24).

1st Division, which for one week of repeated NK night attacks held the high ground overlooking the Bowling Alley. Finally the NK 13th Division gave up the fight, blew up the road in front of the 27th Infantry, and withdrew. Taegu was safe, for a time at least, and the ubiquitous 27th Infantry was returned to its 25th Division west of Masan, where trouble was again brewing.

Before returning to Tokyo I visited all American divisions along the Perimeter and was convinced that in spite of difficulties General Walker and his doughty men, Americans and South Koreans alike, would hold on to their bridgehead. On my return to Washington and after reporting to the President, the Secretary of Defense and the Joint Chiefs, I stated this conviction to the Armed Services Committees of the Congress and to the press. These statements, according to press editorial reaction at the time, did much to reassure the Congress and the public.

The North Korean September Offensive

By the end of August the North Korean attacks had been thrown back all along the front. The United Nations forces were becoming stronger and more experienced with each passing week. Promises of combat troops in addition to the British 27th Brigade, which arrived at Pusan on August 29, had been made by the United Kingdom, Canada, the Netherlands, Turkey, and Thailand. The North Korean high command planned a final all-out effort to drive the United Nations allies from Korea before it was too late.

The attacks launched by the NK I and II Corps during the period of August 31 to September 2 were, in effect, replicas of the August attacks but were better coordinated and on a more savage scale. To meet them General Walker had to use every last resource under his command. He demonstrated again and again his mastery of the flexible defense, the essence of which is the employment of reserves at the proper time and place. But all units were holding overly long frontages, and he had to scramble for reserves, shifting them from one front to another as he sensed the greatest danger. He seemed to be everywhere during this period, moving by jeep or light airplane to wherever the going was toughest, judging enemy capabilities and morale against the same factors on the side of the Americans and South Koreans. Never a patient man, his patience wore thin whenever a subordinate commander showed signs of wavering. On one occasion, according to the historian Appleton, he told a division commander, who had come back to Eighth Army Headquarters to lament over a difficult situation, "If the enemy gets into Taegu, you will find me resisting him in the streets and I'll have some of my trusted people with me and you had better be prepared to do the same. Now get back to your division and fight it!"

At one stage, about September 6, when the North Koreans had captured Pohang and had severed the Pohang-Taegu lateral, had forced back the 1st Cavalry Division to within 15 miles of Taegu, had driven through the 2d Division almost to Yonsan in the Naktong Bulge, and had poured through the 24th Infantry Regiment of the 25th Division almost to Masan, General Walker was forced to consider shortening the Pusan Perimeter by withdrawing to the so-called Davidson Line. In August General MacArthur, looking toward all contingencies, had instructed General Walker to prepare a defensive line closer to Pusan in the event that the U.S. Eighth and the ROK Armies were not able to hold the Naktong River line. This rearward position, on an arc with a radius of about 30 miles from Pusan, had been surveyed and partially delimited on the ground under the supervision of Brigadier General Garrison H. Davidson, of Army football fame. After reviewing the situation with his principal staff officers, Walker directed that tentative orders for the withdrawal be prepared. That night, like many a military commander before him, he wrestled with this decision. Before dawn he reached his decision to stand and fight. The order for withdrawal was never issued.

In all prudence, however, the headquarters of the Eighth Army was moved back to a position just north of Pusan, to avoid loss or damage of its irreplaceable communications equipment. Walker, however, continued to maintain an advanced tactical command post in Taegu, where he remained.

General Walker was most concerned with the situation in the

south, in the sectors of the U.S. 2d and 25th Divisions, where enemy penetrations not only were a direct threat to Pusan but were on the verge of cutting the main Pusan-Taegu line of communications. Fortunately for the hard-pressed 25th Division, Michaelis' 27th Infantry had just rejoined it from the Bowling Alley north of Taegu. Walker, weighing the varied threats around the Perimeter, felt that an NK breakthrough on the 2d Division front was most serious. He alerted the 19th Infantry of the 24th Division, which was in reserve southeast of Taegu, and the 1st Marine Brigade, which was preparing to move to Pusan for MacArthur's projected amphibious counteroffensive. On the morning of September 2 General Walker called Major General Doyle O. Hickey, the able and friendly Deputy Chief of Staff of the Far East Command in Tokyo. Walker described the critical situation on the southern front and the steps he had taken to meet it. He said he knew MacArthur had other plans for the Marines but felt he could not restore the front in the Naktong Bulge without using the Marine Brigade, the freshest reserve he had. Hickey at once replied that MacArthur the day before had approved the use of the Marines whenever Walker should deem it necessary. Walker attached the 2d Marine Brigade to the 2d Division and ordered the 24th Division Headquarters and its 19th Infantry to a position south of Miryang, from which the 19th Regiment could intervene in either the 2d or the 25th Division sectors. The 2d Division was to launch an all-out attack to drive the enemy once again from the Naktong Bulge.

A coordinated counterattack by the Marine Brigade and all elements of the 2d Division, including the 2d Engineer Battalion which fought as infantry, jumped off at dawn on September 3. The attack was heavily supported by the Fifth Air Force and Marine aviation. According to prisoners, this attack, which drove the North Koreans back to the Cloverleaf hills by September 5, was one of the bloodiest and most terrifying experiences sustained by NK troops during the war. The NK 4th Division, of Taejon fame, like its companion 3d Division before it, was all but destroyed. The Marine Brigade was released to the control of the Far East Command on September 6.

The NK attacks against Masan and Taegu and in the east were likewise repulsed with heavy casualties on both sides. By September 12 the NK September offensive was spent. The U.S. Eighth and the ROK Armies under the brilliant leadership of General Walker had won one of the greatest defensive battles in United States military history, rivaling the Battle of the Bulge in World War II.

General Walker paid well-deserved tribute to the Fifth Air Force, saying, "If it had not been for the air support that we received from the Fifth Air Force, we would not have been able to stay in Korea."

But I am sure that General Walker knew, though he was too modest to say so, that the chief victors in this epic struggle were Johnny Walker himself and that habitually underrated soldier, the American doughboy, and his counterpart in the ROK Army. It would shortly be their turn to join in General MacArthur's long-planned counteroffensive.

VI

INCHON

Plans and Preparations

To MOST MEN it would have appeared a hopeless task to right the situation that had taken shape over the two months since June 29, 1950, the day Seoul fell to the North Korean invaders. When General MacArthur flew to Korea in June, and drove to the Han River opposite the city, he observed the outmanned ROK Army streaming to the south in defeat and confusion. Yet by the time the victorious North Koreans had crossed the Han, and even before they commenced their march on Pusan, which they were confident would win the war, General MacArthur had determined in his own mind the broad strategy that would drive the invaders back across the Han and end their dream of a quick and easy conquest of South Korea.

A few days after the fall of Seoul Admiral Sherman, Chief of Naval Operations, radioed Admiral C. Turner Joy, Commander of the Naval Forces in the Far East, advising him that a Marine regimental combat team could be made available for service in Korea whenever General MacArthur desired it. Joy reported this at once to General MacArthur. He found the General happily receptive. MacArthur had already conceived an amphibious assault on the west coast in the enemy's rear. He promptly radioed the JCS for the combat team, and the JCS signaled approval the next day. MacArthur planned to land this team and the 1st Cavalry Division at Inchon and seize the high ground north of Seoul, while General Dean's 24th Division drove the North Koreans back against the Han River. Underestimating the strength and skill of the North Koreans, MacArthur had set a tentative date for this operation as early as July 22.

General MacArthur knew that before this could be done the enemy's attack on Pusan would have to be stopped. It was only after the touch-and-go fighting along the Pusan Perimeter that the aggressors were halted. With full credit to the courage and sacrifices of the men of the U.S. Eighth and the ROK armies, who threw back the North Koreans, the epic battles of the Pusan Perimeter were essentially the story of one man, Lieutenant General Walton C. Walker.

Even more so, the brilliant counteroffensive, spearheaded by the amphibious assault at Inchon, was the masterpiece of one man, General Douglas MacArthur, who conceived the operation and drove it to a successful conclusion in the face of tremendous difficulties.

Operation Bluehearts was the code name assigned to the first plan, which died almost aborning, as the ROK Army and the U.S. 24th Division were unable to stop the North Korean advance. By July 10 it became apparent that the 1st Cavalry Division would have to be used in the holding operation, and Bluehearts was cancelled.

However, a more ambitions plan was already being developed by Brigadier General Edwin K. Wright's Joint Staff Plans and Operations Group. On July 10 General MacArthur radioed the JCS asking that the 1st Marine Provisional Brigade, consisting of the 5th Marine Regiment and a Marine Air Group and auxiliary units, which had been approved by the JCS, be expanded to a full division with appropriate air support.

This request reached Washington while General Vandenberg and I were en route to Tokyo on our visit described in Chapter IV. We met General MacArthur and his staff on July 13. MacArthur explained his reasons for cancelling Bluehearts. He reiterated his determination to attack the enemy's rear by a landing on the west coast as soon as he was sure that the North Korean advance was halted. He had not yet chosen a new target date or a definite point of attack. He favored Inchon, but consideration was being given also to Heiju and Chinnampo, both well north of Inchon.

The following day, after returning to Tokyo from Korea, I conferred with General Almond and most of General Wright's Plans and Operations Group. Before departing from Washington

I had been briefed on possible landing sites on the west coast. The Navy staff in Washington was highly skeptical of the practicability of Inchon because of the narrow sea approaches and the thirty-five-foot tides. With this in mind, at the meeting with General Almond I questioned the feasibility of Inchon. Rear Admiral James H. Doyle, the Navy's expert on amphibious warfare, on Admiral Joy's staff, replied, "It will be extremely difficult and will take considerable destruction ashore, but it can be done." I queried also whether the assault troops would get across the formidable Han River after landing at Inchon. Almond said that amphibious trucks were available in the theater and could be used to ferry troops. He also pointed out that MacArthur planned to drop an airborne regimental combat team, which had been requested on July 8, north of the Han to secure the north bank.

I had no authority to approve or disapprove the plan. How and when the requisite troops could be raised to war strength and fully equipped, as General MacArthur desired, had not been determined by the Defense Department. The Navy and Marine questions concerning the feasibility of landing at Inchon had not been resolved. I remained dubious about Inchon. My experience in the South Pacific and Normandy had strongly impressed me with the difficulties of amphibious operations, which here would be compounded with exceptional problems of tides, tortuous approaches through narrows waters, and time for coordination of the attack elements. But before leaving Tokyo I did tell General MacArthur privately that I felt that one full Marine division could be sent to him.

On my return to Washington I reported to the Joint Chiefs of Staff the broad outlines of General MacArthur's plans and expressed my doubts. I learned that the others of the JCS had agreed to bring the 1st Marine Division up to full strength but had not yet decided to commit it to the Far East, which they had been urged to do by Admiral Arthur W. Radford, Pacific Fleet Commander, and by Lieutenant General Lemuel C. Shepherd, U.S. Marine Corps Commander, Pacific Fleet Marine Force.

On July 19 MacArthur again called for the 1st Marine Division and 1st Marine Air Wing and stipulated that they should arrive in the Far East by September 10, 1950. He requested that men and equipment be sent at once to Japan to bring the 5th Marine Regimental Combat Team, then en route, to war strength.

The Marine Corps had already initiated steps to bring its 1st Division to full strength. Under Presidential authority it called to active duty its entire Organized Ground Reserve, including 1800 officers and more than 31,000 enlisted reservists. To provide additional experienced men, it transferred 6800 regulars from the 2d Marine Division, normally committed to operations with the Atlantic Fleet, to the 1st Marine Division, being assembled at Camp Pendleton, California. Equipment likewise was being moved there from all over the United States. But Admiral Sherman felt it would be too dangerous to strip the Atlantic Fleet Marine Force in order to meet the September 10 deadline. On his recommendations the Joint Chiefs of Staff radioed MacArthur on July 20 that the 1st Marine Division, at full strength, could not reach Japan before November or December.

General MacArthur reacted to this message as he had often done in World War II, when he felt the authorities in Washington were slighting his Pacific Command in favor of Europe. He urged reconsideration, insisting that the availability of the full Marine division by September 10 was "absolutely vital" to the success of his entire plan. He added, "There can be no demand for its use elsewhere which can equal the urgency of the immediate battle mission contemplated for it." The JCS were not considering any other use of the 1st Marine Division just then, but the Chiefs were concerned that the Communists might take advantage of our involvement in Korea to put pressure again on the western Allies in Europe or initiate some new disturbance in the Middle East, as they had done earlier in Berlin and Greece.

The exchange of messages described above took place just at the time that General Dean was making his last stand at Taejon and reports were reaching the JCS in Washington that both flanks of the Eighth Army were being threatened by North Korean Army drives down the east and west coasts. MacArthur had agreed that the attack on Pusan would have to be stopped before the counteroffensive was launched. Consequently, the Joint Chiefs called

MacArthur to a teleconference on July 24 to inquire whether, in the light of developments on the front of the Eighth and ROK Armies, he was still planning on mid-September for the amphibious assault. Undismayed by the fluid situation on the fighting front, MacArthur replied that "barring unforeseen circumstances, and with complete provision for requested replacements, if the full Marine division is provided, the chances to launch the movement in September would be excellent."

The JCS were still concerned more directly with the questionable ability of General Walker's forces to stop the rampaging North Koreans than they were about meeting a mid-September deadline for the counteroffensive. So, in fact, was General MacArthur. Recognizing the threat to Pusan, the base port that was even more essential to the Eighth Army than Seoul was to the enemy, MacArthur took decisive action to bolster Walker's crumbling defenses. The 5th Marine Regimental Combat Team and the 2d Infantry Division, both en route to Japan and both scheduled to participate in the amphibious attack, were diverted directly to Korea and released to General Walker. This diversion seemed even to General MacArthur's planning group to necessitate a delay of the amphibious operation to October 15, and they so recommended. However, a number of factors argued for a September date.

Perhaps this is a good place at which to assess the pros and cons, not only of the date but, more importantly, of the point of attack for the flanking operation. The physical difficulties of a landing at Inchon were related chiefly to the tides and the nature of the seaward approaches. Because of the configuration of the Korean peninsula in relation to the Yellow Sea and the mainland of Asia there are tremendous tides along the Korean west coast, averaging twenty-nine feet and running up as high as thirty-six feet. The many small islands off shore serve to funnel the tides at high speed into Inchon, yet act as buffers to the receding tides. Consequently, over the centuries great mud flats have been deposited as far out as 6000 yards from the shore line at low water. LST's being beached at Inchon could approach only at flood tide and would be stuck in the mud as soon as the tide turned. This condition limited to three or four the number of days in a month that the required thirty-foot tides were available. Low tides were common in the Yellow Sea from May through August, whereas from October onward rough waters would make extremely dangerous the approaches to Inchon through the narrow deep-water "Flying Fish" channel, which threaded the passageway between the islands. Thus, according to the hydrographic records, September 15 was the ideal time for a landing at Inchon. The next suitable date would be October 11, by which time, unless pressure on the Pusan perimeter were relieved, the vital port of Pusan might have fallen.

Of course, an alert enemy, familiar with these local conditions, could read the same charts and arrive at the same optimal dates for a flanking amphibious attack. He thus could be prepared to bomb or shell the approaching troop convoys moving through the restricted channels. Gunfire support vessels would have to anchor in the swift waters of these channels in order to deliver accurate fire support to the landing forces. Karig and others in their *Battle Report* (Holt, Rinehart and Winston, 1952) quote Lieutenant Commander Arlie G. Capps, Admiral Doyle's Gunnery and Training Officer, as fearing that the gunfire support ships might become "sitting ducks out there in the channel."

The tides, currents, and treacherous channel to Inchon required a daylight approach with an assault landing at Inchon in the late afternoon. This would permit little time for consolidating a beachhead before dark.

A further tactical complication was posed by the fortified island of Wolmido, which dominated the approaches to Inchon and the landing areas. There were no beaches in the Inchon area at high tide. In fact, the city was protected from the tides by a twelve-foot stone seawall, which was itself a formidable obstacle. The Marines would first have to seize Wolmido before attacking the city itself. There they would have to use ladders to clamber over the seawall, which could be covered by fire from houses along the waterfront. For the first time in their long history the Marines would be making an amphibious assault directly in the heart of a city.

In addition to these tactical and technical drawbacks to Inchon, which were chiefly the concern of the Navy and the Marine Corps, there was a serious strategic question whether the Eighth Army could break through the North Korean cordon along the Naktong River and drive on Inchon quickly enough before the enemy could concentrate an overwhelming force against the amphibious attackers. In many instances throughout military history the division of forces beyond supporting distances has led to disastrous defeats. The Eighth Army would have to cross the Naktong River and the narrow defiles of the Sobaek Range and advance over 150 miles to reach the Inchon bridgehead.

Although these drawbacks to the landing at Inchon might prove insurmountable, Inchon offered rewards that were certainly tempting. A successful landing there, if followed by a quick seizure of nearby Seoul, would sever the enemy's principal supply routes, which radiated into and out of Seoul. Kimpo airfield, the best in South Korea, would fall as part of the drive on Seoul, providing both a good air logistical terminal and an excellent operating base for fighter bombers. The psychological impact of recapturing the traditional political capital of Korea would be enormous and, if the Eighth Army could strike the hammer blow on the anvil of Inchon in time, the North Korean Army might be destroyed — which was the objective of the exercise.

A theater Commander is always given broad leeway by the JCS in planning and conducting operations. However, in order to discharge their responsibilities to the President, the Joint Chiefs of Staff must have up-to-date information on their field commanders' plans. President Truman never interfered with military operations, but in the Korean war — a war in peacetime, without a formal declaration by the Congress — he was deeply committed personally and wished to be kept constantly informed. General MacArthur did not wish to conceal anything from Washington, but he was not very communicative about his plans. He was skeptical about the security of the information he furnished Washington.

In as precariously balanced an operation as the Inchon counteroffensive the JCS had two alternatives. We could have asked no questions, made no challenge to the plans as we knew them, and allowed General MacArthur to accept complete responsibility for the outcome. The General was perfectly willing and confidently proceeding to do just this, but we could not, as long as we had any doubts concerning its success, have washed our hands of responsibility for the operation. We were not prepared to do this. At a meeting at the White House on August 10 with the President and the Secretary of Defense, at which it was agreed to send the 3d Infantry Division and to assemble a full Marine division for employment in Korea, Admiral Sherman made a comment which he recorded at the time, "I made it clear that I was confident that General MacArthur would make good use of the forces, but that the Joint Chiefs of Staff would have to pass on his plans for amphibious landings."

Not having received any details of the planned operations since my oral report of July 15, the JCS decided to send two of our members to the Far East to review the situation directly with General MacArthur. Admiral Sherman as Chief of Naval Operations, the Chief of Staff most directly concerned with the amphibious phase, and I as Executive Agent for the Far East, were designated. On arrival in Tokyo on August 21 we were cordially received, as always, by General MacArthur. A full briefing and discussion of the Inchon plans was arranged for the late afternoon of August 23. This would give Admiral Sherman, who had not been to Korea, and me an opportunity for a short visit there on August 22.

Later that afternoon, while Admiral Sherman conferred with Admiral Doyle on naval plans for the landing, I had a session with General Almond and the staff of the X Corps, which was to make the assault. The 1st Marine Division and the 7th Infantry Division and supporting troops were to constitute the newly created X Corps. Because time before the projected D Day was short, Admiral Sherman in early August had suggested that the Fleet Marine Force, Pacific, which was located in Honolulu and commanded by General Shepherd, an experienced amphibious commander, should furnish the headquarters and staff for the landing. However, MacArthur had decided to place Almond in command of the X Corps and to have him select his staff largely from General Headquarters in Tokyo. According to Almond, MacArthur considered this best "from the standpoint of his ability to supervise the planning and its future operations." When on August 10 MacArthur surprised Almond by informing him of this decision, Almond protested that he could not serve both as Chief of Staff at General Headquarters and command the Corps in Korea. MacArthur replied, "Let Hickey [Major General Doyle O. Hickey, Deputy Chief of Staff] serve as Chief of Staff while you are away. We will all be back here in a month."

By the time Sherman and I arrived in Tokyo, Almond with characteristic competence had assembled a joint staff, including ten Marine and two Navy officers. The staff had been working secretly on operations plans in an old airplane hangar in the motor pool of the General Headquarters Command in Tokyo. No one else in the headquarters knew of these preparations, not even the most acquisitive newsman.

The next day, August 22, Sherman and I, accompanied by a number of senior Naval and Air Force officers, flew to Korea and were briefed by Walker at his headquarters in Taegu. Since we had not yet met with MacArthur on his plans for Inchon, that matter was not raised. Tentative plans for the counteroffensive had been outlined to Walker by Hickey in early August. Walker had agreed with the concept, but members of his staff doubted seriously whether the Eighth Army would be able to break out of the Perimeter unless heavily reinforced. At the time of our visit on August 22 Walker was too involved in plugging holes in his leaky front to give much thought to a later break-out, and we did not press him on this point.

The following morning I accompanied General Walker on a swing by air along the front, stopping to visit all division commanders in the south, including Brigadier General Craig, the Commander of the 1st Marine Brigade. I observed that, although all commanders were confident of their ability to hold the Perimeter, the troops, especially in the 24th Division, were weary from weeks of almost continuous fighting. They could use some respite before turning to the offensive, but none was in sight.

With these and other uncertainties in mind Admiral Sherman

and I met General MacArthur and his staff for a full-scale review
of the United Nations Commander's counteroffensive plans shortly
after our return to Tokyo from Korea in the late afternoon of
August 23, 1950. Present besides the principals were Admirals
Joy and Doyle, and Generals Almond, Hickey, and Wright, and
members of General Wright's planning group.

After brief opening remarks from General MacArthur, General
Wright outlined the basic plan (Map 7), which called for an
assault landing by the 1st Marine Division of the X Corps directly
in the port of Inchon. After the capture of the city the corps was
to advance as rapidly as possible and seize the Kimpo airfield, the
town of Yongdungpo, and the south bank of the Han River east
thereof. It was then to cross the river, capture Seoul, and secure
the dominant ground to the north. The 7th Infantry Division,
commanded by Major General David G. Barr, was to land after
the Marines, advance on their right flank, and secure the south
bank of the Han southeast of Seoul and the high ground north of
Suwon and west of Kyonganni. Thereafter the X Corps on the
Suwon–Yonganni–Seoul line would form the strategic anvil on
which the Eighth Army, after breaking out of the Pusan Perimeter, would deliver the hammer blows intended to destroy the
bulk of the North Korean Army.

Doyle and his naval and marine planners then presented a
thorough analysis of the naval phases of the landing operation.
They emphasized the difficulties and risks involved and were
frankly pessimistic. Doyle concluded the presentation by stating
that, though the operation was not impossible, he did not recommend it. According to MacArthur's *Reminiscences*, Admiral Sherman, reviewing the Navy briefing, commented, "If every geographical and naval handicap were listed — Inchon has 'em all."

I questioned the ability of the Eighth Army to make a quick
junction with the X Corps at Inchon, particularly since General
Walker's forces would be weakened by the withdrawal of the 1st
Marine Brigade. Failure to make this junction might result in
disaster to the X Corps. I suggested, as an alternative to Inchon,
that consideration be given to a landing at Kunsan, which had few
of Inchon's physical drawbacks, was close to the enemy's main
supply routes through Nonsan and Taejon, and should ensure more

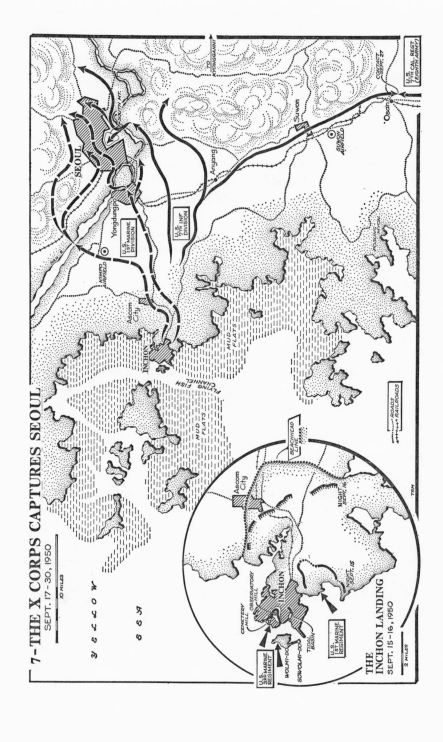

7—THE X CORPS CAPTURES SEOUL
SEPT. 17–30, 1950

10 MILES

YELLOW

SEA

SEOUL

Yongdungp'o

KIMPO AIRFIELD

U.S. 1ST MARINE DIVISION

Ascom City

INCHON

MUD FLATS

FLYING FISH CHANNEL

MUD FLATS

U.S. 7TH INF. DIVISION

Anyang

Suwon

SUWON AIRFIELD

Osan

CONTACT SEPT. 27

U.S. 7TH CAV. REGT. (EIGHTH ARMY)

TO KYONGGANNI

HAN RIV.

THE INCHON LANDING
SEPT. 15–16, 1950

2 MILES

BEACHHEAD LINE

Ascom City

NIGHT SEPT. 16

INCHON

Cemetery Hill
Observatory Hill

U.S. 3RD MARINE REGIMENT

WOLMI-DO

SOWOLMI-DO

TIDAL BASIN

U.S. 1ST MARINE REGIMENT

NIGHT SEPT. 15

ROADS

RAILROADS

TRM

prompt union with the Eighth Army in the vicinity of Taejon. Admiral Sherman seconded my suggestion.

*

General MacArthur sat silently puffing his pipe throughout his naval staff's presentation, which lasted more than an hour, and the remarks made by Admiral Sherman and me. He continued sitting in silence for a few moments as we waited for his reaction. He then spoke quietly, in a matter-of-fact tone at first, gradually building up emphasis with consummate skill. Even discounting the obvious dramatics, this was a masterly exposition of the argument for the daring risk he was determined to take by a landing at Inchon.

MacArthur said that he recognized all of the hazards that the Navy and Marine Corps had so clearly pointed out but that he had confidence in their ability to overcome them. He said that the Navy and Marines had never let him down throughout his campaigns in the Pacific and that he was sure they would not now.

As to a landing at Kunsan, the general insisted that the envelopment would be too shallow, would not effectively cut the enemy communications centered in Seoul, and would permit the North Koreans to fall back on their line of communications while still presenting a continuous front to the X Corps and the Eighth Army.

Our fears that the X Corps at Inchon might be overwhelmed before the Eighth Army could make a junction were ill founded, the general said. He was convinced that the bulk of the Communists were committed against the Pusan Perimeter and that they had inadequate reserves in the vicinity of Inchon and had not properly prepared Inchon for defense.

The very reasons we cited for not landing at Inchon would tend to ensure surprise. "For the enemy commander will reason that no one would be so brash as to make such an attempt." As Wolfe did at Quebec, he would land where the enemy would think it impossible and, with the consequent surprise, gain a decisive victory. MacArthur closed with a stirring peroration:

"If my estimate is inaccurate and should I run into a defense with which I cannot cope, I will be there personally and will immediately withdraw our forces before they are committed to a bloody setback. The only loss then will be my professional reputation. But Inchon will not fail. Inchon will succeed. And it will save 100,000 lives."

The brilliant exposition left the general's audience spellbound. Admiral Joy later recounted, "I must admit that after I had listened to this eloquent and passionate soliloquy, my personal misgivings about the choice of Inchon were erased. I believe that the General had persuaded me, and all others in the room — with the possible exception of Admiral Sherman — that Inchon could be successful."

I was favorably impressed but still had some reservations. There was more at stake than General MacArthur's reputation, great as that was. Thinking back, I realize that the main point that was missing in this briefing — though neither Admiral Sherman nor I focused on it at the time — had to do with the strength of the enemy in the Inchon area and his ability to concentrate there quickly. General MacArthur had stated that the Communists had massed their strength around Walker's defense perimeter, but I do not recall that this point had been convincingly covered by Commander Robert H. McIlwaine, who gave the intelligence summary for Admiral Doyle.

Sherman and many of the naval and marine officers were still dubious. According to Major General Oliver P. Smith, the commander of the 1st Marine Division, the following morning Admirals Sherman, Radford, Joy, and Doyle and Generals Shepherd and Smith met in Joy's office to review their impressions. Smith particularly felt that MacArthur should give consideration to landing at Posung-Myon, about 30 miles south of Inchon, where naval underwater reconnaissance parties had made several undetected landings and had found deep water that would permit landings at any hour of any day, unrestricted by the tide. It was generally agreed that since one of the main objectives, if not the chief one, was to capture Seoul at the earliest practicable date, the landing would have to be made at Inchon. None the less, Shepherd said he was going to see MacArthur before he left Tokyo and make a

final plea for a landing in the Posung-Myon area. He did see
MacArthur, but to no avail.

Sherman also had a final conference with MacArthur, but there
is no mention of its subject matter in Sherman's notes. Sherman
is quoted by Cagle as having said, after leaving MacArthur's
office, "I wish I could share that man's optimism."

General MacArthur had not asked Admiral Sherman or me to
approve his plans; any such approval would have been beyond
our authority as individual members of the JCS. Our visit had
served a useful purpose; I feel that it crystallized the general's
determination to proceed with Inchon, and we were now fully
informed for the first time about these plans, the full risks involved,
and the general's personal confidence in the outcome.

Upon our return to Washington Sherman and I briefed the other
Chiefs, the Secretary of Defense, and the President. After reviewing our reports, the JCS on August 28 sent MacArthur a condi-
tional approval of his plans as follows:

> We concur in making preparations for and executing a turning
> movement by amphibious forces on the west coast of Korea,
> either at Inchon in the event the enemy defenses in the vicinity
> of Inchon prove ineffective, or at a favorable beach south of
> Inchon if one can be located. We further concur in prepara-
> tions, if desired by CINCFE [Commander in Chief, Far East],
> for an envelopment by amphibious forces in the vicinity of
> Kunsan. We understand that alternative plans are being pre-
> pared in order to best exploit the situation as it develops.

General MacArthur issued Operations Order No. 1, General
Headquarters, United Nations Command, on August 30, 1950,
covering the details of the operation. When by September 5 no
copy of this order had been received by the JCS,* nor had any
further information, as requested by the Chiefs in a radio message of August 28, the JCS radioed MacArthur again requesting information on any modification of his plans. He replied
briefly that "the general outline of the plan remains as described

---

* Five copies of this order were sent to the JCS and three to each Chief of Service,
but they were not received in Washington until September 8.

to you." He said that he would send by officer courier by September 11 a detailed description of the planned operation. This would be too late for the JCS to influence the course of action if we or the President felt impelled to interpose.

Reports of the fighting along the Pusan Perimeter in early September boded ill for any early break-out of the Eighth Army in conjunction with the projected Inchon landing. On September 7 the JCS reminded General MacArthur that almost all reserves in the Far East had been committed to the Eighth Army and that all available General Reserve units in the United States, except the 82d Airborne Division, had already been committed to him. No further reinforcements could be expected in the near future, since it would be at least four months before any of the recently federalized National Guard divisions would be ready for action. In view of this situation the JCS radioed MacArthur asking for a fresh evaluation of the Inchon maneuver.

MacArthur sent back a reply at once stating that the embarkation of the troops and the preliminary air and naval preparations were already under way and that there was no question in his mind of the feasibility of the operation. He felt that the situation of the Eighth Army was not critical, though conceivably it might have to contract the Perimeter; positions had already been selected with this contingency in mind. However, there was not the slightest possibility that the Army would be driven from the Pusan beachhead, since the Inchon envelopment would prevent any enemy reinforcement in the south. An early junction of the Eighth Army and the X Corps, while desirable, was not a vital part of the operation. He concluded by again expressing his complete confidence and that of his commanders and staff in the success of the operation.

Impressed with this firm reiteration of confidence from the responsible field commander, the JCS on September 8 radioed him: "We approve your plan and President has been so informed." The reference to the President led MacArthur, as recounted in his *Reminiscences*, to speculate that Mr. Truman had threatened to interfere and overrule the JCS. This was in no sense the case. A routine had been established from the very onset of the Korean

U.S. Joint Chiefs of Staff at beginning of Korean War: Admiral Forrest P. Sherman, Chief of Naval Operations; General Omar N. Bradley, U.S. Army, Chairman; General Hoyt S. Vandenberg, Chief of Staff, U.S. Air Force; and General J. Lawton Collins, Chief of Staff, U.S. Army

A South Korean soldier relaxes on a hillside overlooking railroad yards in Pusan, Korea

General Collins presents the United Nations flag to General MacArthur atop MacArthur's headquarters in Tokyo

General Collins talks with wounded Corporal Ralph E. Hargrove of Ypsilanti, Michigan

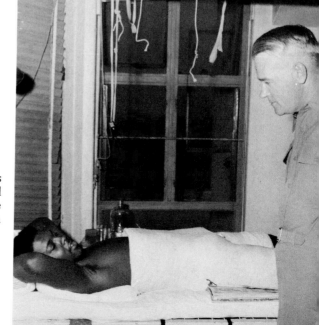

Korean refugees:
Left, above. Moving along the road to Taegu to escape fighting south of the 38th Parallel
Left, below. Jamming aboard trains at a railroad station
Above. Preparing to board a vessel for evacuation from the fighting area north of Pusan

Left. Major General O. P. Smith, USMC, confers with Vice Admiral J. H. Doyle, USN, aboard the USS *Rochester* prior to Inchon invasion

Below. U.S. Marines approaching Blue Beach, Inchon. Clouds of smoke are from fires started by shelling from U.N. ships

One bulldozer pulls another along the muddy shore of Walmido as equipment is unloaded from LST's

Men of the 5th Regiment, 1st Cavalry Division, use a shallow boat to cross the Naktong River west of Taegu

Aerial view of the Chosin Reservoir area

Major General Edward H. Almond, Commanding General X Corps (left), and Vice Admiral Arthur D. Struble, Commander Seventh Fleet, converse aboard the U.S. battleship *Missouri* before General Almond departs for Wonsan

Men of the 8th Cavalry Regiment, 1st Cavalry Division, supported by
tanks, move up to assault positions atop a Communist-held hill in North
Korea

Left. Korean refugees crowded aboard fishing boats
to evacuate Hungnam. They will transfer to U.N.
transports and LST's

A Korean carries his aged father across the icy Han River southeast of
Seoul in their flight south to escape the onrushing Communists

war, in which the JCS kept the President informed on the current
situation in Korea. This was done by General Bradley, who was
Chairman, and in his absence by one of the Chiefs. When Admiral
Sherman and I returned from Tokyo in August we had briefed the
President and undoubtedly told him of our concern over the
feasibility of the Inchon landing. In Sherman's Memorandum for
the Record, in connection with events in late June and early July,
1950, there is a brief entry dated September 6, just prior to the
JCS September 8 dispatch to MacArthur, in reference to his final
evaluation of the plans for Inchon. It reads: "Briefed President at
9:30. After the staff left, the September operation was discussed."
The record does not indicate the nature of the discussion or
whether Sherman was alone with the President. A subsequent entry in this memorandum, dated September 8, says, "JCS reported
to President receipt of optimistic reply from General MacArthur
and of our consequent approval of Inchon landing." It should be
noted that this memo indicates that the *JCS informed* the President of the *JCS* approval. I doubt whether we would have *dis-
approved* a theater Commander's plans without the concurrence of
the President. We accepted full responsibility for our own actions
in querying MacArthur on his plans, expressing to him our concern
about their feasibility, and giving our final approval. I have
no recollection of President Truman's ever expressing any doubt
about the success of Inchon or of his seeking to override any
action or decision of the JCS in regard to that operation. In his
memoirs the President wrote:

> General Collins and Admiral Sherman had left for Tokyo on
> August 19 for their detailed conference on General MacArthur's
> plans for an offensive, and on their return they had placed these
> plans before me for *my information and advised me that the
> Joint Chiefs had approved the plans.* It was a daring strategic
> conception. I had the greatest confidence that it would suc-
> ceed.*

* The italics are mine.

Movement to Inchon

While these discussions were taking place, Vice Admiral Arthur
D. Struble, who had been assigned command of Joint Task Force
7, which was to conduct the Inchon operation, was assembling
troop transports, landing craft, carriers, cruisers, destroyers, minesweepers, and other supporting craft and equipment at Yokohama,
Kobe, and Sasebo in Japan and at Pusan.

As if there were not enough natural obstacles to the Inchon
operation, the elements aimed a knockout blow at the Joint Task
Force, as its various components moved toward the attack area.
Typhoon "Kezia," which had been brewing near the Mariana
Islands, was taking dead aim at southern Japan. Admiral Struble,
who had been Chief of Staff to Vice Admiral Alan G. Kirk, commanding the U.S. Naval Forces for the Normandy landings in
World War II, must have thought back to June 4, 1944, D Day
minus 1, when foul weather poured into the English Channel
from the Atlantic and forced a postponement of D Day. Because
of the tidal conditions at Inchon there was even less leeway with
respect to time than in Normandy. In this case, with a view to
getting ahead of "Kezia" which, hopefully, would follow the
normal pattern of western Pacific typhoons and veer north, Admiral Struble ordered the convoy out of Kobe a day ahead of
schedule. He had his flagship, the cruiser *Rochester,* sail from
Yokosuka on September 11.

Admiral Doyle, in command of the Attack Force, left Kobe the
same day aboard the *Mount McKinley,* accompanied by General
Smith and their staffs. General MacArthur had chosen to join
Doyle in *Mount McKinley,* where he would be closer to the assault action than in *Rochester.* After plowing through the heaviest
seas Doyle had ever encountered, the *Mount McKinley* turned
into Sasebo on September 12 to pick up Generals MacArthur,
Almond, and Shepherd, who had flown down from Tokyo.
MacArthur had invited Shepherd along as an adviser. Fortunately,
as the convoys passed the island of Chejudo, off the southern tip
of Korea, on September 13, the Yellow Sea ahead was relatively
calm.

The attack plan called for the capture of the islands Wolmido and Sowolmido by the 3d Battalion, 5th Marines, under Lieutenant Colonel Robert D. Taplett on the morning of D Day, September 15, as a prelude to the main landings by the 5th Marine Regiment (less the 3d Battalion) on Red Beach at the northern edge of Inchon and by the 1st Marine Regiment on Blue Beach south of the city. Because of the broad mud banks these later landings would have to be made at the height of the incoming tide, at 5:30 P.M.

Wolmido was known to be heavily fortified. Its guns would have to be knocked out before the Advanced Attack Group carrying the 3d Battalion could safely approach the landing. Therefore a daily air bombardment of the island commencing September 10 was determined on; it was to be followed by naval gunfire on September 13 and 14, even though this would disclose an impending attack. To ensure destruction of Wolmido's batteries, Rear Admiral J. M. Higgins, the Gunfire Support Group commander, decided on a bold maneuver. Rather than risk ship collision or running aground during a night approach, Higgins chose to attack in broad daylight on September 13. He hoped also to goad the North Koreans on Wolmido to open fire and thus disclose their positions. A new hazard to the operation was exposed — and an unexpected advantage to the daylight approach at low tide thereby appeared — when several mines were discovered by the destroyers in the "Flying Fish" channel. Pausing only to detonate the mines with 40mm shells, the destroyers closed to within 800 yards of Wolmido with guns blazing. Farther back the cruisers poured in salvoes from their 6- and 8-inch guns, and Navy fighters bombed away. The guns on Wolmido remained strangely silent, but after enduring a half-hour's pounding they finally opened up. Though they scored hits on three destroyers, the guns were quickly silenced once their positions were revealed. The destroyers, having completed their misson, withdrew. As they did so, they discovered and destroyed eight more mines. Luckily, these proved to be the only remaining mines sown by the enemy in the approaches to Inchon. The following day, September 14, the Gunfire Support Group encountered no obstructions and practically no return fire from Wolmido, whose defenders had been almost stunned into submission. Wolmido was ready to be taken.

That night, under cover of darkness and navigating the tortuous approach channel by radar, the Advance Attack Group under Captain Norman W. Sears, U.S. Navy, bringing the 3d Battalion, 5th Marines, moved into the inner harbor of Inchon. Captain Sears quietly anchored his small convoy so as to place the now impotent island between the ships and the enemy batteries along the Inchon waterfront. All was now ready for the dawn assault.

In spite of hell, in the form of typhoon "Kezia," rough water and a myriad other difficulties, the U.S. Navy had done a magnificent job in bringing the Joint Task Force through on schedule without a major mishap or the loss of a single vessel. This achievement was a tribute not only to the leadership, experience, and judgment of Admirals Struble, Doyle, and Higgins, but also to the skill, discipline, and devotion of all hands. The next job was up to the Marines. They were ready and competent.

The Marines Storm Ashore

The 1st Marine Division plan fixed H Hour for the assault on Wolmido's Green Beach at 6:30 A.M., to be followed late in the afternoon by the main landings of the 5th Marines (less the 3d Battalion) on Red Beach and the 1st Marine Regiment on Blue Beach (Map 7).

While Captain Sears' Advance Attack Group was positioning itself opposite Green Beach, the *Mount McKinley*, with General MacArthur and the Attack Force commanders crowding the flag bridge, moved into the narrows just before dawn. As the faint outline of Wolmido emerged from the gray morning haze, the leader of the first group of Marine Corsairs overhead rolled over and plunged down with the bombs that opened the forty-five-minute preparation. The guns of the destroyers and cruisers, including those of *Mount McKinley*, roared into action, their jets of flame illuminating the bridge with each salvo. By 6:00 A.M. the assault troops had embarked, and their LCVP's could be seen circling back of the line of departure. Three thousand screaming rockets from three rocket ships added a dramatic Roman-candle finale to the bombardment, after which the first line of LCVP's streaked for Green Beach.

Five days of pounding, September 10 to 14, had so decimated Wolmido's defenders and driven them underground that only a few scattered shots were received as the Marines hit the beach. Most of the surviving defenders surrendered without a fight. At 6:55 A.M. the observers on the bridge of *Mount McKinley* spotted an American flag, secured by Sergeant Alvin E. Smith to a shell-torn tree on the crest. At this signal General MacArthur, happy with the initial success, rose from his chair and said, "That's it. Let's get a cup of coffee."

By 8:00 A.M. all of Wolmido had fallen to the 3d Battalion, which quickly turned to the reduction of Sowolmido; that was completed by noon. General MacArthur promptly sent off a brief report to the JCS:

"First phase landing successful with losses light. Surprise apparently complete. All goes well and on schedule."

The 3d Battalion, 5th Marines, had not lost a man killed in action, had suffered only seventeen wounded, and counted 136 prisoners and 108 North Koreans dead. Thus far the intelligence of the Commander in Chief, Far East, as to the inadequacy of Inchon's defenses was proving correct. No enemy reaction from the city could be spotted as the awesome tide fell back from its early morning high of over thirty feet, isolating the 3d Battalion by a sea of mud.

In the late afternoon the now welcomed flood tide began to roll in, bearing with it the main assault groups destined for Red and Blue Beaches. Another forty-five-minute bombing and gunfire preparation was to precede the H Hour landing, scheduled for 5:30 P.M. The opening salvoes at 4:45 signaled the start of the LCVP's on their long trek to the beaches. Once again the elements seemed to be allied with the enemy as the critical moment of landing approached. Sudden gusts of wind and rain swept stinging spray into the faces of the coxswains of the LCVP's, making it difficult for them to hold course. On the bridge of *Mount McKinley* General MacArthur and his commanders and staff strained their eyes and ears while they listened to a blow-by-blow account of developments from air observers aloft, who alone could penetrate the rain and smoke rising from the landing areas.

Not even the aerial observers could discern the immediate reaction as the leading LCVP's disappeared from view in the murk of rain and smoke. The 5th Marines, Lieutenant Colonel Raymond L. Murray commanding, scaled the seawall on Red Beach with their ladders. They met only scattered fire as they moved toward a cemetery-covered hill, where an enemy mortar position had been spotted a few days before. After some spasmodic resistance on the left flank of Red Beach a platoon of Company A outflanked the mortar position on Cemetery Hill. As the platoon reached the crest, the dazed and spiritless mortar men threw down their weapons and meekly surrendered. The Marine history records that "hardly a shot had been fired by the 2d Platoon, still without a single casualty, and the capture of Cemetery Hill had required about ten minutes."

Observatory Hill a half-mile to the south was tougher. The 5th Marines, who had been fighting in the Naktong Bulge only ten days before, had had no time for a rehearsal of their attack and little time to work out the details of the landing. Confusion inevitably resulted. Incoming waves of LCVP's did not arrive on schedule, and some landed in wrong areas. This slowed the attack on Observatory Hill. As nightfall approached, the attack was more seriously hampered when LST's, bringing supplies into Blue Beach, drew some mortar and machine-gun fire from the direction of the Hill. Thinking that the marines had not been able to advance inland, some of the LST's opened fire, spraying the crests of Cemetery and Observatory Hills and the south flank of Red Beach. As Lieutenant Colonel Harold S. Roise's 2d Battalion moved up from the beach on the right flank, it was swept by fire from the LST's, killing one man and wounding twenty-three others. Slowed by these misfortunes, the 5th Marines did not secure their D Day objective until past nightfall. At 10:00 P.M. the 3d Battalion, which had been isolated on Wolmido throughout the afternoon, crossed the causeway to shore and rejoined the 5th Regimental Combat Team.

On the other side of Inchon the 1st Marine Regiment, Colonel Lewis B. Puller commanding, was having greater difficulties. Having been assembled at Camp Pendleton, California, after the outbreak of fighting in Korea, it had been brought to full strength by hastily gathered small detachments and individuals, both regular and reserve, from all over the country. There had been no time for any cohesive training before sailing for Japan, little time for detailed planning with supporting naval units after arrival in Japan, and none for rehearsals. Officers scarcely knew their own men or their counterparts in the Navy who would put them ashore. In fact, this newly created regiment had never even practiced as a tactical entity until it landed on Blue Beach.

The supporting amphibious units of the Navy suffered comparable handicaps. Inadequate maps and aerial photos of the landing areas and uncertainty about currents, depths of water over the mud flats, and exit routes from the beach made detailed tactical planning impossible in advance.

Successive waves of landing craft lost direction, crossed one another's paths, and groped their way ashore, often to the wrong areas. Fortunately, lack of enemy resistance at the beach permitted the leadership and initiative of unit commanders to bring some order out of these chaotic conditions.

Meanwhile the advance inland by the 1st Marines was making good progress against little resistance. Throughout the night scattered groups of Marines joined their front-line units. By dawn the first day's objectives were well in hand.

The total Marine casualties on D Day, September 15, were twenty killed in action, one dead of wounds, and 174 wounded. General MacArthur reported to the JCS:

"Our losses are light. The clockwork coordination and cooperation between services was noteworthy . . . The command distinguished itself. The whole operation is proceeding on schedule."

Commencing early the following morning, September 16, the 5th and 1st Marines completed the encirclement of Inchon, leaving to South Korean Marines the task of mopping up the city. The troops encountered no resistance, except from haphazard moves by enemy tanks, which were quickly knocked out by Marine-supporting aircraft and tanks. By the end of D Day plus 1 the initial objective line, some 3 miles inland, had been secured.

Enemy communications had been so badly interrupted that NK headquarters in Seoul had no idea of the location of the 1st Marines' front lines. This was clearly shown shortly after sunrise on September 17, when a column of six T-34 tanks and infantry without any advance guard moved down the road from Seoul into the jaws of a 5th Marine outpost. The Marines, scarcely believing their eyes, waited until the enemy was within pointblank range. Unlike Brad Smith's men in the opening battle of the war, they were fully equipped with 3.5-inch rockets and supported by M-26 tanks. A hail of fire of all arms suddenly engulfed the enemy columns. Within minutes all six T-34's were destroyed and some 200 of the NK infantrymen killed.

General MacArthur, accompanied by Admiral Struble, Generals Almond, Shepherd, and Smith, and a coterie of staff officers, correspondents, and photographers, after landing at Inchon early that morning and visiting the command posts of the 1st Marine Division and the 1st Marine Regiment, had moved into the 5th Marine Regiment zone just after the tank ambush. Much to General Smith's dismay, the group of visitors inspected the burned-out rubble, oblivious of the possibility of fire from potential enemy positions to the front not yet reconnoitered by Marine columns. The group had scarcely departed from the command post of the 5th Marine Regimental Combat Team when seven armed NK soldiers were flushed from a culvert on which General Mac-Arthur's jeep had been parked during the inspection.

The 5th Marine Regiment moved forward rapidly on September 17 and by dark had captured the southern end of the Kimpo airfield. The small group of Red defenders were taken by surprise and had not even mined the runway. Kimpo was cleared during the morning of September 18, and by late afternoon advanced sections of Marine Air Group 33 flew in from Japan, while the 5th Marines proceeded toward the Han River. They were joined on September 18 by ROK Marines who had been relieved in Inchon by the Army's 2d Engineer Brigade. At nightfall on September

19 the South Koreans and the 5th Marines had secured the south bank of the Han along their entire front and were preparing for a crossing the following morning.

Enemy reaction to the Inchon landing had been slow and desultory. The NK 18th Division in Seoul, known also as the Seoul Defense Division, which had been scheduled to depart for the Naktong front before the landing occurred, was belatedly ordered to counterattack and recapture Inchon. Its leading elements on September 17 checked the 1st Marine Regiment, which was moving along the Seoul highway toward Yongdungpo, the industrial suburb of Seoul on the south bank of the Han. Artillery and mines continued to slow the 1st Marines on September 18 and 19 before the enemy fell back into Yongdungpo. There the NK 18th Division put up a stubborn fight until driven from the city on September 21.

With the fall of Yongdungpo the NK resistance opposite Seoul collapsed, and by September 23 the 1st Marines had moved up to the Han River southwest of the city and prepared for a crossing the following morning.

The 7th Infantry Division Covers the South Flank

While the 1st Marine Regiment was advancing on Yongdungpo, Major General Barr's 7th Infantry Division, the U.S. Army's half of the X Corps, was arriving in Inchon. On the morning of September 19 the 2d Battalion, 32d Infantry Regiment, relieved the 2d Battalion, 1st Marines, south of the Seoul-Inchon road, and the 7th Division assumed responsibility for the X Corps' south flank. The next day command of operations ashore passed from Admiral Struble to General Almond, whose X Corps command post was established in Inchon. By September 22 the 7th Division had secured the Suwon airfield, which could accommodate C-54 transport planes, essential for the supply of the X Corps. The 32d Infantry, flaring out to the northeast, secured the south bank of the Han on September 24 and was ready to cross the river for its part in the assault on Seoul.

Action on the Eighth Army Front

While these advances in the Inchon area were proceeding on
schedule, the Eighth Army along the Naktong was having difficulty breaking out of the Perimeter. Anticipating that word of the
Inchon landing would lower the morale of the NK forces opposing him, General Walker had obtained approval from General
MacArthur to delay his attack until September 16. Walker may
also have hoped that the enemy would begin to shift some divisions to the north. However, either through design or faulty
communications, news of Inchon apparently did not reach the NK
command in the south for several days. The 87th Regiment of
the NK 9th Division was the only enemy unit moved to the north
from the Naktong area, and it reached Yongdungpo on September
20, barely in time to join in the defense of that town.

The main effort of the Eighth Army was to be made along the
Taegu-Taejon-Suwon axis by the I Corps under Major General
Frank W. Milburn. The corps was unable to break the enemy
cordon until September 19. On that date after three days of fierce
fighting the 5th Regiment Combat Team, Colonel John L. Throckmorton commanding, captured the key town of Waegwan on the
Naktong, making possible the crossing of the river by the 24th
Division. Thereafter enemy resistance began to crumble, though
no real signs of a breakthrough appeared for another three days.

MacArthur had not counted on a quick junction of the Eighth
Army with the X Corps, but when the Army was unable to make
any sizable advance by September 19, he instructed General
Wright to prepare to implement Plan 100-C, one of the original
alternatives to Inchon. This called for the amphibious movement
of the two United States divisions and an ROK division from the
Eighth Army via Pusan to a landing at Kunsan. Walker objected
to this move and when, on September 22, the NK armies began
to fall back everywhere, Plan 100-C was abandoned. The NK
withdrawal turned into a rout in the last week of September as
the Eighth and ROK armies pursued relentlessly. On September
27 elements of the 7th Cavalry Regiment of Walker's Eighth

Army met the 31st Infantry, which General Barr had sent south from Suwon to close the trap between his 7th Infantry Division and the Eighth Army.

Some scattered NK units, abandoning their heavy equipment, took refuge in the more inaccessible mountain areas and remained as guerrillas, but not more than 25,000 or 30,000 disorganized troops got back to North Korea, most of them assembling in the Pyonggang-Kumhwa-Chorwon area, which later became known as the "Iron Triangle." The NK "People's Army," which 'had stormed across the Han so confidently only three months before, had been practically destroyed by General MacArthur's brilliant maneuver.

The Capture of Seoul (See Map 7)

While these events were transpiring, the 1st Marine Division had been brought up to full strength with the arrival of its third regiment, the 7th Marines, at Inchon. By September 24 all three regiments had crossed the Han but were held up along the western edge of Seoul by the dogged resistance of the NK 25th Brigade, which had been moved down from Chorwon on September 20. MacArthur and Almond were anxious to capture Seoul not later than September 25, three months to the day since the initial attack of the North Koreans. Impatient with the slow progress of the frontal attacks of the Marine Division, Almond on September 24 changed the original plan of the X Corps, which had called for the seizure of Seoul by the 1st Marine Division alone. He shifted the left boundary of the 7th Infantry Division and directed Barr to have the 32d Infantry Regiment and the ROK 17th Infantry, attached to it, cross the Han on September 25 and attack the city from the southeast. The North Koreans were surprised by this smart maneuver and offered little resistance to the 32d Infantry in its capture of South Mountain, a dominant hill in the eastern section of the city.

Simultaneously the 1st Marine Division launched its main attack against Seoul, employing all three regiments. The NK 25th Brigade continued to resist block by block within the city, limiting the advance of the 1st and 5th Regiments to about 2000 yards. The 7th Regiment protected the division's open north flank.

Shortly before dark an air-observer report reaching General Almond indicated that enemy columns were streaming to the north out of Seoul. Almond directed General Smith to push his attack throughout the night. Although the air report had some factual foundation, the Marines, hit with counterattacks before they got their own attacks under way, made little or no advance before dawn.

Nonetheless, just before midnight on September 25 General Almond, apparently basing his press release on the air-observer report and the capture of South Mountain, announced the liberation of Seoul. The next day the Marines continued to encounter the same deadly street fighting that they had feared they would face in Inchon, and by nightfall of September 26 the Americans held only half the city. MacArthur followed Almond's declaration by issuing on September 26 an official United Nations communiqué announcing, "Seoul, the capital of the Republic of Korea, is again in friendly hands. United Nations forces, including the 17th Regiment of the ROK Army and elements of the U.S. 7th and 1st Marine Divisions, have completed the envelopment and seizure of the city."

Actually, fighting in Seoul continued throughout September 27 and 28 before the last groups of the North Korean invaders were ferreted out. The next day MacArthur returned to Seoul with President Syngman Rhee. In a moving ceremony in the National Assembly Hall, in the presence of Rhee's cabinet, members of the legislature, Generals Walker and Almond, and representatives of the units that had liberated Seoul, General MacArthur officially returned the capital city to the redoubtable Syngman Rhee. President Rhee, choked with emotion, outstretched his arms as if to embrace the American deliverers, as he cried out, "How can I ever explain to you my own undying gratitude and that of the Korean people?"

MacArthur flew back to Tokyo after the ceremony, the plaudits of the United Nations and all America ringing in his ears. President Truman wired him:

Few operations in military history can match either the delaying action where you traded space for time in which to build up
your forces, or the brilliant maneuver which has now resulted in
the liberation of Seoul.

The JCS paid their own tribute to the general in a message
which read in part:

> Your transition from defensive to offensive operations was
> magnificently planned, timed and executed . . . We remain
> completely confident that the great task entrusted to you by the
> United Nations will be carried to a successful conclusion.

General MacArthur richly earned the praises heaped upon him
by the grateful American and Korean peoples. While paying full
tribute to the amazing success of the Inchon-Seoul campaign,
many military historians, particularly students of amphibious warfare, caution that Inchon should not be taken as a model for the
future.

David Rees, in his book *Korea — The Limited War,* has written
perhaps its most dispassionate and objective appraisal:

> Inchon, then, could not have happened under any other com-
> mander but MacArthur. It sprang from his overpowering per-
> sonality and self-confidence, and his plan was supported by no
> one else for it looked back to an age of warfare unencumbered
> by specialist objections and peripatetic Joint Chiefs. It remains
> an astonishing achievement precisely because it was a triumph
> not of military logic and science, but of imagination and intui-
> tion. It was justified on no other grounds but the most over-
> whelming, the most simple; it succeeded and remains a Twen-
> tieth Century Cannae ever to be studied.

Right he is. But the operation should be studied in the light
of what followed. In my judgment the Joint Chiefs were fully
justified in raising the questions regarding Inchon that we did.
The success of Inchon was so great, and the subsequent prestige
of General MacArthur was so overpowering, that the Chiefs hesi-
tated thereafter to question later plans and decisions of the gen-

eral, which should have been challenged. In this we must share with General MacArthur some of the responsibility for actions that led to defeats in North Korea.

Inchon marked the peak of the extraordinary career of one of America's most brilliant soldiers. From then on he seemed to march like a Greek hero of old to an unkind and inexorable fate.

VII

U.N. FORCES CROSS INTO NORTH KOREA

Dilemma at the 38th Parallel

THE CAPTURE of Inchon and Seoul ended the first phase of the Korean war but created new dilemmas as difficult as those that followed the NK invasion of South Korea.

Should the victorious United Nations Command stop at the 38th Parallel? Should it simply drive the North Koreans back to where they came from, or should the North Korean Army be destroyed completely? Should all of Korea be occupied by United Nations forces and a united Korean government be established under the protection of the United Nations? What would be the reaction of the Soviets and Communist China under any of these conditions?

These questions had to be considered in view of the United Nations Security Council resolutions of June 25, June 27, and July 7. The June 25 resolution had condemned the North Korean attack, had demanded the withdrawal of NK forces to north of the 38th Parallel, and had called on all U.N. members to "render every assistance to the United Nations in the execution of this resolution and to refrain from giving assistance to the North Korean authorities." (See p. 12.) The second had recommended that "the Members of the United Nations furnish such assistance to the Republic of Korea as may be necessary *to repel the armed attack and to restore international peace and security in the area.*" * The third had provided for a unified command under the United States and had reiterated the objective given in the second.

However, the brief mandate included in these resolutions was

* The italics are mine.

far from definitive, particularly with respect to the phrase "to restore international peace and security in the area." Even as the 24th ROK Army and the U.S. 24th Division were falling back on Taejon, President Truman had called on the National Security Council to study the question whether United Nations forces should be sent across the 38th Parallel. In mid-July 1950 on the recommendation of General Bolté, I had suggested to the JCS that a study be initiated by the Joint Strategic Survey Committee in anticipation of the National Security Council's paper. Meanwhile, the Intelligence Division of the Army General Staff was already working on a study of its own, as was the Central Intelligence Agency. Information contained in these studies was made available to the JCS.

The fragmentary early instructions sent General MacArthur by the JCS had, of course, made no reference to future operations. However, when General Vandenberg and I visited General MacArthur in mid-July 1950, we found that he was already looking ahead. He told us, "I intend to destroy and not [merely] to drive back the North Korean forces. . . . I may have to occupy all of North Korea."

Later, on my next visit to Korea in August, this time with Admiral Sherman, we discussed with General MacArthur the possible follow-up of a successful landing at Inchon. We agreed with the General that he should be authorized to continue the attack across the 38th Parallel to destroy the North Korean forces, which otherwise would be a recurrent threat to the independence of South Korea.

Before directing any such action, the JCS had to await the outcome of the National Security Council's study. By September 1 the Council had completed its study, which was forwarded to the Departments of State and Defense for comment. Secretary Johnson sent it to the JCS for recommendation.

The study was a long, somewhat rambling paper, whose central idea was that conditions were too uncertain for the United States to commit itself to any definite course of action. Not enough was known of the intentions of the Russians or the Chinese or, indeed, of the United Nations members actively supporting the action in

Korea. Without United Nations support General MacArthur should not be permitted to cross the 38th Parallel. Although the staff of the National Security Council agreed that the resolutions of the United Nations Security Council provided a sound legal basis for crossing the Parallel, it felt that the United Nations forces should not do so for merely local tactical reasons. If they were required to cross into North Korea to compel the withdrawal of NK units from South Korea or to destroy NK forces, General MacArthur should be given special authority. It was surmised that the military situation would be stabilized on the 38th Parallel, and it was suggested that the United Nations offer surrender terms to the NK government as soon as victory of the United Nations forces was assured. If Soviet or Chinese Communist forces entered North Korea, General MacArthur should limit his advance to the old positions along the 38th Parallel. If major Russian units entered the fighting at any stage, the United Nations forces should go on the defensive at once and report to Washington for instructions. The only hint of what those instructions should be was contained in the broad conclusion that the United States should not tie up its resources in a major war in Korea, an area of little strategic importance to it. Taking a different tack in the event that the Chinese Communists alone intruded, the study recommended that General MacArthur continue the fighting only so long as he had a reasonable chance of successful resistance against Chinese attack, though he should be authorized to initiate appropriate air and naval action against Communist China. The United States should then seek United Nations condemnation of the Chinese Communists as aggressors.

This curiously contradictory document received a cold review by the JCS. The Chiefs disagreed with the assumption that the military situation would or should be stabilized at the 38th Parallel. We argued that a limited advance to the Parallel would solve nothing, militarily or politically, since this would leave Korea divided by an arbitrary boundary difficult to defend but easy for North Korean guerillas to infiltrate. On the other hand, a successful drive to the North could unite Korea under a single government acceptable to the United Nations and could secure a defensible natural frontier along the Yalu and Tumen Rivers. We felt that General MacArthur's mission required the destruction of the NK forces and that no prior restrictions should be placed on his crossing the Parallel if it became necessary to do so in order to accomplish this mission. The chief contra argument that we considered was that an extension of operations to the north would provide additional excuse for Soviet recalcitrance in the United Nations and could lead to the active intervention of the Soviets or the Chinese Communists. We anticipated, however, that the main strength of the NK Army would be broken in South Korea and that operations north of the Parallel would be chiefly of a mopping-up nature, which should be conducted by South Korean troops.

The JCS recommended that our views be embodied in a final review of the study before it was returned to the National Security Council and submitted to the President. The JCS recommendations were approved by the Secretary of Defense. Most of our views, along with the cautions of the National Security Council's staff, were included in the final paper, which was approved by the President on September 11. However, perhaps because of a temporary hiatus at the office of the Secretary of Defense, resulting from the replacement, the following day, of Louis Johnson with General George C. Marshall, no instructions were sent to the JCS to prepare an implementing directive for General MacArthur. On September 15 the Chiefs did dispatch to MacArthur's headquarters a summary of the conclusions of the National Security Council study, covering operations north of the 38th Parallel and courses of action in the event of Communist intervention. Despite his immediate concern with the outcome of Inchon the General requested the JCS to send him a copy of the complete study. The Chiefs did so by an officer courier.

On September 25 General Bradley forwarded to General Marshall for approval a directive covering future operations of the United Nations Command. The proposed order dealt chiefly with military matters; other aspects of national policy would have to be covered by other departments of the government, principally the State Department. After several days of waiting, during which the Army staff fretted over the delay in getting definite instructions to General MacArthur, the State Department added to the JCS draft some instructions on the return of Seoul to the ROK government of Syngman Rhee. Because of the importance of this directive General Marshall secured the approval of the President. The JCS transmitted the order to General MacArthur on September 27.

General MacArthur was specifically informed as follows:

Your military objective is the destruction of the North Korean armed forces. In attaining this objective you are authorized to conduct military operations, including amphibious and airborne landings or ground operations north of the 38th Parallel in Korea, provided that at the time of such operations there has been no entry into North Korea by major Soviet or Chinese Communist Forces, no announcement of intended entry, nor a threat to counter our operations militarily in North Korea. Under no circumstances, however, will your forces cross the Manchurian or USSR borders of Korea and, as a matter of policy, no non-Korean ground forces will be used in the northeast provinces bordering the Soviet Union or in the area along the Manchurian border. Furthermore, support of your operations north or south of the 38th Parallel will not include Air or Naval action against Manchuria or against USSR territory.

Later paragraphs expanded on the basic instructions quoted above and then went on:

When organized armed resistance by North Korean forces has been brought substantially to an end, you should direct the ROK forces to take the lead in disarming remaining North Korean units and enforcing the terms of surrender. Guerilla activities should be dealt with primarily by the forces of the Republic of Korea, with minimum participation by United Nations contingents.

Circumstances obtaining at the time will determine the character of and necessity for occupation of North Korea. Your plans for such occupation will be forwarded for approval to the Joint

Chiefs of Staff. You will also submit your plan for future operations north of the 38th Parallel to the Joint Chiefs of Staff for approval.

A day or two after these instructions had been received by General MacArthur news dispatches from the Far East reported that General Walker had said that the Eighth Army would halt at the Parallel, presumably to await permission to cross. Though these reports were unconfirmed, Secretary Marshall sent a personal message to MacArthur, cautioning that such an announcement might cause embarrassment in the United Nations, in which it was desirable to avoid a specific vote on crossing the 38th Parallel. Concerning this crossing the Secretary stated, "We want you to feel unhampered tactically and strategically to proceed north of the 38th Parallel."

General MacArthur reported back to the Secretary of Defense that, though he doubted Walker had made such a statement, he had cautioned the Army commander that any reference to a crossing would be made by General Headquarters or direct from Washington. He added that unless and until the aggressors capitulated, he regarded all of Korea open for operations.

While these questions were being thrashed out in the Defense Department, they were being studied by the State Department and discussed in the Congress and the press. Public opinion and political considerations had to be weighed by the President and his advisers. Senator William F. Knowland, the Republican leader in the Senate, had stated that failure to pursue the NK aggressors across the 38th Parallel would be appeasement of the Communists, a charge avoided by Democrats and Republicans alike, particularly in that election year. By and large, news commentators, columnists, and editorial writers indicated a strong public opinion in favor of continuing military operations to eliminate the Communist satellite state of North Korea and thus, hopefully, prevent a recurrence of the Korean war.

World opinion also had to be considered, especially as reflected in the United Nations, under whose ægis the war was being fought. United Nations sanction for crossing the 38th Parallel was highly desirable. The State Department was satisfied that the United Nations resolutions of June 27 and July 7 provided adequate authorization, but President Truman insisted on a more specific new authorization. By now the Russian representative, Jakob Malik, had rejoined the United Nations Security Council, with his misplaced veto, so it was deemed advisable to skip the Council and apply directly to the U.N. General Assembly for support in crossing the Parallel. On October 7, 1950, the General Assembly adopted a resolution, which was presented by the United Kingdom and seven other nations. Without mentioning the 38th Parallel, the resolution recommended that:

(a) All appropriate steps be taken to ensure conditions of stability throughout Korea, and

(b) All constituent acts be taken, including the holding of elections, under the auspices of the United Nations, for the establishment of a unified, independent, and democratic government in the sovereign state of Korea.

This resolution also established a new commission, the United Nations Commission for the Unification and Rehabilitation of Korea. A copy of the resolution was sent by the JCS to General MacArthur for his information, but no directive to unify Korea was ever included in the missions assigned to him.

In any event neither of the objectives included in the October 7 resolution could be achieved unless the United Nations forces entered North Korea. There remained no question but that the U.N. General Assembly, President Truman, the U.S. Secretaries of State and Defense, and the U.S. Joint Chiefs of Staff all had approved the crossing of the 38th Parallel. Most of the questions concerning the wisdom of this decision came after the event.

Wake Island Conference

Despite the general accord among the countries participating in the United Nations' action in Korea regarding the wisdom of crossing the 38th Parallel, some doubts had begun to arise concerning the ultimate objectives of the United Nations and how far their forces should advance. Through roundabout diplomatic channels there had been reports of Chinese threats of intervention, and intelligence agencies had received rumors of troop movements north of the Yalu. President Truman was determined to prevent any expansion of the United Nations "police action" into a full-scale war with China or Russia, but he was not sure that his field commander in Korea saw eye to eye with him in this regard. General MacArthur had always taken an aloof attitude toward the Administration and had never indicated any interest in visiting Washington for consultations with the President, the State or Defense Department, or the JCS. In fact, he had not returned to the United States since his retirement from the Army in 1937 while serving in the Philippine Islands, a fact that Mr. Truman felt left the General out of touch with what "home folks" were thinking. In August the President had sent Ambassador Harriman and General Ridgway to Tokyo to acquaint General MacArthur with the President's views of world affairs, particularly with respect to Formosa and China. Harriman reported that although MacArthur accepted Mr. Truman's position in regard to Formosa, he did so without full conviction. A subsequent letter from the General to the Veterans of Foreign Wars seemed to contradict the President's policy.

President Truman had never had any direct contact with General MacArthur. Now, with a crossing of the 38th Parallel by the Eighth Army in the offing, the time had come when he felt it was essential for the two men to get together for a review of the Korean situation. The President could have called the General to a meeting in Washington, but this would have taken him away from his command for too long a period. Never a stickler for protocol, he decided to meet MacArthur somewhere in the Pacific. At General Marshall's suggestion Wake Island was selected as the meeting place.

On October 11 President Truman made a public announcement of the meeting, in part as follows:

Gen. MacArthur and I are making a quick trip over the coming weekend to meet in the Pacific. . . . I shall discuss with him the final phase of United Nations action in Korea. . . . We have absolutely no interest in obtaining any special position for the United States in Korea, nor do we wish to retain bases or other military installations in that country. We should like to get our armed forces out and back to their other duties at the earliest moment consistent with the fulfillment of our obligations as a member of the United Nations. Naturally, I shall take advantage of this opportunity to discuss with General Mac-Arthur other matters within his responsibility.

Originally the President thought of taking all of the Joint Chiefs of Staff with him, but later he decided this would be inadvisable. He settled on taking Chairman of the JCS Bradley and Secretary of the Army Pace as military advisers and Assistant Secretary of State Rusk, Ambassador Harriman, and Ambassador-at-Large Jessup. Ambassador Muccio and Major General Courtney Whitney, General MacArthur's military secretary, accompanied Mac-Arthur. Admiral Radford sat in on the main conference.

The President and the General greeted one another cordially at the airstrip as the President landed at 6:30 A.M. on October 15. After the usual picture-taking the two drove in an old Chevrolet to the quonset-hut office of the local airline manager. There they talked alone for some while before joining the official party for the main conference in another building.

Unknown to either the President or General MacArthur, and reportedly without instructions from anyone, Miss Vernice Anderson, secretary to Ambassador Jessup, was in the next room, the door of which was open, taking shorthand notes throughout this conference. Bradley and others in the President's party openly took notes, which were combined later into a top secret memorandum. A total of fifty-nine copies of this memorandum were distributed to officials of the White House and of the State and Army Departments, to the JCS, and to General MacArthur's headquarters. As always seems to happen in Washington in the case of such controversial memoranda, especially when so widely disseminated, a copy was "leaked" to the press. It was later published in full by Rovere and Schlesinger in *The MacArthur Controversy*. Dur-

ing the congressional hearings* on the relief of General Mac-
Arthur the General took umbrage at the fact that any "record"
of the conference had been kept. He said that he had not read
the copy of the memorandum when it was received at his headquarters but simply had it filed. He never acknowledged the
phrases about nonintervention by China attributed to him, but in
exchange with Senator Richard B. Russell had this to say:

> *The Chairman:* So you are not in a position to state whether
> or not there are inaccuracies in that report or whether it is a
> reasonably accurate statement of what transpired on Wake
> Island?
> *Gen. MacArthur:* No, sir; I have no way of telling you that.
> I have no doubt that in general they are an accurate report of
> what took place.

Someone at General Headquarters must have read the notes of
this important meeting with the President, but there was no challenge of their accuracy made at that time.

In addition to providing an opportunity for the President and
the General to become acquainted or, at least, to size up one
another, the conference at Wake Island is of historical interest
largely because of statements made by General MacArthur in
regard to the progress of the war, the likelihood of Chinese intervention, and the probable consequences if the Chinese Communists did intervene.

According to the informal notes of the conference, Mr. Truman
opened the meeting by asking the General to give his views on the
problems facing the United States in rehabilitating Korea. Mac-
Arthur was extremely optimistic in describing the status of military operations, venturing his belief that formal resistance by the
North Koreans would be over by Thanksgiving. The enemy had
only about 100,000 men left, and these were poorly trained, led,
and equipped. They were fighting obstinately but only to save
face.

* U.S. 66th Congress 1st Session, Hearings before the Senate Committees on
Foreign Relations and Armed Services, "Military Situation in the Far East,"
Washington, D.C., 1951, hereafter cited as the MacArthur Hearings.

The General sketched his plan to land the X Corps at Wonsan and predicted that it would cut across to Pyongyang in one week in a maneuver that he compared to Inchon. He noted that the North Koreans had once again made the fatal mistake of not deploying in depth and predicted, "When the gap is closed, the same thing will happen in the north as happened in the south." If all went according to schedule, the Eighth Army would be withdrawn to Japan by Christmas. A reconstituted X Corps, consisting of two American divisions and some smaller units from other nations, would remain in Korea to carry out security missions and to assist the United Nations Commission for the Unification and Rehabilitation of Korea. The General hoped that elections could be held before the first of the year, avoiding a prolonged military occupation.

This led to a discussion of the problems of unifying the country after the war was over and of the rehabilitation of the vast areas, on both sides of the 38th Parallel, damaged by the fighting and bombing.

At this point President Truman asked what turned out to be the most significant question of the conference. As reported in the memorandum it was:

> *Pres. Truman:* What are the chances for Chinese or Soviet interference?
>
> *Gen. MacArthur:* Very little. Had they interfered in the first or second months it would have been decisive. We are no longer fearful of their intervention. We no longer stand hat in hand. The Chinese have 300,000 men in Manchuria. Of these, probably not more than 100/125,000 are distributed along the Yalu River. Only 50/60,000 could be gotten across the Yalu River. They have no air force. Now that we have bases for our Air Force in Korea, if the Chinese tried to get down to Pyongyang there would be the greatest slaughter. . . .

As for the Russians, the General continued, it was a little different. They had no ground troops in Korea, and winter would set in before they could get a division there. The Russians did have strong air forces in Siberia, but they were no match for our

Air Force. A Chinese ground attack supported by Russian air was unlikely, because their air-ground coordination would be poor, and the Russians would be as likely to bomb the Chinese as to hit our troops.

General Bradley, perhaps carried away by General MacArthur's optimism and aware of the need of troops to meet United States commitments to newly created NATO in Europe, asked whether the 2d or 3d Division could be released from the Far East Command by January. MacArthur readily agreed to make either available for shipment to Europe at that time.

At the end of the conference President Truman said that he and General MacArthur had discussed Formosa fully in their private meeting. "There is no need to cover that subject again. The General and I are in complete agreement." However, in the MacArthur Hearings the General insisted that the agreement was only that there was no need to review Formosa again in the main conference. There is no doubt that differences over Formosa still remained.

After this discussion there were meetings on "technical matters" between members of the two groups. General MacArthur talked with Secretary Pace and General Bradley, and Ambassador Muccio met with State Department representatives. Good-byes at the air strip were cordial but on General MacArthur's part restrained. President Truman presented to the General a fourth oak-leaf cluster for his Distinguished Service Medal and in answer to a question from the press about how the conference had gone replied enthusiastically, "Perfectly. . . . I've never had a more satisfactory conference since I've been President." But with the insight of a good newsman Tony Laviero of the *New York Times* accurately summed up the sensing of the press: "President Truman left Wake highly pleased with the results, like an insurance salesman who had at last signed up an important prospect, while the latter appeared dubious about the extent of the coverage."

The two men had at least met face to face for the first time — and the last. Mr. Truman was apparently convinced that he had persuaded the General to accept his views on Korean policy. Later events were to prove that this was not the case. As indicated in his *Reminiscences,* the General remained scornful of Mr. Truman's knowledge of the Far East and world affairs. More important for his own future, he underestimated the courage and determination of this little man who happened to be the President of the United States.

Plans for the Advance into North Korea

While few persons in position of authority in October 1950 questioned the desirability of carrying the war into North Korea, there were then and still remain different opinions on MacArthur's method of implementing the JCS directive of October 7 and his command arrangements to control the operation.

The brilliance of Inchon and the rapid capture of Seoul tended to obscure the fact that General Almond's X Corps had not been able fully to provide the anvil against which General Walker's Eighth Army and the ROK Army were to hammer the NK Army to destruction. The X Corps did all that actually could be expected of it, but it simply could not extend its lines to cover all escape routes west of the Taebaek Mountains and found it impossible to cover the trails through the mountains or the east coast road. Three fourths of the NK Army was destroyed or captured, but the remainder, including a number of the senior commanders and staff officers, was able to slip away through the mountains or along the coastal road. Realizing this possibility, Almond had, on September 21, requested MacArthur to switch a ROK division from Walker's army to the X Corps. But it would have taken too long to effect the transfer, and Walker, who was having his own troubles breaking out of the Pusan bridgehead, demurred. MacArthur turned down Almond's request, though it galled the General to know that the North Koreans were surrendering only when cut off and that thousands were escaping north of the border.

General MacArthur became more than ever convinced that it would be necessary to cross the 38th Parallel in order fully to destroy the NK Army. Even before receiving the September 27 directive he had instructed General Wright to develop plans for

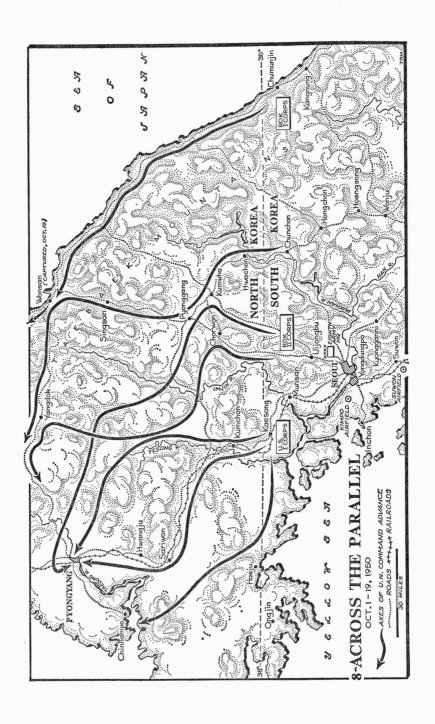

8-ACROSS THE PARALLEL
OCT. 1-19, 1950

AXES OF U.N. COMMAND ADVANCE
ROADS
RAILROADS

30 MILES

an amphibious landing well north of the Parallel, either in the
vicinity of Chinampo on the west coast or of Wonsan on the east
coast, coupled with an overland drive by the bulk of the Eighth
Army.

It would have been easier logistically and less time-consuming
to have made a second amphibious landing on the west coast
north of Inchon in the vicinity of Chinampo than to have done
so on the east coast. According to Wright, however, even before
Inchon MacArthur had leaned toward a double envelopment of
the NK forces facing the Pusan Perimeter by landings on both
coasts, an idea that had to be dropped because of inadequate
forces available. Preliminary studies of Wonsan as a possible
landing site had been made. Under conditions existing after
Inchon, Wonsan offered a number of advantages. A prompt landing there would serve to cut off NK forces retreating in the east
and would provide an east coast port for logistical support of
later operations to the north. Its harbor facilities were reasonably
good, and it was located at the narrow waist of Korea, with the
shortest overland rail and highway connections east of Pyongyang
and north to the industrial area of Hamhung-Hungnam (Map 8).

By September 27 Wright and his planning group were able to
present a plan in consonance with MacArthur's concept. Wright
recommended that the Eighth Army drive to the north from the
Seoul area to seize Pyongyang while the X Corps launch an
amphibious assault on Wonsan. He estimated that the latter
attack could be made within ten days after the X Corps received
orders to load out, provided shipping could be assembled in time.

MacArthur accepted this proposal, which met his specifications.
He informed the JCS on September 28 that if the NK Army failed
to accept a surrender proclamation, which he had been authorized
to issue on October 1, he intended to cross into North Korea.
He outlined his plan of action briefly: the Eighth Army would
advance on Pyongyang via Kaesong and Sariwon, the X Corps
landing amphibiously at Wonsan and thereafter making a junction
with the Eighth Army which, presumably, would be by an attack
to the west along the Wonson-Pyongyang corridor. MacArthur
said he would use only ROK troops north of the Chungju-

Yongwon-Hungnam line. The Eighth Army attack would commence between October 15 and October 30. Details of the plan
would be furnished the JCS later.

This time, perhaps somewhat overawed by the success of
Inchon, some aspects of which we had questioned, the Joint
Chiefs did not wait for receipt of the details. We approved the
plan as outlined and on September 29 forwarded it to the Secretary
of Defense for final action, urging quick approval, since it was
possible that some ROK forces might even then be crossing the
38th Parallel. General Marshall and President Truman agreed to
the plan at once, and on September 29 the JCS radioed General
MacArthur to proceed with his plan as scheduled.

The campaign for the destruction of the remaining elements of
the NK Army was spelled out in United Nations Command
Operations Plan 9-50, issued on September 29. The plan followed
the outline submitted to the JCS. The date for the advance of
the Eighth Army was fixed as twelve days after its troops passed
through the X Corps. The Wonsan landing would follow in three
to seven days.

But the advance of the Eighth Army had to await the re-
stocking of food, fuel, and munitions. This was dependent on
opening rail and highway communications north of Pusan, which
had been disrupted by our bombing during the battles of the
Pusan Perimeter. The logistic situation was further complicated
by the fact that the 7th Infantry Division of the X Corps would
have to move overland to Pusan, where it would be loaded out
for Wonsan, while the 1st Marine Division and X Corps troops
would sail from Inchon. These moves were bound to delay the
inflow of essential supplies for both the X Corps and the Eighth
Army. The harbors of Pusan and Inchon were already taxed to the
limit of their capacity, and few if any additional cargo planes
were available to increase supply by air.

While the logistical build-up went on, the ROK 3d Division on
the east coast crossed into North Korea on October 1 with
practically no opposition. These troops were still under General
Walker's command. Walker had not tried to hold them back,
since their advance was in consonance with General MacArthur's

plan as first outlined to his senior commanders in Seoul on September 29.

The rapid drive of the ROK 3d Division did give MacArthur some second thoughts about the landing of the X Corps at Wonsan. On October 2 he notified the JCS of the ROK crossing and commented that the projected amphibious maneuver of the X Corps might not be necessary if the ROK advance continued against only light resistance. However, an overland move to the north by both the Eighth Army and the X Corps would have worsened the already difficult logistic situation, since the supply line from the main base at Pusan lengthened with each mile of advance. Even though MacArthur had cautioned against any further bombing of rail lines north of Seoul, the retreating North Koreans were bound to destroy bridges and block some of the many railroad tunnels. Another port was essential on the east coast to support operations in northeast Korea, and Wonsan was the logical choice. These logistical considerations, linked perhaps with the lure of another amphibious success, threw the balance in General MacArthur's mind in favor of the amphibious assault.*

MacArthur's uncertainty regarding the Wonsan landing was short-lived. On the same day, October 2, that he had radioed the JCS, he issued a precautionary order confirming his original plan to destroy the North Korean forces south of the Chongju-Kunuri-Yongwon-Hamhung-Hungnam line. The Eighth Army was to attack on A Day, to be announced later. After it had captured Pyongyang and the X Corps had taken Wonsan, each would attack toward the other via the Pyongyang-Wonsan corridor, to cut off all enemy escape routes. MacArthur would exercise overall command of the combined operations. Walker would command all United Nations army forces in the overland drive, including the British 27th Infantry Brigade and the Philippine Battalion

---

* In a letter to Colonel John Meade, acting Chief of Military, Department of the Army, General Almond wrote on July 8, 1955: "I think Gen. MacArthur must have had in his mind the brilliance of strategic maneuver which had been so successful in the Pacific War in World War II and which had been demonstrated at Inchon and that, furthermore, Gen. MacArthur had confidence in the fact that a large force landed on the flank of the retreating enemy and the East Korean territory would facilitate the physical occupation of North Korea in the most expeditious manner possible."

Combat Team, the former of which had arrived in Korea in late August and the latter on September 19. Almond's X Corps would be under the direct control of MacArthur, with Joy in command of the amphibious movement until Almond took over after the landing. The 187th Airborne Regimental Combat Team would be in General Headquarters reserve.

At the time this order was issued there was little or nothing about the planned operations that anyone in Washington could challenge. Certainly the JCS raised no question about the strategy to be employed, though I and, I think, Bradley were skeptical about the command arrangements. After the war Major General Leven C. Allen, Walker's Chief of Staff, told the historian Appleman that Walker wanted to employ the X Corps — if it were placed under his command — to capture Pyongyang, while the remainder of the Eighth Army, after following the X Corps initially, would veer off to the northeast and move on Wonsan through the area of Chorwon, Pyonggang (not Pyongyang), and Singosan. Walker felt this would save considerable time, since the X Corps was already positioned for a drive on Pyongyang, whereas the Eighth Army, especially the ROK troops on the east coast, could reach Wonsan in much shorter time than the X Corps moving by water. Such a plan had been outlined by Colonel John A. Dabney, Operations G-3, Eighth Army, to General Walker, as soon as it became known at Eighth Army Headquarters on September 29 that the X Corps was to land at Wonsan. As Dabney later commented to Appleman, Walker said he agreed with Dabney's plan but refused to forward it to General Headquarters, since he had already made his views known and had received contrary orders.

Appleman's evaluation of Allen's recollection of General Walker's intentions and Colonel Dabney's comment on Appleman's text of *South to the Naktong, North to the Yalu*, one of the authoritative histories of the Korean war, are interesting, if not conclusive. According to Appleman, Walker and his principal staff officers felt it would be a mistake not to press the pursuit of the defeated enemy. To halt for a period of almost two weeks while the X Corps was loaded out of Inchon and Pusan and then moved by ship around to Wonsan, would permit the escape of a large part of the NK forces. According to Appleman, Walker believed that Wonsan would fall to the ROK I Corps before Almond could land at Wonsan and that United Nations forces, moving directly on Pyongyang, could capture it before the X Corps could move there from Wonsan. The Eighth Army staff agreed that the port of Wonsan would be required for the support of whatever forces operated subsequently in the northeast sector of North Korea. The question was as to the quickest and most effective method of capturing Wonsan considering the difficult logistical situation. General George L. Eberle, G-4 Supply, General Head-quarters, believed that both the X Corps and the Eighth Army could be supplied from Pusan and Inchon until Wonsan was opened.

Unfortunately, there is no available written record of the Dab-ney-Walker plan, if there was one at the time. MacArthur did not consult either Walker or Almond about his plans for operations after the fall of Seoul. On September 26, when Walker radioed MacArthur requesting that he be kept advised of plans for the X Corps, he was told only that after the capture of Seoul the X Corps would be placed in General Headquarters reserve and that its future operations would be directed by MacArthur; these op-erations would be revealed to Walker "at an early date." Almond later informed Colonel Meade that MacArthur had not con-sulted him with respect to the X Corps' operations after Seoul. Almond had sent a staff officer to Tokyo about September 23 to inquire into future plans for the corps; he was informed only that such plans were being evolved and would be settled shortly.

Command Arrangements for the Attack into North Korea

It was not within the province of the Joint Chiefs of Staff to challenge MacArthur's system of command for the attack across the 38th Parallel; such matters are the prerogative of a com-mander. Some of MacArthur's own principal staff officers sub-sequently reported to the military historians that they were surprised that the X Corps was not integrated into the Eighth Army after Inchon. General Almond recalled, "It had always been my understanding that when the Inchon operation was completed, the X Corps troops would be absorbed by Eighth Army." Generals Hickey and Wright are reported to have advised that this be done, and General Eberle felt likewise. General Wright in a letter to Schnabel on July 14, 1955, stated flatly, "I do not and did not concur in the desirability of the [Wonsan] operation as a X Corps venture. In my opinion, the X Corps should have become an element of Eighth Army immediately upon conclusion of the Inchon landing."

On the other hand, General MacArthur in a letter to Colonel Edward Snedeker, United States Marine Corps, on February 26, 1956, said, "If such dissension [sic] existed it was never brought to my attention. To the contrary, the decision to retain a function of General Headquarters command and coordination between Eighth Army and the X Corps until such time as a juncture between the two forces had been effected was, so far as I know, based upon the unanimous thinking of the senior members of my staff. It but followed standard military practice in the handling and control of widely separated forces where lateral communications were difficult, if not impossible. I doubt, furthermore, that General Eberle entertained the viewpoint that the X Corps supply problem would have been simplified if X Corps had been a part of the Eighth Army."

These divergent views within the United Nations Command, both with respect to the relative merits of an overland drive versus an amphibious maneuver to capture Wonsan and with respect to the command relationship of the Eighth Army and the X Corps, pointed up one of the few weaknesses of MacArthur as a commander. Unquestionably, he discussed future plans and operations with some members of his staff, including Almond while Almond was his Chief of Staff, but rarely did he do so with his field commanders; he told them what to do. This is highly desirable in many situations but not necessarily so when the top commander is distant from the scene of combat, not in frequent immediate contact with his principal subordinate commanders, and out of direct touch with enemy reactions. While General MacArthur was in Tokyo and Generals Walker and Almond were operating in Korea somewhat independently of one another, the difficulties of command and communications increased as the operations north of the 38th Parallel developed.

ROK I Corps Captures Wonsan and Hungnam

In compliance with MacArthur's warning order of October 2, 1950, the Eighth Army on October 3 issued its own preparatory order for the advance into North Korea. This order directed General Milburn's I Corps, consisting of the 1st Cavalry Division, the 24th Infantry Division, the ROK 1st Division, and the newly constituted British Brigade, to concentrate in an area west of the Imjin River. The IX Corps, General Coulter commanding, which included the 2d and 25th Divisions, was to protect the line of communications from Seoul back to Pusan and, together with ROK police forces, destroy remaining enemy forces in South Korea. The ROK Army was directed to advance its II Corps, including the ROK 6th, 7th, and 8th Divisions, into the Chunchon-Uijongbu area in the central highlands east of the U.S. I Corps. The ROK 3d and Capital Divisions, composing the ROK I Corps, were ordered to move up the east coast to the Yongpo-Chumunjin area. All units were to be prepared to cross the 38th Parallel on Eighth Army orders.

The ROK I Corps did not wait for such orders (Map 8). As a foreboding of difficulties with President Syngman Rhee that were to come later, Rhee announced at a mass meeting in Pusan on September 19, 1950, "We have to advance as far as the Manchurian border until not a single enemy soldier is left in our country." He said that he did not expect the United Nations forces to stop at the 38th Parallel but that, if they did, "we will not allow ourselves to stop." And the ROK Army did not stop. All divisions of the ROK I and II Corps crossed the Parallel before any American unit. On the east coast the ROK 3d Division, followed by the Capital Division, kept constant pressure on the retreating NK 5th Division. Traveling night and day, mostly on foot, they averaged 15 miles a day. The opposition was tougher and the going slower in the central highlands, but by October 11 elements of the II Corps were converging on Pyonggang (not Pyongyang) via Chorwon and Kumhwa, halfway to Wonsan. However, the ROK I Corps beat them to Wonsan. On October 10, troops of both its 3d and Capital Divisions entered Wonsan, taking heavy enemy shelling as they did so, and the next day cleared the city and the airfield on the narrow peninsula to the east. That afternoon Generals Walker and Partridge flew into the field. Promptly the next day Partridge had twenty-two cargo planes fly in 131 tons of supplies for the ROK I Corps.

During the next week, while the ROK 3d Division secured Wonsan and awaited the expected landing of the X Corps, the Capital Division moved 50 miles up the coast against light opposition and occupied both Hamhung and the port of Hungnam. In a period of seventeen days the ROK I Corps had advanced over 160 miles and captured the two important ports on the Korean east coast — a remarkably fine job.

The Eighth Army Enters North Korea

The crossing of the 38th Parallel by the Eighth Army under General MacArthur's warning order of October 2 had to await his designation of A Day. The ROK I Corps had initiated its advance on September 30, but even into the second week of October the Eighth Army was still critically short of ammunition and other supplies. The Army was 200 miles north of its railhead at Waegwan, back on the Naktong River, and Inchon was of little help, since its facilities were largely tied up for the first half of October with loading out of the X Corps. Walker grew more impatient with each day of delay in advancing the Eighth Army, a delay that was permitting the North Koreans to regroup their forces. Intelligence reports indicated feverish activity in the vicinity of Pyongyang, where new units, which had not fought in the south, were moving to the defense of the NK capital city. Walker had had no word from General Headquarters since the warning order of October 2, which had indicated that the Eighth

Army would attack between October 15 and 30. Finally, on October 7 a call from Walker's Chief of Staff, Allen, to Hickey in Tokyo brought the reply that Walker was authorized to move out when ready. Even though reserves of supplies were dangerously low, Johnnie Walker ordered the advance to begin on October 9, Gay's 1st Cavalry Division in the center of Milburn's I Corps attacking Kaesong, supported by the 24th Infantry Division on its left and General Paik Sun Yup's ROK 1st Division on its right (Map 8).

The NK forces, all newly created, initially put up stiff opposition, but by October 14 a pincer movement by two cavalry regiments had captured Kumchon. Thereafter NK resistance weakened, and a mad scramble began between units of the 24th Infantry Division and the 1st Cavalry Division to see which would be first to reach Sariwon, the next key point, 50 miles to the north and halfway to Pyongyang. As elements of both divisions converged on Sariwon, pockets of the enemy were cut off, and during the night movements some of these groups became mixed with the attacking columns. In the resulting confusion some units of the British Brigade attached to the 1st Cavalry Division were mistaken by the North Koreans for Russians rumored to be coming to their aid. As the British Brigade entered Sariwon on October 17, a column of the 7th Cavalry Regiment under Lieutenant Colonel Peter D. Clainos moved up on secondary roads to the northeast. General Gay, following the action in a light plane, noted that the roads north of Sariwon were clogged with escaping enemy. He dropped a message to Clainos, directing him to send, after capturing Hwangju, a battalion south toward Sariwon to intercept the enemy. Clainos' troops took the surrender of many NK groups of soldiers, in one case after duping a Korean platoon into believing that the Americans were Russians. Some 1700 NK soldiers surrendered that evening.

Colonel Clainos, who had established radio communications with the British Brigade in Sariwon, radioed Lieutenant Colonel Charles H. Green, commanding the 3d Australian Battalion on the brigade's night-defense perimeter, that he would enter the perimeter before midnight with a column of troops and prisoners mounted in trucks with headlights ablaze. As Colonel Clainos crossed the friendly outpost he heard an Australian soldier remark to another, "Now what do you make of this? Here we are, all set for a coordinated attack in the morning, and the bloody Yanks come in at midnight from the north, with their lights burning, and bringing the whole damned North Korean Army as prisoners!"

Sariwon fell to the United Nations forces on October 17. A race then began between American and British units, Paik's 1st ROK Division, and the ROK II Corps, all trying to be the first to enter the practically defenseless city of Pyongyang. On October 19 the leading regiment of the 1st Cavalry Division entered the southern edge of Pyongyang almost simultaneously with the ROK 1st Division, moving in from the east. By dark of October 19 the heart of Pyongyang was in Paik's hands, with the 5th Cavalry Regiment in the southern section and the 8th Regiment of the ROK 7th Division, ROK II Corps, in the northern section.

Thus, as General Walker and his staff had anticipated, before a single unit of the X Corps had landed at Wonsan, both Wonsan and Pyongyang had fallen to the Eighth and ROK Armies under his direct command. Units of the ROK II Corps had succeeded in moving overland to the Wonsan-Pyongyang road and after the capture of Wonsan had performed the maneuver, originally conceived by General MacArthur for the X Corps, of moving along that road to assist in the seizure of Pyongyang. Through no fault of its own the 1st Marine Division had not yet sailed from Inchon.

The X Corps Moves to Wonsan

On the same day, October 9, that the Eighth Army initiated its attack across the 38th Parallel, the 1st Marine Division began loading out of Inchon. Troops and equipment for an amphibious landing must be "combat loaded"; that is, the men who are to make the assault and the equipment and supplies they will need immediately after landing must be loaded on the same ships. This type of loading takes more time and calls for special landing craft and more shipping than is required for an unopposed landing or for bulk loading of reserve supplies. The combat loads of the

Marines to be used at Wonsan came into the Inchon port area largely by trucks and combat vehicles from the Seoul area and had to be put aboard LST's from the harbor beaches, which could be used only at high tide. Vehicles to accompany the troops had to be waterproofed and deck-loaded securely on transports. Normally a base port has its own complement of trucks for internal movement of cargo, while the vehicles of outgoing troops are being loaded on transports. Inchon did not have sufficient trucks to permit this, adding further delay.

This time-consuming procedure, which had been anticipated by the supply and logistical staff, required ten days. Meanwhile, two Marine battalions that had boarded their LST's on October 10 had to remain in their cramped quarters on these packed ships until Joint Task Force 7, under Admiral Struble, was ready to sail October 16 on its 830-mile voyage from Inchon to Wonsan. At convoy speed the task force would reach the Wonsan area about October 20. Wonsan had fallen to the ROK 3d Division on October 10.

Meanwhile, the other half of the X Corps, the 7th Infantry Division, which had been relieved in the Seoul area by units of the Eighth Army on September 30, began its movement to Pusan by truck and rail on October 5. Several times during its long journey attacks from enemy groups that had been bypassed in the forward rush of the Eighth Army had to be beaten off. But by October 12 the 7th Division was assembled in the vicinity of Pusan. Troops began loading on October 16. Since the division was to follow the 1st Marines ashore at Wonsan, units did not have to be prepared for immediate combat upon landing. The loading on transports and cargo ships of troops and supplies was completed in one day. The division did not know it then, but it was to lie idly afloat in Pusan harbor for the next ten days. Someone in the long chain of command had failed to notify the 7th Division of the postponement of D Day caused by enemy mine fields in Wonsan harbor.

Even before Task Force 7 was ready to sail, a new impediment to landing at Wonsan had developed. Underwater mines, which our Navy had feared might imperil the Inchon operation, were discovered in the sea approaches to Wonsan and Hungnam. With more time available than at Inchon, the North Koreans, supervised by a party of Russians, it was later learned, had laid approximately 3000 mines, not only in the approaches to Wonsan but in the harbor itself and on the beaches. Admiral Struble promptly directed minesweeping to begin five days earlier than planned and assembled all available minesweepers. Sweeping began at Wonsan on October 10. It was quickly realized that the Navy was up against one of the most formidable mine fields in naval history. Recognizing the size of the clearing job to be done, Admirals Struble and Joy recommended to General MacArthur that D Day be set back to October 20. General MacArthur approved this change on October 10. The command ship *U.S.S. McKinley*, with Attack Force Commander Admiral Doyle, General Almond, and General Smith aboard, proceeded to the Wonsan area, arriving there October 20. The assault ships carrying the 1st Marine Division were directed to delay arriving off Wonsan by sailing north for twelve hours and then south for an equal period while awaiting orders from Admiral Doyle. This they did from October 19 to October 25 in what the frustrated Marines called "Operation Yo-Yo." It was not until October 28 that the combat elements of the division were ashore.

By now the ROK Capital Division of the ROK I Corps had captured Hungnam and was continuing to move up the coast. Meanwhile the X Corps mission was changed from a move west, to assist in the capture of Pyongyang, to an advance northwest toward the Manchurian border. It was then decided that the 7th Infantry Division, still at anchor in Pusan, would be landed over the beaches at Iwon, 150 miles north of Wonsan, on LST's. This required that its unit equipment be unloaded from transports in Pusan and transferred to LST's. On October 27 the 17th Regimental Combat Team from the 7th Infantry Division left Pusan for Iwon. Fortunately, the minesweepers found no mines at Iwon, and the landing was peaceful. The ROK Capital Division had passed through several days before. Except for most of its tanks, General Barr's 7th Division was ashore in the Iwon area by November 9.

An Evaluation

It is easy to "Monday-morning-quarterback" an operation long after its completion. The way the amphibious movement of the X Corps worked out, the movement proved unnecessary, but it did place the corps where General MacArthur wanted it ultimately: on the east flank of the Eighth Army in northern Korea. The ports of Wonsan and Hungnam were essential for supply of whatever troops were to operate in the northeast, so they would have had to be cleared of mines in any event. No time was lost in this Navy task, which was by no means a wasted effort.

One unquestioned result of the amphibious movement of the X Corps was the delay it caused in the supply of the Eighth Army. In its move from the Naktong bridgehead to its junction with the X Corps the Eighth Army had outrun its supply lines, which were still based on Pusan. When it reached Seoul, its nearest railroad supply point was at Waegwan on the Naktong River, 200 miles away. Inchon was completely tied up for almost two weeks with the loading out of the 1st Marine Division, while truck and rail traffic from Pusan over the damaged roads was snarled by the rearward movement of the 7th Infantry Division down to Pusan. The Eighth Army supply situation never fully recovered from this delay before a new menace from China arose in the north.

It is impossible to assess with any certainty the effect of the lull in the pursuit of the North Koreans in the west. It is an axiom of military tactics to press relentlessly on the heels of a defeated enemy. This was not done after the fall of Seoul. Only the X Corps was in position to do so, in conjunction with the smashing drive of the ROK Army in the east. This possibility was recognized by Walker, the senior commander in the field. He had promptly flown into Wonsan after its capture and could sense and see with his own eyes the extent of the North Korean collapse. It probably was too late then to change the plans for the movement of Almond's corps by sea, though the 1st Marine Division had just started to load out of Inchon. But Walker could not have changed these plans if he had wished to. He had no authority to introduce any flexibility into the operation, because overall control was still being exercised by MacArthur from Tokyo, some 800 miles away, and the X Corps was not under his command but received its orders direct from General Headquarters. This system was both necessary and effective during the Inchon operation; it left much to be desired thereafter.

The decision having been made to land the X Corps at Wonsan, retention of control of the corps by General Headquarters, as at Inchon, was essential. However, there is little question but that the corps, once ashore there, should have been incorporated into the Eighth Army at once. After the Korean war the historian Appleman contacted all of the principal staff officers of General Headquarters. Hickey, who was the acting Chief of Staff, Wright, who was the chief planner, and Eberle, who was the logistical chief, all of them experienced soldiers, said they had favored the attachment of the X Corps to the Eighth Army, though MacArthur later stated that none of his staff had advocated this to him. Perhaps one clue to why no one had expressed his views on this subject to the Commander in Chief was indicated by Almond in his letter dated July 8, 1955, to Colonel Meade, in which Almond stated, "Whether 'several principal advisors' advised Gen. MacArthur to place X Corps under Eighth Army after the Inchon landing, I do not know. It should be noted, however, that Gen. MacArthur was at all times fully capable of making up his own mind without benefit of advice."

Not only did General MacArthur not attach the X Corps to the Eighth Army, even after Wonsan, but he promptly squelched an intimation from General Walker that the latter was thinking in terms of a broader mission for the Eighth Army after the capture of Wonsan by the ROK I Corps. MacArthur radioed Walker that he intended to transfer this corps from the operational control of the Eighth Army to that of the X Corps when Almond's headquarters was established ashore. This, in effect, would place the X Corps, which would then consist actually of two corps, on a par with the Eighth Army. Following the landing of the X Corps at Wonsan the ROK I Corps was in fact passed to Almond's control.

Thus it was made clear that the remote control of the United Nations forces in Korea would continue to be exercised by General Headquarters in Tokyo — at a time when a new campaign to advance to the Manchurian border was getting under way in the face of ominous moves by the Chinese Communists beyond the Yalu.

VIII

COMMUNIST CHINA INTERVENES

Unheeded Warnings

EVEN BEFORE the decision to have the United Nations forces cross the 38th Parallel, danger signals were being posted by the Russians and Chinese Communists. On August 4 Jakob Malik, the Soviet representative to the United Nations, proposed that the "internal civil war" in Korea be discussed in the United Nations, with representatives of Communist China present, and that all foreign troops be withdrawn. On August 22 he said that continuation of the United Nations action would lead to a broadening of the conflict. On the insistence of the United States and Britain the Security Council voted down Malik's August 4 proposal and also a later demand that the Chinese Communists be permitted to come to the United Nations to press their charges of aggression by the United States. This action of the Security Council, combined with the defeat of the North Koreans at Inchon and Seoul, led to a series of warnings from top Chinese officials.

On September 30 Chou En-lai, Peking's Foreign Minister, announced in typical Communist phraseology, "The Chinese people absolutely will not tolerate foreign aggression, nor will they supinely tolerate their neighbors' being savagely invaded by the imperialists."

On October 3 Chou formally summoned the Indian Ambassador to Peking, D. K. M. Pannikar, to a midnight conference at Chou's residence. Chou advised Pannikar that, if American troops crossed the 38th Parallel, China would be forced to intervene. He said that if only South Koreans entered the North, he would not interfere. Chou En-lai knew that this warning would be passed on through the British government to Washington — as it was. Because of this roundabout approach and because it hardly seemed likely that, if the Chinese were serious, they would disclose their intentions in advance, United States intelligence agencies discounted the warning. Pannikar was suspected of having Communist leanings. A short while later, again through Indian channels, he reported that the Chinese would not intervene. The United States intelligence community generally agreed that Chou's threats were a bluff, primarily a last-ditch attempt to intimidate the United States, and probably covered a less drastic plan of action, such as offering sanctuary to the North Korean leaders.

On the military side firsthand intelligence about Chinese intentions was difficult to attain. Ninety percent of the intelligence information at the Department of the Army came from sources in the Far East Command. General MacArthur had been directed, in one of the earliest orders from Washington, to stay clear of the Soviet and Manchurian borders. This order was designed to avoid any excuse for direct Communist intervention. It also precluded air and ground reconnaissance beyond the Yalu or close thereto. General Willoughby, the Far East Command's Intelligence officer, G-2, was thus limited to indirect sources of military intelligence. Teleconferences were held each day between Army G-2 officers in the Pentagon and Willoughby's staff in Tokyo. The Army G-2 also received daily an intelligence summary from the United Nations Command. This somewhat duplicated the telecon information but included an attempt at evaluation of the often contradictory reports. In addition, the Central Intelligence Agency combined reports from its own sources, chiefly the Chinese Nationalist Government on Formosa and others operating out of Hongkong, with reports from the United Nations Command and sought to discern Communist China's intentions. All of these summary reports were made available to the JCS, and presumably were seen by or were available to General MacArthur.

On September 27 the JCS directed MacArthur to make a special effort to determine whether China intended to intervene. The next day he radioed back assurance that at that time there were no indications of Chinese entry into North Korea. Yet only one week later, on October 3, the day of Chou En-lai's warning to Ambassador Pannikar, the United Nations Command intelligence summary reported some evidence that twenty Chinese divisions were already in North Korea and had been there since September 10. Commenting on the warning from Chou En-lai and the other recent Chinese threats, this summary noted, "Even though the utterances . . . are in the form of propaganda, they cannot be fully ignored since they emit from presumably responsible leaders in the Chinese and North Korean Communist Governments. The enemy retains a potential of reinforcement by CCF [Chinese Communist forces] troops."

The next day, covering the reported entry of nine Chinese divisions into North Korea, the General Headquarters intelligence summary observed that recent reports were taking on a "sinister connotation." It again concluded that the potential "exists for Chinese forces to openly intervene in the Korean War, if United Nations forces cross the 38th Parallel."

In a series of intelligence summaries between October 8 and 14 the Far East Command's G-2 reported that "while exaggerations and canards are always evident, the potential of [the Chinese] massing at the Antung and other Manchurian crossings [of the Yalu] appears conclusive." Yet, whatever misgivings Willoughby may have had about the Chinese threat, there is no recorded indication that he attempted personally to dissuade MacArthur from crossing the 38th Parallel. Instead, continuing reports of Chinese troop movements and threats were discounted for lack of conclusive evidence or were characterized by MacArthur's G-2 as "probably in a category of diplomatic blackmail."

President Truman had kept abreast of these reports through periodic intelligence briefings. While agreeing that they probably constituted attempts at blackmail, he was sufficiently concerned about the possibility of Chinese intervention to have the JCS send MacArthur instructions covering such an eventuality. Consequently, on October 9 the Chiefs sent him a directive that stated, "Hereafter, in the event of an open or covert employment anywhere in Korea of major Chinese Communist units, without prior announcement, you should continue the action as long as, in your judgment, action by forces now under your control offers a reasonable chance of success. In any case, you will obtain authorization from Washington prior to taking any military action against objectives in Chinese territory."

On October 12 it was reported to President Truman that though the Chinese Communists lacked necessary air and naval support, they could intervene effectively but "not necessarily decisively." The President was told that in spite of Chou En-lai's threats and Chinese troop movements in Manchuria there were no conclusive indications of Chinese intentions. It was felt that the Chinese would hesitate to endanger their chances of a seat in the United Nations by intervening. If they did intervene, without help from Soviet air and naval support, which might not be forthcoming, they would suffer heavy casualties. In summary, this report said that, although full-scale Communist intervention in Korea should be regarded as a continuing possibility, a consideration of all known factors led to the conclusion that, barring a Soviet decision for global war, such action was not probable in 1950. During this period intervention probably would be confined to continued covert assistance to the North Koreans.

As was to prove the case in later years, notably the Cuban affair in the 1960's, the Central Intelligence Agency and all other United States intelligence agencies which based their conclusions on probable intentions of the enemy rather than on his capabilities were wrong. This time the Central Intelligence Agency had plenty of company; everybody was wrong.

Plans for the Advance to the NK Frontier

As General MacArthur returned to Tokyo from the Wake Island conference, optimism prevailed throughout all echelons of the United Nations Command and in Washington. Intent on making good on his forecast of victory by Thanksgiving, MacArthur on October 17 issued U.N. Operations Order No. 4 to initiate what, hopefully, would be the final phase of the war (Map

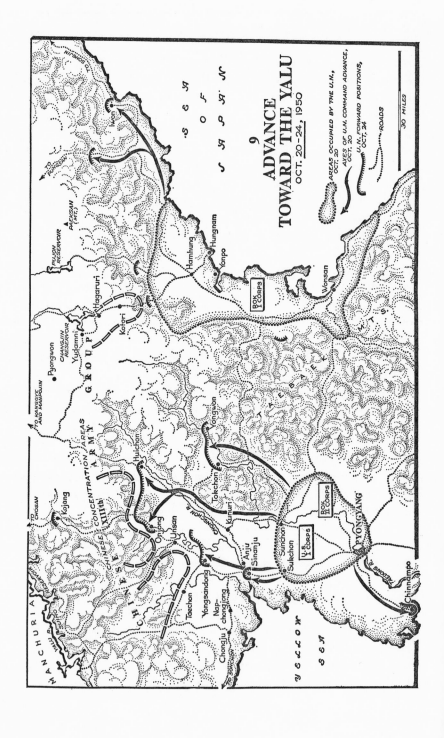

9

ADVANCE
TOWARD THE YALU
OCT. 20–24, 1950

AREAS OCCUPIED BY THE U.N.,
OCT. 20

AXES OF U.N. COMMAND ADVANCE,
OCT. 20

U.N. FORWARD POSITIONS,
OCT. 24

ROADS

30 MILES

MANCHURIA

CHOSAN

Kojang

Kanggye

TO KANGGYE
AND MANPOJIN

S E A   O F   J A P A N

Iwon

TO PUNGSAN

PAEKSAN
(MT.)

PUJON
RESERVOR

Hamhung

Hungnam

Tonpo

Pyongwon

CHANGJIN
RESERVOR

Yudamni

Hagaruri

Kotori

Wonsan

G R O U P

C O N C E N T R A T I O N   A R E A S

C H I N E S E   XIIIth   A R M Y

Huichon

Yongwon

ROK
I CORPS

Unsan

Onjong

Kunuri

Tokchon

T A E B A E K   M T S.

Taechon

Yongsandong

Nap-
chongjong

Chongju

TO SUIHO

Anju
Sinanju

Sukchon

Sunchon

ROK
II CORPS

U.S.
I CORPS

PYONGYANG

Chinnampo

Y E L L O W   S E A

YALU R.

SUIHO

CHINESE

9). This order assigned a new objective for the United Nations Forces, running from Sonchon on the west coast to Pyongwon, northwest of the Changjin Reservoir, and thence via Pongsan to Songjin on the Sea of Japan. This line was about 40 miles south of the Manchurian border most of the way but almost 100 miles from the Russian frontier on the east coast. A boundary between the Eighth Army and the reinforced X Corps was drawn as indicated on Map 9. The north-south leg of the boundary followed the crest of the high Taebaek range, with peaks up to 7400 feet, between the watershed of the Chongchon River on the west and the streams flowing down the eastern slopes to the Sea of Japan. Lateral communication between the X Corps and the Eighth Army, across the Taebaek range, would become more and more difficult as the units advanced north of the Wonsan-Pyongyang corridor and as the Eighth Army veered to the north-west in its drive across the Chongchon toward the Yalu. The X Corps, with headquarters at Wonsan, had only radio and teletype communications with Eighth Army headquarters, which moved up to Pyongyang on October 24.

Operations Order No. 4 removed the restrictions on the use of non-Korean troops north of the Chongju-Kunuri-Yongwon-Hamhung line, restrictions that had been stipulated by the JCS instructions of September 27, 1950. All units, without regard to their composition, were to press forward to the assigned objective line. Although the western end of this line at Sonchon was not far in advance of the JCS limiting line, in its center and on the east coast it was from 50 to 100 miles ahead of the JCS line. This was the first, but not the last, stretching of MacArthur's orders beyond JCS instructions. If the Chiefs noted this — and I have no recollection that we did — we offered no objection.

The 187th Airborne RCT Drops North of Pyongyang

In order to cut off as many as possible of the enemy troops and North Korean government officials fleeing from Pyongyang and, if possible, to rescue American and ROK prisoners known to be held captive in that vicinity, Operations Order No. 4 called for an airdrop of the 187th Airborne Regimental Combat Team north of Pyongyang on the front of the U.S. I Corps. This RCT had been held in General Headquarters reserve at the Kimpo airfield after it had assisted the X Corps in clearing the south bank of the Han River in the battle for Seoul.

Two roads branched north from Pyongyang. About 30 miles away a transverse road connected them between the small towns of Sukchon on the west and Sunchon on the east, about 17 miles apart. It was planned to drop the RCT, Colonel Frank S. Bowen commanding, less one battalion, at Sukchon and the 2d Battalion, under Lieutenant Colonel W. J. Beyle, at Sunchon. Each group was reinforced with artillery and antitank weapons and engineering, medical, communications, and other service troops. A successful drop was made against only light resistance on October 20. Sukchon and Sunchon were quickly seized, blocking positions set up to the north and south, and contact established with elements of the ROK 6th Division, the left flank unit of the ROK II Corps, which was advancing in the east zone of the Eighth Army. In all, 4000 troops and more than 600 tons of equipment and supplies, including jeeps, machine guns, 90mm antitank guns, 105mm howitzers, and mobile radio equipment, were dropped. This airborne operation, the first by American troops since World War II, demonstrated the tremendous advance made since that time in parachuting heavy weapons, transport, and supplies essential for the survival of airborne troops.

General MacArthur and members of his staff had flown from Tokyo to witness the air drop. Afterwards they had gone down to Pyongyang. There at an informal meeting with reporters MacArthur said that 30,000 NK troops, about half the surviving enemy forces in North Korea, had been trapped between the 187th combat team and the U.S. and ROK I Corps, and he predicted that they would be captured or destroyed. He characterized the airborne operation as an "expert performance" and added, "This closes the trap on the enemy." The following day in Tokyo he said, "The war is very definitely coming to an end very shortly."

Unfortunately, these optimistic forecasts did not materialize. Because of the slowness in initiating the pursuit by the Eighth

Army after Seoul, which contributed to the delay in launching the airborne operation, the bulk of enemy forces north of Pyongyang had by October 20 withdrawn north of Sukchon-Sunchon and probably were already north of the Chongchon River. The NK government installations had been moved on October 12 from Pyongyang and by October 20 had been set up in a temporary new capital in the mountain fastness of Kanggye, near the Manchurian frontier. No important NK officials were captured. Moreover, most of the American and ROK prisoners had also been moved northward, only to be massacred in cold blood as the pursuing allies closed in on their captors. In the subsequent operations the 187th Airborne RCT did trap the NK 239th Regiment, about 2500 strong, between the 187th's Sukchon position and the British 27th Infantry Brigade, which was leading the advance of the U.S. I Corps north of Pyongyang. The NK 239th Regiment was practically destroyed. In three days of combat the 187th had captured 3818 NK prisoners and had suffered a total of 111 casualties, of which 46 were jump injuries. It had passed to Eighth Army control after the jump landing and was withdrawn to Pyongyang on October 23.

The Eighth Army Advances to the Chongchon (See Map 9)

Pyongyang was cleared of the enemy on October 20, the day the 187th Regimental Combat Team dropped on Sukchon and Sunchon. The Eighth Army moved out at once corps abreast, the ROK II Corps on the right and the U.S. I Corps on the left. By October 23 the British 27th Infantry Brigade, under tactical control of the U.S. 24th Division, on the left of the I Corps advanced from Sukchon to Sinanju near the mouth of the Chongchon River. That same day General Paik's ROK 1st Division had reached the river at Kunuri and had moved downstream to Anju. By dark on October 24 all three regiments of the ROK division were across the Chongchon, prepared to attack on the northeast toward Unsan.

As these units crossed the Chongchon General MacArthur on

October 24 issued new instructions removing all remaining restrictions on the use of United Nations ground forces in areas close to the North Korean border. Commanders were authorized to employ any and all forces necessary to secure all of North Korea. Although MacArthur did caution that United Nations forces other than ROK should be withdrawn from border areas "as feasible" and replaced with ROK units, his instructions were clearly counter to the policy of the Administration as formulated in the study of September 11 made by the National Security Council, a copy of which had been sent to him at his request on September 18, 1950. They were also contrary to a specific statement of this policy contained in a directive from the JCS, dated September 27, 1950, quoted in Chapter VII (pages 147–8). Upon learning of MacArthur's new order the JCS promptly radioed him, stating that it was not in accord with our September 27 directive, and asked for an explanation.

MacArthur replied at once that he had acted as a matter of military necessity, because ROK forces lacked sufficient strength and experienced leadership to seize and secure the critical areas along the border. He pointed out that the September 27 limitation on the employment of non-ROK troops close to the frontiers was not an order but simply a statement of policy which, he felt, had been modified by the letter of September 30 from the Secretary of Defense, General Marshall, which stated, "We want you to feel unhampered tactically and strategically to proceed north of the parallel."

He assured the Chiefs that he understood their concern but hinted at dire consequences of any other course of action. He concluded by stating that the entire subject was covered at the Wake Island conference. There is no record that the question of using only ROK troops near the borders was discussed at Wake, but the General may have raised it in his private talk with the President. Neither Mr. Truman nor General MacArthur mentions the subject in their memoirs. In any event, it was too late for the JCS to stop the movement of American forces north of the restraining line. The JCS at least tacitly accepted MacArthur's defense of his order and made no move to countermand it. However, the matter did not end here. It was raised again by me during the MacArthur Hearings, in answer to a question.

Beyond the Chongchon to the Yalu

The Chongchon River parallels the Yalu at a distance of about 65 miles, both streams flowing from northeast to southwest (Maps 10 and 12). The valley of the Chongchon varies in width from 3 miles near the river's source in the rough mountains of north central Korea to 20 miles of open rolling country below Sinanju, where the Chongchon empties into the Yellow Sea. The Yalu rises in the northeast corner of Korea in the Taebaek range, flows generally westward through a deep gorge, and then turns to the southwest near Chosan. Thence it runs in deep-cut, winding loops until it reaches the site of the high Suiho hydroelectric dam, built by the Japanese during their long tenure of Korea. This dam backs up a reservoir that extends for 60 miles, branching into numerous fjordlike valleys in the steep mountains on both sides of the Manchurian border. Below the dam the Yalu broadens and meanders to the Yellow Sea.

The main crossing of the Yalu above the dam is at Manpojin, where the road and railroad from Kanggye enters Manchuria. A secondary railroad spans the river just below the dam, but the more important crossings are at Sinuiju-Antung, where the main railroad and highway come down from Mukden and continue south to Pyongyang and Seoul.

The divide between the Chongchon and the Yalu would have to be seized and held, as a minimum, by the Eighth Army if the Army was to be able to dominate the Yalu crossings. The dividing ridge line curves back and forth from the Yalu, being nearest that river opposite the Suiho dam. From the crest of the divide spiny ridges with narrow intervening valleys run down to the rivers on either side. Whoever controls these ridges controls the roads that run up the valleys from the Chongchon to the divide and thence down on the north side to the Yalu. The villages of Taechon, Unsan, and Onjong lie at the southern entrances to three of the

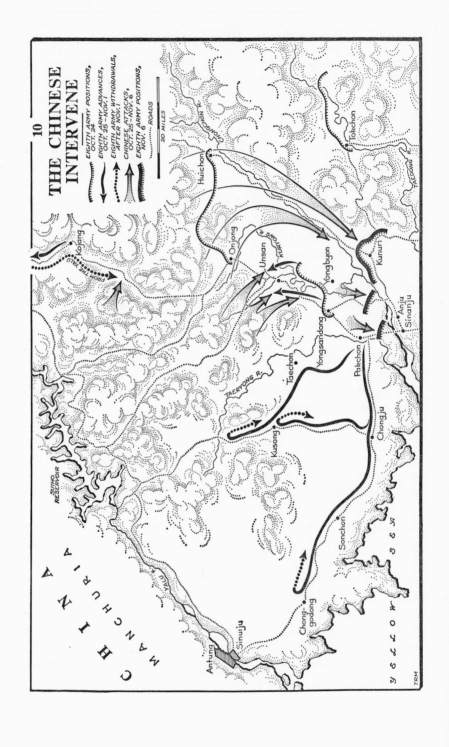

THE CHINESE
INTERVENE

EIGHTH ARMY POSITIONS,
OCT. 24

EIGHTH ARMY ADVANCES,
OCT. 25–NOV. 1

EIGHTH ARMY WITHDRAWALS,
AFTER NOV. 1

CHINESE ATTACKS,
OCT. 25–NOV. 6

EIGHTH ARMY POSITIONS,
NOV. 6

ROADS

20 MILES

CHINA

MANCHURIA

SUIHO
RESERVOIR

YALU R.

Antung

Sinuiju

Chong-
godong

Sonchon

Chongju

Pakchon

Kusong

Taechon

TAERYONG R.

Yongsandong

Anju
Sinanju

Kunuri

Yongbyon

Unsan

KURYONG R.

E. Onjong

Huichon

CHONGCHON R.

Kojang

Tokchon

TAEDONG R.

YELLOW SEA

HOSAN STRIP

TRM

valleys. They and the adjacent areas were to become the scene of bitter fighting, disastrous to the United Nations cause.

The Eighth Army operations north of the Chongchon started as a continuation of the pursuit of the North Korean forces routed at Pyongyang. Little or no resistance was expected and, as is usually the procedure in a pursuit, all United Nations troops were urged to press forward without regard to lateral contact between units. The 6th Division of the ROK II Corps had the easiest going. Moving up the valley of the Chongchon, it reached Huichon on October 23 and then turned northwest toward its objective, the village of Chosan on the Yalu. Its leading regiment, the 7th Regiment, bivouacked the night of October 24–25 at Kojang, 18 miles south of Chosan. The next morning Major Harry Fleming, military adviser to the regiment, moved up to Chosan with its reconnaissance platoon. There the platoon observed North Koreans fleeing across a floating footbridge into Manchuria. It set up machine guns to stop this traffic. After reconnoitering the town the platoon left a small party behind in Chosan to await the arrival of the 7th Regiment the next day. The platoon returned to Kojang. It proved to be the first and only unit under Eighth Army command ever to reach the Yalu.

Collapse of the ROK II Corps

While the ROK 6th Division's 7th Regiment was marching un-opposed toward the Yalu, its 2d Regiment moved north out of Onjong. Within a few miles the leading 3d Battalion came under fire (Map 10). The troops piled out of their vehicles and deployed to drive off what they thought to be a North Korean roadblock. Actually, it was held by Chinese who poured down from the ridges and cut the battalion to pieces. That evening Chinese troops cut off the 2d Battalion, badly mauled it, and, before dawn on October 26, attacked Onjong. Apparently shocked by the violence of the Chinese onslaught, the ROK troops broke in panic. Three miles out of Onjong they were cut off by a Chinese roadblock. By this time not a single company was intact. They simply scattered into the hills without a fight.

The same fate befell elements of the ROK 6th and 8th Division when, under orders of the ROK II Corps commander, they attacked from Huichon toward Onjong in an effort to recover the artillery and other equipment lost there. They were badly beaten by the Chinese and lost all of their own artillery and many vehicles.

These reverses in the Onjong area effectively cut off the 7th Regiment, the leading unit of the ROK 6th Division, which was now isolated at Kojang.

The 7th Regiment, not knowing of the disaster in its rear, was about to move up to Chosan on October 27 when it received orders to withdraw. It started south the following morning but quickly ran into a Chinese roadblock, and the entire regiment was soon engaged. Close air support held off the enemy until dark, but during the night many ROK soldiers disappeared into the hills, and by morning all resistance ended. Of the 3552 officers and men of that regiment a total of only 875 escaped to Kunuri and rejoined the division.

By October 29 the ROK II Corps, badly crippled, had been driven back both north and south of the Chongchon, causing General Walker to release the ROK 7th Division from the U.S. I Corps, to which it had been attached following the capture of Pyongyang, to bolster the ROK II Corps. He ordered the ROK corps to establish a defensive position with its 8th Division north of the Chongchon and the 7th Division south of the river extending the line toward Tokchon. The Chinese Communists continued their drive to outflank the ROK II Corps. Alarmed at this threat to the open right flank of the Eighth Army, Walker assembled the U.S. 2d Division in the vicinity of Sunchon for emergency use.

Danger on the I Corps Front

West of the ROK II Corps the U.S. I Corps crossed the Chongchon on October 25 with its ROK 1st Division and U.S. 24th Division abreast, the ROK troops on the right. Its 1st Cavalry Division was held in reserve at Pyongyang.

The ROK division was the first to run into trouble just north of Unsan. Stopped by interdiction fire at a bridge, its two leading regiments were heavily engaged by mid-afternoon. A captured enemy soldier was definitely identified as Chinese. He said there were 10,000 Chinese troops in the hills northwest of Unsan and 10,000 more to the east toward Huichon. This report was relayed to Army Headquarters. Word that the enemy to the front were Chinese rather than North Koreans spread rapidly through the ROK troops, bringing chills of apprehension even more ominous than the first snow of approaching winter, which hit at the same time. Worse yet, by the morning of October 26 it was clear that during the night the enemy had almost surrounded Unsan.

In the afternoon of October 26 ROK 1st division commander, General Paik, examined a number of enemy dead and confirmed that they were all Chinese. He reported to General Milburn, Commander of the U.S. I Corps, that his division was engaged with a full Chinese division of at least 10,000 men, not a mixed Chinese-Korean organization.

As late as October 26 Eighth Army intelligence officers discounted prisoner reports of Chinese intervention in strength, but by October 28 General Walker had become so concerned with the situation along the Chongchon that he ordered the 1st Cavalry Division to move up from Pyongyang, pass through the ROK 1st Division, and attack as far as the Yalu; General Gay therefore moved his command post to Yonsandong.

The situation at Unsan had improved somewhat on October 27 and 28 after an air drop of ammunition and supplies. However, when the 8th Cavalry Regiment, Colonel R. D. Palmer commanding, relieved ROK 1st Division forces at Unsan, it took over a dangerous salient in the U.S. I Corps front, with a gap on its left of 15 miles to the nearest unit of the 24th Division. By nightfall of November 1 the 8th Cavalry was disposed in a semicircle north, west, and southwest of Unsan, the ROK 1st Division extending its position to the east and southeast facing the disintegrating ROK II Corps.

Disaster at Unsan

The Chinese covered their troop movements in the Eighth Army area by setting numerous fires in the hills south of the Yalu, making it difficult for reconnaissance planes to spot enemy locations. Realizing the threat to his 1st Cavalry Division in its dispersed and exposed position, Hap Gay telephoned I Corps headquarters on November 1 requesting authority to withdraw the 8th Regiment from Unsan. This request was refused. Apparently, Milburn and the I Corps staff did not accept fully the reports of strong Chinese forces on the Corps front until General Walker telephoned Milburn on the afternoon of November 1. Walker told Milburn that the ROK II Corps had disintegrated, leaving the U.S. I Corps' right flank unprotected. Walker instructed Milburn to protect his flank and to assume control of any ROK troops that came into his area.

Milburn at once took steps to have the 1st Cavalry Division establish a blocking force on the Kunuri-Anju road southwest of Kunuri and went himself to the ROK II Corps command post at Kunuri. There he found the Corps headquarters about to move to Sunchon, 25 miles to the rear. The Corps Commander, General Yu Jae Hung, said he did not know the location of most of his units and that they were disorganized. Milburn told him that he would have to hold Kunuri and that a Cavalry blocking force west of Kunuri would support him.

During the afternoon of November 1 the Chinese cut the road south of Unsan and were attacking the 1st Battalion of the 8th Cavalry Regiment and the 15th Regiment of the ROK 1st Division. By midnight the ROK regiment was overwhelmed, most of them killed or captured. This permitted the enemy to move south past the right flank of the Cavalry battalion.

While these ominous events were occurring, a meeting was being held by General Milburn at I Corps headquarters in Anju, starting at 8:00 P.M. The division commanders and key staff officers were present. General Milburn said his corps would pass to the defensive at once. The 8th Cavalry Regiment and the ROK 15th Regiment were to be withdrawn from Unsan to positions along the Yonsandong-Yongbyon east-west road.

The decision to withdraw had been made too late. About 1:00 A.M. on November 2 a Chinese force cut the withdrawal route of the 1st and 2d Battalions of the 8th Cavalry Regiment southeast of Unsan. By dawn the regiment was almost completely surrounded. Some units and groups of men of those two Battalions were able to break through the Chinese roadblocks with heavy losses, but the bulk of the 3d Battalion was trapped by the Chinese cordon. An effort was made by the 5th Cavalry Regiment under Colonel Harold K. Johnson (later Chief of Staff of the U.S. Army) to break through the Communist ring and reach this battalion, but all efforts failed. Late on the afternoon of November 2 Milburn, after conferring with Gay, decided that it would not be possible with the forces available to rescue the battalion. In view of the threat to the whole right flank of his I Corps he ordered the immediate withdrawal of the 1st Cavalry Division south of the Chongchon River. The abandonment to the enemy of any unit runs counter to the traditions of the United States Army. Sadly, and with bitter gall, Hap Gay, scion of General George Patton, ordered Colonel Johnson to break off his attack.

In a remarkable display of courage and tenacity that measured up to the highest traditions of American Cavalry the dwindling group of men within the shrinking perimeter of the 3d Battalion held out for two harrowing nights and days. In the late afternoon of November 4 the remaining able-bodied men under a handful of officers, screened by the smoke of a Chinese artillery preparation for a final attack, slipped out of the perimeter to the east. Captain Clarence R. Anderson, the battalion surgeon, volunteered to stay with the wounded, who included the heroic battalion commander, Major Robert J. Ormond, who, though badly wounded, had helped hold his battalion together. Major Ormond died the next day. Some 200 men and a few surviving officers shortly after daylight on November 4 broke through a gap in the enemy lines. Though they managed to reach the mountains, they were again surrounded the next day after marching overnight in a rainstorm. Even then they refused to surrender and, on the decision of the officers remaining, broke up into small groups hoping to filter out. Most were killed or captured. On November 6 the 3d

Battalion, 8th Cavalry Regiment, ceased to exist as a unit. It died gallantly.

More than 600 officers and men of the 8th Cavalry Regiment were lost at Unsan, most from the 3d Battalion. Among them were Major Ormond, most of his staff, five company commanders, two medical officers, and a chaplain. It was later learned that elements of two Chinese divisions had fought at Unsan. They also lost heavily.

The Eighth Army Holds a Bridgehead on the Chongchon

In the western half of the U.S. I Corps sector the pursuit of the North Koreans in late October had gone well. By October 29 the British Brigade had captured Chongju, after which General Church, commanding the 24th Infantry Division, passed the U.S. 21st Infantry through the Commonwealth men who had earned a rest. A night attack by Colonel Richard W. Stephen's 21st Infantry regiment broke through the NK's delaying position south of Songchon, and by November 1 the 21st had reached Chonggo-dong, only 18 miles from Sinanju on the Yalu.

The enemy in this division's sector were all North Koreans. The division soldiers were unaware of the Chinese attacks in the Onjong-Unsan area. The Americans were dismayed when, on orders from I Corps, they were told to halt and dig in. They didn't know it, but where they stopped was to mark the farthest advance toward the Manchurian border of any Americans in the Eighth Army. It was a fitting coincidence that their leading battalion was the 1st, which had been commanded by Lieutenant Colonel Brad Smith in the first American battle in Korea at Osan on July 5, four months before.

During this period three relatively separate and uncoordinated operations within the Eighth Army had been taking place: the battle of ROK II Corps on the east, the fighting of the 1st Cavalry and ROK 1st Divisions in the vicinity of Unsan, and the advance of the 24th Division in the west. Convinced at last that the Eighth Army was up against powerful Chinese Communist forces, General Walker stepped in on October 31 to bring order to the headlong pursuit. He told General Milburn to limit the 24th Division's advance to conform with the critical situation in the Unsan area.

Walker was anxious to hold a bridgehead over the Chongchon with a view to a later resumption of the offensive. The British Brigade and the 19th Regiment of the 24th Division were to hold north of the river covering the bridges and tank fords in the vicinity of Anju. The units were withdrawn to these positions by November 3. The ROK 1st Division pulled back across the Chongchon on November 4.

Things were more difficult to the east near Kunuri. Colonel Throckmorton's 5th Regimental Combat Team had been placed north of Kunuri to back up elements of the ROK II Corps, which had been driven by the Chinese into a narrow area against the corps' boundary. Recognizing that Hill 622 northeast of Kunuri commanded the whole lower valley of the Chongchon, the Chinese made an all-out effort to take it. However, the ROK 7th and 8th Divisions of the battered ROK II Corps still had some fight left and with the help of Johnny Throckmorton's ever-tough combat team held their ground and saved the right flank of the Eighth Army south of the Chongchon.

Simultaneously with these actions stiff fighting was going on north of the river east of the British Brigade. During the next several days the CCF 119th and 120th Divisions (Chinese Communist forces) made repeated day and night attacks to break through or between the British Brigade and the 24th Division. They had occasional temporary successes but each time were beaten back by counterattacks.

Finally, on November 6, the Chinese broke off their attacks and withdrew into the hills to the north. The Eighth Army had held its bridgehead. Undaunted and spurred on by General Mac-Arthur, it began planning at once for a resumption of the offensive.

The X Corps Advances

While these events were transpiring in the zone of the Eighth Army, General Almond with the U.S. X Corps and 1st ROK Corps was proceeding with his own campaign, practically independently and beyond supporting distance of the Eighth Army. (Map 11.) It is 100 miles by air from Wonsan to the Chongchon River at Sinanju and almost 150 miles from Hungnam to the Suiho dam on the Yalu. In between these points the rugged Taebaek range raises a formidable barrier to any east-west troop movement.

This range broadens out in northeast Korea into a jumble of wild, almost trackless mountains, which extend down to the sea all the way from Hungnam to the Russian frontier. The principal route across the Taebaeks north of the Wonsan-Pyongyang highway connects the industrial area of Hamhung-Hungnam with the Changjin Reservoir at Hagaruri and then continues on through Kanggye to the Yalu at Manpojin. To the east a fair road runs along the coast and from it a few poorer roads wind up to Pungsan and thence to Hyesanjin on the upper Yalu.

The objective initially assigned X Corps by MacArthur's Operation Order No. 4 was the Pyongwon-Pungsan-Songjin line. This was later changed for the X Corps, as for the Eighth Army, to call for the seizure of all of North Korea. Almond's plan of operations was that the ROK I Corps continue its drive up the coast to the Russian frontier, that the U.S. 7th Division of the X Corps, under General Barr, advance from Iwon via Pungsan to Hyesanjin, and that the 1st Marine Division remain in the Wonsan-Hungnam area, responsible for the corps rear area and lines of communications. Later the Marines were to be relieved by the U.S. 3d Infantry Division, which was expected to arrive shortly from Japan. The Marines were then to move from Hamhung to the Changjin Reservoir and thereafter continue northward, as determined by the tactical situation at the time.

The ROK I Corps Drives North (See Map 11)

Without waiting for the relief of the 1st Marine Division the ROK I Corps had started the 26th Regiment of its 3d Division up the road to the Changjin Reservoir, while the Capital Division moved along the coast road. On October 25 leading battalions of this regiment became engaged with an enemy force about halfway to the Changjin Reservoir. A captured Chinese soldier said he belonged to the 5th Regiment of the Chinese 8th Army and that 3000 to 4000 Chinese were in the area. The ROK regiment slowly continued its advance until stopped by a strong force of Chinese supported by NK tanks. The ROK troops did succeed in capturing a number of Chinese before being forced to take up a defensive position. On October 30 Almond questioned through an interpreter a group of these prisoners at the ROK I Corps command post in Hamhung. They were identified as belonging to the CCF 124th Division. They told Almond that they had entered North Korea with their division at Manpojin in mid-October and had marched from there on foot at night, their mortars carried by pack animals. The men were well clothed and in good shape, though they said they had not eaten for three days. Almond sent a personal message to MacArthur confirming the presence of the Chinese Communists in North Korea.

Undeterred by the evidence of Chinese intervention, the X Corps pushed ahead toward the Manchurian and Siberian frontiers. The ROK Capital Division fought its way north along the coastal road, supported by U.S. Navy air strikes and gunfire, against stubborn resistance from the NK 41st Division. The industrial center of Chongjin, 65 miles south of the Siberian boundary, was captured on November 26.

In a little less than two months since it crossed the 38th Parallel the ROK I Corps had advanced by foot and vehicle 425 miles to Chongjin, fighting a good portion of the way. Still equipped with cotton fatigue clothing, worn-out shoes, and old U.S. Army overcoats, the ROK troops also had to fight the cold; by mid-November the temperature in northeast Korea had dropped well below zero.

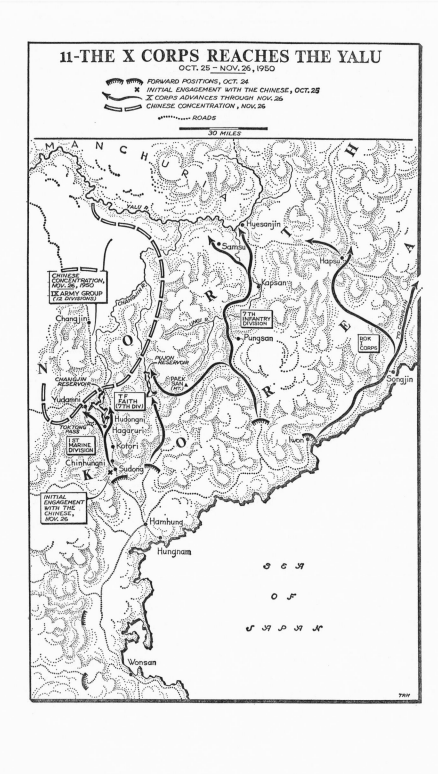

11-THE X CORPS REACHES THE YALU
OCT. 25 – NOV. 26, 1950

FORWARD POSITIONS, OCT. 24
✗ INITIAL ENGAGEMENT WITH THE CHINESE, OCT. 25
X CORPS ADVANCES THROUGH NOV. 26
CHINESE CONCENTRATION, NOV. 26
••••••••••• ROADS

30 MILES

MANCHURIA

YALU R.

Hyesanjin

Samsu

Hapsu

CHINESE
CONCENTRATION,
NOV. 26, 1950
IX ARMY GROUP
(12 DIVISIONS)

CHANGJIN R.

Kapsan

Changjin

UNGI R.

7 TH
INFANTRY
DIVISION

Pungsan

ROK
I
CORPS

TO CHONGJIN

PUJON
RESERVOIR

PAEK
SAN
(MT.)

Songjin

N

CHANGJIN
RESERVOIR

Yudamni

T F
FAITH
(7TH DIV)

TOKTONG
PASS

Hudongni

Hagaruri

1ST
MARINE
DIVISION

Kotori

Iwon

Chinhungni

Sudong

K

INITIAL
ENGAGEMENT
WITH THE
CHINESE,
NOV. 26

Hamhung

Hungnam

SEA

OF

JAPAN

Wonsan

TRH

It was not till the end of the month that LST's could bring the South Korean troops any warm winter clothing. That the ROK I Corps did so well probably can be traced to the improved leadership after its failures around Pohangdong in late August and the assistance of some exceptionally able men of the U.S. Korean Military Advisory Group.

The U.S. 7th Division Reaches the Yalu (See Map 11)

West of the ROK I Corps the 17th Infantry Regiment, the leading unit of the U.S. 7th Division, X Corps, had its baptism by fire on November 1, when it drove off a strong North Korean attack. On its left the 31st Infantry Regiment, after landing at Iwon on November 3–4, advanced into the mountains toward the Pujon Reservoir. On November 8 it ran into a battalion of Chinese troops on the eastern slopes of Paeksan, a 7700-foot peak near the southern end of the reservoir. This was the first encounter of Americans with the Chinese Communists forces on the front of the X Corps. The Chinese unit was later identified as part of the CCF 126th Division.

On November 12 the X Corps ordered the 7th Division to continue its attack to the north. Barr directed the 17th Regiment, commanded by Colonel Herbert B. Powell, to take Kapsan and then move up to Hyesanjin on the Yalu; the 31st was to advance on the left of the 17th, and the 32d was to seize the southeast shore of the Pujan Reservoir. To reach Kapsan the 17th had to cross the waist-deep Ungi River in 7° below-zero weather against small arms and mortar fire. Two days later it captured Kapsan, and after advancing on foot 19 miles over icy roads against scattered NK opposition it entered Hyesanjin on November 21 without further opposition.

Upon receiving word that the 17th Regiment had reached the Yalu General MacArthur radioed General Almond, "Heartiest congratulations, Ned, and tell Dave Barr that the 7th Division hit the jackpot." Almond also wired congratulations to the 7th Division. Apparently, neither Barr, Almond, nor MacArthur was greatly concerned about the fact that five days earlier a patrol of the 31st Regiment had encountered a group of about 200 Chinese soldiers at the north end of the Pujon Reservoir, who withdrew after a brief fight. Leaving strong detachments to hold the mountain passes east of the reservoir leading into the rear area of the 7th Division, General Barr did take steps to gather his division in the area Hyesanjin-Samsu-Kapsan.

The 7th Marines Reach the Changjin Reservoir (See Map 11)

The arrival of the U.S. 3d Infantry Division in Korea in early November freed the 1st Marine Division of its mission of protecting the X Corps base and line of communications in the Wonsan-Hungnam area. On October 30 the X Corps ordered the Marines to relieve the ROK I Corps troops on the road to the Changjin Reservoir.

This road climbs some 4000 feet from sea level at Hamhung to a high plateau at the south end of the reservoir, a distance of almost 60 miles. In one winding stretch of 8 miles it rises 2500 feet from Chinhungni to the Kotori plateau. It was at the beginning of this steepest stretch of road, near the village of Sudong, that the CCF 124th Division had established its initial blocking position.

The 7th Marine Regiment led the Marine division from Hamhung on November 1. After relieving the ROK I Corps the following morning it moved out and promptly ran into Chinese opposition. Little headway was made that day. The regiment bivouacked for the night with its battalions in column along the road.

About midnight the CCF 370th Regiment launched an attack designed to separate the two leading Marine battalions and cut them off from the third. By daylight the Chinese Communist forces had gained a dominant position overlooking a key bridge between the Marine battalions. The Marines called in their supporting air which, combined with determined infantry action, drove the Chinese from their blocking positions, killing about 700. After this bloody engagement the 7th Marine Regiment met little resistance, and on November 4 it entered Sudong. On November

10 it moved through the pass to Kotori, which was only 7 miles from its objective, Hagaruri, without further opposition.

Biting 35-miles winds and 8° below-zero weather suddenly hit the plateau the first night, November 10–11, that the 7th Marines spent there. The shock of a 40° drop in temperature after days of strenuous climbing and fighting caused 200 men to collapse from cold in the next few days. Water-soluble medicines froze, and plasma and morphine could be administered only when artificially warmed. Under these circumstances neither Colonel Homer Litzenberg, the regiment's commanding officer, nor General Smith, commander of the division, was in any hurry to push on to Hagaruri. Smith was growing more and more concerned about the isolated position of his troops, particularly of his wide-open left flank. He wished to improve and secure his supply line through the pass, and most of all wanted to concentrate the division in the Hagaruri area before any further advance toward the Yalu.

When the 7th Marines did enter Hagaruri on November 14, it found the town burned out from earlier bombings. The few natives who remained said that the 3000 Chinese soldiers who had occupied Hagaruri had left three days before, moving out to the north and west. That night the temperature dropped to 15° below zero and snow covered the roads, making it imperative to have an airstrip near Hagaruri to supplement supply by road and to ensure rapid evacuation of the sick and wounded. Work on an airstrip began November 19. Engineers improved the road through the pass, making it passable for trucks.

Meanwhile the 7th Marine Regiment took up a perimeter defense around Hagaruri, and General Smith began his moves to concentrate his division. A battalion of Lieutenant Colonel Murray's 5th Marines arrived at Koturi on November 16, as the 7th Marines assumed responsibility for guarding the supply line back to Hamhung. Colonel Puller's 1st Marine Regiment was still in the vicinity of Hamhung, covering the road west of that city and helping guard the division rear area from guerrillas.

There is little question that General Smith deliberately dragged his feet in complying with X Corps orders to move on to the north from Hagaruri. An entry in his log dated November 23, 1950, reads in part as follows:

> In accordance with Corps orders the 7th [Regiment] is moving to a blocking position at Yudamni. The regiment has been slowed down by enemy roadblocks and snowdrifts. From the time we started the advance north I have been concerned about my exposed left flank. The Corps has not shared this concern. To reach Yudamni it is necessary to go about 15 miles from Hagaruri over a high mountain pass. In accordance with Corps orders I had to push the 5th Marines up the east side of the reservoir en route to the Manchurian border. I did not want to push Murray too far or get Litzenberg out on a limb at Yudamni until I could close up Puller in rear of them. I therefore did not press Murray to advance rapidly and I directed Litzenberg to occupy for the time being a suitable blocking position west of Hagaruri and not over the mountain pass. I hoped there might be some change in the orders on the conservative side. This change did not materialize and I had to direct Litzenberg to go on to Yudamni.

The sound tactical judgment that General Smith displayed during this period, as he did consistently throughout the war, was to prove the salvation of the 1st Marine Division in the weeks to follow.

Reactions to Chinese Entry

When General MacArthur learned of the halt of the Eighth Army, he had General Hickey call General Walker for an explanation. In a letter to MacArthur on November 6 Walker gave a spirited defense of his action. After reviewing conditions prevailing after the capture of Pyongyang, he wrote, in part:

> An ambush and surprise attack by fresh, well-organized and well-trained units, some of which were Chinese Communist Forces, began a sequence of events leading to complete collapse and distintegration of ROK II Corps of three divisions. Contributing factors were intense, psychological fear of Chinese

intervention and previous complacency and over-confidence in all ROK ranks. . . . The collapse [of ROK II Corps] on the east flank together with heavy attack on the 1st ROK Division and 8th Cavalry RCT on the east flank of the I U.S. Corps seriously threatened the only road supplying the I Corps and dictated temporary withdrawal of exposed columns of 24th Infantry Division on the west, a regrouping of forces, an active defense, a build-up of supplies pending resumption of offensive and advance to the border. . . .

There has never been and there is now no intention for this Army to take up or remain on a passive perimeter or any other type of defense. Every effort is being made to retain an adequate bridgehead to facilitate the resumption of the attack as soon as conditions permit. All units continue to execute local attacks to restore or improve lines. Plans have been prepared for resumption of the offensive employing all forces available to the Army to meet the new factor of organized Chinese Communist forces. These plans will be put into action at the earliest possible moment and are dependent only upon the security of the right flank, the marshalling of the attack troops and the restoration of vital supplies. In this connection there now exists in the forward areas only one day of fire. Opening of port of Chinampo and extension of railroad to Pyongyang is essential to movement of supplies and troops.

In the face of such a forthright defense MacArthur did not further press his challenge of the doughty Eighth Army commander.

Logistical and Intelligence Problems

During the period of optimism in October following the Wake Island conference there had been serious talk in Washington of cutting back on supplies and replacements intended for the Far East Command. Many of the measures that had been taken to support the Korean war had not been specifically authorized by Congress, and Secretary of the Army Pace was concerned that the Army had had to obligate funds and spend some money that was not yet appropriated. He directed a careful review of Army programs that might be curtailed in the event of an early end to the fighting. Millions of dollars had been wasted in the Pacific theater at the end of World War II, because great quantities of equipment and supplies had to be abandoned without adequate storage facilities. The Army wished to minimize such losses this time, in addition to cutting the cost of bringing back excess men and equipment from the Far East.

The JCS were also interested in shifting two divisions to Europe, if possible, to meet our NATO commitments there. Canada, Britain, France, Greece, and other countries had offered to send brigades or smaller units to participate in the United Nations effort in Korea. These would all require United States assistance and logistical support. General Bolté, Army G-3, recommended, and I agreed, that some of these contributions could safely be reduced, and the JCS concurred. However, in order better to gauge the actual situation in the field, I sent Bolté to the Far East Command on October 31, 1950. He conferred with Mac-Arthur, who earlier had agreed generally with the cutback program. The next day he flew to Korea and talked with General Walker, all corps commanders and some division commanders. This was just at the time that the Chinese began their intervention. Bolté at once cabled Washington, recommending that full support of the Far East Command be continued.

At the same time Robert A. Lovett, Deputy Secretary of Defense, disturbed by reports of Chinese actions, suggested that the JCS reconsider plans intended to reduce contributions of fighting units from other of the United Nations. I concurred in these recommendations from Lovett and Bolté, and on November 6 the JCS took steps to stop all plans for retrenchment.

Confusing and conflicting intelligence reports about Chinese Communist capabilities and intentions were still being received by the JCS. On November 3 the Chiefs requested General Mac-Arthur to furnish his estimation of the Korean situation "in light of what appears to be overt intervention by Chinese Communist units."

MacArthur replied that it was impossible to appraise the "actualities" of Chinese intervention. He suggested that the Chinese might be following one or more of four possible courses of action: open intervention in full force, covert intervention concealed for diplomatic reasons, use of "volunteers" to gain a foothold in Korea, and entry on the assumption of encountering only ROK forces that could easily be defeated. As to the first course, he said that "while it is a distinct possibility, and many foreign experts predict such action, there are many fundamental logical reasons against it and sufficient evidence has not yet come to hand to warrant its immediate acceptance." Finally, he advised the JCS, "I recommend against hasty conclusions which might be premature and believe that final appraisement should await a more complete accumulation of military facts."

The calm and measured tone of this reply gave no hint of impending emergency. This is difficult to understand in view of General Almond's personal report on October 30 definitely identifying the CCF 124th Division in the area of the Changjin Reservoir and the confirmation on October 25 from General Paik of the presence of Chinese troops north of the Chongchon River on the front of the Eighth Army.

Actually, Chinese troops had been crossing into North Korea via the Yalu bridges in great numbers, and by November 5 General Willoughby, MacArthur's G-2, warned that the CCF had the capacity to launch a major counteroffensive. Finally alarmed, General MacArthur ordered his air force to go all out to blast away the Korean ends of these bridges and to destroy "every means of communication and every installation, factory, city and village" south of the Yalu, save only Rashin on the Russian border, the Suiho dam, and other hydroelectric plants. Information that Far East Command B-29's were to be employed to attack the bridges over the Yalu between Antung and Sinuiju was disclosed to the Army staff in Washington during a routine daily telecon on November 6. However, General Stratemeyer, MacArthur's air commander, apparently feeling that this directive was of exceptional interest, radioed directly to Air Force Headquarters in Washington the gist of his instructions from MacArthur. This information was promptly passed to Deputy Secretary Lovett.

Lovett, doubting that the chances of destroying these bridges warranted the risk of hitting the Manchurian city of Antung, at once informed Secretary of State Acheson, who called in Dean Rusk, then Assistant Secretary of State for Far Eastern Affairs. Rusk reminded Acheson that our government had promised the British that we would take no action that might involve attacks on Manchuria without first consulting them. The United States was then pressing the U.N. Security Council for a resolution calling on the Chinese to cease their intervention in Korea. Rusk felt that this resolution, which was important for continued United Nations support of any future action by United Nations forces in Korea against the Chinese Communist forces, would be endangered by any accidental bombing of Manchuria. He feared also the possibility of China's invoking the mutual defense treaty with the Soviet Union. Acheson and Lovett concluded that the attack should be held up pending clarification of the situation in Korea.

General Marshall, the Secretary of Defense, concurred in their judgment. Lovett then directed Finletter, the Secretary of the Air Force, to inform the JCS that the bombing should be postponed pending direct approval of the President. Acheson called President Truman in Independence, where the President had gone to vote in the mid-term elections. After hearing Acheson's report the President said that he would approve the bombing only if there were an immediate and serious threat to the security of the United Nations Command.

Considering that MacArthur only two days before had cautioned against "hasty conclusions which might be premature" and had seemingly discounted JCS fears of a serious Chinese threat, his sudden alarm and the precipitous order for bombing of the Yalu bridges had a touch of panic, which disturbed Washington military and civilian authorities alike. The JCS, in accordance with the President's decision, directed General MacArthur to suspend any bombing of the Yalu bridges. We told him that the matter was being considered at the government level and that one factor was the United States' commitment not to take any action affecting Manchuria without consulting the British. He was requested to furnish at once his current estimate of the situation and his reasons for ordering the bombing of the bridges. Meanwhile all bombing within 5 miles of the Manchurian border was to be suspended.

In his reply MacArthur admitted for the first time that the situation was serious, and protested — as he was to do in the future when any limitation was placed on his freedom of action — that the halting of the bombing would be "paid for dearly in American and other United Nations blood." In an extraordinary request that, in effect, asked the President to share with him the responsibility for an action in the field, he requested that the order be referred to the President for reconsideration: "I believe your instructions may well result in a calamity of major proportion for which I cannot accept the responsibility without his [the President's] personal and direct understanding of the situation."

Surprised at the sudden sense of urgency revealed in this message, General Bradley telephoned directly to the President and read the dispatch to him. Though still concerned over the possible international consequences of an error in bombing, President Truman had little alternative under the conditions as newly painted by General MacArthur. He told Bradley to authorize MacArthur to go ahead with his plans.

The JCS message reflected the President's concern and that of the State and Defense Departments:

> The situation depicted in your message [of Nov. 6] is considerably changed from that reported in last sentence your message [Nov. 4] which was our last report from you. We agree that the destruction of the Yalu bridges would contribute materially to the security of the forces under your command unless this action resulted in increased Chinese Communist effort and even Soviet contribution in response to what they might well construe as an attack on Manchuria. Such a result would not only endanger your forces but would enlarge the area of conflict and U.S. involvement to a most dangerous degree.
>
> However . . . you are authorized to go ahead with your planned bombing in Korea near the frontier including targets at Sinuiju and Korean end of Yalu bridges provided you still find such action essential to safety of your forces. The above does not authorize the bombing of any dams or power plants on the Yalu River.

Because of necessity of maintaining optimum position with United Nations policy and directives and because it is vital in the national interests of the U.S. to localize the fighting in Korea, it is important that extreme care be taken to avoid violation of Manchurian territory and air-space and to report promptly hostile action from Manchuria.

It is essential to be kept informed of important changes in situation as they occur and that your estimate as requested in our . . . [message of Nov. 6] be submitted as soon as possible.

MacArthur replied at once with his estimate, which confirmed that the Chinese threat was real and growing and that it could force a withdrawal of United Nations forces if permitted to increase in strength. Yet he announced his intention of renewing the Eighth Army's attack, perhaps within ten days, stating that only by such a "reconnaissance in force" could the enemy's strength be determined. Meanwhile intelligence agencies in Washington, pooling information from all sources, estimated that 30,000 to 40,000 Chinese were already in Korea and that as many as 350,000 enemy troops could be transferred and supported there within a month or two.[*]

[*] It was during this period, according to Martin Lichterman on p. 602 of his study, *To the Yalu and Back,* that:

Secretary Marshall and the Joint Chiefs of Staff asked Secretary Acheson to go to the President and recommend an order to CINCFE to halt his advance and consolidate his positions, but said that the military themselves would not make any recommendations. Acheson pointed out that he had discussed the matter with President Truman, but that he could not advise the President on military matters when the military leaders themselves were not ready to advise. Thus, in the end, nothing was done and the drama in Korea hastened to its tragic denouement.

This statement was supported by Lichterman by reference to a letter from Acheson to him, dated Jan. 30, 1957; an interview with Acheson, March 27, 1957; and an interview with Dean Rusk, March 26, 1957.

This reported action is so out-of-character as to General Marshall, to say nothing of the members of the JCS, that I checked it with Dean Acheson on April 22, 1969. I showed Acheson the entire page 602 of Lichterman's study and called his attention to the above quote. Acheson recalled the discussions with Marshall and the JCS, then read aloud his carbon copy of the Jan. 30, 1957 letter to Lichterman, which contained no such statement as that attributed to him by Lichterman. Mr. Acheson could not recall his ever making any such statement. He concluded emphatically, "That just isn't so."

I am positive that no such request was made to Secretary Acheson by Secretary Marshall or the JCS at any meeting attended by me.

Starting November 8, the Far East Air Force bombed all the main Yalu bridges from Sinuiju to Hyseanjin. Under the restrictions imposed from Washington the bombing was relatively ineffective yet unusually hazardous for our fliers. To avoid flying over Manchuria or having misses land there, bombing runs had to be made at right angles to the bridges while enemy antiaircraft safely emplaced in Manchuria could fire on our bombers without fear of any counter fire. Russian-built MIG-15's, presumably flown by Chinese pilots, likewise attacked our planes, at first only during the bomb runs, but by mid-November large groups of enemy jets, based in Manchuria, were intercepting the bombers well inside Korea. When hard-pressed by our fighters, the MIG's would break off and seek refuge in Manchuria without danger of pursuit beyond the border. General MacArthur protested this situation and suggested to the JCS that our airmen be allowed to pursue enemy attackers a specified distance of 6 to 8 miles into Manchuria.

We agreed that this should be done, as did Secretary Marshall, who, in testimony during the MacArthur Hearings, said Secretary Acheson and President Truman likewise concurred. However, our political leaders felt that we should not unilaterally authorize "hot pursuit" over Manchuria. To do so without consulting other countries supplying troops to the Commander in Chief of the U.N. Command under the original United Nations resolutions, which had not encompassed direct confrontation with China, might well cause a rift between the United States and our United Nations allies. Efforts of the State Department to secure from the allies an agreement to such pursuit proved futile. As a result, our fliers were never authorized to pursue the enemy over Manchuria.

Throughout November the Far East Command bombers, joined by U.S. Navy carrier-based planes, made almost daily attacks on the bridges. They succeeded, at great cost, in cutting four of the several international bridges and damaging most of the others. However, by the end of the month many stretches of the Yalu were frozen, and the Chinese employed pontoon bridges where needed. Despite every effort to avoid it, some bombs landed in Manchuria, furnishing the Communists with propaganda for both internal and external use. The campaign to destroy the bridges was suspended on December 5.

General MacArthur's Mission Re-examined

The JCS instructions to General MacArthur dated September 27, which were to guide his actions after crossing the 38th Parallel, had defined his basic objective as "the destruction of the North Korean armed forces." In accordance with the decision of the National Security Council MacArthur was authorized to conduct military operations "provided that at the time of such operations there has been no entry into North Korea by major Soviet or Chinese Communist Forces, no announcement of intended entry, nor a threat to counter our operations militarily in North Korea." Since major Chinese forces had been reported by both the Eighth Army and X Corps, we advised MacArthur that his mission might have to be re-examined.

MacArthur realized at once that such reconsideration by Washington might lead to the abandonment of his drive to the Yalu, reversion to a defensive posture, and further action limited to a consolidation of the areas occupied since Inchon. These possibilities were loathsome to him. He protested vigorously to the Chiefs, pointing out that on October 10 we had told him that in the event of open or covert intervention of major Chinese Communist units without prior announcement he was to continue the action as long as in his judgment the forces available to him had a reasonable chance of success. He reiterated his faith in the effectiveness of air interdiction to prevent Chinese reinforcements from crossing the Yalu in time to prevent him from destroying those Chinese units already in North Korea, and stated his intention to launch an attack about November 15 to destroy those forces and to keep going until his troops reached the border.

As to the JCS comment that our government had a commitment to consult with the British in regard to any new course of action that might involve China, MacArthur, possibly referring to a then-current news report that British Foreign Minister Ernest Bevin favored a buffer zone south of the Yalu, departed in his reply from the normal role of an American military commander. He caustically commented on what he termed "the widely reported British desire to appease the Chinese Communists by giving them a strip of Northern Korea" and cited the Munich pact of 1938 as a precedent of their current attitude. "To give up any portion of North Korea to the aggression of the Chinese Communists would be the greatest defeat of the free world in recent times. Indeed to yield to so immoral a proposition would bankrupt our leadership and influence in Asia and render untenable our position both politically and militarily." He suggested that the United States press the United Nations for a resolution condemning the Chinese Communists and calling on them to withdraw from North Korea on pain of military sanctions by the United Nations if they failed to do so. MacArthur ended his note of protest by assuring the JCS that complete victory could be achieved if "our determination and indomitable will do not desert us." Perhaps he was heartened in this belief by the reports of the Chinese withdrawals on the front of the Eighth Army after the first week of November.

MacArthur's protest that his mission should not be changed underscored the urgent necessity for an authoritative review of United States policy in the light of the Chinese intervention. President Truman directed the National Security Council to meet on November 9 for this purpose.

As was usually the case, the JCS was called on for an analysis of the situation and its recommendations. These were submitted to Secretary Marshall for consideration by the National Security Council. After analyzing various considerations that might influence the Chinese to intervene in Korea, the Chiefs stated that, in our judgment, the continued involvement of the United States in Korea would be in the interest of Russia and world Communism through its imposition of a heavy drain on our military and economic strength. We still considered Korea strategically unimportant in the context of a possible global war, in which Russia, not China, would be the chief antagonist. We doubted whether China would attempt to drive the United Nations forces from all of Korea without material assistance from Soviet naval and air power. In such event it would be clear that World War III was under way and the United States (and the United Nations) should withdraw from Korea as quickly as possible.

If the Chinese intervened in full strength but without military assistance from the Soviets, three courses of action were open: to continue the action as planned; to set up a defensive position short of the North Korean northern border; or to withdraw from Korea. To succeed with the first course might require additional United Nations forces, even if no more Chinese troops entered. Without committing ourselves definitely, the Chiefs indicated that the second course was perfectly feasible and perhaps expedient in the face of the military and political uncertainties raised by the Chinese entry. Voluntary withdrawal from the Korean peninsula was rejected.

The JCS recommended that every effort be made to settle the problem of Chinese intervention by political means. As to MacArthur's assigned mission, we were willing to await clarification of the Chinese Communist forces' military objectives before interfering in his plan to drive to the Yalu. And with respect to the United States' overall military posture, we recommended that plans and preparations be made on the basis that the risk of global war had been substantially increased by the Chinese action in Korea.

General Bradley represented the JCS at the National Security Council meeting, which was attended by the Secretaries of State and Defense, General Bedell Smith, then head of the Central Intelligence Agency, and other members of the council. President Truman was not present.*

Bradley outlined the possible intentions of the Chinese Communists as analyzed by the JCS. He ventured a personal opinion that the United Nations forces could hold in the general area of their existing positions, but he could not say what Chinese pressure they would be able to stand without being forced to bomb the Chinese bases in Manchuria. However, the JCS had agreed

---

* The only available statement of what transpired at this meeting is that contained in President Truman's *Memoirs*, Vol. II, pp. 378–380, which is paraphrased in Colonel Schnabel's official U.S. Army History, "Policy and Direction — The First Year," still in manuscript form, Chap. XIII, pp. 47–49.

that any decision to attack Chinese territory should be a United Nations decision, since under current United Nations resolutions, which were the basis for our operations in Korea, such an attack was forbidden. Bradley said that he doubted that bombing of the Yalu bridges would stop the Chinese from entering Korea in strength. General Smith interpolated that the Yalu would soon be frozen over and thus passable almost anywhere.

Secretary Marshall pointed out that the X Corps was widely dispersed and had little depth, to which Bradley replied that this was accounted for by the fact that MacArthur had been directed to occupy all of Korea.

Secretary Acheson inquired whether there was any line that was better from a military point of view than the current positions. Bradley said that the farther back it was, the easier it would be to support logistically, but that any rearward movement would depress the Koreans' morale and lessen their will to fight.

Acheson then speculated on the possibility of persuading the Chinese to agree on a 20-mile-wide demilitarized zone, 10 miles on each side of the Yalu, to meet their concern with the electrical output of the Yalu dams, which supplied some of their power to Manchuria, and to reassure them that the border would not be violated. He went on to say that the trouble with any such proposal was that the Chinese then would insist on the withdrawal of all foreign troops, which would abandon Korea to the Communists.

After considering the views of all those present, the Council recommended to the President certain interim measures. It felt that the overt actions of the Chinese thus far were insufficient basis for determining a firm strategy and that intensive efforts should be made to ascertain the real intentions of the Communists. Meanwhile, the current instructions to General MacArthur should remain unchanged. Political action should be started in the United Nations to seek support of an overwhelming majority of members in demanding the prompt withdrawal of Chinese forces from Korea. Political channels should be used also to explore Chinese intentions and to seek some political-economic basis for stabilizing peacefully the Manchurian and North Korean frontier problems of electric power, water rights, and allied matters. And, in agreement with the JCS, the National Security Council recommended that the United States develop its overall plans and policies on the basis that the risk of global war had been increased by the Chinese intervention.

So far as I know, the President took no formal action on these recommendations, though all were put into effect. In retrospect, the most important outcome of this meeting was that it permitted General MacArthur to go ahead with his plans for an attack, or reconnaissance in force, to the Yalu, a move that was destined to lead to one of the few military defeats in United States history.

IX

THE CHINESE COUNTEROFFENSIVE

The Eighth Army and X Corps Prepare to Renew the Attack

As THE EIGHTH ARMY prepared to renew its November offensive, General Walker's chief concern was a shortage of ammunition and other supplies in the forward areas. But by mid-November the port of Chinampo north of Inchon was operating well, and road and rail lines in the Army's rear had been improved, making possible an increased forward flow of supplies, supplemented by cargo airlift. By November 20 the critical logistics problem in the Eighth Army area had been solved. Moreover, the Army had been strengthened by bringing up Major General Coulter's U.S. IX Corps and placing it between the U.S. I Corps and the ROK II Corps. General Walker set November 24 for the resumption of the attack to the Yalu.

General Almond's X Corps on the east coast was better off logistically than the Eighth Army, being supplied through the near-by ports of Wonsan, Hungnam, and Iwon; LST's were directly supplying the ROK I Corps over the many beaches in its zone. However, as the 7th Infantry Division and the 1st Marine Division advanced inland, their supply lines stretched out 100 or more miles over steep mountain roads. Furthermore, the regiments of these divisions were widely dispersed, with little or no direct connection, over a front of 85 miles by air from Hyesanjin on the Yalu to Yudamni, west of the Changjin Reservoir.

The X Corps had been advancing to the north independently of the Eighth Army, intent on its mission of occupying all of North Korea east of the Taebaek range. The stunning blow dealt the Eighth Army by the Chinese in late October brought to General Almond and to General Wright's Joint Staff Plans and Operations Group at General Headquarters a realization of the relative isolation of the corps from the Eighth Army. The southernmost offensive element of the corps, the 7th Marine Regiment at Yudamni, was almost 90 miles, as a crow flies, northeast of the bulk of the Eighth Army near Kunuri. There was no unit of the Eighth Army directly opposite the X Corps north of an east-west line through Hamhung. The entire area north of such a line, from the X Corps boundary to the Yellow Sea, was open to the enemy. The U.S. 3d Infantry Division, responsible for guarding the corps area south of this line, manned defensive roadblocks on the trails crossing the Taebaek Mountains. But 50 miles by rough roads separated these posts from the easternmost blocking positions of the Eighth Army. On only one occasion in November had a patrol from the Eighth Army and the X Corps met in the intervening no-man's land. It had taken the patrol, moving on footpaths and periodically harassed by NK guerrillas, a full five days to reach an outpost on the corps' west boundary. Thus, what was going on in the widening gap between the two forces was unknown.

MacArthur seemed undisturbed by this situation, apparently discounting the possibility of a massive Chinese attack and counting on the rugged barrier of the Taebaek Mountains to protect the west flank of the X Corps. Later, during the congressional hearings, he said in answer to a question by Senator Russell:

> The disposition of the forces was made upon the basis of the enemy that existed, and the orders that I had to defeat them.
>
> That enemy was the North Korean group, and our forces had practically destroyed them. We would have completely destroyed them, if the Chinese had not intervened.
>
> We were limited, as I say, by the two conditions: the size of the force I had—and the mission that was given me.
>
> My mission was to clear out all North Korea, to unify it and to liberalize it.*

* As indicated in Chapter VII, page 147 no military mission to unify Korea was ever assigned to General MacArthur. In later testimony at the MacArthur Hearings (pp. 362 and 2085) General Marshall and Secretary Acheson confirmed this.

The number of troops I had was limited, and those conditions indicated the disposition of the troops I had.

As a matter of fact, the disposition of these troops, in my opinion, could not have been improved upon, had I known the Chinese were going to attack.

The difficulty that arose was not the disposition of the troops, but the overwhelming number of the enemy forces, and the extraordinary limitations that were placed upon me in the use of my air.

The JCS were somewhat disturbed by the exposed position of the X Corps, but we took no direct action to change the situation, as General Bradley testified in answer to a question during the MacArthur Hearings:

Well, Senator, we were a little bit worried, looking at the map from here, as to those dispositions, and we asked General MacArthur if he needed any additional or changed directives and he said he did not. We did not send him any message as to our worries about the disposition because you cannot fight a battle and conduct a battle from 7,000 miles away, which we were. You must let your field commander fight that battle.

He might have added that just as the JCS could not conduct the battle from 7000 miles away, neither could General MacArthur from a distance of 700 miles.

The attitude of the Joint Chiefs toward General MacArthur at that time was well illustrated as General Bradley continued:

Gen. MacArthur is a man of long distinguished service, and experience, and I think it would be quite improper to try to tell him from here how exactly to dispose his divisions, and so we did not do so.

Bradley did say that if he had been the commander he would have made different dispositions. Yet, when Secretary Marshall, during the National Security Council meeting on November 9, questioned the deployment of the X Corps, which he felt was in some danger because of its great dispersion and lack of depth,

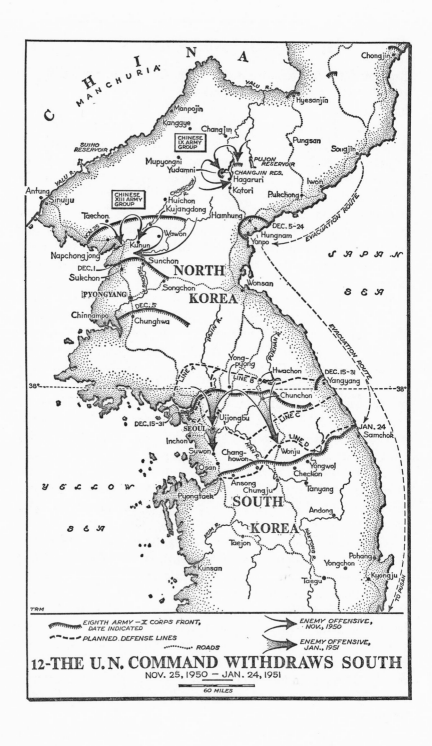

12-THE U. N. COMMAND WITHDRAWS SOUTH
NOV. 25, 1950 — JAN. 24, 1951

EIGHTH ARMY — X CORPS FRONT, DATE INDICATED

PLANNED DEFENSE LINES

ROADS

ENEMY OFFENSIVE, NOV., 1950

ENEMY OFFENSIVE, JAN., 1951

60 MILES

Bradley defended the disposition as having been required by the JCS directive to MacArthur to occupy all of North Korea and to hold elections.

Wright's planning group was less inhibited than the JCS in suggesting changes. They were concerned not only with the position of the X Corps but with its direction of attack and objectives. The Eighth Army was to make the main effort in the renewed attack. Wright's group could not see how the corps, if it continued its attack to the north, east of the Taebaeks, could give any direct assistance to the Eighth Army. Furthermore, its northerly movement would increase the exposure of its west flank. This had been pointed out to General Almond by General Smith, commander of the 1st Marine Division, to no avail.

The planning group believed that the only way for the X Corps to assist Walker was to attack to the northwest, threatening the flank and rear of any Chinese forces that might try to turn the east flank of the Eighth Army via the gap between the two major forces. First, the X Corps would have to clear the reservoir area and seize the town of Changjin, north thereof, before it could safely drive northwest with two divisions. Wright said its objective should be to cut the Chinese Manpojin-Kanggye-Mupyongni main supply route (Map 12). General Hickey, Acting Chief of Staff in the Far East Command, approved this staff study, and on November 15 MacArthur directed Almond to develop an alternative plan for reorienting his attack to the west after reaching the vicinity of Changjin. This alternative plan would be executed on orders from MacArthur.

Meanwhile, General Willoughby, MacArthur's Intelligence officer, continued to report a crucial build-up of forces in the Changjin-Pujon reservoir area northwest of Hungnam. In a telecon with Washington on November 17 he indicated the vulnerability of the west flank of the X Corps and of the corps' main supply route from Hungnam to the Changjin Reservoir. Almost 10,000 enemy troops had been located west of this route, from Hungnam to Hagaruri, and the enemy was reported as having the equivalent of four divisions in the reservoir area. Presumably, this information was passed on to MacArthur and to the X Corps by Willoughby.

In accordance with MacArthur's instructions of November 15, Almond directed the preparation of plans for an attack to the northwest by the 1st Marine Division along the Hagaruri-Mupyongni axis, with the 7th Infantry Division providing protection to the Marines' right flank by assigning a regimental combat team to seize Changjin (Map 12). He also directed that the Hamhung-Hagaruri road be developed as a main supply road for the corps. The plan was taken to Tokyo by a staff officer, discussed with the staff, and approved by MacArthur with only one modification, which moved the new boundary between the X Corps and the Eighth Army farther west and south. Almond was to designate his own D Day. He set the date as 8:00 A.M., November 27.

As long as the operations of the X Corps had been limited to the area east of the main ridge line of the Taebaek range, and the enemy consisted only of the remnants of the defeated North Korean army, the corps had sufficient wherewithal to accomplish its mission of clearing all of North Korea within its zone. But with this new directive to move to the northwest across the Taebaeks to assist the Eighth Army, in the face of strong Chinese Communist forces and with no diminution of its original tasks, the X Corps was given a mission impossible of accomplishment.

The one-page corps Operations Order No. 7, dated November 25, 1950, would have required a considerable shifting of troops to line them up in their new zones of action. It required the 1st Marine Division and the 7th Infantry Division to attack initially in different directions, the Marines to the northwest and the 7th Division to the north and then northwest, with the mission of cutting the Manpojin-Kanggye-Mupyongni main supply route of the CCF and destroying enemy forces between the Taebaeks and the Yalu 70 air miles away. Studying this order and its Intelligence G-2 annex, which indicated the presence of elements of four CCF divisions in the corps' zone of action, one is forced to wonder whether the men who prepared and approved it really believed that it was susceptible of successful implementation with the forces available.

Certainly Smith, commanding the Marines, had doubts about

the outcome, as was indicated in his log written at the time. Commenting on his mission, he concluded with the most perceptive understatement of the war: "Our line of communications will be very tenuous."

An Intuitive Estimate

After the Chinese withdrawal following their initial success against the Eighth Army in late October General MacArthur, at the request of the JCS, had given this view of the Chinese intervention:

> Unquestionably . . . organized units of the CCF have been and are being used against UN forces; that while it is impossible to determine accurately the precise strength, it is enough to have taken the initiative in the west and to have slowed appreciably our offensive in the east. The pattern seems established that such forces will be used and increased at will, probably without a formal declaration of hostilities. If this enemy build-up continues, it can easily reach a point preventing our resumption of the offensive and even force a retrograde movement.

Yet, two days later, he reported optimistically to the Joint Chiefs:

> I believe that with my air power, now unrestricted so far as Korea is concerned except as to hydroelectric installations, I can deny reinforcements coming across the Yalu in sufficient strength to prevent the destruction of those forces now arrayed against me in North Korea.

MacArthur's confidence in air power had been built largely on his experience in the Pacific during World War II, where naval and land-based aviation wrecked Japanese fixed installations in the brilliant island-hopping campaign from the South Pacific to Tokyo and destroyed their naval forces at sea. But the installations and the troops that garrisoned them were relatively immobile, and the naval forces could not long be concealed at sea. This was not true of the highly mobile, flexible armies of the Chinese, which could live off the land and otherwise sustain themselves with supplies caried on A-frames on the backs of men, and which could march great distances overnight and then disappear in daylight in the woods and ravines of North Korea. MacArthur's overreliance on air power, coupled with his lack of personal knowledge of the actual situation on the ground — a knowledge that could have been gained only from frequent direct contact with commanders and troops in the field — led him to a wholly unrealistic appraisal of the projected operation of the Eighth Army and the X Corps.

In his mind's eye he pictured a giant pincer movement between the X Corps and the Eighth Army that would crush the enemy forces and end the war. In a communiqué from General Headquarters a few hours before the Eighth Army jumped off on November 24 the general announced:

> The United Nations massive compression envelopment in North Korea against the new Red Armies operating there is now approaching its decisive effort. The isolating component of the pincer, our air forces of all types, have for the past three weeks, in a sustained attack of model coordination and effectiveness, successfully interdicted enemy lines of support from the North so that further reinforcement therefrom has been sharply curtailed and essential supplies markedly limited. The eastern sector of the pincer, with noteworthy and effective naval support, has steadily advanced in a brilliant tactical movement and has now reached a commanding enveloping position, cutting in two the northern reaches of the enemy's geographical potential. This morning the western sector of the pincers moves forward in general assault in an effort to complete the compression and close the vise. If successful, this should for all practical purposes end the war, restore peace and security to Korea, enable the prompt withdrawal of United Nations Military Forces.

Then later the same day, in a special communiqué to the United Nations, he said:

> The giant UN pincer moved according to schedule today. The air forces, in full strength, completely interdicted the rear areas and an air reconnaissance behind the enemy line, and

along the entire length of the Yalu River border, showed little sign of hostile military activity. The left wing of the envelopment advanced against stubborn and failing resistance. The right wing, gallantly supported by naval air and surface action, continued to exploit its commanding position.

Our losses were extraordinarily light. The logistic situation is fully geared to sustain offensive operations. The justice of our course and the promise of early completion of our mission is reflected in the morale of troops and commanders alike.

If David Reese was correct in attributing General MacArthur's success at Inchon to imagination and intuition rather than to military logic and science, the failure of the North Korean campaign against the Chinese Communist forces could equally be attributed to imagination and intuition, which took the place of first-hand, up-to-date knowledge of the military situation, a tough, realistic appraisal of Chinese Communist capabilities, and a sound evaluation of air power under conditions existing in Korea.

The Actual Situation

The actual situation of the Chinese forces in North Korea was in sharp contrast to the bright picture conjured up by General MacArthur. Unknown to MacArthur four CCF armies had crossed from Manchuria into North Korea between October 14 and October 20, two by way of Antung-Sinuiju, near the mouth of the Yalu, and two farther north via Manpojin.

All were part of Lin Piao's Fourth Field Army which, in the early part of the Communist insurrection against Chiang Kai-shek, had cut the Nationalist line of communications to Manchuria and had overrun that vast province. As Chiang's forces had withdrawn to south China, the Fourth Field Army had fought its way from Manchuria to Hainan Island, off China's south coast, where it had made a successful amphibious landing in the spring of 1950. By that autumn it was back in Manchuria, battle-hardened and acclimated to north Asia's bitter weather. And it was ably led by Communist China's most experienced soldiers. Lin Piao and his subordinate commanders had been almost continually in the field for three years and had acquired vast experience in the techniques of the camouflage, guerrilla warfare, night attacks, and enveloping maneuver, best suited to their troops, organization, and equipment.

Thus, as the United Nations forces prepared to renew the attack in late November, the Eighth Army of four United States divisions, three ROK divisions, and a British and a Turkish brigade was actually confronted by eighteen divisions of the CCF XIII Army Group. Similarly, the X Corps of three United States divisions and two ROK divisions was taking on twelve divisions of the CCF IX Army Group. The combined CCF armies comprised almost 300,000 fighting infantrymen supported by cavalry, artillery, and service units, a far stronger force than the United Nations Command.

Besides the Chinese forces twelve divisions of the NK Army, totalling 65,800 men, were now ready to re-enter the fighting. After the rout of the NK Army north of Pyongyang in October 1950 it had split into two groups; one had moved into the mountains in the Kanggye area, and the other had withdrawn into Manchuria. Both groups had been rehabilitated and re-equipped, obviously by the Chinese. They were to follow the Chinese forces and were to be prepared to exploit any break in the ROK Army front.

The CCF operations in Korea apparently were planned and controlled by a joint CCF-NK army headquarters in Mukden, under the direction of General Peng Teh-huai, the Deputy Commander in Chief of the Chinese Communist Army. A subordinate headquarters, located near Kanggye in North Korea, under Kim Il Sung, the Commander in Chief of the North Korean Army, was nominally in charge of the Communist operations, but there is little doubt that the actual control was exercised by Peng Teh-huai.

Attack and Counterattack

As the Eighth Army moved up to its jump-off positions for the November 24 attack, the enemy to its front had broken direct contact and seemed to be withdrawing to positions farther north. General MacArthur, suspicious of this lack of contact on the Eighth Army front and now somewhat worried about the gap between Walker's and Almond's commands, directed General Stratemeyer's Far East Air Force to patrol the gap with great care. This was done with twelve to sixteen sorties in daylight and a half-dozen sorties at night, but no enemy forces were detected in this broken terrain.

In telecons with the Army staff in Washington on November 24 and 25 General Willoughby, in one of his more optimistic reports — which frequently seemed to alternate with pessimistic estimates — said the Chinese Communists had "embarked on their Korean venture in some cases with only three days' rations" and that constant pressure from United Nations ground forces and aerial bombing had undoubtedly depleted their reserves of ammunition. He indicated that if the Chinese did try to stop the Eighth Army, they would be at a disadvantage. His final estimate prior to the November 24 attack was that the Eighth Army would be opposed by about 83,000 North Koreans and between 40,000 and 80,000 men of the Chinese Communist Forces.

Nonetheless, battle-wise Johnnie Walker prescribed a closely coordinated attack with the U.S. I Corps, the U.S. IX Corps, and the ROK II Corps abreast from west to east. The advance was to be by successive phase lines, the initial objective being the Napchongjong-Taechon-Onjong-Huichon-Kukhwacham-Inchori line, less than a third of the way to the Yalu. Advance from this line was to be on subsequent army orders. The basic elements of this plan had been relayed by General Wright from General Headquarters to X Corps on November 10. In turn, Walker had been informed of X Corps plans by visiting staff officers from General Headquarters on November 24.

The Eighth Army's attack got off to a good start with only light enemy contact for the first two days. Then, as dusk fell on November 25, the Chinese Communists slashed into the allied forces without warning and with overwhelming strength (Map 12). Aiming their major effort against the unstable ROK II Corps and its junction with the IX Corps, the Chinese forces crushed the

Eighth Army's right flank and opened gaps in the IX Corps' front, forcing it back. Units of the ROK II Corps broke and fled in the darkness, apparently terrified at the viciousness of the Chinese attack. Farther west the 25th Division of the I Corps held its ground initially but, threatened with envelopment of its right flank, had to withdraw, as did the other units on its left, to conform to the roll-back of the Army's right.

At noon on November 27 Walker called General Headquarters, reporting the situation, and the next day informed MacArthur that the enemy force opposing him was estimated at 200,000 Chinese and that the IX Corps had withdrawn 11 miles to face the axis of the Chinese attack that was sweeping through the sector of the ROK II Corps.

On the front of the X Corps the CCF troops had waited until that corps' attack, which had started on November 27, and had penetrated to the outskirts of Changjin (Map 12). Then, in one sudden blow on November 28 the CCF IX Army Group cut the main supply route of the X Corps both west and south of Hagaruri, threatening the lifeline of both the 1st Marine Division and the 7th Infantry Division. Bridges were blown at several points. That night a heavy attack was launched against Hagaruri, while farther north the 7th Division was hit, resulting in the isolation of two battalions east of the Changjin Reservoir.

Any doubts of Chinese strength and intentions were thus violently torn aside. On November 28 General MacArthur radioed the JCS:

> The Chinese military forces are committed in North Korea in great and ever-increasing strength. No pretext of minor support under the guise of volunteerism or other subterfuge has the slightest validity. We face an entirely new war. . . .
> It is quite evident that our present strength of force is not sufficient to meet this undeclared war by the Chinese with the inherent advantages that accrue thereby to them. The resulting situation presents an entire new picture which broadens the potentialities to world-embracing considerations beyond the sphere of decision by the Theater Commander. This command

has done everything humanly possible within its capabilities but is now faced with conditions beyond its control and its strength. . . . My strategic plan for the immediate future is to pass from the offensive to the defensive with such local adjustments as may be required by a constantly fluid situation.

Faced with an emergency situation, MacArthur did something that normally he would have decried. He called a "council of war" in Tokyo the night of November 28, summoning Generals Walker and Almond from their commands in Korea at a time they could ill afford to be away. They met MacArthur and Generals Hickey, Wright, Willoughby, and Whitney at the residence of the general in the American Embassy compound. The meeting lasted from 9:50 P.M. on November 28 to 1:30 A.M. on November 29. The discussion covered all aspects of the situation and possible corrective actions. Because at that time the situation of the Eighth Army appeared to be more serious than that of the X Corps, consideration was given to the possibility of the X Corps' aiding the Army. In light of the November 27 attack plan of the X Corps, Almond's views are of interest. Wright had suggested that the 3d Division be sent west across the Taebaek range to join Walker's army and to attack CCF forces on its east flank. Almond strongly objected. He pointed out that the road across the Taebaeks shown on the map did not exist on the ground. Furthermore, the bitter winter weather and the difficulty of supplying the division, combined with the possibility of strong Chinese forces operating in the gap between Walker's and his command, made any such relief expedition extremely hazardous. MacArthur agreed with Almond that the latter's first task was to extricate the Marines and the two battalions of the 7th Division that had been cut off in the Changjin Reservoir area. MacArthur ordered Walker to withdraw as far as necessary to prevent the CCF troops from outflanking his command and told Almond to keep in contact with the forces opposing him but to concentrate his corps in the Hamhung-Hungnam area. He later ordered, then cancelled, an attack by a task force of the 3d Division to link up with the east flank of the Eighth Army.

Almost simultaneously with this conference the National Security Council was meeting in Washington at the call of the President, who on the morning of November 28 had been briefed by Bradley on the adverse turn of events in Korea. As usual, Bradley represented the JCS before the Council. Secretary Marshall declared that neither the United States nor the United Nations should become embroiled in a war with China over Korea and that whatever we did should be within the framework of the United Nations. Bradley supported this position. There was general agreement that it was necessary to take steps at once to strengthen our armed forces. The President said he would send a supplemental budget to the Congress to cover the additional costs.

The JCS, with the approval of the President, accepted MacArthur's estimate of the situation and approved his shifting from the offensive to the defensive. Concerned with the exposed position of the X Corps and the apparent lack of coordination between that Corps and the Eighth Army, the JCS queried MacArthur regarding these points. On November 30 MacArthur replied that the X Corps "geographically threatened" the main supply lines of the Chinese units bearing down on the east flank of the Eighth Army. (This was difficult to understand in view of his orders to the X Corps to concentrate in the Hamhung-Hungnam area, with the Taebaek range intervening). Despite the fact that the Chinese had already cut the main supply route of the X Corps in several places and had isolated some elements of the 7th Division MacArthur discounted the threat posed by the overextended dispositions of the X Corps. In reference to a suggestion that, if possible, a continuous defensive line be established he said that even at the narrow waist of Korea a continuous line would be too long for his reduced forces and that logistical support would be difficult because of the Taebaek range, which would split the front.

Retreat of the IX Corps

Meanwhile, events in the IX Corps sector of the Eighth Army along the Chongchon River north of Kunuri were nearing the crucial stage. As the IX Corps fell back across the Chongchon in late November, the Chinese armies struck hard through the crumpled ROK II Corps in an effort to envelop the east flank of the Eighth Army. The Turkish Brigade attached to the IX Corps had been directed to hold Wawon, east of Kunuri, to cover the withdrawal of the U.S. 2d Division, Major General Lawrence B. Keiser commanding, the easternmost division of the corps which had participated in the battles of the Naktong Perimeter. The brigade commander, Brigadier General Tashin Yasici, knew little English and apparently had difficulty in understanding instructions. This was true at all command levels in the Turkish Brigade. Most oral suggestions from attached American military advisers had to be transmitted through interpreters and were frequently misunderstood. Communications with the 2d Division and IX Corps were not maintained, partly through lack or loss of communications equipment. On two occasions instructions to the Turkish Brigade were not carried out fully. On November 29 General Yasici, after withstanding several Chinese attacks, chose to withdraw to the southwest, without orders, further exposing the east flank of the 2d Division as well as his own. Nonetheless, the stand of the Turkish Brigade at Wawon probably prevented the Chinese from cutting off the 2d Division north of Kunuri.*

South of Kunuri the danger to the 2d Division deepened. During the next few days, as the division fended off blows from both flanks, the Chinese slipped strong forces around to the east and cut the division's escape route south of Kunuri on the road to Sunchon. Efforts made by elements of the British Brigade, which had been in reserve south of Sunchon, to break the Chinese road-

---

* The Turkish Brigade later became a highly effective force. There was never any question of the fighting qualities or the fortitude of the Turkish soldier. During one of my visits to a hospital in Tokyo I was introduced to a Turk whose left arm had been partially paralyzed by a shell fragment during the action at Wawon. This soldier spoke little English and could not comprehend the American surgeon's questions seeking to determine the extent of damage to the nerves in the arm. The surgeon had the man extend his left hand, and the doctor, using a heavy operating needle, pricked successively the fingers of the outstretched hand. The soldier's face was expressionless and he did not wince. Finally, the doctor pricked one of his own fingers and quickly withdrew his hand with an "Ouch." Whereupon the soldier grabbed the needle, rammed it through the palm of his left hand, pulled it through, then gave it back to the surgeon, and in his deep guttural voice said, "Me — Turk!"

block had failed in the face of superior Chinese forces. In an action reminiscent of the 24th Division's ordeal at Taejon the 2d Division en route to Sunchon on November 30 to December 1 had to run the gauntlet of a narrow defile and a pass under murderous enemy fire from the high ground on either side. The road was intermittently blocked with burning trucks, which could only be pushed aside by tanks or bulldozers. Much of the artillery, transport, communications, and engineering equipment had to be abandoned before or during the run through the defile. Little coordinated control could be exercised, and many small units and individuals made their way through on foot as best they could. A check made on December 1 as the 2d Division assembled near Sukchon revealed that in the last few days of November the division had lost almost 5000 officers and men, about one third of its authorized strength. Equipment losses included sixty-four artillery pieces, hundreds of trucks and tractors, almost all of its engineering equipment, and much of its signal equipment. On December 1 General Keiser began moving his depleted division to Chunghwa, south of Pyongyang, while the 1st Cavalry Division spread its thin lines even thinner to cover the right center of a newly forming defensive position of the Eighth Army, the Sukchon-Sunchon-Songchon line, facing northeast.

The X Corps Withdraws to Hungnam

After the November 28 commanders' conference in Tokyo General Almond proceeded at once to concentrate the X Corps in the Hamhung-Hungnam area. His first task was to extricate units of the 1st Marines and the 7th Infantry Divisions that were under attack in the Changjin Reservoir area (Map 12). Since the bulk of General Barr's 7th was well to the north, Almond placed its 1st Battalion of the 32d Regiment and 3d Battalion of the 31st Regiment and supporting artillery, which were isolated east of the reservoir and were being commanded by Lieutenant Colonel Don C. Faith, Jr., under control of General Smith, the Marine division commander, whose command post was at Hagaruri, the center of action. Smith was directed to withdraw his 5th and 7th Marine

Regiments from Yudamni and, in coordination with Barr, to work out some way of rescuing Colonel Faith's command. Then the combined Marine and Army forces were to fight their way down the Hagaruri-Kotori main supply route to Hungnam. The 7th Division (less the 31st Regiment) was to withdraw via the Hyesanjin-Pungsan-Pukchong road. The ROK 3d Division, farthest north of the ROK I Corps, was to concentrate on the coast at Songjin, where General Almond arranged with Admiral Joy to pick up the regiment and sea-lift it to Hungnam. The ROK Capital Division was to withdraw via the coastal road. Supplies in the Wonsan area were to be evacuated, after which that port would be abandoned. The 3d Division would cover the concentration of the X Corps in the Yonpo-Hungnam-Hamhung area.

Generals Barr and Smith agreed that no relief force could break through to Task Force Faith until the 5th and 7th Marines were concentrated at Hagaruri which was being held only by the 3d Battalion, 1st Marine Regiment, and a mixture of Marine and Army service troops. Fearing that Faith might not be able to hold out until the Marines from Yudamni could reach Hagaruri, General Smith had no alternative but to direct him to fight his way back to Hagaruri. The Marines would furnish close air support.

The 5th and 7th Marines and Task Force Faith initiated their moves on December 1. The Marines staged an orderly, well-planned move in a single column. The going was tough; Chinese resistance combined with snow-covered, steeply pitched roads and sub-zero weather to slow their progress. By the afternoon of December 3, the column had reached the top of the pass. The going downhill to Hagaruri was easier. Largely because of excellent air support, the Chinese offered little resistance and the regiments reached Hagaruri intact, with minimum loss of equipment but bringing along some 1500 casualties.

Don Faith's two battalions, weakened by several days of assaults from the 80th CCF Division, had a more harrowing and less successful outcome. Before starting, Colonel Faith had destroyed the howitzers of the 57th Field Artillery Battalion's excess supplies, and all but twenty-two vehicles, just enough to carry the wounded, who then totalled 600. The column moved out in good order at 1:00 P.M., December 1, on the road just east of the Chang-jin Reservoir. It drew fire at once, as expected, but what came next was not expected. Four United States pilots, flying in support of the task force, miscalculated their runs and dropped napalm on the leading troops. Several men burned to death and the two leading companies scattered to avoid the resulting fires.

After some delay Faith had the column moving again, only to be struck repeatedly by harassing Chinese groups, causing delays and increasing casualties. While leading a flanking attack to break through a roadblock Colonel Faith was mortally wounded.

With the loss of its commander and many key subordinate leaders, the task force began to disintegrate, more and more men seeking to avoid the persistent enemy fire along the road by trekking their way south along the reservoir ice. Many of the trucks, jammed with the increasing number of wounded, had flat tires and several were beyond repair. Major Robert E. Jones, who had taken over from Don Faith, was forced to make the grim decision to leave behind, with guards, many of the wounded.

Night had fallen by the time the force reached the village of Hudangni, halfway to Hagaruri. There fire from the village completed the disintegration of the column. An effort to drive the enemy from the village failed. Finally, the truck column made a desperate effort to run the vehicles with the wounded through the village. Chinese fire killed the drivers of the leading trucks and raked the other vehicles and accompanying troops. Everyone who could scattered, most of the men moving toward the reservoir. As the firing finally died down, only the immobile wounded and the dead remained at Hudongni. Among them was Colonel Don Faith, who sat dead of his wounds in the cab of a two-and-a-half-ton truck.

A small task force of Army troops and tanks tried to break through from Hagagaru to Hudongni without success. Fortunately, the Chinese made little or no effort to cut off the men escaping along the ice and did administer aid to the wounded in Hudongni. Of the 2500 troops originally making up Task Force Faith slightly more than 1000 reached Hagaruri. Of this number only 385 were still fit to fight. They were re-equipped from Marine stocks at Hagaruri and, with other Army troops there, were formed into a provisional battalion, attached to the 7th Marine Regiment for the final drive out of Hagaruri to Hungnam. This skillful withdrawal under constant Chinese pressure was completed on December 11.

During the period between October 26, 1950, when the 1st Marine Division landed at Wonsan, and December 11 the division suffered 704 killed in action or dead of wounds, 187 missing, and 3489 wounded in action, for a total of 4380 battle casualties, or approximately double the number for the Inchon-Seoul campaign. In addition there were almost 6000 nonbattle casualties, most of which were from frostbite. Under the circumstances General Smith did extremely well to bring his division out in fighting shape. Not the least of the Marine accomplishments was the evacuation by air of all the wounded, Army and Marine alike, from the hastily built airstrips at Hagaruri and Koturi.

The battle casualties of all United Nations forces in the ill-fated campaign of the X Corps in North Korea totalled approximately 11,500, of which 705 were killed in action and 4779 were missing during the period of heavy fighting, November 27 to December 10 — a heavy toll. The campaign did tie down a considerable number of North Korean forces and crippled a large part of the CCF IX Army Group, which might otherwise have been turned against the Eighth Army with even more dire results.

Repercussions in Washington and Europe

Turning back our account to late November, as reports of the reverses of the Eighth Army along the Chongchon River reached Tokyo, General MacArthur radioed the JCS on November 30 that the Eighth Army would not be able to make a stand in the forseeable future and would have to move to rearward positions by successive stages. He now felt that the CCF forces intended to destroy all United Nations forces in Korea and take over the entire country.

Greatly disturbed by this report, the JCS in reply, on December

1, reverted to our already expressed concern with respect to the X Corps and its relationship to the Eighth Army. We pointed out that the planned concentration of the X Corps in the Hamhung-Hungnam area, instead of posing a threat to the Chinese then operating against the east flank of the Eighth Army, as stated by General MacArthur, actually widened the gap between the X Corps and the Army, affording additional opportunity to the CCF Army to intervene strong forces between the two major United Nations commands. We agreed that the first task was to extricate the Marines and the units of the 7th Division units east of the Changjin Reservoir, but we again suggested that, once this was done, the operations and positioning of the Eighth Army and the X Corps "should be sufficiently coordinated to prevent large enemy forces from passing between them or outflanking either of them." We authorized MacArthur to ignore the entire region northeast of the narrow waist of the country except for such operations as were necessary for the military security of his command.

MacArthur remained adamant in opposing the JCS proposals, reiterating his objections already cited. He added that while the morale and efficiency of the United Nations forces had been fine, the troops were mentally and physically fatigued after five months of almost incessant combat, were understrength, and had lost much equipment. By contrast, the CCF troops were fresh, at full strength in men and materiel, and in top fighting condition. He said that because of the nature of the terrain and the distance from the sea where the major fighting was occurring the effectiveness of his air power and our Navy's potential gunfire support were greatly reduced. Unless massive ground reinforcements were promptly furnished, the United Nations Command would be forced into successive withdrawals, declining in strength with each withdrawal, or would become cooped up in beachheads, which offered little hope of decisive action. He concluded:

This small command, actually under present conditions, is facing the entire Chinese nation in an undeclared war, and unless some positive and immediate action is taken, hope for success cannot be justified and steady attrition leading to final destruction can reasonably be contemplated.

Following our established policy of not overriding the theater commander, the JCS on December 4, again with the approval of the President, told General MacArthur that we now considered the safety of the United Nations forces to have first priority and approved the consolidation of these forces into beachheads, the X Corps to be based on Hungnam-Wonsan and the Eighth Army on Inchon and Pusan.

While these exchanges were taking place, our United Nations and NATO allies were becoming alarmed at newspaper and other reports of the situation in Korea and the possibilities of precipitate action by the United States or by MacArthur that might lead to war with Communist China. It was difficult for authorities in Washington to get a clear picture of the rapidly changing condition in Korea. In order to have some firsthand information and to obtain directly from MacArthur his estimate of the capabilities of the forces then available to him and his views about a possible cease-fire, it was decided to send me, as Executive Agent for the JCS, to consult with him and his principal field commanders. Accompanied by a small staff, I arrived in Tokyo on December 4. After a brief meeting with MacArthur we flew directly to Seoul, where General Walker then had his headquarters, arriving there at dusk. During the evening Walker filled me in on events following the Chinese attack. He said that the U.S. 2d Division and the Turkish Brigade had been badly hurt, but the 1st Cavalry and 24th and 25th Divisions were in good shape. Of units of the ROK II Corps only the 5th Division was in fair condition; the others would have to be rehabilitated and re-equipped. He pointed out the location of his troops, which were then falling back to positions just north of Pyongyang. Walker did not think he could hold Pyongyang for long. He feared that with the X Corps' contracting into the Hamhung area beyond the Taebaek range the CCF forces might pour through the gap left by the ROK II Corps on his right flank. If he was required to hold Seoul and the area north of the Han River, the Eighth Army might be threatened with encirclement. We were agreed that a forced evacuation by way of Inchon would be very costly in men and materiel. On the other hand, Walker was confident he could withdraw on Pusan without further serious losses and, if reinforced with the X Corps, could hold the old Pusan Perimeter indefinitely.

The next day, December 5, I spent with General Walker, visiting General Milburn's I Corps headquarters and the command post of the 25th Division. We also made an aerial reconnaissance of part of the Eighth Army's projected delaying positions south of the Taedong and Han Rivers.

Leaving Seoul the following morning for X Corps headquarters at Hamhung, I had the impression that, although the situation in the Eighth Army was sticky, there was no panic. As I left Kimpo airfield, I was asked by newsmen whether we would use the atomic bomb as a tactical weapon against the Chinese invaders. I replied, "Certainly not from what I saw yesterday." Then, in reply to a query whether there was a possibility that the Eighth Army would be enveloped by the Chinese driving down its right flank, I said, "I think the Eighth Army can take care of itself."

General Almond met me at the Yonpo airstrip just south of Hungnam. After a briefing at his command post in Hungnam we visited the headquarters of the 3d Division and Dave Barr's 7th Division which, less the two battalions of the 31st Regiment attached to the 2d Marine Division, had already closed in the Hungnam beachhead. We also made a flight over the final defensive positions covering the beachhead and flew part of the way over the 1st Marine Division's escape route, but we could not get all the way, because of bad weather.

General Almond felt that the 1st Marine Division, then fighting its way back from Hagaruri, would get through without further heavy losses and that the X Corps would be concentrated in the beachhead in the next few days. Almond was confident he could hold the Hamhung-Hungnam area for a considerable period and that the corps could be evacuated without any great difficulty when and if ordered to do so. I agreed with his estimate.

I returned to Tokyo on December 6 and conferred at once with Generals MacArthur, Stratemeyer, Hickey, Wright, and Willoughby and Admiral Joy for a thorough review of actions that might be taken in Korea. Three sets of conditions were considered, as a framework for the discussion. The first two assumed a continuation of an all-out attack by the Chinese Communist forces; the third was based on a possible Chinese agreement not to advance south of the 38th Parallel.

The first case was examined under the assumption that existing restrictions against allied bombing north of the Yalu would be continued, that there would be no blockade of China, that there would be no reinforcements to the United Nations Command from Formosa, that there would be no substantial reinforcements from the United States until April 1951, when four National Guard divisions might be available and, finally, that the atomic bomb might be used in North Korea. General MacArthur protested strongly that any such limitations would be tantamount to surrender. Under these conditions an armistice might be helpful for political purposes but would not be essential militarily, since the United Nations forces would have to be withdrawn from Korea and this could be done safely from Hungnam and Pusan with or without an armistice.

In the second situation it was assumed that an effective naval blockade of China would be established, air reconnaissance and bombing of the Chinese mainland would be permitted, Chinese Nationalist forces would be exploited to the maximum, and the atomic bomb might be used if tactically appropriate. General MacArthur said that under such conditions he should be directed to hold in Korea as far north as possible and that he would move the X Corps overland to join the Eighth Army in the Pusan bridgehead.

In the third case, General MacArthur felt that, if the Chinese agreed not to cross the 38th Parallel, the United Nations should accept an armistice. The NK forces as well as the CCF forces should remain north of the 38th Parallel, NK guerrillas in the south should be withdrawn, the Eighth Army should continue to cover Seoul-Inchon while the X Corps withdrew to Pusan, and a United Nations commission should oversee the implementation of the armistice. MacArthur felt that this would be the best course to follow, unless the United Nations should decide to act as assumed in the second case. In any event Chiang Kai-shek should be permitted to send troops to Korea without delay, and the participating United Nations powers should increase their fighting contingents to at least 75,000. He concluded by saying that unless substantial reinforcements were sent quickly, the United Nations Command should pull out of Korea.

I agreed that if the United Nations did not support fully the operations in Korea in the face of continued all-out Chinese attack, General MacArthur should be directed to take the necessary steps to safeguard his command and prepare plans for evacuation from Korea. While I did not presume to argue the point with General MacArthur, I did not feel that, even with the limitations likely to be placed upon the United Nations Command, the Chinese could force its withdrawal from Korea. I based this judgment primarily on the views expressed by the field commanders, Walker and Almond. Upon arrival in Washington on December 8 I was besieged by newsmen at the airport, all naturally concerned about the Korean situation. Without going into details I said simply that the United Nations forces would be able to take care of themselves without further serious losses.

The day I had left for Korea the British Prime Minister, Mr. Clement Attlee, had arrived in Washington for discussions with President Truman. The British and our European allies were fearful that if we became involved in a war with China, we would be unable to meet our commitments to NATO. They were concerned about the possibility of our employing the atomic bomb and were distrustful of General MacArthur. Mr. Truman and Mr. Attlee met daily at the White House, along with the Secretaries of State and Defense and the British Ambassador to the United States. These discussions were winding up when I returned from Tokyo on December 8.

After reporting to the JCS General Bradley and I went to the White House at the invitation of the President to brief the British-American conferees on the highlights of my trip. It was a distinguished gathering, headed by Mr. Truman and Mr. Attlee, Secretaries Acheson and Marshall, and the British Ambassador, Sir

Oliver Franks, whom we met in the oval Cabinet Room adjacent to the President's office. Using a large-scale map of Korea for background, I reviewed the recent operations. I pointed out that, if the Chinese continued their all-out attack, it would not be possible to hold the Seoul-Inchon area. However, I quoted General Walker's conviction that he could retain a sizable bridgehead based on Pusan, particularly when reinforced by the X Corps — a reinforcement that by then MacArthur had agreed to — when that corps was withdrawn from Hungnam. I concluded by expressing my personal judgment that, although the military situation remained serious, it was no longer critical.

In the final conclusions of the conferees it was agreed that a cease-fire and peaceful solution of the conflict were desirable in the immediate future, if they could be secured on honorable terms. However, such a solution would not be bartered with the Chinese Communists in exchange for our withdrawing protection from Formosa or Indo-China. If no solution could be obtained, the American and British troops would fight on in Korea unless they were forced out. The Secretary of State so informed General MacArthur.

During the trying days following the Chinese Communist attack it had become evident to the President and to his principal political and military advisers that drastic action would have to be taken to strengthen our military forces and to build up our industrial mobilization potential for meeting our commitments to the newly created NATO and for facing a possible major war against China. The National Security Council, acting on November 22 on recommendations of the JCS, had approved expansion of the United States Army to eighteen combat divisions, to be achieved by June 30, 1954. On December 5 the JCS recommended, and on December 14 the National Security Council approved, a plan to accomplish this expansion — with comparable increases in the Navy and Air Force — by June 1952. Accordingly, the President called two additional National Guard divisions, the 31st and 47th, to active federal service effective in January, 1951.

Finally, after long debate in the National Security Council and lengthy consultation with congressional leaders of both parties President Truman on December 15, 1950, in a radio address to the nation declared that a state of national emergency existed. The following day he signed a proclamation announcing that the military, naval, air, and civilian defenses of the nation were to be strengthened as rapidly as possible and calling on citizens in all walks of life to make the necessary sacrifices.

Withdrawal of the X Corps and Eighth Army and Death of General Walker

While I was conferring with General Almond in Hungnam on December 6, the question of a possible forced evacuation of Korea was being discussed by General MacArthur with his planning staff in Tokyo. General Wright urged that, without waiting for it to be forced out, the X Corps be sea-lifted from Hungnam to Pusan or Pohangdong and then become part of the Eighth Army. Thereafter the Eighth Army would be strong enough to withdraw successively, if necessary, to the Pusan Perimeter.

MacArthur was reluctant to place Almond under Walker's command but, after thinking the matter over, on December 7 approved Wright's recommendations and notified both Walker and Almond accordingly:

> Current planning calls for a withdrawal in successive positions, if necessary, to the Pusan area. Eighth Army will hold the Seoul area for the maximum time possible short of entailing such envelopment as would prevent its withdrawal to the south. Planning further envisions the early withdrawal of X Corps from the Hungnam area and junction with Eighth Army as practicable. At such time, X Corps will pass command to the Eighth Army.

The JCS upon learning of this message radioed their concurrence, adding that they felt the X Corps should be evacuated as soon as practicable. On December 8 MacArthur issued detailed orders to put these plans into effect. Nine lines, designated "A" to "I," were listed for possible occupation by the Eighth Army, the southernmost one conforming generally to the trace of the old Naktong perimeter (Map 12). Positions "A" to "D" were north of Seoul, which Walker was not to surrender unless there was a definite enemy threat of envelopment. Position "D" was Mac-Arthur's first designation of a continuous line across the Korean peninsula. It ran from the south bank of the Imjin River to about 15 miles north of Samchock on the east coast, about the same length as the earlier rejected Pyongyang-Wonsan line.

On December 11 MacArthur flew to Korea for the first time since October 21, when he had witnessed the air drop of the 187th Airborne Brigade launching the attack on Pyongyang. He visited both X Corps and Eighth Army headquarters and discussed with his field commanders their withdrawal plans.

The CCF 27th Army, perhaps recuperating from its heavy battle casualties and losses to the weather in the bitter fighting in the Changjin area, made little effort to overrun the Hungnam beachhead or to disrupt the evacuation of the X Corps, which was handled skillfully. One hundred and ninety-three shiploads of men and materiel were evacuated on naval transports while the Air Force and Navy provided air cover, bombing, and gunfire support. Approximately 105,000 combat troops, 98,000 Korean civilian refugees, 17,500 vehicles, and 350,000 tons of bulk cargo were sea-lifted, and 3600 troops, 196 vehicles, 1300 tons of cargo, and several hundred refugees were flown out by the Fifth Air Force from the Yonpo airfield. No serviceable equipment or supplies were left behind, though it was necessary to blow up some ammunition, bombs, gasoline, and oil in the final destruction of the port facilities.

While the X Corps was moving out, the Eighth Army continued its displacements south. By mid-December it was on line "B," extending from the Imjin River through Yongpyong and Huachon to Yangyang on the east coast. These displacements had not been forced by the CCF Army, which failed to press a pursuit. However, intelligence reports revealed that the CCF Army was occupying Pyongyang, and probes by NK forces seemed to be screening Chinese movements. General Walker still feared an outflanking maneuver against his insecure right flank before it could be firmly anchored. To help in this regard the ROK I Corps from Hungnam was disembarked near Samchok on the east coast. In addition, Walker had notified Almond that the X Corps, upon passing to Eighth Army command, would be re-equipped by Brigadier General Crump Garvin's 2d Logistical Command at Pusan, after which it was to be prepared to move promptly into the forward area.

American intelligence agencies were puzzled by the lack of aggressive Chinese follow-up. General Willoughby speculated that the CCF forces had expected a stand by the Eighth Army north of Pyongyang and that, when this did not develop, they were thrown off stride. General MacArthur directed General Walker to push strong reconnaissance groups through the NK screen to determine enemy dispositions and intentions.

In the course of checking on these actions, on December 23, Walker was driving north from Seoul headed for Uijongbu. As his jeep was passing two trucks halted on the narrow road, it was struck by a Korean truck which had pulled out from behind the parked vehicles. Walker's jeep overturned, and its occupants were thrown out. General Walker was killed almost instantly. As it was for his World War II army commander, General Patton, before him, it was a sad and inglorious ending for a fine battle-field commander.

On one of my early trips to the Far East Command I had discussed with General MacArthur a possible successor to General Walker in the event that anything should happen to the latter. Walker was almost constantly in the field, visiting front-line commanders and his troops and riding about in an open, un-armored jeep. In a fluid situation anything could happen. Mac-Arthur had said that if Walker were lost, he would want as Walker's successor General Matthew B. Ridgway, my West Point classmate, who was then serving as Deputy Chief of Staff for Operations and Administration. I had agreed thoroughly with his choice. As soon as MacArthur learned of Walker's death, he personally advised me by telephone and requested that Ridgway be sent at once. I informed the President and Secretaries Marshall and Pace immediately, and the President promptly designated General Ridgway the new commander of the Eighth Army. I caught Matt by telephone at a small dinner party at the home of a friend and gave him the word. Always a great soldier, Ridgway, without delaying to spend Christmas with his family, left Washington the following day. He arrived in Tokyo shortly before midnight on Christmas Day.

X

RIDGWAY TAKES COMMAND

Preliminaries

MATT RIDGWAY was eminently qualified to command the Eighth Army. He had a brilliant record in World War II as commander of the 82nd Airborne Division in Sicily and Normandy and later as commander of the XVIII Airborne Corps. As a young officer he had served in China at Tientsin and in the Philippines and was familiar with the Orient and its ways. While a Deputy Chief of Staff for Operations and Administration he had visited Japan and Korea, and he had kept in daily touch with the situation in Korea since the outbreak of war. But perhaps his most important qualification was that he had the full confidence of both General MacArthur and the Joint Chiefs of Staff. Matt and I had known one another as classmates at West Point, and he had served in my VII Corps in Normandy and in General Bradley's First Army and Twelfth Army Group in France and Germany. He had represented me at times at JCS meetings and was well and favorably known to the other Chiefs. Finally, he had the initiative, drive, and aggressive spirit that were badly needed in the Eighth Army after its reversals at the hands of the overwhelming Chinese forces.

MacArthur was not overly optimistic as Ridgway reported to him on December 26. The best MacArthur hoped for was "inflicting a broadening defeat making possible the retention and security of South Korea." He went on to say, "We are now operating in a mission vacuum while diplomacy attempts to feel its way." Any quick military success that Ridgway might achieve would assist the United States and allied United Nations officials in deciding whether the United Nations Command could or would remain in Korea. The only instructions MacArthur gave Ridgway were to hold in Korea as far north as possible "in the most advanced positions in which you can maintain yourself." He was to hold Seoul for political and psychological reasons but not allow it to become a fixed position.

Ridgway recounts that in the course of this private discussion MacArthur revealed marked changes in his points of view on two subjects of great importance. First, he cautioned Ridgway that the ability of tactical air power to stop the movement of enemy troops and supplies — on which, besides strategic bombardment, he had relied so heavily — was much exaggerated. Second, and of vital import, he was now prepared to turn over full control of military operations in Korea to Ridgway. When, near the end of their meeting, Ridgway asked whether the General would object to a decision to attack, MacArthur replied, "The Eighth Army is yours, Matt. Do what you think is best."

True to his word, MacArthur stayed aloof from tactical operations from the time Ridgway assumed command of the United Nations forces until March 1951, after the Eighth Army had begun its counteroffensive. During this period MacArthur was in Korea only twice. Thereafter he visited Eighth Army headquarters weekly but continued to give Ridgway a free hand in running the Army. One of Ridgway's most valuable assets was his willingness to accept responsibility for his own actions. MacArthur had made it clear that Ridgway did not have to obtain confirmation from General Headquarters for any proposed operation, and Ridgway did not do so. In proper deference to MacArthur, however, Ridgway always notified him of his intentions in advance of any major move. MacArthur never questioned Ridgway, in contrast to the tight control he had always maintained over General Walker.

Before leaving for Korea on December 26 Ridgway had conferred with the senior Air and Navy commanders at General Headquarters, General Stratemeyer and Admiral Joy, and with General Hickey and other principal staff officers. He was familiar with them all because of his visit with Averell Harriman earlier in the year and had known Stratemeyer from cadet days.

Ridgway had intended to launch an attack soon after he assumed command in Korea. The atmosphere he encountered at Eighth Army headquarters at Taegu, where he landed late on December 26, gave him pause. He immediately felt that the main command post was too far to the rear and too populated with staff officers who should have been nearer to the front, in closer touch with the troops. At dawn the next morning he flew to the advanced command post at Seoul. There he met at once the American corps commanders, Milburn and Coulter, and the Eighth Army's Deputy Chief of Staff, Colonel William A. Collier. They discussed various means of improving the combat potential of the Eighth Army and the possibilities of holding a bridgehead north of the Han River. Ridgway emphasized the necessity of better lateral communication, particularly between Coulter's IX Corps and the ROK III Corps, and close coordination in planning and action between the I and IX Corps.

Ridgway next called on our able American Ambassador, John Muccio, from whom he received valuable information — that, strangely, did not come from military intelligence — which indicated to Ridgway a dangerous threat from the direction of Wonju through a gap leading to the Army's right rear. Ridgway took immediate action. The nearest available reserve was the 2d Infantry Division, now under a new commander, Major General Robert B. McClure, but still not fully recovered from the mauling it received while withdrawing from Kunuri. Ridgway ordered McClure to move up to block the opening. As so often happens when a commander is able, he was also lucky, the move of the 2d Division being just in time to check the enemy, who was about to exploit the gap.

Muccio accompanied Ridgway when the latter called to pay his respects to President Syngman Rhee at the President's modest home in Seoul. Rumors of a possible withdrawal from Korea were circulating in Seoul. The President gave no indication of his concern but greeted the new commander with cool appraisal. When Ridgway forthrightly extended his hand and said, "I'm glad to see you, Mr. President, glad to be here, and I mean to stay," the doughty old patriot's wrinkled face broke into a smile, and he grasped Ridgway's extended hand in both of his. Matt Ridgway had made a friend.

The necessary formalities over, Ridgway took off for a personal view and assessment of his new command. For the next three days he traveled by light plane, helicopter, and jeep along the front, studying the terrain, evaluating commanders, and gauging the spirit of his army. He visited every corps and division commander west of the Taebaek Mountains, missing only the Capital Division on the quiet east coast. He also arranged to meet General Almond, who had arrived at Kyongju, near Pohangdong, from Hungnam on December 26. Everywhere he talked to officers and soldiers of all ranks, looking in vain for the drive and élan he associated with American troops.

Ridgway was back at his Taegu command post on the evening of December 30, much disturbed by what he had learned on his reconnaissance. He realized the ordeal the men of the Eighth Army had been through in the preceding six months. They had been hastily gathered together from around the world into units never fully up to strength or fully armed and equipped and were fighting in a strange land in an undeclared war that they did not fully understand. Yet Ridgway could not avoid the hard conclusion that the Army he inherited was a dispirited command. In his own words:

> There was a definite air of nervousness, of gloomy foreboding, of uncertainty, a spirit of apprehension as to what the future held. . . . It was clear to me that our troops had lost confidence. I could read it in their eyes, in their walk. I could read it in the faces of their leaders, from sergeants right on up to the top. They were unresponsive, reluctant to talk. I had to drag information out of them. There was a complete lack of that alertness, that aggressiveness, that you find in troops whose spirit is high.

It was also apparent to Ridgway's experienced eye that the attack he had hoped to launch was out of the question. Furthermore, he had noted weaknesses along the front, which would have to be shored up. There was mounting evidence that the Chinese were about to renew their attack — probably, as was their wont, on the coming New Year holiday. He would have little time for preparation to meet the new offensive.

Ridgway estimated that his chances of holding against the Chinese onslaught depended chiefly on the judicious commitment of his few available reserves and on revitalizing the fighting spirit of the Army. The disposition of the Army was still essentially the same as under General Walker, Milburn's I Corps covering the approaches from Pyongyang to Seoul, Coulter's IX Corps deployed across the Wonsan-Seoul corridor, the ROK III, II, and I Corps, in that order from west to east, extending the front into the Taebaek range, and the ROK Capital Division still anchoring the right flank on the east coast.

Ridgway had been aghast at the Army G-2's lack of information on the locations and capabilities of the enemy, a lack that he took steps to correct by ordering vigorous patrolling to the front. It did appear that the weight of enemy forces was aimed directly at Seoul along the Wonsan-Seoul axis, with a strong secondary effort southwest from Chunchon and Wonju, designed to outflank the I and IX Corps north of Seoul. Such an envelopment would come through the shaky ROK Army.

The only solid reserve available to counter this threat was the X Corps, the divisions of which were still unloading in the Pusan area. As a preliminary caution, Ridgway passed the Second Division to Almond's command, since he planned ultimately, as had General Walker, to place the X Corps in the east-central, Chongchon sector, then held by the ROK III Corps; this would narrow the front held by ROK forces. At the same time he pressed Garvin's Logistical Command and Almond to speed up the unloading and re-equipping of the 1st Marine Division and the 7th Infantry Division. As soon as the 7th Division was ready, he had Almond move it up to join the 2d Division backing up the ROK III Corps, and he put the 1st Marine Division and the 3d Infantry Division into army reserve.

Concurrently Ridgway was quietly but firmly bearing down on combat leaders and staff officers at all echelons in an effort to change their defeatist attitude. By exhortation and personal example he reoriented their thinking toward the front. Not only was aggressive patrolling demanded of all units, particularly at night, but no further withdrawals were to be made unless inescapable, and any such were to be fighting withdrawals, in which close contact was maintained and maximal punishment dealt the enemy. But it was some time before Ridgway's own aggressive spirit began to seep down through the United Nations Command.

The Chinese Renew the Attack

Anticipating the CCF attack, General Ridgway flew up to Seoul on December 31 and made a swing along the western front by jeep that afternoon. The Chinese began their "Third Phase Offensive" shortly before dark, initially picking on ROK divisions on the fronts of the I and IX Corps and then broadening the attack during the night to include the ROK III Corps. A wedge was driven between the ROK 1st and 6th Divisions at the junction of the two western corps, which the Chinese were bound to exploit. Few reports from the ROK III Corps reached the Army's advance command post during the night, but lack of information from the usually reliable American advisers was ominous.

As Ridgway started by jeep for the front of the ROK 1st and 6th Divisions near dawn of New Year's Day, he was shocked to encounter a column of oncoming trucks packed with ROK soldiers who were clearly fleeing to the rear. He jumped from his jeep and tried unsuccessfully to wave the column to a halt. He returned to the Eighth Army command post and ordered straggler points established where retreating troops could be stopped and reassembled. He then headed back north to the command posts of the I and IX Corps. He was relieved to find the bulk of the troops still in position and the two ROK division commanders taking steps to bolster the shoulders of the enemy penetration.

However, reports from the ROK III Corps now reached Ridgway, telling of strong enemy attacks since dawn, while increasing pressure was developing on the front of the I and IX Corps farther west. Loath as he was to order a withdrawal — instead of an attack, only six days after taking command — Ridgway decided that the wisest thing to do at this stage was to have the I and IX Corps fall back to a bridgehead position covering

Seoul and to move all ROK forces back to a narrower front east of Seoul. Oral instructions accordingly were given personally to Milburn and Coulter at noon on January 1, 1951. Ridgway wanted the withdrawal made in daylight, so as to take advantage of air and observed-artillery support. He directed that strong groups of infantry and armor be posted on high ground covering the routes of withdrawal and that these forces counterattack enemy penetrations and disrupt the enemy follow-up before they themselves pulled back to the bridgehead. He issued similar instructions to the three ROK corps during the afternoon.

Unfortunately, these plans were not always carried out. The ROK 6th Division on the IX Corps front became disorganized when struck by an enemy flank attack, and by dark of January 1 it was streaming rearward out of control. General Gay had to stretch out the 1st Cavalry Division to cover the ROK 6th Division sector besides his own. On the I Corps front the British 29th Brigade, which had arrived in Korea in October, under its dauntless commander, Brigadier T. Brodie, withdrew grudgingly. The brigade and Bill Kean's 25th Division were deployed in the I Corps sector of the bridgehead by midnight. General Milburn had ordered them to hold there "at all costs." In a move that exemplified the definitive leadership with which Ridgway had taken command of the United Nations forces he countermanded this part of Milburn's order. He had not designated the bridgehead a final defensive position, and he felt that such an order to a major unit was a prerogative of the Army commander. He wished chiefly to make clear to the men of all ranks that, although he counted on them to fight hard, he and all their leaders were concerned for their safety, would not risk their lives needlessly, nor abandon any units that were cut off; there would be no more Unsans. But although Ridgway did not wish any needless sacrifices, he did insist that his orders for counterattacks to punish the enemy during withdrawals be carried out. He admonished both Milburn and Coulter for failure in this regard.

As the Chinese attack hit the bridgehead on January 3, a chaotic situation developed in the sector of the ROK Army. In an effort to stabilize this front Ridgway passed control of three ROK divisions to the X Corps, but until the U.S. 7th Division and the 1st Marine Division of the X Corps were up in position, he had no certainty of how long the east flank would hold. With the broad Han River at his back he could not afford to risk having the I and IX Corps trapped north of the river by an enemy break through the X Corps front. In addition to some 75,000 troops and their equipment thousands of ROK government officials and foreign nationals would have to be moved across the frozen river, to say nothing of the hordes of refugees who would be streaming out of Seoul. This would have to be done before the enemy arrived within artillery range of the river crossings. Thus an early decision to retire south of the Han would be required to safeguard his command and minimize civilian loss of life.

Shortly after noon on January 3 Milburn and Coulter were told to initiate their movements as soon as their coordinated plans were completed. When safely across the Han, the I Corps was to cover the final evacuation of Inchon and the Seoul and Kimpo airfields. The IX Corps was to defend the south bank of the river from Yongdungpo east to the junction of the Han and Pukhan Rivers, where it was to tie in with Almond's X Corps.

All permanent bridges over the Han had been destroyed in earlier battles and had not been repaired. Two military floating bridges and a redecked railway bridge would have to be reserved for military traffic after 3:00 P.M., leaving only five floating foot-bridges and the heavy ice of the frozen river for the unofficial civilian exodus.

As a result of careful planning and tight control the withdrawal of all troops and equipment was carried out without a major hitch. But it was with a saddened heart that General Ridgway watched from the river bank, as his troops and heavy equipment swayed their way across the precarious bridges and hundreds of thousands of South Koreans fled across the ice, many for the second time.* He had not come to Korea to surrender Seoul, and in his own mind he was determined to take it back again some day.

For the present, however, further withdrawals were inescapable.

---

* General Ridgway has given a poignant description of this scene in his memoirs, *Soldier* (Harper & Brothers, pp. 213–14).

By the morning of January 4 Chinese patrols were observed on the Kimpo peninsula to the left rear of the I Corps and were reported crossing the Han east of the IX Corps. Farther east in the sector of the X Corps and the ROK Army the situation was still chaotic. Late on January 4 Ridgway issued the order that the move to the Pyongtaek-Ansong-Changhowon-Samchock (known as Line D) commence at noon the next day. The I and IX Corps reached Line D on January 7 with little or no enemy follow-up (Map 12).

In the more fluid sector of the X Corps and the east thereof conditions were still threatening, even though the enemy consisted largely of rehabilitated North Korean units and guerrillas. Futile efforts of the U.S. 2d Division to hold the key road center of Wonju led to the appointment by General Almond of another new division commander, Major General Clark L. Ruffner, Almond's X Corps Chief of Staff. A 15-mile gap developed between Chechon and Yongwol.

However, vigorous patrolling and local counterattacks from elements of General Barr's 7th Division and other units of the X Corps, combined with effective corps artillery fire and close air support, was taking a toll of the NK troops. The bitter cold and increasing shortages of medical supplies and ammunition and the heavy losses of personnel forced a halt to the NK offensive. By the end of January the 2d Division had reoccupied Wonju, and the X Corps had begun to organize a solid front generally along Line D. General Almond had done a good job under difficult conditions.

Re-evaluation of MacArthur's Mission

The reverses suffered by the United Nations Command in December and the shortage of trained reserves with which to reinforce the Eighth Army convinced the JCS that the mission assigned MacArthur in the directive of September 27 of 1950 (see Chapter VII, pages 147–8) would have to be revised. That directive had authorized the crossing of the 38th Parallel and spelled out MacArthur's mission thereafter. In a radio message dated December 30, 1950, from the JCS to General MacArthur he was now told to defend in successive positions. Nine such positions lettered "A" to "I," all north of the old Naktong Perimeter defenses, and three additional lines within that perimeter had been designated by MacArthur on a map I had brought back from Tokyo after my last visit (Map 12). MacArthur was directed to damage the enemy as much as possible, subject to the primary consideration of the safety of his troops and his continuing responsibility for the defense of Japan. The JCS radio message continued:

> It seems to us that if you are forced back to positions in the vicinity of the Kum River and a line generally eastward therefrom, and if thereafter the Chinese Communists mass large forces against your positions with an evident capability of forcing us out of Korea, it then would be necessary, under those conditions, to direct you to commence a withdrawal to Japan.
>
> Your views are requested as to the above outlined conditions which should determine a decision to initiate evacuation, particularly in light of your continuing primary mission of defending Japan for which only troops of the Eighth Army are available.
>
> Following the receipt of your views we will give you a definite directive as to the conditions under which you should initiate evacuation.

MacArthur replied that it would not be necessary to reach an anticipatory decision to evacuate until his forces were actually forced back to what he called the "beachhead line." There was some confusion over which of the designated lines was intended. The JCS finally advised MacArthur that when the Eighth Army reached the so-called Davidson line, which the Eighth Army engineer, Brigadier General Garrison H. Davidson, had traced in August 1950 in an arc roughly 30 miles north of Pusan, the time for final decision to withdraw would have arrived. This was the first time that the Chiefs stepped in and gave the Commander in Chief of the U.N. Command a specific order on a matter of seeming detail. Actually, the timing of a decision to evacuate had not only military, but tremendous political significance, and in this instance we felt we had to narrow down the period of decision.

The December 30 directive from the JCS to MacArthur had two

interdependent and, from MacArthur's viewpoint, conflicting possible courses of action. On the one hand he was told to defend Korea, subject to the proviso that he must save his command from destruction and still be prepared to defend Japan from invasion. On the other he was to withdraw without further ado. The clear intent of the directive, as framed by the JCS, was that the second course was dependent on the progress of the first. If he found in the course of the withdrawal that he could no longer defend Korea without serious risk of destruction of his command and the baring of Japan to invasion, then he should evacuate. The Chiefs indicated that this decision should be made when and if the Davidson line was reached.

MacArthur radioed the JCS on January 10, stating that the two courses of action were incompatible in that they could not be carried out simultaneously. What he seemed to be shooting for was a spelling-out of the continuing political objectives that should govern the decision whether the United Nations forces should remain in Korea and under what conditions. I must admit that I personally, and, I believe, the JCS as a group, had considerable sympathy for MacArthur in the dilemma presented to him by this directive. In our regular periodic meetings with representatives of the State Department the Chiefs constantly tried to pin down at any particular time after the Chinese intervention, just what our remaining political objectives were in Korea, but our diplomatic colleagues would always counter with the query "What are your military capabilities?" The discussion would almost invariably come down to the age-old question of the chicken and the egg. The Chiefs could only deduce that our State Department co-workers, torn as they were by the often conflicting domestic and international political considerations, wanted us to attain the maximal military results within our military capabilities. But the military would have to assume all the responsibility if things went wrong.

MacArthur pointed up his dilemma — and ours — when he stated in his radio message of January 10, 1951, that the determining factor was just how far the United States was prepared to go in order to retain the United Nations Command in Korea.

If the primary interest of the United States in the Far East was to pin down a large part of the Chinese military potential, then, as he said in the same message, "the military course is implicit in political policy and we should be prepared to accept whatever casualties result and any attendant hazard to Japan's security. . . . The issue really boils down to the question of whether or not the United States intends to evacuate Korea, and involves a decision of the highest national and international importance, far above the competence of a theater commander, guided largely by incidents affecting the tactical situation developing on a very limited field of action."

Since from MacArthur's point of view the JCS directive in effect left in the hands of the Chinese Communists the determination of whether or not the United Nations Command would evacuate, the general wanted to know whether the objective of our political policy was to maintain a military position in Korea indefinitely or for a limited time, or whether it was to minimize losses by evacuating as soon as possible. He concluded, "As I have pointed out before, under the extraordinary limitations and conditions imposed upon the command in Korea, its military position in Korea is untenable, but it can hold for any length of time, up to its complete destruction, if overriding political considerations so dictate."

This message was shown to President Truman by Secretary Marshall. The President later wrote:

> I was deeply disturbed. The Far East Commander was, in effect, reporting that the course of action decided upon by the National Security Council and the Joint Chiefs of Staff and approved by me was not feasible. He was saying that we would be driven off the peninsula, or at the very least suffer terrible losses.

Of course, if this was General MacArthur's belief, it was his duty to say so. The President called a special session of the National Security Council on January 12 to consider the general's message. He told his advisers that he wanted MacArthur to be kept informed of both political and military matters affecting Korea. He doubted whether many of the advices that had been sent the general in the past had actually been seen by him. To ensure that the general was fully informed of the political aspects of the situation as viewed by the nation's leaders in Washington, the President decided, as he has related in his memoirs, to send MacArthur a personal letter, which in part was as follows:

> . . . I wish in this telegram to let you have my views as to our basic national and international purposes in continuing the resistance to aggression in Korea. We need your judgment as to the maximum effort which could reasonably be expected from the United Nations forces under your command to support the resistance to aggression which we are trying rapidly to organize on a world-wide basis. This present telegram is not to be taken in any sense as a directive. Its purpose is to give you something of what is in our minds regarding the political factors.

The President then listed a series of purposes that would be served by a successful resistance in Korea, the first two of which were as follows:

> (a) To demonstrate that aggression will not be accepted by us or by the United Nations and to provide a rallying point around which the spirits and energies of the free world can be mobilized to meet the world-wide threat which the Soviet Union now poses.
> (b) To deflate the dangerously exaggerated political and military prestige of Communist China which now threatens to undermine the resistance of non-Communist Asia and [threatens] to consolidate the hold of Communism on China itself. . . .

The message also said:

> 2. Our course of action at this time should be such as to consolidate the great majority of the United Nations. This majority is not merely part of the organization but is also the nations whom we would desperately need to count on as allies

in the event the Soviet Union moves against us. Further, pending the build-up of our national strength, we must act with great prudence insofar as extending the area of hostilities is concerned. Steps which might in themselves be fully justified and which might lend some assistance to the campaign in Korea would not be beneficial if they thereby involved Japan or Western Europe in large-scale hostilities.

3. We recognize, of course, that continued resistance might not be militarily possible with the limited forces with which you are being called upon to meet large Chinese armies. Further, in the present world situation, your forces must be preserved as an effective instrument for the defense of Japan and elsewhere. . . . In the worst case, it would be important that, if we must withdraw from Korea, it be clear to the world that that course is forced upon us by military necessity and that we shall not accept the result politically or militarily until the aggression has been rectified.

4. In reaching a final decision about Korea, I shall have to give constant thought to the main threat from the Soviet Union and to the need for a rapid expansion of our armed forces to meet this great danger. . . .

The President concluded by paying tribute to General MacArthur and to the performance of his troops under most difficult circumstances.

JCS Representatives Again Visit Korea

The key point made by General MacArthur in his foreboding radio message of January 10, which could not be gauged definitely from Washington, was whether the military position of the United Nations Command was actually "untenable." Despite the reversals being sustained by the Eighth and ROK Armies and their disappointing lack of confidence and aggressive spirit, General Ridgway was not dismayed. His own faith in the ultimate capability of his command was indicated in personal letters to me and to General Haislip, dated January 3 and January 11 respectively, the latter at the very time that General MacArthur was challenging the JCS directive of December 30. Ridgway was in no way being disloyal to MacArthur's command; he was unaware of MacArthur's protest. In his letter to me he said:

> Everything is going fine. We shall be in for some difficult days but I am completely confident of the ability of the Eighth Army to accomplish every mission assigned.

And in his letter to Haislip on January 11 Ridgway wrote:

> The power is here. The strength and the means we have — short perhaps of Soviet military intervention. My one overriding problem, dominating all others, is to achieve the spiritual awakening of the latent capabilities of this command. If God permits me to do that, we shall achieve more, far more, than our people believe possible.

The JCS did not change our December 30 directive. In a radio message dated January 12, 1951, we acknowledged that the United Nations Command could not stave off a sustained CCF drive for any great length of time, but we said that it would be in the national interest to hold as long as possible so as to permit diplomatic and military consultations with other United Nations members, to maintain United States prestige throughout the world, and to sustain confidence in the United Nations and, among our allies, in NATO.

The Chiefs were concerned, as was the President, that MacArthur should fully understand his new directive. The time had come for another visit to Tokyo and Korea by members of the JCS for personal visits with the General and his field commanders. This time General Vandenberg and I were selected.

The day we arrived in Tokyo, January 15, General Ridgway had launched a limited-objective attack against an enemy concentration that had been discovered north of the I Corps between Osan and Suwon. Despite opposition from his staff Ridgway seized this first opportunity to test and demonstrate the improving outlook of his army. He ordered a limited but coordinated attack from the I Corps, using infantry, tanks, and close air support.

The attack was given the code name "Wolfhound" for Mike Michaelis' 27th Infantry Regiment, the "Wolfhounds" of the 25th Division. The corps was to deliver a heavy blow against the enemy and then withdraw, leaving a covering force behind.

After an initial conference with MacArthur in Tokyo Vandenberg and I flew at once to Korea, where Operation Wolfhound was in progress. For the next two days Vandenberg visited air units and installations and made an air and ground reconnaissance of the combat zone, while I toured the front with Ridgway. I talked to corps and division commanders and a number of junior and noncommissioned officers. I could feel in the Eighth Army the improved spirit that Ridgway had already imparted to his men. As I rode along with Matt Ridgway my mind went back to the times we visited one another during the crucial days of the Battle of the Bulge during World War II, when we commanded adjacent corps on the north side of the Bulge and were trying to convince Field Marshal Montgomery that no enemy was going to break through our positions.

I left Korea fully convinced that the Eighth Army would once again stand and fight, the confident words of Matt Ridgway at the inescapable parting press conference ringing in my ears: "There is no shadow of doubt in my mind that the Eighth Army can take care of itself."

As soon as we landed in Tokyo I radioed to General Bradley a summary of my observations in Korea, an extract of which follows:

> Just returned Tokyo from Korea. Eighth Army in good shape and improving daily under Ridgway's leadership. Morale very satisfactory considering conditions. ROK forces lack confidence and instinctively fear Chinese but are still capable of resistance against NK troops. No signs of disaffection or collapse though this could change quickly in event of serious reverses.
>
> Barring unforeseen development, Ridgway confident he can obtain two to three months' delay before having to initiate evacuation. Does not want to do this before Army is back in old beachhead.
>
> Chinese have not made any move so far to push south from

Han River. When counterattacked they have usually fled. They are having supply difficulties and there are many indications of low morale.

Ridgway taking steps to check NK infiltration on front of X Corps.

On the whole, English Army now in position and prepared to punish severely any mass attack.

Before departing Tokyo on January 19 for Washington Vandenberg and I again met MacArthur and his principal staff officers. A summary of our report to the JCS is as follows:

At our first meeting, Gen. MacArthur read the President's letter, and said it had cleared up his questions as to how long and under what conditions the Eighth Army should remain in Korea. He said he interpreted the letter as a directive to remain in Korea indefinitely, which the UN forces could do, though in this case he could not assume responsibility for the risk of leaving Japan defenseless.

We called attention to the fact that the President's message clearly stated it was not a directive, but that in the conference with the President just prior to our departure it was generally agreed that the decision to evacuate Korea should be delayed as long as possible, without endangering the Eighth Army or the security of Japan. The objective was to permit full time for political action by the UN, and in the meantime to inflict maximum punishment on the Chinese. We also pointed out that even if a decision was made to send reinforcements to Japan it would take at least six weeks for them to arrive and that in the interim his basic mission of securing Japan remained unchanged.

General MacArthur stated that a withdrawal from Korea would have repercussions throughout Asia and would unquestionably result in the loss of Hongkong, Indochina and the remainder of Southeast Asia. He declared, with some emotion, that his command should not be held responsible for the defense of Japan while required to hold in Korea. Although there were no open indications of Russian moves to attack Japan, they had the capability with forces now in Sakhalin and the Vladivostok area. Since this threat was always present he urged that the four National Guard divisions, which he had understood were mobilized for this purpose, should be sent to Japan at once. (We pointed out that he had been advised that these divisions had not been called up for the defense of Japan.)

At our second conference after returning to Japan from Korea, I read the message I had just sent to General Bradley [quoted above], and General Vandenberg outlined the results of his inspection of Air Force activities, which he had found highly satisfactory.

After some discussion of the Korean evacuation problem, General MacArthur reviewed the military situation and stated that in his opinion the UN forces could hold a beachhead in Korea indefinitely. He felt that with our continued domination of the sea and air, Chinese forces would never be able to bring up adequate supplies, over their lengthening lines of communications, to enable them to drive the UN forces from Korea. He reiterated his belief that a decision to evacuate Korea was a political matter and should not be decided on military grounds.

He again urged that reinforcements be sent at once to Japan, and indicated that he would be satisfied with two National Guard divisions. He stated that he was proceeding with the development of the Japanese police forces, and that as rapidly as he could furnish equipment, he could organize four light Japanese divisions. He felt that this force, with the two American National Guard divisions, would provide adequate security for Japan until the conclusion of the Korean conflict.

When Van and I arrived back in Washington, I found that my message to Bradley had been shown to President Truman. After reporting to the JCS we briefed the President on our observations. The President and his chief advisers, who had access to our reports, were reassured. For the first time since the previous November responsible authorities in Washington were no longer pessimistic about our being driven out of Korea and, though it was realized that rough times were still ahead of us, no longer was there much talk of evacuation. General Ridgway alone was responsible for this dramatic change.

No one knew better than Ridgway, however, that his task of transforming the Eighth Army from a tired, dispirited organiza-

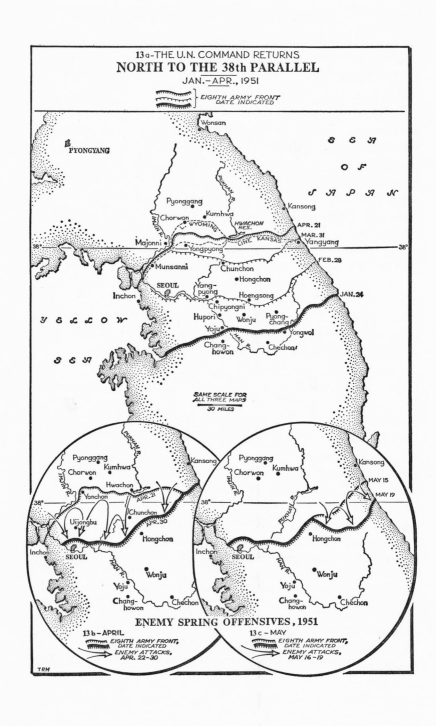

13a–THE U.N. COMMAND RETURNS
NORTH TO THE 38th PARALLEL
JAN.–APR., 1951

EIGHTH ARMY FRONT
DATE INDICATED

SAME SCALE FOR
ALL THREE MAPS
30 MILES

ENEMY SPRING OFFENSIVES, 1951

13 b – APRIL
EIGHTH ARMY FRONT,
DATE INDICATED
ENEMY ATTACKS,
APR. 22–30

13 c – MAY
EIGHTH ARMY FRONT,
DATE INDICATED
ENEMY ATTACKS,
MAY 16–19

TRM

tion into one with confidence and spirit had only begun. Operation Wolfhound had demonstrated that Mike Michaelis and his 35th Regiment still had initiative and drive, but this spirit was not yet widespread. During my stay with Ridgway in Korea he had pointed out the need for fresh leadership, especially in divisional commands. He attributed the lack of aggressiveness of some commanders to the wear and tear of four to six months of hard fighting and the reverses of recent weeks.

Secretary Pace and I had already determined a policy of rotating senior commanders in Korea to training posts at home, where their Korean experience could be put to good use. Ridgway wanted the commanders who were simply worn out to be returned to the States under this policy, without any stigma. I agreed. Ridgway said he intended to move General Coulter to Army Headquarters as his Deputy Commander, to look after his many administrative and service responsibilities. He especially desired Major General Bryant E. Moore, who had served with distinction under both of us in Europe, to be Coulter's replacement. Coulter was recommended for a third star. I approved both moves.

Operation Thunderbolt

With Operation Wolfhound as an example General Ridgway instructed his American corps commanders to devise similar operations. The I and IX Corps did follow up with two limited reconnaissances-in-force without locating any large enemy forces south of the Han River. Ridgway then ordered a stronger and deeper penetration. Operation Thunderbolt called for a reconnaissance to be made by the I and IX Corps, each employing one American division, reinforced with armor and, at the discretion of the corps commanders, one ROK regiment. Even now Ridgway took every precaution to ensure that the troops did not bite off more than they could chew and that they would obtain the maximal air and naval gunfire support possible. As a final move to check on enemy dispositions Ridgway flew over the objective area with General Earl Partridge, the fine commander of the Fifth Air Force, who would furnish air support. This rare reconnaissance by two senior commanders, at low altitude, to a depth of 20 miles over enemy territory, showed no strong enemy concentrations. Ridgway was convinced that his forces could go all the way to the Han and might be able to hold on to the ground gained.

The I and IX Corps started Operation Thunderbolt on January 25 (Map 13a). Elements of three divisions of the Chinese 50th Army, XIII Army Group, were encountered by I Corps, but in each instance the Chinese withdrew after brisk counterattacks. Farther east the IX Corps ran into so much stiffer resistance from the CCF 38th Army that General Ridgway authorized Coulter to reinforce his 1st Cavalry Division with the 24th Division, now commanded by Major General Blackshear Bryan. The I Corps likewise was told to add the 3d Division and the 25th Division. By January 30 Operation Thunderbolt had become a full-scale attack by four United States divisions, the Turkish Brigade, and two ROK regiments. Ridgway planned to broaden the operation to the east by having Almond's X Corps and the ROK II Corps attack respectively toward Chipyongni and Hongchon, where the ROK II and the newly created ROK V Corps were resting after having abandoned Wonju. This, called Operation Roundup, was to commence about February 5 and to be coordinated by General Almond.

The combined Thunderbolt-Roundup attack made good headway in the west but had tougher going in the mountainous terrain of the X Corps zone. By February 10 the 25th Division had entered Inchon, which had been abandoned by the enemy the day before, as had the Kimpo airfield.

MacArthur Visits Ridgway

Shortly after the start of Operation Thunderbolt Ridgway had written to MacArthur outlining his plans for future operations. He saw little point in a general advance beyond the Han River and considered that any attempt to capture Seoul would be foolish militarily as long as the great disparity in strength between the CCF forces and his command remained. Similarly, he felt that the 38th Parallel would be indefensible with his present forces.

After receipt of this letter MacArthur flew to Korea on February 13 for his second visit since Ridgway had taken command of the United Nations forces. Ridgway took advantage of the visit to review again his plans with MacArthur. MacArthur agreed generally with the plans but emphasized that the Eighth Army should hold strongly to the line of the Han. Ridgway assured him that he intended to hold the Han line on the front of the I and IX Corps even in the face of a Chinese attack then under way, which had opened a 12-mile gap on the front of the X Corps east of Chipyongni, a point held by Colonel Paul Freeman's 23d Regiment of the 2d Division. The east corner of the gap had fallen back to Wonju after the capture of Hoengson on February 13, despite a gallant stand there by the Netherlands Battalion, in which its commander, Lieutenant Colonel M. P. A. den Ouden, was killed. The Chinese poured into the gap, creating a deep salient that threatened the positions of the I and X Corps.

Defensive Battles of Wonju and Chipyongni

Ridgway decided to reduce the salient in the classical way, by holding the shoulders and counterattacking against the flanks. He directed Almond to have Freeman's 23d Regiment, 2d Division, stay in Chipyongni, and released to Almond the 7th Infantry Division, now commanded by Major General Claude B. Ferenbaugh, to bolster the 2d Division in the Wonju area. Ridgway then visited Moore's IX Corps command post and briefed him on the plans for eliminating the salient. Moore had already assembled Colonel Marcel L. Crombez's 5th Cavalry Regiment south of Yoju for possible counterattack against the west flank of the penetration.

Efforts to stabilize the east shoulder around Wonju were proving difficult, but after failing to overrun Wonju or crack through the 7th Division the North Koreans could no longer withstand their losses from hunger, cold, and allied bombardment and fire. By February 18 they broke contact and backed off to the north.

Meanwhile, at Chipyongni Freeman's 23d Regiment, reinforced by the French Battalion, the 1st Ranger Company, artillery and engineers, was regaining for the 2d Division some of the luster it had lost in earlier engagements. Completely surrounded for five days, the 23d Regiment stood off attacks from elements of five Chinese divisions. Freeman was badly wounded in the leg by a mortar shell on February 14. General Almond had Lieutenant Colonel John H. Chiles flown into Chipyongni to take command, but Freeman refused evacuation and remained in command until mid-morning on February 15, when he had to be hospitalized.

The Chinese had blocked the Chipyongni-Yoju supply road south of Chipyongni and slowed down efforts of the 27th British Brigade to open the road. Learning of the slow advance of the British, General Moore on the afternoon of February 14 ordered Colonel Crombez to move from Yoju to Chipyongni via a road west of the British. Moore reinforced his regiment with tanks, artillery, and engineers. Crombez got his task force east of the Han before midnight but was forced to halt at Hupori, some 8 miles south of Chipyongni, while his engineers built a bypass around a blown bridge. He renewed the attack in the morning but soon ran into a Chinese battalion dug in on a hill commanding the road. It was mid-afternoon before the Chinese could be driven off.

Figuring that the Chinese would be manning other positions south of Chipyongni, Crombez doubted whether his troopers could fight their way to the beleagured city before dark (unknown to him, the last available reserve in Chipyongni had been committed that afternoon), but he believed an armored column might get through. He decided to give it a try. He organized a special force of twenty-three tanks from Company D, 6th Tank Battalion, and Company A, 70th Tank Battalion. He mounted 160 men of Company L on the tanks for protection of the tanks during any halt. Four engineers, to remove any mines encountered, were to ride in one of the leading tanks with Crombez. It would not be possible to bring up the ambulances and supply train until after the road was opened, but Chiles, whom Crombez had contacted by radio, urged him to come, "trains or no trains."

Before departing at 3:45 P.M. Crombez had his artillery and supporting air pound the hills bordering the road ahead of him. Despite the bombardment the Chinese resisted stubbornly, and several stops had to be made before the column broke through a last narrow pass into Chipyongni. Crombez still had all his tanks, though three were damaged. Three tankers were killed and four wounded. Only twenty-three of the men of Company L went all the way, many of them wounded. Twelve were killed, and about half the remainder were wounded or lost in action.

The breakthrough of Crombez' column ended the Chinese effort to take Chipyongni. They suffered nearly 5000 casualties, including 79 prisoners who identified the five Chinese divisions of which elements had participated in the attack. Fortunately, the Chinese attacks had been made piecemeal by company-size forces. Even so, the 23d Regiment lost 52 killed, 259 wounded, and 42 missing.

The Chinese withdrawal from Chipyongni signaled an enemy pull-back all along the central front. By February 19 the X Corps and the ROK Army to its east were back approximately where they were when the enemy counteroffensive began. General Ridgway regarded the defense of Chipyongni as the turning point in the revitalization of the Eighth Army and felt that Colonel Crombez' decision to fight his way through to Chipyongni symbolized the new aggressive spirit of his command. Ridgway was ready at once to capitalize on his victory with a bold, two-pronged thrust into the withdrawing enemy, a thrust he called Operation Killer.

Ridgway Presses His Attack (See Map 13a)

Determined not to give the retreating enemy any rest or time to reorganize, General Ridgway planned to launch Operation Killer on February 21. As its name implied — a name that caused us sensitive souls in Washington to ask whether that term were really necessary — the objective was to destroy the Chinese and NK forces east of the upper reaches of the Han River.

In its first week the IX Corps, whose east boundary had been shifted to include Wonju, had advanced 10 miles above Chipyongni, and by February 24 the 1st Marine Division, now under that corps, had seized the high ground north of Hoengsong.

Tragedy hit the corps that same day when its new commander, General Moore, died of exposure and a heart attack after the crash of his helicopter into the frozen Han River. General Ridgway placed General Smith, commander of the Marine division, temporarily in command of the corps, until Major General William M. Hoge, who had distinguished himself with the bold seizure of the Remagen Bridge in World War II, arrived in Korea on March 5.

Operation Killer had not quite lived up to its name or to General Ridgway's hopes of destroying large forces of the CCF and NK armies, chiefly because of foul weather and an early spring thaw that disrupted road and rail movement. Undaunted, Ridgway with MacArthur's approval on March 7 launched Operation Ripper, the objectives of which were to destroy enemy forces, materiel, and supplies, to capture Hongchon and Chunchon, and to seize line "Idaho," just south of the 38th Parallel. Though Seoul was not included as a specific objective, a crossing of the Han by the 25th Division east of the city, followed by a crossing of the ROK 1st Division to the west, forced the CCF forces to abandon the city. By March 15 the capital was once again in United Nations hands. A drive made by the I Corps northwest of Seoul, aided by a drop of the 187th Airborne Regimental Combat Team, quickly brought the corps to the Imjin River. Chunchon fell on March 19. By the end of March all geographical objectives of Operation Ripper had been attained, but the main body of the enemy had escaped into North Korea, where there were indications that he was preparing for a spring offensive.

To keep the CCF forces off balance and to gain a stronger defensive position if one became necessary, Ridgway planned a new attack, called Operation Rugged. It was to carry to the "Kansas" line, which ran just north of the 38th Parallel from Yongpyong on the Imjin River through the Hwachong Reservoir to Yangyang on the east coast. Ridgway informed MacArthur of this plan on March 22. MacArthur gave his approval but instructed Ridgway not to move north of the Parallel in force until he had been specifically authorized to do so. Plans were under way in Washington to initiate a negotiated settlement.

To Cross or Not To Cross the 38th Parallel,
That Was the Question

General Ridgway's early successes in January had dispelled Washington's fears that the United Nations forces might be driven out of Korea. As the United Nations Command moved north toward the 38th Parallel, the State and Defense Departments turned their attention to future courses of action. On February 6, 1951, the JCS had a meeting with representatives of the Department of State to discuss five possible courses, as outlined by the State Department representatives: an all-out military effort to clear all of Korea and unify the country by force; complete abandonment of Korea; extension of hostilities to China; an indefinite stalemate at approximately the existing front lines; and a peaceful settlement through negotiations.

This discussion arrived at the same impasse as did those in January. In the later report of the JCS to the Senate Committee on Korean Operations (MacArthur Hearings) we said:

> During the course of the discussion it became apparent to the Joint Chiefs of Staff that the Department of State would prefer not to express political objectives with respect to Korea until military capabilities there were established. On the other hand, the consensus of the opinions of the Joint Chiefs of Staff was that a political decision was required before there could be suitable determination of military courses of action.

Speaking for the JCS at the Hearings, General Bradley indicated that the Chiefs realized that until the outcome of Ridgway's step-by-step operations was more clearly discerned, it would be difficult for the State Department or the United Nations to determine a sound political guidance for the military leaders. The State Department representatives were laboring under the same basic difficulty as the Chiefs: the lack of a clear United States or United Nations *policy* with respect to Korea in the light of the existing circumstances. Such a policy could be determined only by the National Security Council for the United States — and, for all practical purposes, for the United Nations — and by the heads of state of the nations actively participating in the war. On the other hand, the National Security Council needed recommendations from the State Department staff and the JCS to assist it in determining the basic policy. This was what the State-JCS discussions were struggling to provide. But under our American philosophy that the military should be subservient to civilian control — to which the JCS fully subscribed — it follows as a corollary that military considerations should rarely be the deciding factor in determining national policy. Consequently, in the absence of any new political guidance we recommended no change in the current conduct of an aggressive defense.

The State Department informed the United Nations member countries actually participating in the Korean war of the five alternative courses of action that it had suggested in the February 6 meeting with the JCS. Great concern arose among these allies as the United Nations forces approached the 38th Parallel. Secretary Acheson was convinced from soundings made in the United Nations that practically all its members, including a majority of those contributing forces in Korea, were strongly opposed to any general advance across the Parallel.

On February 23 Secretary Acheson sent Secretary Marshall the draft of a memorandum dealing with Korea, which he suggested be sent to the President. Acheson asked Marshall to consider revising the JCS directive of September 27 so as to limit the advance of the United Nations Command. Acheson said that any decision to send substantial forces across the Parallel would require prior agreement of governments furnishing troops to Korea. Any unilateral action of the United States might lead to the withdrawal of certain allies from the war. Acheson conceded that all of South Korea would have to be freed, which would constitute a victory for the United Nations cause, since it would thwart the basic objective of the North Korean Communists in initiating the war. He recognized that as long as the fighting continued, General MacArthur should be free to employ naval and air power north of the Parallel and to take whatever ground action was necessary to interrupt enemy offensive preparations. What he cautioned against was a general allied advance into North Korea.

In an unusual step Secretary Marshall referred this memorandum to the service Secretaries besides the JCS.* Secretaries Pace of the Army, Finletter of the Air Force, and Daniel A. Kimball of the Navy found the Acheson proposals reasonable. All three agreed that the United Nations forces should not make an advance across the 38th Parallel except to acquire favorable terrain for defense. However, when Pace and Finletter proposed that the United States adopt this as a policy and announce it publicly, Secretary Kimball demurred. He felt discussing such a policy with other governments or announcing publicly that the United Nations forces were more or less bound to the 38th Parallel would hamper effective military action. He advocated, instead, that other governments having troops in Korea be informed that General MacArthur had been advised not to make any new major move without prior consultation.

On our part the Chiefs disagreed with Mr. Acheson's proposals. We judged that as long as the United Nations political objectives had not been changed, its military forces should not be forbidden for political reasons to cross the 38th Parallel. The JCS and Generals MacArthur and Ridgway contended that any directive stopping the United Nations forces at the Parallel would impose no such restriction on the CCF or the NK armies but would permit them to build up their own forces in preparation for another invasion of South Korea. MacArthur had to have freedom of maneuver to ensure the safety of the United Nations forces. Pressing again for the decision on the United States' political objectives in Korea, the JCS summed up our recommendations to Secretary Marshall:

> Until this governmental decision is reached there should be no change in that part of the directive to Gen. MacArthur which

---

* So far as I know, this was the first time that a question of major military significance was referred to the service Secretaries for comment. It would have been unfortunate if they had been consulted regularly on such matters, because this would have tended to interpose them between the JCS and the Secretary of Defense, which was not contemplated by the National Defense Act of 1947, as amended in 1949.

now permits him so to dispose his forces either north or south of the 38th Parallel as best to provide for their security.

Because of these cogent objections Secretary Marshall informed Secretary Acheson that he believed the memorandum should not be sent to the President. Secretary Marshall agreed with the JCS that there was a risk in disclosing to the enemy an American decision to remain south of the Parallel. He felt that the United Nations forces had to have freedom of action and maneuver and that it was too early from a military viewpoint to reach a final decision on crossing. Secretary Marshall supported the position of the JCS on the necessity of making definitive the United States' political objectives in Korea. He suggested that the political and military factors should be worked out in the National Security Council, in which their senior staff was considering the problem. He suggested also that the President be advised that the JCS had reported that General MacArthur had indicated his intention to continue the advance until the enemy's main line of resistance was developed and that, if no such strong position was located south of the 38th Parallel, MacArthur would so report to the JCS and await instructions before proceeding farther.

Nothing specific came of the exchange of letters between the Secretaries of Defense and State. But Ridgway could not stand still while Washington debated. His actions in the field, by default of political decisions in Washington, became the determining factor in the gradual evolution of a policy of sorts. The advances gained by Operations Killer and Ripper convinced the National Security Council and the State and Defense Department planners that the United Nations forces were getting the upper hand over the Communists in Korea. Perhaps it was obvious to the Chinese that in the face of overwhelming allied air power they could not operate successfully far from their Manchurian base. The Washington planners agreed that the Chinese might now be amenable to a political settlement. Both the State and Defense Departments felt that the best way to initiate the move toward a negotiated peace would be a public appeal to the Communists by President Truman as the executive agent for the United Nations.

The State Department had prepared a draft statement, on which general agreement was reached at a meeting on March 19 between the Secretaries of State and Defense, Deputy Secretary of Defense Lovett, the JCS, and staff assistants from the State Department. On March 20 we sent the following message to General MacArthur:

> State planning a Presidential announcement shortly that with clearing of bulk of South Korea of aggressors, United Nations now prepared to discuss conditions of settlement in Korea. United Nations feeling exists that further diplomatic efforts toward settlement should be made before any advance with major forces north of the thirty-eighth parallel. Time will be required to determine diplomatic reactions and permit new negotiations that may develop.
>
> Recognizing that the parallel has no military significance, State has asked Joint Chiefs of Staff what authority you should have to permit sufficient freedom of action for next few weeks to provide security for United Nations forces and maintain contact with the enemy. Your recommendation desired.

General MacArthur replied on March 21 that his present directive was adequate and asked that no further limitations be imposed upon him.

United Nations Forces Re-enter North Korea (See Map 13a)

Having received no new instructions from the JCS, General MacArthur gave final approval to General Ridgway's plan for Operation Rugged, which commenced March 22. The attack moved steadily forward and reached generally to the 38th Parallel by March 30. On April 3 MacArthur flew to Korea to discuss with Ridgway the next step, which would reach all the way to the "Kansas" line across the North Korean border. They reviewed recent intelligence and the possibility of an enemy counterattack. Ridgway informed MacArthur that he had decided not to attack across the Imjin River and that the strongest defensive line he could seize was "Kansas." MacArthur agreed and told Ridgway he wanted him to make a strong fight for this line but that any advance beyond it should be carefully limited and controlled.

MacArthur notified the JCS on April 5 that Operation Rugged was making progress and that Ridgway intended to follow up with another, called Operation Dauntless, to seize an extension of line "Kansas" in the west-central zone (Map 13a). This extension, called "Wyoming," would place the United Nations forces along the southern base of the Chorwon-Pyonggang-Kumhwa triangle — later to become known as the "Iron Triangle" — where the enemy was accumulating supplies and reinforcements. MacArthur reported that when the "Wyoming-Kansas" line was secured, he intended to limit further operations to battalion-sized patrols in order to maintain enemy contact. He was convinced that existing logistical limitations, combined with terrain, weather, and enemy dispositions, would make any further allied advance infeasible.

General MacArthur had reported on March 31 that a major renewal of the Chinese offensive might be expected any time in April. He estimated that the Chinese Communist forces had 274,000 troops in North Korea and almost 500,000 additional forces in Manchuria. The North Koreans had nearly 200,000 men, including guerrillas, available to join any attack.

In the face of these formidable numbers General Ridgway made plans to check the expected offensive by rolling to the rear with the enemy's punch. On April 12 he issued a plan for a possible withdrawal, called Operation Audacious. This was communicated in strictest confidence to senior commanders only. It provided for an orderly fighting withdrawal by successive phase lines and would be initiated only on Ridgway's orders.

But before this should become necessary and, in fact, before the line "Wyoming" could be attained, there were new United Nations commanders in Tokyo and Korea.

XI

THE RELIEF OF GENERAL MACARTHUR

MacArthur Offers to Negotiate

PRESIDENT TRUMAN's proposed announcement of his conditions for an armistice was never made. While the draft of this announcement, which had been agreed to by the Departments of State and Defense on March 19, 1951, was being circulated for clearance by the nations furnishing troops to the United Nations Command, General MacArthur on March 24 issued a public statement regarding the Korean conflict. In this communiqué he pointed out the military weaknesses of Communist China in comparison with the nations supporting the United Nations Command. He concluded:

> The enemy therefore must by now be painfully aware that a decision of the United Nations to depart from its tolerant effort to contain the war to the area of Korea, through expansion of our military operations to his coastal areas and interior bases, would doom Red China to the risk of imminent military collapse.
> These basic facts being established, there should be no insuperable difficulty arriving at decisions on the Korean problem if the issues are resolved on their own merits without being burdened by extraneous matters not directly related to Korea, such as Formosa and China's seat in the United Nations.
> The Korean nation and people which have been so cruelly ravaged must not be sacrificed. That is the paramount concern. Apart from the military area of the problem where the issues are resolved in the course of combat, the fundamental questions continue to be political in nature and must find their answer in the diplomatic sphere.

Within the area of my authority as military commander, how-ever, it should be needless to say I stand ready at any time to confer in the field with the commander in chief of the enemy forces in an earnest effort to find any military means whereby the realization of the political objectives of the United Nations in Korea, to which no nation may justly take exceptions, might be accomplished without further bloodshed.

The draft of the intended announcement by the President had not been furnished to MacArthur, but on March 21 he had been advised of it and told that it was being discussed with our allies. Despite this knowledge the general's announcement, ad-dressed, as he later wrote in his *Reminiscences,* "to my troops, to Korea, to Japan and to the world at large," was issued with-out any reference to or clearance by Washington.

When MacArthur's pronouncement — which was promptly dubbed by some as an ultimatum to the Communists — hit the headlines, the State Department was shocked, and the Pres-ident was furious. At the time the general's statement was made the President's draft announcement had been cleared with most of the thirteen nations having troops in Korea. There was an immediate outcry from some of these countries, notably England and France, fearful that MacArthur's communiqué might presage a broadening of the war in the event that the Communists did not agree to an armistice. A meeting was called at once on March 24 by the Secretary of State, which was attended by Secretary Acheson and members of his staff, Deputy Secretary of Defense Lovett, and the Joint Chiefs of Staff, at which the dilemma presented by the general's announcement was fully discussed. It was concluded that the idea of having the President make his announcement should be dropped, losing, according to Sec-retary Marshall, "whatever chance there may have been at that time to negotiate a settlement of the Korean conflict."

Later that afternoon the same group conferred with the Pres-ident. Mr. Truman later wrote that he had already made up his mind to relieve General MacArthur, but I cannot recall and can find no record that the question of dismissal was raised at this meeting. The President did direct General Bradley to call

General MacArthur's attention again to a directive of December 6, 1950, which (quoted on page 280) required that all public statements by government officials and military commanders dealing with foreign policy or military policy be cleared by the State or Defense Department. MacArthur's announcement had not been submitted to either. Bradley sent the following radio message:

> From JCS personal for MacArthur
> The President has directed that your attention be called to his order as transmitted 6 December 1950. In view of the information given you 20 March 51 any further statements by you must be coordinated as prescribed in the order of 6 December.
> The President has also directed that in the event Communist military leaders request an armistice in the field, you immediately report that fact to the JCS for instructions.
>   BRADLEY

Earlier Danger Signals

General MacArthur's pronouncement of March 24 was not the first instance of what Mr. Truman now regarded as "insubordination." Mr. Truman had been concerned for some time with the general's tendency to express publicly his views on the Far East that were at variance with United States Government policy.

The President's first uneasiness with respect to MacArthur came not from any utterance of the general's but from MacArthur's trip to Formosa on July 31, 1950, shortly after the outbreak of the Korean war. During my visit of July 10 to July 15 to Tokyo and Korea the general had discussed with me the Communist Chinese threat to Formosa, which island was located in his area of responsibility. He had told me that as soon as the situation in Korea was reasonably stabilized, he intended to visit Formosa for talks with Generalissimo Chiang Kai-shek, whose forces had taken refuge on Formosa the year before, after having been forced out of mainland China by the Communists. With a view to preventing a broadening of the Korean war Mr. Truman had directed MacArthur to interpose the U.S. Seventh Fleet between Formosa and the mainland for the dual purpose of securing Formosa from Communist attack and of preventing an attack from Chiang on the mainland.

In July of 1950 the Communists had begun to concentrate forces in China opposite Formosa, causing the JCS to recommend to the Secretary of Defense that the Nationalists be permitted to break up these concentrations, even if it meant attacks on the mainland. MacArthur heartily agreed and notified the Chiefs that he would visit Formosa shortly to make a personal survey of the situation, because there had been conflicting reports coming out of Formosa concerning the status of the Chiang government and its armed forces.

General MacArthur, accompanied by Admiral Struble, flew to Formosa on July 31 amid a flurry of speculation in the American and world press about the purpose of the visit. He remained on the island for two days, conferring with the Generalissimo, but not until five days after his return to Tokyo did he report on the visit to the JCS. Meanwhile, press speculation over whether any commitments had been made to Chiang continued to build up. The State and Defense Department and the White House were worried, particularly since the American Embassy in Taipeh had reported to the State Department that General MacArthur was about to transfer United States fighter squadrons to Formosa, a report that later proved to be unfounded. Adding heat to the speculative fever, the Generalissimo made a public announcement that hinted at extensive agreements between General MacArthur and himself.

However ill-founded, these rumors and alarms caused the President to direct Louis Johnson, then Secretary of Defense, to send a stern message of caution to MacArthur, stating, "No one other than the President as Commander in Chief has the authority to order or authorize preventive actions against concentrations on the mainland. The most vital national interest requires that no action of ours precipitate general war or give excuse to others to do so."

General MacArthur replied at once that he fully understood the President's wishes and was complying meticulously. He fol-

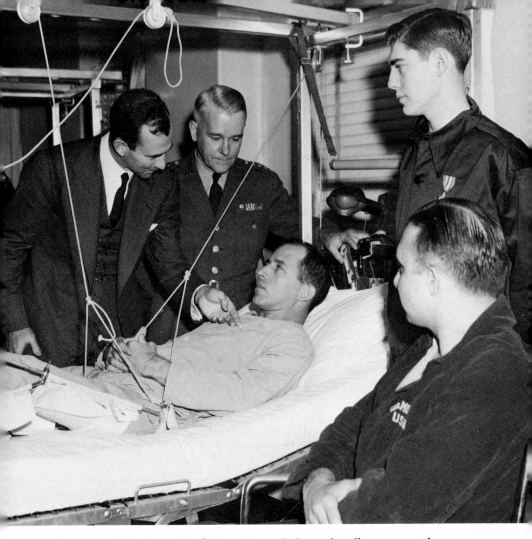

Secretary of the Army Frank Pace, Jr., and General Collins present the first Korean service ribbons to three wounded veterans

Men of the 187th Airborne Regimental Combat Team, U.S. Eighth Army, charge over the top of Hill 299, north of Seoul, through Chinese Communist fire

Members of the 1st Battalion, 24th Infantry Regiment, 25th Division, trudge up the rocky mountainside ten miles south of Chorwon on the west central front

Helicopter pilot prepares to take off for the 1st Mobile Army Surgical Hospital, Korea, with a wounded man enclosed in the stretcher attached to the right side

Paratroopers of the 187th Airborne Regimental Combat Team float earth-ward from C-119 planes to cut off retreating Communist units, south of Munsan

Tanks of the 72d Tank Battalion attached to the 2d U.S. Infantry Division move into position to support infantry of the ROK 8th Division attacking Communist positions in the Central Highlands, North Korea

Admiral Forrest P. Sherman, Chief of Naval Operations, and Lieutenant General Edward H. Almond, Commanding General U.S. X Corps, prepare to leave Corps airstrip to visit 1st Marine Division in Korea

Pfc. Robert V. Lombardi of Bronx, New York (*left*), and Pfc. Floyd R. Turberville of Tunnel Spring, Alabama, Company M, 23d Regiment, U.S. 2d Infantry Division, fire their mortar at Chinese Communist positions on Heartbreak Ridge

Chief of Naval Operations Admiral William M. Fechteler, escorted by Captain W. R. Smedberg III, inspecting United States Marines aboard the USS *Iowa*

Left. General Collins stands with other Army generals after his arrival at the X Corps airstrip to begin an inspection tour of the Corps area. *Left to right:* An unidentified Republic of Korea Major General; General Collins; General Matthew B. Ridgway, Commander in Chief, U.N. Command; General James A. Van Fleet, Commanding General, U.S. Eighth Army; Major General Clovis E. Byers, Commanding General, U.S. X Corps; and Major General Paik Sun Yup, Commanding General, 1st ROK Corps

Riflemen of Company L, 21st Regiment, 24th U.S. Infantry Division, return to their bunkers along the reverse slope of the ridge line commanding the heights of Kumsong

Major General William K. Harrison attends one of the daily meetings of the Military Armistice Commission at the United Nations base camp, Munsan-ni

Chinese Communist forces in one of the thirty compounds of the United Nations prisoner of war camp on Kojo-do

Major General William F. Dean, former Commanding General, 24th Infantry Division, after being presented Korea's highest award, the Taeguk Medal with Gold Star, by President Syngman Rhee. Looking on is General Mark W. Clark, Commander in Chief, U.N. Command.

lowed up with a complete report of his conference with Chiang. He confirmed Chiang's willingness to cooperate and said Chiang's forces had real potential if given additional equipment and training. He reported that he had ordered periodic sweeps of the Formosa Straits by elements of the Seventh Fleet, occasional reconnaissance flights over adjacent areas of China, and familiarization flights by small groups of United States aircraft that would include temporary and refueling landings on Formosa. All of these actions were fully in accord with the President's original instructions for the defense of Formosa, as transmitted to Mac-Arthur by the JCS on June 27, 1950.

MacArthur had taken umbrage at the distorted press reports of his Formosa visit and in a detailed public rebuttal had said, in part:

This visit has been maliciously misrepresented to the public by those who invariably in the past have propagandized a policy of defeatism and appeasement in the Pacific.

To make sure that MacArthur was fully cognizant of the Government's policy toward the Far East, Mr. Truman sent Averell Harriman, one of his closest advisers and a former friend of Mac-Arthur, to Tokyo to confer with the general. Harriman was accompanied by General Ridgway and General Lauris Norstad, the Deputy Chief of Staff for Operations, United States Air Force. According to the General's comments on this visit in his *Reminiscences* and the lengthy quotation from Harriman's report in Mr. Truman's *Memoirs,* the two men had a frank but somewhat wary discussion of the major political and foreign-policy problems involved in the Korea-Formosa situation. MacArthur later wrote of the Harriman visit, "He left me with a feeling of concern and uneasiness that the situation in the Far East was little understood and mistakenly downgraded in high circles in Washington." On his part, Harriman assured the President that MacArthur had not overstepped proper military bounds in the general's visit to Formosa. But at one point in his report Harriman summarized his impression of the general's attitude: "For reasons which are rather difficult to explain, I did not feel that we came to a full agreement on the way we believed things should be handled on Formosa with the Generalissimo. He accepted the President's position and will act accordingly, but without full conviction."

This early lack of rapport between the President and MacArthur with respect to Formosa unquestionably cast a pall over their relationship, which was to be darkened by subsequent events, the first of which followed quickly.

Perhaps taking its cue from some of the articles in the American press concerning the general's visit to Formosa, the Peiping régime in August 1950 charged the United States with aggression in Formosa and asked the U.N. Security Council to order the withdrawal of all United States armed forces which, it alleged, had invaded Formosa. President Truman felt impelled to refute this charge through our Ambassador to the United Nations, Warren Austin, who furnished the U.N. Secretary General, Trygve Lie, with a full account of the official American policy in regard to Formosa. Ambassador Austin quoted the President's recent statement to the American Congress, in which he declared that the United States would not seek any special position or privilege on Formosa.

The U.N. Security Council was still mulling over a charge made by Jakob Malik, the Russian delegate, accusing the United States of aggression in connection with our neutralization of Formosa, when a paper prepared by MacArthur, to be read for him before a national meeting of the Veterans of Foreign Wars in Chicago, was released to the press on August 26 by the public relations office at General Headquarters in Tokyo.

In this paper MacArthur stated that our strategic frontier in the Pacific had been advanced, as a result of the defeat of Japan in World War II, from the Hawaii-Midway-Guam-Philippines line to the chain of islands extending "in an arc from the Aleutians to the Marianas held by us and our free allies. From this island chain we can dominate by air power every Asiatic port from Vladivostok to Singapore and prevent any hostile movement into the Pacific. . . . If we hold this line we may have peace — lose it and war is inevitable."

This could be, and was, interpreted not only by the State Department and the White House but by many of our allies in the United Nations, as well as by the Communists, that we intended to establish and hold air bases on Formosa. MacArthur continued with one of his often repeated remarks: "Nothing could be more fallacious than the threadbare argument by those who advocate appeasement and defeatism in the Pacific [that] if we defend Formosa we alienate continental Asia. Those who speak thus do not understand the Orient."

A copy of MacArthur's letter to the veterans was brought to Mr. Truman from the White House press room two days before its scheduled delivery date. Mr. Truman interpreted it as being critical of and contrary to his announced policy toward Formosa, which Ambassador Austin had spelled out to the U.N. Secretary General only the day before, and which MacArthur had assured Harriman that he would support. The President felt that the MacArthur statement would serve to confuse the United Nations and the world about just what the real policy of the United States was. Furthermore, he regarded its issuance as violating the traditional American relationship of the military to civilian control, aside from the impropriety of a public declaration of views by the commander of United Nations forces in the field while Formosa was being debated in the U.N. Security Council.

In his memoirs Mr. Truman has said that at that time he gave serious thought to relieving MacArthur as Commander in Chief in the Far East and replacing him with Bradley but decided not to do so. He also said that on August 26, he read MacArthur's letter to a meeting of Acheson, Johnson, John W. Snyder, Secretary of the Treasury (and a close political adviser to President Truman), Harriman, and the JCS. (I have no recollection of this meeting, which apparently occurred while I was en route back from Tokyo. I testified at the MacArthur Hearings, p. 1294, that "as a member of the Chiefs I was not consulted as to the basis of the objection to the letter.") As a result of this meeting the President directed Johnson to radio MacArthur to withdraw his statement "because various features with respect to Formosa are in conflict with the policy of the United States and its position in the United Nations."

MacArthur immediately radioed back protesting that his message had been carefully drafted to support fully the President's statement of June 27 with respect to Formosa. Surprisingly, he apparently felt that he could divorce his views as a private citizen from his official position as Commander in Chief, United Nations Command, in Korea — something no government official has ever succeeded in doing. He claimed that his statements in the letter were "purely my personal ones." He called attention to the fact that the Veterans of Foreign Wars undoubtedly had given wide distribution to the speech in the customary advance press releases. Under the circumstances he advised Secretary Johnson that retraction of his message would be a grave mistake. The general did not mention, and probably did not know, that the *U.S. News and World Report* already had a copy.

MacArthur's reclama had no effect. He was required to notify the National Commander of the Veterans of Foreign Wars that he had been directed to withdraw his message — a bitter pill for a proud and sensitive man to swallow publicly. In retrospect he may have been right in considering that suppression of the message would be a mistake. Its enforced withdrawal did attract world attention to the statement, which the *U.S. News and World Report* published in full on September 1. However, the President felt that the impression of hidden United States intentions of retaining control of Formosa for military purposes — which he believed would be read into the message by the Communists and dissident elements in the United Nations — made it imperative for him to repudiate the general's statement, despite the obvious drawbacks of suppressing it. And MacArthur should have foreseen that his statement could provide false propaganda to the Soviets, as it did. It was picked up at once on the Russian radio, and shortly thereafter in a speech before the U.N. General Assembly the Soviet Ambassador, Andrei Vishinsky, twisted the intent of the general's remarks, saying, "None other than General MacArthur recently informed, with cynical candor, the whole world about the decision of the ruling circles of the United States of America at all costs to turn Taiwan into an American base in the Far East."

Whatever the effect of the letter on world opinion, it made a lasting impression on Mr. Truman. Though he tried to soften the blow to MacArthur's personal feelings by later messages, the incident further clouded the relationship of the two men and weakened the confidence of the President in his proconsul in the Far East.

After Inchon

The prestige of General MacArthur after Inchon was so great that the JCS leaned over backward not to contravene his occasional strayings from military directives. Even the President, in going to Wake Island, made a special effort to become acquainted with the general whom he had never met. From all indications he came away from Wake well impressed with his field commander.

On his part, MacArthur was later to write in his *Reminiscences:*

> The conference at Wake Island made me realize that a curious, and sinister, change was taking place in Washington. The original courageous decision of Harry Truman to meet and defeat Communism in Asia was apparently being chipped away by the constant pounding whispers of timidity and cynicism. The President seemed to be swayed by the blandishments of some of the more selfish politicians of the United Nations. He seemed to be in the anomalous position of openly expressing fears of over-calculated risks that he had fearlessly taken only a few months before.
>
> This put me as a field commander in an especially difficult situation. Up to now I had been engaged in warfare as it had been conducted through the ages — to fight to win. But I could see now that the Korean War was developing into something quite different. There seemed to be a deliberate underestimating of the importance of the conflict to which the government had committed — and was expending — the lives of United States fighting men.

It is difficult to gauge how much of these comments was actually the feeling of MacArthur at the time of the Wake Island conference and how much was the result of bitterness at his being relieved of command.

For some time after the Wake Island conference General Mac-
Arthur limited his recommendations strictly to military channels.
When I made my third wartime trip to Tokyo in early December
of 1950, I had sought MacArthur's recommendations concerning
how best to counter the Chinese intervention. He had proposed
the bombing of China, the institution of a naval blockade, and
other measures. These I had reported to the JCS, and the general
had followed up with several messages to the Chiefs urging various actions. We had given careful consideration to these suggestions and on January 12, 1951, had submitted to the Secretary
of Defense a study analyzing sixteen possible courses of action if
conditions in Korea should worsen to the point where we might
have to evacuate to Japan. This study was forwarded by Secretary Marshall to the National Security Council. On my next trip
to the Far East with General Vandenberg in January, 1951, I read
the JCS memorandum to General MacArthur on January 15. The
JCS and MacArthur were in general agreement on the sixteen
points in the memorandum, which included a naval and economic
blockade of China, the initiation of naval and air attacks on objectives in China in the event that the Communists attacked any of
our forces outside Korea, the continuation of bombing of military
targets in Korea, and other measures. However, I made clear to
the general that these proposals were tentative and their implementation was dependent largely on whether we would have to
evacuate Korea. Actually, all but four were implemented. These
four dealt with an economic and naval blockade of China, which
would have affected the trade of some of our allies besides that
of the Soviet Union, the removal of restrictions on aerial reconnaissance of Manchuria and Communist China coastal waters,
and the removal of restrictions on the operations of Chinese Nationalist forces on Taiwan against the mainland. As a result of
the improved conditions in Korea created by Ridgway's skillful
operations, Vandenberg and I reported to the JCS our judgment
that we would not be forced out of Korea, and the JCS supported
the action of the National Security Council in not implementing
these four courses of action.

Over the following months MacArthur complained more and

more about the failure to make effective all sixteen recommendations. And as the general's estimation of Chinese intentions and capabilities proved to be wrong, he became more sensitive to criticisms that began to appear in the domestic and foreign press and began to yield to the temptation to defend himself in the public forum.

In December of 1950 he hit out vehemently in the *U.S. News and World Report* and the *New York Times*, charging that limitations placed on his operations were an enormous handicap "without precedent in military history" — which was true, though most United States field commanders have had to operate under restrictive directives, as have Pershing in Mexico and Eisenhower in Europe. But this new limited war, which was being fought, not just by the United States, but by international forces under the ægis of the United Nations, was also without precedent. As Mr. Truman later phrased his growing differences with the general: "General MacArthur was ready to risk general war and I was not."

President Truman was particularly incensed by General MacArthur's statements during this period. In later years he wrote that prior to the launching of the ill-fated offensive of November 24, 1950, toward the Yalu, MacArthur had "talked as if he had the answer to all the questions. But when it turned out that it was not so, he let all the world know that he would have won except for the fact that we would not let him have his way. I should have relieved Gen. MacArthur then and there. . . . There was no excuse for the statements he now began to make to certain people as soon as the offensive had failed. . . . Within a matter of four days he found time to publicize in four different ways his view that the only reason for his troubles was the order from Washington to limit the hostilities to Korea . . . and made it quite plain that no blame whatsoever attached to him or his staff."

Determined to put a stop to such statements, whatever their source, President Truman on December 5, 1950, sent to Cabinet members and the heads of all executive departments a directive requiring government officials to clear with the State Department all foreign-policy statements and with Defense all public statements dealing with military policy. The directive specified that it applied to all top officials whether located in Washington or in the field. The JCS sent a copy of this broad instruction to General MacArthur on December 6 and also forwarded to him a copy of the following specific directive, which the President had transmitted to the Secretaries of State and Defense:

> In addition to the policy expressed in memorandum of this date to the heads of departments, concerning the clearance of speeches and statements, I wish the following steps to be taken:
> Officials overseas, including military commanders and diplomatic representatives, should be ordered to exercise extreme caution in public statements, to clear all but routine statements with their departments, and to refrain from direct communication on military or foreign policy with newspapers, magazines or other publicity media in the United States.

The JCS added:

> The above is transmitted to you for guidance and appropriate action.

It was this directive that MacArthur ignored or, possibly, had forgotten, when he made his pronouncement of March 24, 1951, with its offer to negotiate an armistice in the field.

The Final Straw: Congressman Martin Publishes a Letter

Mr. Truman's ire over General MacArthur's pronouncement of March 24 had scarcely cooled when another unfortunate incident touched him to the quick. On March 20, a few days before MacArthur's offer to negotiate, the general had replied to a personal letter from Congressman Joseph W. Martin, Republican Minority Leader in the House of Representatives. On March 8 Martin had written the general that he was scheduled shortly to make a radio address suggesting that Chiang's forces on Formosa might be employed in the opening of a second front against the Chinese Communists to relieve the pressure on our forces in Korea. Martin had stated:

I would deem it a great help if I could have your views on this point, either on a confidential basis or otherwise.

In his reply, in which he made no mention of any restriction on its use, General MacArthur wrote in part:

My views and recommendations with respect to the situation created by Red China's entry into the war against us in Korea have been submitted to Washington in most complete detail. Generally these views are well known and generally understood, as they follow the conventional pattern of meeting force with the maximum counterforce as we have never failed to do in the past. Your view with respect to the utilization of the Chinese forces on Formosa is in conflict with neither logic nor this tradition.

It seems strangely difficult for some to realize that here in Asia is where the Communist conspirators have elected to make their play for global conquest, and that we have joined the issue thus raised on the battlefield; that here we fight Europe's war with arms while the diplomats there still fight it with words; that if we lose this war to Communism in Asia the fall of Europe is inevitable, win it and Europe most probably would avoid war and yet preserve freedom. As you point out, we must win. There is no substitute for victory.

This letter clearly revealed the extent to which MacArthur's frustration over the limitations placed on his operations had gotten the better of his judgment. His reversion to his World War II pique at the priority given the European theater over the Pacific broke out again in the non-sequitur comparison of the Korean war with the situation in Europe. This was as untimely and unseemly as it was illogical. The general chose to forget, or ignore, the gallant fight of the Greeks to save their country from Communism and the fortitude of the Berliners in defying Russia throughout the trying days of the Berlin airlift. Though their contributions to General MacArthur's United Nations Command were small, seven European countries had sent combat units, and three others had furnished medical units. The general should have known that his letter to the Republican Minority Leader would be made public, with inevitable political repercussions.

Congressman Martin's reading, on April 5, 1951, on the floor of the House of Representatives, of his correspondence with the general and its subsequent spread in the *Congressional Record* were the final incidents that goaded the President into action. The following day Mr. Truman called to a meeting the Secretaries of State and Defense, Harriman, and Bradley. The President has written that he had already made up his mind to relieve Mac-Arthur, but he announced no decision at this meeting, though the question of "what should be done about General MacArthur" was discussed for an hour. According to Mr. Truman, Harriman felt the general should have been relieved in 1949, when MacArthur pleaded he could not come to Washington to discuss an important economic issue that was up before the Japanese Diet. Marshall advised caution, saying he wished to reflect on the matter. Bradley was reported to have said that the general had been insubordinate and deserved to be relieved but that he wanted to obtain the views of the JCS. The President did ask Marshall to bring to his attention all pertinent messages exchanged between the Pentagon and MacArthur's headquarters.

Early the next day, Saturday, April 7, the President and the same group met again. It was agreed that the question of the action that should be taken with respect to MacArthur should be considered by each individually over the weekend. The President directed Secretary Marshall to secure the views of the Joint Chiefs of Staff on the possible relief of the general.

I had left Washington on Thursday, April 5, to give a talk at the Air War College in Montgomery, Alabama, and to inspect the 4th Infantry Division at Fort Benning, Georgia, and knew nothing of these meetings until I returned Saturday evening. Meanwhile, late on April 5, according to Admiral Sherman's testimony at the MacArthur Hearings, General Bradley had advised the other Chiefs that consideration was being given at the White House to the relief of General MacArthur and suggested that the Chiefs be thinking about it, since they might be called on for their views or recommendations.

Bradley called the JCS together in his office at 2:00 P.M., Sunday, April 8, and informed us that the President was considering relieving General MacArthur and that Secretary Marshall wanted to have our strictly military viewpoints. I cannot recall all the details of our discussion, but we reviewed the various incidents and the general's differences with the policies of the President. I remember saying — as I later testified — that I felt the President was entitled to have a commander in the field whose views were more in consonance with the basic policies of his government and who was more responsive to the will of the President as Commander in Chief.

Consideration was given to recommending the retention of MacArthur as Supreme Commander in Japan, but we all thought that the problems of occupation and defense of Japan were so intimately tied with Korea that it would be infeasible to have two commanders in Japan. At the end of our discussion, in which all of us actively participated, it was agreed unanimously that we should concur in the relief of General MacArthur by the President. I do not recall it with certainty, but I am quite sure we concluded then that General Ridgway was the logical choice for his successor.

It was a sad and sober group of men that reported to Secretary Marshall in his office at 4:00 P.M. It was not easy to be a party to the dismissal of a distinguished soldier. The Secretary asked each of us individually for his views. We each gave them orally. Then the Secretary asked for our conclusion, which Bradley, as Chairman, stated was that we concurred in the President's proposal to relieve MacArthur. As was frequently the case when Secretary Marshall received staff reports orally, he made no comment of his own but simply said that Bradley should present the views of the JCS to the President at a meeting Monday morning.

Bradley was the only member of the JCS present at this meeting, which was attended by Acheson, Marshall, and Harriman. He reported that the Chiefs had all agreed MacArthur should be relieved. Marshall and the others each concurred, whereupon the President announced his decision.

Bradley had presented orally the views of the JCS. After the meeting he went back to his office and dictated a draft memorandum for the record, spelling out the three principal reasons cited by the Chiefs of Staff for their concurrence in the relief. This draft was circulated to the Chiefs, with the caution that nothing should be added that was not discussed by them at their meetings with Bradley and Marshall on Sunday afternoon, April 8. The three reasons given by the JCS for our support of the relief of Mac-Arthur were as follows:

1. That by his public statements and official communications Gen. MacArthur had indicated that he was not in sympathy with the decision to try to limit the conflict to Korea. This made it difficult for him to carry out the JCS directives. It was necessary to have a commander in the field more responsive to control from Washington.

2. Gen. MacArthur had failed to comply with the President's directive to clear statements on policy before making such statements public. He had taken independent action in proposing publicly to negotiate an armistice directly with the enemy field commander despite the fact that he knew the President had such a proposal under consideration at a government level.

3. The JCS felt the military in our country must be controlled by civilian authority. Gen. MacArthur's statements and actions ran counter to this basic principle.

After the decisive meeting with the President Secretary Marshall met with General Bradley and me and asked me to draft the messages that would have to be sent to Generals MacArthur, Ridgway, and James A. Van Fleet, who was to succeed Ridgway. (As in the case of General Ridgway's succession to General Walker's command of the Eighth Army, I, as Army Chief of Staff, had obtained prior agreement wtih Secretaries Pace and Marshall that Lieutenant General Van Fleet should be appointed Commanding General, Eighth Army, if anything happened to Ridgway. President Truman approved Van Fleet's appointment.)

The draft orders were submitted to Secretary Marshall, who presented them on Tuesday afternoon, April 10, at a meeting with the President of the same four principals, Acheson, Marshall, Harriman, and Bradley, who had been advisers of the President throughout. Secretary Marshall testified during the MacArthur Hearings:

> We met again, the same group, with the President, and there submitted these drafts of his directive to General MacArthur for his relief, and of his statement, his public statement, that was to be made, and of the draft of the order that I was to issue to Gen. Ridgway to take command.
>
> These were in draft form. There were minor adjustments made in them and then they were prepared for issue.

According to Secretary Marshall's testimony, the original plan of the group advisory to the President was to have the dismissal order delivered personally to General MacArthur by Secretary of the Army Pace, the Executive Agent for the Department of Defense, who happened to be on an inspection visit to the Far East Command. Specific instructions were dispatched to Pace that he was to deliver the order to the general at the Embassy before the latter went to his office for his daily business. The order was to have been delivered at 8:00 P.M., Wednesday, April 11, Washington time, which was 10:00 A.M., April 12, Tokyo time. It is not clear, but apparently it was intended that the relief would become effective at a later date or, in Secretary Marshall's words, "was named for some date ahead." Unfortunately, Secretary Pace had gone to Korea — not knowing anything of the impending relief — and the instructions did not reach him in time because of a breakdown in a power unit in Pusan.

Late Tuesday, April 10, in Washington there were indications that the action to be taken had become known publicly and was to be published by a Chicago newspaper the following morning. The President then decided to advance the transmission of the official notification to General MacArthur by approximately twenty hours. The exact timing of the public release was made so as to coincide with the arrival in Tokyo of a hurriedly revised dispatch sent directly to General Headquarters.

President Truman's announcement was as follows:

> With deep regret I have concluded that General of the Army Douglas MacArthur is unable to give his wholehearted support to the policies of the United States Government and of the United Nations in matters pertaining to his official duties. In view of the specific responsibilities imposed upon me by the Constitution of the United States and the added responsibilities entrusted to me by the United Nations, I have decided that I must make a change of command in the Far East. I have, therefore, relieved General MacArthur of his commands and have designated Lieutenant General Matthew B. Ridgway as his successor.
>
> Full and vigorous debate on matters of national policy is a vital element in the constitutional system of our free democracy. It is fundamental, however, that military commanders must be governed by the policies and directives issued to them in the manner provided by our laws and the Constitution. In time of crisis, this consideration is particularly compelling.
>
> General MacArthur's place in history as one of our greatest commanders is fully established. The Nation owes him a debt of gratitude for the distinguished and exceptional service which he has rendered his country in posts of great responsibility. For that reason, I repeat my regret at the necessity for the action I feel compelled to take in his case.

According to General MacArthur, the first inkling that he had been relieved came from his wife at the Embassy residence where they had just finished lunch. An aide had telephoned that he had heard a special news bulletin that interrupted a program to say, "President Truman has just relieved General MacArthur from his Far Eastern and Korean Commands and from the direction of the occupation of Japan." Apparently, the official dispatch did not reach the general until a half-hour or so later. It was a sad and deplorable way to terminate the military career of a distinguished soldier.

Upon receipt of the dispatch, General MacArthur directed his Chief of Staff, General Hickey, to telephone General Ridgway in Korea at once to inform him of the President's orders. He turned over to Hickey the functions of command until Ridgway could fly to Tokyo to take over in person.

Ridgway happened to be at the front in Korea with Secretary Pace when a war correspondent, who evidently had heard a radio announcement of Ridgway's new assignment, asked Ridgway whether congratulations were not in order. Not knowing anything of the dramatic events that had been transpiring, Ridgway could only respond briefly that he didn't know what the man was talking about. For some reason the correspondent did not enlighten him, and Ridgway continued on the tour of the front with Pace, who likewise knew nothing of the role that had been intended for him to play in the relief of MacArthur. It was not until several hours later that Ridgway learned of his elevation to command of the United States forces in the Far East and the United Nations Command in Korea.

He left for Tokyo at noon the following day, April 12, 1951, for a brief conference with MacArthur and to pay his respects to his former commander. Matt Ridgway has payed tribute to the "indomitable spirit" of General MacArthur, who received him "with the greatest courtesy. . . . He was entirely himself — composed, quiet, temperate, friendly, and helpful to the man who was to succeed him. He made some allusions to the fact that he had been summarily relieved, but there was no trace of bitterness or anger in his tone. I thought it was a fine tribute to the resilience of this great man that he could accept so calmly, with no outward sign of shock, what must have been a devastating blow to a professional soldier standing at the peak of his career."

Ridgway flew back to Korea the same evening, where he remained until General Van Fleet arrived to assume command of the Eighth Army on April 14.

The Senate Hearings

General MacArthur returned home to the adulation of crowds everywhere, a tumultuous reception in San Francisco, an emotion-filled address to a joint session of the Congress, a ticker-tape parade in New York, and then a more sober inquiry into his relief by the combined Foreign Relations and Armed Services Committees of the United States Senate. Later he received the official thanks of the Congress of the United States.

The Senate hearings, conducted in closed executive sessions of the joint committees, began May 3, 1951, and lasted for seven weeks. More than two million words of testimony were taken from thirteen witnesses. The stated purpose of the inquiry was to examine the military situation in the Far East and the circumstances surrounding the recall of General MacArthur. Including appendices, the printed record totaled 3691 pages. It was cleared on a daily basis by Vice Admiral Arthur C. Davis, the Director of the Joint Staff of the JCS. Admiral Davis had been designated by the Defense Department, at the request of Senator Russell, to act as censor of any sensitive military information that should be deleted from the public record. Such deletions were subject to review by two members of the Joint Committee.

The inquiry was supposed to be nonpartisan, and the Chairman, Senator Richard B. Russell of Georgia, and some committee members of both parties tried to keep it so. But General MacArthur, a popular hero and prominent Republican, who had permitted his name to be entered in the 1948 Wisconsin presidential primary, had been relieved of his commands by a Democratic president, and with a presidential election coming up the next year it was inevitable that politics would enter the deliberations. The undeclared war in Korea was not going very well, and the Senate committees, always sensitive of their prerogatives and responsibilities with respect to the conduct of war and foreign affairs, wanted to know why. The skeptical temper of the senators was indicated at once by the requirement that all witnesses testify under oath, a procedure rarely required of such distinguished persons as the Secretaries of State and Defense and military men of the stature of Generals MacArthur and Bradley.

The Committee Chairman had to be reminded by a member to swear in General MacArthur, the first witness. The general referred to his address to the Congress in lieu of any preliminary statement, then submitted himself to questions. Under the procedure followed throughout each member was allotted a limited time for questioning. By and large, the general was treated with

kid gloves by all committee members and drew praise from Democrats and Republicans alike for his accomplishments and lifetime
of distinguished service.

But the next witness, Secretary Marshall, and all who followed
who were in any way connected with the relief were subjected to
intensive grilling, generally following a critical pattern set by most
Republican members, and to a more friendly treatment from most
of the Democrats, palpably designed to counter Republican arguments. The questions bounced around, with much repetition
and little semblance of order, from such subjects as the relief of
General MacArthur to the strategic importance of Formosa, to the
Yalta conference, to the alleged Communist penetration of the
State Department, to the Wedemeyer report on China, to the
authorship of the Atlantic Charter, to the relations between General Stilwell and Chiang Kai-shek. Actually, more time was spent
in attacking and defending the Administration's policies in the
Far East than in enquiring into the circumstances surrounding the
recall of General MacArthur, though the Chiefs of Staff were
queried over and over again on our unanimous support of the
recall.

Not only did the Chiefs of Staff support the relief of General
MacArthur, we backed the efforts of the Administration to prevent the Korean war from expanding into a war with Russia or
China, or both. General Bradley in one statement summarized the
basic differences between General MacArthur and the JCS in this
respect:

> While a field commander very properly estimates his needs
> from the viewpoint of operations in his own theater or sphere
> of action, those responsible for higher direction must necessarily
> base their actions on broader aspects, and on the needs, actual
> or prospective, of several theaters. The Joint Chiefs of Staff,
> in view of their global responsibilities and their perspective with
> respect to the world-wide strategic situation, are in a better
> position than any single theater commander to assess the risk of
> general war. Moreover, the Joint Chiefs of Staff are best able
> to judge our own military resources with which to meet that
> risk. . . .
> From a global viewpoint — and with the security of our

Nation of prime importance — our military mission is to support a policy of preventing Communism from gaining the manpower, the resources, the raw materials, and the industrial capacity essential to world domination. If Soviet Russia ever controls the entire Eurasian land mass, then the Soviet-satellite imperialism may have the broad base upon which to build the military power to rule the world. . . .

Korea, in spite of the importance of the engagement, must be looked upon with proper perspective. It is just one engagement, just one phase of this battle. . . .

As long as we keep the conflict within its present scope, we are holding to a minimum the forces we must commit and tie down. . . .

The strategic alternative, enlargement of the war in Korea to include Red China, would probably delight the Kremlin more than anything else we could do. . . .

Red China is not the powerful nation seeking to dominate the world. Frankly, in the opinion of the Joint Chiefs of Staff, this strategy would involve us in the wrong war, at the wrong place, at the wrong time, and with the wrong enemy.

General Vandenberg and I were queried extensively about why the JCS did not support bombing of the Communist bases in Manchuria. My views were expressed in this exchange with Senator Russell B. Long, Democrat of Louisiana:

Senator Long. But it is your feeling that to undertake to directly punish the Chinese by bombing within China would tend to unify them and to commit their government to a principle that they were going to fight an all-out war with the United States, whatever the cost?

General Collins. I firmly believe that. . . . and the trouble is . . . when you start bombing, to make it effective you wouldn't only have to bomb the airfields where there are planes, but you would have to bomb the storage houses, the warehouses, and things of that sort. . . .

Now where do you stop? Once you embark on the business of bombing, the other man is going to move away from you. Well, he just moves a little deeper and then you get deeper, and the first thing you know, you are involved in the bombing of cities and all sorts of things, aside from the bombing of strictly military installations such as airfields.

It was at this point, according to my recollection (the public record shows a deletion here), that I expressed my constant fear that a few incendiary bombs might be dropped some night, in reprisal, on Pusan, our lone major port and main supply base in Korea. It was terribly vulnerable to such an attack.

Reinforcing the point I had made about the extent of bombing of Manchuria that would be required to be really effective, General Vandenberg testified in his opposition to bombing north of the Yalu with the totally inadequate air force we had at that time:

> Air power, and especially the application of strategic air power, should go to the heart of the industrial centers to become reasonably efficient. Now, the source of materiel that is coming to the Chinese Communists and the North Koreans is from Russia. Therefore, hitting across the Yalu, we could destroy or lay waste to all of Manchuria and the principal cities of China if we used the full power of the United States Air Force. . . . However, in doing that we are bound to get attrition. If we use less than the full power of the United States Air Force, in my opinion it might not and probably would not be conclusive. . . . the attrition that would inevitably be brought upon us by bombing north of the Yalu would leave us, in my opinion, naked for several years to come, and therefore I did not advocate it.

With reference to General MacArthur's advocacy of a naval blockade of China Admiral Sherman testified, in part:

> A blockade, to be completely successful, should cut off all access to vital strategic materials or equipment. However, since a naval blockade of China alone assumes a neutral Russia, it would be impossible to stop the flow of materials overland from Russia.
>
> Russia would very probably demand unimpeded access to Port Arthur and Dairen, over which it exercises military rights and other privileges under Sino-Soviet treaties. . . .
>
> The blockade could not be tight without allied cooperation.

The fact is that our allies have been unwilling to join in a naval blockade of China . . .

. . . the reason why I feel that the United States has been well advised not to attempt, unilaterally, by force, to establish this naval blockade is that the object is to stop the shipment of material into China, and for us to send the United States Navy out to cut off shipments under the flags of our allies would, in my opinion, defeat our wider purposes.

As the hearings proceeded, Senator Charles W. Tobey, Republican of New Hampshire, chided his colleagues on "the utter futility of much that is going on here . . . We are asking questions many of them very, very piddling . . . When we get all through Mr. MacArthur will still be deposed from his position, Mr. Marshall will still be the man in charge of the defense of this country, the Joint Chiefs of Staff will still be the same as they are now . . . there is a distinct, political trend in a lot of these hearings, subconsciously at least . . . I think the whole thing is unfortunate. I wish we could ring the curtain down."

His statement was challenged by Senator Wayne Morse, and his fellow senators also obviously disagreed with him, as did the public. In my judgment the hearings were worthwhile. Not only did they expose the pros and cons of our Far East policy to review; they produced a record that is a gold mine of information on the Korean war and the confused attitudes of the American Congress, confronted for the first time with the frustrations of a limited war. In any event, the hearings meandered on and on. But at the end it was obvious that there could be no agreement on a report to the Congress.

Chairman Russell did succeed in obtaining unanimous agreement to a "Statement Affirming Faith in Country," designed to assure our friends and allies and to warn Communist aggressors that "the objectives of the people of the United States are unchanged by anything that has transpired during this ordeal of controversy. We are unshaken in our determination to defend ourselves and to assist to the limit of our capabilities all of those free nations determined to survive in freedom."

The Republican members of the joint committees, with the exception of Senators Henry Cabot Lodge, Wayne Morse, Leverett Saltonstall, and Charles W. Tobey, prepared and issued to the public a report of their personal findings. It is of interest that only six of forty-eight "findings" of this group dealt in any way with the relief of General MacArthur and only two of eight listed "conclusions" covered this subject. The second of the eight conclusions stated, "The removal of Gen. MacArthur was within the constitutional power of the President, but the circumstances were a shock to the national pride." The third conclusion read, "There was no serious disagreement between Gen. MacArthur and the Joint Chiefs of Staff as to military strategy in Korea." The remaining conclusions were:

1. The inquiry was in the public interest.

4. Our armed forces acquitted themselves with gallantry.

5. The administration's Far East policy has been a catastrophic failure.

6. The foreign policy of the United States since the middle 1940's has been based on expediency rather than the principles of liberty and justice.

7. The United States should never again become involved in a war without the consent of Congress.

8. Cessation of hostilities, based upon the restoration of the status quo at the thirty-eighth parallel, will be a victory for aggression.

The report was signed by Styles Bridges, Alexander Wiley, H. Alexander Smith, Bourke B. Hickenlooper, William F. Knowland, Harry P. Cain, Owen Brewster, and Ralph E. Flanders.

There was at least a modicum of truth in what Senator Tobey had said. Nothing was changed by the hearings. The war went on pretty much as it had before the relief of General MacArthur but with much less strain between the field command and the political and military leaders in Washington. The chief importance of the outcome of the clash between the General and the President was that the great American tradition of civilian control of the military was once again courageously asserted. To the list of things that Senator Tobey predicted would be unchanged he might have added that Mr. Truman would still be very much the President of the United States.

XII

STALEMATE

Van Fleet Takes Over the Eighth Army

GENERAL JAMES A. VAN FLEET has had a unique career in the Army, in the latter phase of which I happened to have a role. Van was two years ahead of me at West Point, a member of the distinguished class of 1915, which included Dwight D. Eisenhower and Omar N. Bradley. As I remember, Van had not played football at the Point until Coach Charlie Daly persuaded the husky cadet to give it a try in his junior year. Van quickly developed into one of the most versatile backs the Army team had in those days of nonspecialists, helping mightily to lick the Navy 20 to 0 in the fall of 1914.

Out in the service Van Fleet did well, but in the early days of World War II he became the victim of a strange mix-up in the usually clear mind of General George C. Marshall, Army Chief of Staff. During the 1930's Lieutenant Colonel Marshall, then Assistant Commandant of the Infantry School at Fort Benning, had an officer on the faculty with almost the same name as Van Fleet. For certain disciplinary reasons Colonel Marshall had taken an adverse attitude toward this man. After the outbreak of World War II Van Fleet was recommended more than once for promotion to Brigadier General, but each time the recommendation had reached the Chief of Staff it was turned down by General Marshall, thinking the man involved was his former Benning instructor.

When I arrived in England in January 1943 to take command of the VII Corps, I discovered that Van Fleet was a colonel commanding the 8th Infantry Regiment, which had been designated the assault regiment of my 4th Infantry Division. On my first inspection of the regiment I found it in topnotch condition and was greatly impressed with its commander. I telephoned my observations to General Bradley and added, "We are wasting the potential of Van Fleet as a regimental commander. He ought to be in command of a division."

Brad's reply was "Well, Joe, he is in your Corps. Do something about it."

I replied, "If Van does as well on D Day and thereafter as I feel sure he will, I will recommend him at once to be a BG."

Van Fleet met all my expectations. He was promoted promptly and was soon put in command of the 90th Infantry Division, which he converted from one of the poorest divisions in Europe to one of the very best. He ended the war in command of a corps.

After I became Chief of Staff I recommended him to General Marshall, then Secretary of State, for heading the military assistance group being sent to Greece to aid the Greeks in combatting the Communist effort to take over that country. Again Van Fleet did a magnificent job. In my judgment he contributed more than any other person, including even Queen Fredrica or Marshal Papagos, to saving Greece from the Communists.

So it was with full confidence that, when Ridgway was sent to Tokyo to become Commander in Chief, Far East, and Commander in Chief, United Nations Command, I recommended Van Fleet as his successor. Van was cast in the same mold as Ridgway as a fighting man. I knew that he could take over the Eighth Army without a falter in its high morale and aggressive spirit. I felt also that Ridgway and Van Fleet would work well together. This they did, with only minor difficulties, which I did not foresee.

When Van Fleet took command on April 14, 1951, the Eighth Army held the "Kansas" line, which had been well prepared for defense (Map 13a). It ran from Munsanni along the Imjin River to near Majonni, then east of the Hwachon Reservoir, and on to Yangyang on the east coast. Van Fleet was anxious to keep up the forward momentum that Ridgway had initiated. However, all intelligence reports pointed to an early renewal of the Chinese offensive with the sixty divisions they still had available. Consequently, Ridgway restricted any advance of the Eighth Army to the "Wyoming" line, a northerly extension of "Kansas" between Majonni and Hwachon, and cautioned Van Fleet to maintain close lateral communications between units as the Army advanced.

Van Fleet's troops were edging their way forward of "Kansas" when the Chinese struck on the night of April 22 (Map 13b). Their main effort was directed toward Seoul, with secondary drives in the Yenchon-Hwachon area and in the mountains farther east. The Eighth Army held everywhere except in the center, where Van Fleet had his first experience with a ROK division breaking under attack. As the division fell back in disorder, Van Fleet decided to withdraw the Army to the "Kansas" line and halt there. However, under pressure from almost a half-million Chinese the Eighth Army was forced back almost 20 miles below "Kansas." It did manage to stop the Communist advance north of Seoul. The enemy offensive was called off in early May after beating itself out and suffering tremendous casualties in a futile effort to capture the city. Van Fleet had won his first battle. Moreover, he had won the confidence of the U.N. Command. Like Ridgway before him, he had been at the front almost constantly and had thus established himself with his men as their kind of soldier.

The Communists' spring campaign was not over, however. They still had in Korea Chinese and North Korean forces totaling almost 750,000 and an equal number across the Yalu in Manchuria, an aggregate total far outnumbering Van Fleet's 270,000 U.S. Army, Marine, and allied troops plus 235,000 in the ROK Army. Ridgway and Van Fleet knew that to keep the enemy off balance and to maintain the high morale of the U.N. Command they could not sit still, awaiting a renewal of the Communist attack. In early May Van Fleet had each front-line division begin probing attacks all along the front, clearing the Kimpo peninsula west of Seoul and recapturing Uijungbu and Chunchon, north and east of the capital. He was planning a general advance for May 12, but intelligence reports, which by now were quite reliable, indicated an imminent launching of a large-scale enemy attack. Van Fleet was forced to postpone his own offensive while readying his forces for the Communist onslaught. This came on the afternoon of May 16 with a drive of five Chinese armies down the Chunchon-Hongchon axis, 50 miles east of Seoul, against the U.S. IX and X Corps (Map 13c).

General Ridgway had been following closely the developments in Korea as the enemy shifted the weight of his forces eastward from north of Seoul, leaving only four armies in a 40-mile sector west of Chunchon. Ridgway estimated that it would take the Chinese at least a week to disengage from their drive on Hongchon and shift the mass of their forces to the western sector. He radioed Van Fleet on May 18, pointing out the opportunity for the Eighth Army to deliver a strong attack up the Uijonbu-Chorwon corridor against the enemy's weakened west flank, with the objective of relieving the pressure on the IX and X Corps. If this strategy proved successful, it would open "unlimited opportunities for major exploitation." After confirming the latest intelligence with a personal reconnaissance of the front General Ridgway on May 20 ordered Van Fleet to attack at once, not only along the Uijongbu-Chorwon axis but across the entire front.

The Chinese were caught overextended and completely by surprise. Their attack toward Hongchon ground to a halt as they belatedly strove to meet the Eighth Army's counterattack. The Americans made substantial gains against weakening resistance. By the end of May they had advanced back north almost to line "Kansas." More importantly, they reported killing more enemy than ever before in a comparable period and counted 10,000 prisoners, most of them Chinese. Ridgway reported to the JCS that huge quantities of enemy materiel were captured, including more artillery, mortars, and automatic weapons than had ever before been seized. Poor medical service and a shortage of food added to noticeable deterioration of Chinese and North Korean combat morale.

General Ridgway reported that, by contrast, the Eighth Army "was at near full strength with morale excellent and logistic capabilities little affected to date by deteriorating weather." He concluded with a bold prediction: "I, therefore, believe that for the next 60 days, the United States Government should be able to count with reasonable assurance upon a military situation in Korea offering optimum advantages in support of its diplomatic negotiations."

However, as we shall see in a later section of this chapter, pursuing the enemy beyond the "Kansas-Wyoming" line was not feasible.

Review of Ridgway's Directives

Keeping one eye on operations in Korea, General Ridgway had been taking a hard look at his dual roles of Commander in Chief of the United States forces in the Far East and Commander in Chief of the United Nations Command. One of his first acts was to have his Chief of Staff catalogue all of the orders, directives, and restrictions received by General MacArthur since the outbreak of war that were still in effect. In analyzing these instructions Ridgway ran into the same seeming conflicts that General MacArthur had, between his strictly American role and his international assignment.

Most of the difficulties arose from a consideration of the relative priorities of the Far East Commander's basic mission of protecting Japan and the United Nations Commander's responsibilities under the United Nations' somewhat vague mandate of June 27, 1950, "to repel the armed attack and restore international peace and security to the area [Korea]." Ridgway raised a specific point of possible conflict when, on April 17, 1951, he requested the JCS to authorize him to withdraw, at his discretion, the United Nations forces from Korea in the event of Russian intervention there and to use them in defense of Japan. Ridgway undoubtedly knew that he would not be permitted to employ any United Nations forces, other than those of the United States, in defense of Japan. Possibly his real intent was to seek clarification of his own authority in case Russia intervened in Korea or attacked Japan.

The JCS replied at once that, although we agreed in principle to the withdrawal of United Nations forces in the event of Russian intervention, we retained the authority to control such a withdrawal. Ridgway's query did cause the JCS to call on me as

Executive Agent to prepare an up-to-date set of instructions for his combined Far East and United Nations commands. The Army G-3 staff, under General Maxwell D. Taylor, after a thorough analysis of all current JCS directives to both commands, prepared a new directive, which sought to eliminate any ambiguities or conflicts. I reviewed and approved this draft which, after concurrence by the JCS, was forwarded to the Secretary of Defense and then to the President for final approval. The new directive was dispatched to General Ridgway on May 1.

Its chief divergence from prior instructions was that for the first time since the initial drive of United Nations Command into North Korea, when its advance was limited to the Yalu River, a limitation was placed by the JCS on any general advance to the north beyond the "Kansas-Wyoming" line: it would require prior approval from the JCS. Ridgway himself had placed a comparable restriction on the Eighth Army in his earlier instructions to Van Fleet dated April 22.

Meanwhile Ridgway had prepared a draft of instructions based on his own concept of what his duties and responsibilities should be in the two commands. He requested the JCS to approve it and return it to him as a directive. His draft did not reach Washington until after the President had approved the JCS directive.

When Ridgway compared the JCS instructions with his draft, he found that they did not fully agree and stated that he did not completely understand them. He radioed the JCS that he was sending to Washington a staff officer "thoroughly familiar with our problems and point of view." He continued, "I request that he be permitted to consult with your planners on current ambiguities and conflicting instructions." He asked also to be allowed to operate under his own proposed instructions pending issuance of a new directive developed by the staff consultations. The JCS agreed to receive Colonel Roy C. Heflebower, Ridgway's staff officer, but refused to suspend our current instructions. Any necessary clarifications agreed upon would be covered by radio dispatches.

The procedure proposed by General Ridgway was never employed by General MacArthur during his exchanges with the Chiefs of Staff. It was easier and came more naturally to Ridgway, who was a former Army Deputy Chief of Staff, familiar with the recent planning methods of the Department of the Army and the JCS, and who knew personally each member of the JCS, all of whom were his contemporaries. Matt also knew that he did not have to pull any punches in making his views known.

I was puzzled about what were the ambiguities and uncertainties to which Ridgway referred. I had G-3 carefully compare the JCS instructions with Ridgway's version. G-3 reported two main points of divergence. General Ridgway recommended that he be allowed to order troops to cross the Manchurian and Soviet borders, if he felt this necessary. In contrast, the JCS strictly prohibited such action, which obviously, with its threat of broadening the war, would require both political and military clearance from Washington. The second point of difference was that Ridgway felt that all American forces in the Far East ought to be assigned to the United Nations forces under his United Nations Command, whereas the 40th and 45th Divisions in Japan were excluded from this command. The Chiefs were unwilling to leave the defenses of Japan to the inchoate Japanese National Police Reserve, a constabulary force started by General MacArthur.

In addition to the points made by Colonel Heflebower, and reinforcing them, General Ridgway on May 9 protested that his U.N. Command's mission to destroy the North Korean and Chinese forces in Korea was impossible so long as he could make no advance with major forces beyond the "Kansas-Wyoming" line. He stated further that the limitation placed on his authority to determine when he might withdraw from Korea conflicted on the one hand with restrictions on his U.N. Command operations, which were subject to the insurance of the "security of forces under your command," and on the other hand clashed with his basic mission as Far East Commander, which required him to defend Japan. Ridgway felt that he should be permitted to decide when, under any critical conditions caused by Soviet action, he should initiate withdrawal from Korea in order to strengthen the defense of Japan.

These, and several minor points, were reviewed by the Army G-3 staff with Colonel Heflebower during the period of May 11 to May 23. We made every effort to meet Ridgway's requests.

I finally submitted to the JCS a new directive for Ridgway, which clearly separated and delineated his responsibilities under his two hats. This directive was reviewed and approved by the JCS and dispatched to Ridgway on May 31, 1951.

Little or no change was made in his duties as Far East Commander, but it was spelled out that the 40th and 45th Divisions would be used only in defense of Japan except on specific authority from the JCS and that only United States forces would be employed in defense of Formosa and the Pescadores.

A major change was made in his duties as U.N. Commander. While the JCS was working on its revision of the directive to Ridgway, the National Security Council was reviewing our national policy toward the Korean war, which shifted the emphasis from a solution based largely on military action to one that would rely primarily on political negotiations. The considerations that brought about this change will be examined in a later section in this chapter. Suffice it now to say that the new policy warranted for the first time a clear-cut, definitive statement of the U.N. Commander's mission. Instead of merely quoting the imprecise wording of the United Nations resolution of June 27, 1950, the revised directive was as follows:

Mission. As CINCUNC [Commander in Chief, United Nations Command] you will, consistent with the security of your forces, inflict maximum personnel and materiel losses on the forces of North Korea and Communist China operating within the geographic boundaries of Korea and adjacent waters, in order to create conditions favorable to a settlement of the Korean conflict which would as a minimum:

a. Terminate hostilities under appropriate armistice arrangements.

b. Establish authority of the ROK over all Korea south of a northern boundary so located as to facilitate, to the maximum extent possible, both administration and military defense, and in no case south of the 38th Parallel.

c. Provide for withdrawal by stages of non-Korean armed forces from Korea.

d. Permit the building of sufficient ROK military power to deter or repel a renewed North Korean aggression.

The restrictions on operations that were then in effect were retained, including the limitation on any general advance beyond "some line through the Hwachon reservoir," which corresponded generally to the "Kansas-Wyoming" line. Later on, modest advances beyond this line were permitted.

In the event of open or covert intervention in Korea by major Soviet forces the U.N. Command would assume the defensive and report the facts to the JCS. However, there would be no restrictions on the conduct of air or naval operations in Korea or adjacent waters.

Ridgway was to plan on evacuation of the United Nations from Korea, subject to JCS approval at the time, in case of a Soviet attack against United States forces in the Far East outside Korea. Pending further instructions, he was not to count on any United Nations forces other than American for the defense of the Far East Command.

In accordance with a new United States policy with regard to the organization of forces that we would support, Ridgway was told to submit to the JCS his plans for developing as rapidly as possible dependable ROK units capable of assuming the major burden of the United Nations forces in Korea.

Concerning the possibility of an armistice Ridgway was told to report to the JCS any feelers from the enemy. For his background information he was furnished a copy as a study of the minimal conditions desired for an armistice; the study had been made by the JCS and submitted to the Secretary of Defense.

The new instructions were accepted fully by General Ridgway. For the first time since he had assumed overall command he knew clearly his responsibilities and the limits of his authority. This directive was to remain essentially unchanged throughout his service in the Far East.

Washington Reviews Korean Policies

As the fighting in Korea ebbed back and forth in the spring of 1951, it became evident that neither side would win a decisive military victory. In spite of the success of the Eighth Army in crushing two successive Communist offensives in April and May the Chinese still had far greater uncommitted war potential in Manchuria than was available in Korea to the U.N. Command. The initial determination of the United Nations allies to support the United Nations action in Korea was waning, and the American public, never too enthusiastic about their first involvement in a limited war in peacetime, were becoming disenchanted. The political leaders within the Administration and on Capitol Hill were leaning strongly toward negotiating an end to the fighting.

Consequently, the Joint Chiefs were called to a meeting on March 19, 1951, with Secretaries Acheson and Marshall, at which the pros and cons of a possible cease-fire that might lead to an armistice were thoroughly discussed. The Chiefs were asked to review the tentative terms that they had prepared in the dark days of December 1950, when it appeared that the U.N. Command might be driven out of Korea. This they did in a memorandum to Secretary Marshall dated March 27.

Conditions had changed greatly since the previous winter. Buoyed by the successes of Ridgway and Van Fleet in early 1951, the Chiefs could not see many advantages in an armistice. They argued that any negotiated agreement that would put an end to the heavy casualties then being inflicted on the Chinese forces, and yet permit them to remain in Korea, would be greatly to the advantage of the Communists. On the other hand, such an agreement would require the retention of large United Nations forces in the country, placing a heavy drain on allied resources, principally United States resources, of men, money, and materiel. Thus, from strictly military considerations the JCS judged that an armistice at that time would not, of itself, constitute an acceptable solution of the Korean situation. However, the Chiefs knew the war was a severe drain on our own resources, and realized that, in light of recent reverses suffered by the Communists, it might be advisable to attempt a negotiated settlement, if such a settlement did not prejudice our essential interests and objectives in the Far East.

Following up on this memorandum, the JCS on April 5, 1951, furnished to the Secretary of Defense for transmittal to the National Security Council a study in which we analyzed the situation in Korea and outlined the military posture that the United States should maintain. For the first time we conceded that "the Korean problem cannot be resolved in a manner satisfactory to the United States by military action alone." The Korean situation was a symptom of world tensions. It could not be resolved by po-litical-military action in Korea alone, but would be resolved only when and if there was a relaxation of world tensions.

Though the JCS said so only by inference, there was no ques-tion but that a military stalemate had been reached between the U.N. Command and the Chinese and North Korean forces. The best feasible future course for the U.N. Command would depend largely on action taken by the Soviet Union. If Russia intervened in Korea, either with large-scale "volunteer" forces or as part of a general war, the U.N. Command should be with-drawn from Korea, and the President should then declare a gen-eral mobilization. If Russia did not start a general war, the United Nations forces should remain in Korea and continue to put pressure on the Communists with a view to securing an armistice that would satisfy our objectives.

The Chiefs concluded with four recommendations that were later integrated into a new National Security Council policy statement of American objectives and procedures to be followed in the Far East. These were:

1. The U.S. forces in Korea should pursue their current military course of action until a political settlement could be reached which would not jeopardize United States' positions with respect to Russia, Formosa, and the seating of Communist China in the United Nations.

2. Dependable South Korean units should be developed as rapidly as possible and in sufficient strength to take over the major burden from the United Nations forces.

3. Preparations should be made immediately for action by naval and air forces against the China mainland in the event of a broadening of the war by the Communists.

4. Urgent steps should be taken to ascertain the policies and objectives of the allies toward Korea specifically and the Far

East in general, to determine what support the United States could expect from them if, while continuing the present military action in Korea, operations against mainland China were initiated by the United States.

While these matters were being correlated with the views of the State Department and other agencies of the government and reviewed at the highest levels of the Administration, the press reports of the MacArthur Hearings were stimulating interest in, and beclouding, the issues involved. It was imperative that at least within the Administration a clear, workable statement of military and political policy on the possibility of ending hostilities be determined. The National Security Council met on May 2 to consider the JCS memorandum of April 5 and other papers dealing with the problems of Asia. On May 17 President Truman approved the National Security Council's statement of policy, a guide for all United States agencies in the government's effort to combat the spread of Communism not only in Korea but throughout southeast Asia and the Pacific area. In doing so the United States, without sacrificing its vital interests, would, as far as possible, work through the United Nations and make every effort to avoid a general war with the Soviet Union or an extension of the current hostilities with China outside Korea, particularly without the support of our major allies. With respect to Korea and Formosa the Council adopted, with minor modifications, the courses of action and recommendations of the JCS contained in our memorandum of April 5, and confirmed the ultimate objective of the United States, which was to solve the Korean situation primarily by political negotiations, as distinguished from military means alone, so as to provide for a united, independent, and democratic Korea. The United States would keep up the current course of action in Korea in furtherance of an acceptable armistice.

Talk and Fight

The National Security Council's policy of May 17, 1951, determined the course of the U.N. Command's combat operations for the two long years that were to elapse between its approval and the signing of the armistice on July 27, 1953.

During this period the main purpose of the United Nations operations was to keep pressure on the enemy and to inflict maximal casualties on the Chinese and North Koreans in order to force an agreement that would end the fighting. The conflict became a grueling war of attrition, somewhat comparable to Ulysses S. Grant's campaign of 1865. There were no dramatic operations like Inchon and the Chinese drive from the Yalu — only deadly struggles for razorback ridges and bleak hilltops on which men died for the slight advantage of straightening a bulge in the front line or gaining better observation for themselves or denying it to the enemy.

While the National Security Council was formulating its policy, General Van Fleet proposed to General Ridgway that he be permitted to launch a combined amphibious and overland operation toward Wonsan to pinch off and destroy a large fraction of the Chinese and NK forces northeast of the Hwachon Reservoir.

Ridgway turned down the plan. The objective area was well beyond the "Kansas-Wyoming" line, which had been set by the JCS directive of May 1 and confirmed by the Council's statement of May 17 as the northern limit of any advance of the Eighth Army. But Ridgway had his own fundamental objection. Since in his judgment, with which the JCS agreed, it was not possible under existing conditions to clear all Korea of enemy forces, he could see little point in risking a large-scale combined operation, which might result in heavy casualties, on the dubious chance of inflicting an indeterminate number of casualties on an enemy that could better stand the losses. Ridgway's idea was to continue an orderly advance to line "Wyoming" while holding "Kansas," and he so advised Van Fleet, who adjusted accordingly. Van Fleet ordered fortification of "Kansas" as a permanent defensive position, while pushing cautiously ahead to "Wyoming," which was reached by mid-June.

For some undisclosed reasons, perhaps political, Van Fleet later protested to the press in 1952 and again at a congressional hearing in 1953 that in early June 1951 he had the Communists "on the run" and "I was crying to turn me loose." These statements do not jibe with the estimation of the situation that he sent Ridgway on June 9, 1951. He wrote then, "The terrain in the Wyoming-Kansas area, when fortified, is suitable both for defense and as a base for limited offensives. However, a general advance beyond this area would nullify our advantages to a large extent. I propose, therefore, to retain EUSAK [Eighth U.S. Army in Korea] forces in this general area upon conclusion of the current operation, and to keep the enemy off balance by limited offensive action."

Van Fleet reiterated essentially this same view when on June 25 Ridgway sent a staff officer, Lieutenant Colonel A. D. Surles, Jr., to Korea to get Van Fleet's judgment whether it was feasible or desirable for the Eighth Army to seize the high ground between his existing front line and the optimal cease-fire line for an armistice.

Van Fleet did not favor an advance by the Eighth Army to seize the high ground in question. An advance in the east would be costly in American lives and would have little tactical advantage. While an advance in the west would be relatively easy, Van Fleet felt that it would unduly expose the Eighth Army's flank to offensive action by the enemy. According to Colonel Surles' report to Ridgway, Van Fleet concluded that the cost in lives and the resulting exposure of the Eighth Army was too much to wager on the chance that there might be a cease-fire.

Van Fleet's estimate then was sound. Although the Chinese had suffered heavily in the Eighth Army's counteroffensive in May, they had plenty of fight left, as they proved in their fierce resistance in mid-June to the U.N. Command's efforts to seize the "Iron Triangle" (Pyonggang-Chorwon-Kumhwa). The Chinese still had in Korea five armies, four artillery divisions, two cavalry divisions, and two NK corps, totaling almost 450,000 men. Thousands upon thousands of fresh Chinese troops were moving down from Manchuria, where there were far more reserves than were available to the U.N. Command. A third factor that mitigated against any sustained allied advance north of "Kansas-Wyoming" was the rugged terrain and inadequate transport and communications facilities. The highly mechanized Eighth Army was dependent for full effectiveness on good road and rail facilities, which in North Korea had been largely destroyed or heavily damaged by allied bombing. The farther the Eighth Army advanced from Pusan and Inchon, the greater its supply problems became, whereas the supply of the Chinese forces was eased. General MacArthur had frequently pointed this out.

These considerations and General Ridgway's mission having ruled out any large-scale offensive operations, at least for the immediate future, Ridgway and Van Fleet began looking ahead to a possible armistice. They agreed that the best defensive position to be held during an armistice would be along the "Kansas" line. Ridgway had been advised by the JCS that an armistice probably would provide for a demilitarized zone 20 miles wide. It was also estimated that the center line of this zone would be the actual line of contact at the time the cease-fire became effective and that troops on both sides would have to withdraw 10 miles from the line of contact. Hence, as a minimum, the United Nations forces should hold a cease-fire line at least 20 miles beyond "Kansas," in order to be able to retain an outpost zone 10 miles deep in advance of "Kansas." With this in prospect the JCS considered the advisability of removing the existing restrictions on any advance beyond "Kansas-Wyoming." Vandenberg and I wondered if it might not be wise to let Ridgway operate in strength as far north as his resources would permit.

On June 20 we queried Ridgway about what he thought of a possible change in his directive that would remove any tactical restrictions on his advancing to the north so as to be in a better position for an armistice.

Ridgway replied to the JCS concurring in the proposed removal of any tactical restrictions on an advance by the Eighth Army but did not indicate that he was planning anything other than local operations. He suggested that a cease-fire line preferably should extend from the confluence of the Han and Yesong Rivers in the west and thence generally northeast past Chorwon and Kumhwa to Kosong (20 miles north of Kansong), on the east coast. He called attention to the fact that this line was below the 38th Parallel on the west coast, but said the difficulties of defending the isolated Ongjin and Yonan peninsulas (Map 2) did not warrant including them within the cease-fire line. Their loss would be more than compensated for by the more important area to be included north of the Parallel in the Chorwon-Kumhwa area and east of the Hwachon Reservoir.

On July 10, 1951, the JCS informed Ridgway that President Truman had approved the removal of restrictions on tactical operations to secure his recommended cease-fire line. But Ridgway and Van Fleet, after touring the front together on June 22, had already decided not to advance north of "Kansas-Wyoming." They agreed that a movement 20 miles beyond "Kansas" was feasible but that the probable cost in casualties was too great to pay, particularly in view of the strong enemy reaction to allied probings on the central front and confirmed combat intelligence that the Communists were about to launch a new offensive.

Renewed Fighting: The Punchbowl and Heartbreak Ridge

Van Fleet beat the enemy to the punch. The removal of restrictions on limited advances to reach the desired cease-fire line permitted an advance on the eastern front. Northeast of the Hwachon Reservoir was a circular valley which came to be known as "the Punchbowl" (Map 14). The valley itself had little military significance, but the high ridges that rimmed it provided direct observation of the United Nations defenses and supply routes in that sector of the "Kansas" front. Van Fleet decided, with Ridgway's concurrence, to clear the Punchbowl. This task was assigned to the X Corps, now commanded by Major General Clovis E. Byers.

The eastern rim of the bowl was held by dug-in elements of three NK divisions. The battle opened with eleven days of bitter fighting by the ROK I Corps of General Paik before the North Koreans were driven from the southeast rim. It was not until September 5, 1951, that attacks by the ROK 5th Division and the U.S. 1st Marine Division against the northwest and northeast rims, combined with an assault of "Bloody Ridge" on the southwest by the U.S. 2d Division, cleared all heights overlooking the

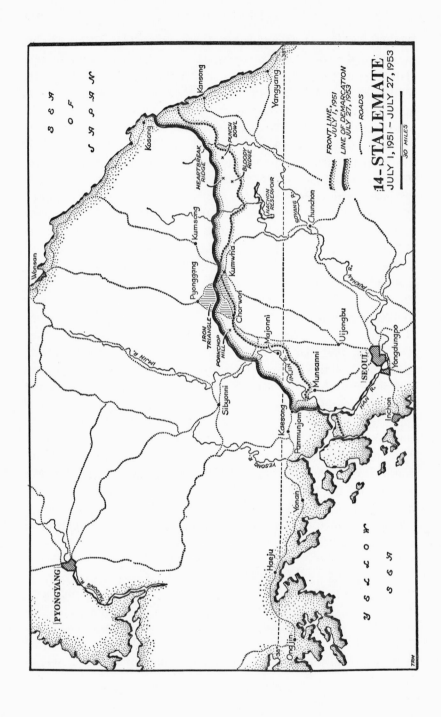

14 - STALEMATE

JULY 1, 1951 – JULY 27, 1953

FRONT LINE,
JULY 1, 1951
LINE OF DEMARCATION
JULY 27, 1953
ROADS

30 MILES

SEA OF JAPAN

YELLOW SEA

PYONGYANG

Wonsan

Kosong

Kansong

Yangyang

HEARTBREAK RIDGE

PUNCH BOWL

BLOODY RIDGE

Kumsong

Pjonggang

Kumwha

HWACHON RESERVOIR

Chunchon

SOYANG R.

IRON TRIANGLE

PORKCHOP HILL

Chorwon

Majonni

Munsanni

Uijongbu

PUKHAN R.

Sibyonni

IMJIN R.

IMJIN R.

Kaesong

Panmunjom

HAN R.

SEOUL

Yongdungpo

Inchon

YESONG R.

Yonan

Haeju

Ongjin

TAEDONG R.

IMJIN R.

TBM

Punchbowl except those to the northwest. The latter heights formed a spine-like ridge which news correspondents soon dubbed "Heartbreak Ridge." Held by parts of three NK divisions, later reinforced by the Chinese 204th Division, it was one of the most formidable positions on the entire battle front. It took a solid month of bloody fighting, from September 13 to October 13, by Major General Robert N. Young's 2d Division, reinforced by the French Battalion under Lieutenant Colonel Ralph Monclar, to rout the Chinese and NK forces from Heartbreak Ridge.

These battles were costly to both sides in men and materiel. While not decisive, they did prevent any renewal of Communist offensive operations and secured a strong defensive line for the U.N. Command while the armistice negotiations continued.

Van Fleet, anxious to keep up the fighting trim of his forces, had difficulty reconciling himself to the *de facto* stalemate. Throughout the fall of 1951 he made successive recommendations to Ridgway for various offensives, but Ridgway felt that none of them offered gains commensurate with the casualties they would cost. On November 12 Ridgway instructed Van Fleet to assume an "active defense," limiting offensive operations to the capture of outpost positions, while being prepared to exploit opportunities to inflict heavy casualties on the enemy. The JCS supported this decision. We felt that the existing main line of contact would be satisfactory as the line of demarcation for a demilitarized zone and could not be greatly improved without undue losses. Actually, a tentative agreement on this line was reached by the armistice negotiators on November 27, 1951, as will be detailed in the next chapter.

Upon being informed of the agreement Van Fleet instructed his corps commanders:

> Eighth Army should clearly demonstrate a willingness to reach an agreement while preparing for offensive action if negotiations are unduly prolonged to this end. A willingness to reach an agreement will be demonstrated by: Reducing operations to the minimum essential to maintain present positions regardless of the agreed-upon military demarcation line. Coun-

terattacks to regain key terrain lost to enemy assault will be the only offensive action taken unless otherwise directed by this headquarters. Every effort will be made to prevent unnecessary casualties.

When war correspondents learned of the Eighth Army order, they reported that the order had brought the ground fighting to a complete halt. While this report was essentially correct, it caused embarrassment to General Ridgway and our negotiators. Washington was particularly incensed by a press association dispatch hinting that the White House was responsible for the order which, in effect, offered the enemy what amounted to a cease-fire. President Truman felt impelled to issue a strong statement to counter this impression, and General Ridgway, apparently irritated by the opening sentences of Van Fleet's order and the public furore, mildly rapped Van's knuckles for assuming "a function entirely outside its [the Eighth Army's] field of responsibility."

The American public in November of 1951 was not yet fully resigned to a peace without military victory. The unfavorable publicity resulting from the Van Fleet order led to a prompt renewal of active patrolling and shelling along the demarcation line. However, there was no resumption of large-scale operations. The U.N. Command continued to put pressure on the Communists through air and sea actions, but the ground forces settled down to a winter of cold frustration.

Air Interdiction

As ground action waned, the U.N. Command turned to its great superiority of air power to continue pressure on the Communists and to try to prevent a build-up of their military strength. A vast interdiction bombing campaign, dubbed Operation Strangle, against enemy rail and highway communications was launched by Air Force, Navy, and Marine Corps planes. The Communists countered with heavier concentrations of antiaircraft and a skillful organization of their great manpower resources to make repairs. According to a later Air Force study, the NK railroad bureau had three brigades of 7700 men, each employed full time on railroad repair. Groups of fifty skilled repairmen were assigned to each rail center, and ten-man teams were deployed every few miles along main-line tracks, ready to respond to reports from rail workers of breaks in the lines. The emergency repair groups moved in promptly and, with the help of local civilian labor, refilled holes and rebuilt road beds. At night, or under cover of bad weather, skilled groups replaced damaged rails and ties. After dark trucks and indefatigable bearers with A-frames on their backs distributed supplies from the railheads to the troops. The U.S. Fifth Air Force estimated that at one time 500,000 soldiers and civilians were engaged in countering Operation Strangle. As was proven in Germany in World War II and demonstrated again in Korea and later in Vietnam, no amount of aerial bombing can prevent completely the forward movement of supplies, particularly in regions where ample manpower is available.

This does not mean that Operation Strangle was of only slight value. Though Van Fleet did complain of the diversion of fighter bombers from close-support missions — which were of less importance in the static defense — he pointed out that the interdiction program denied to the enemy railheads close to the front in critical areas and limited the Reds' ability to match the Eighth Army's supply of ammunition, artillery, and other weapons employed at the front.

Rotation of National Guard Divisions from Japan

In the fall of 1951 I had recommended to the JCS that the two National Guard divisions, the 40th and 45th, which had been stationed in Japan while completing their training, be shipped to Korea in exchange for the 24th Infantry Division and the 1st Cavalry Division. General Ridgway objected to the replacement of his battle-tested divisions by untried new units. He urged, instead, the removal of restrictions we had imposed on the use of the National Guard divisions to supply individual replacements.

As Army Chief of Staff, I knew that such a move would bring down justifiable wrath from the National Guard Association at home and its supporters in the Congress. The men of these units had been called to duty and sent to the Far East to meet an emergency situation. They expected, and were entitled, to see action in Korea. The JCS approved my recommendation that these divisions be rotated to Korea before the terms of service of their men expired in August 1952. The exchange with the 24th and 1st Divisions was completed without any untoward incident by February of 1952. This was followed by the rotation of the original French battalion with a fresh battalion from France and similar exchanges of other United Nations units, thereby retaining the commitments and interest of our United Nations allies.

Rebuilding the ROK Army

One of the major features of the National Security Council's study of May 17 was the provision calling for the development of ROK military forces capable ultimately of taking over the role of the U.N. Command. Even before the formulation of this policy the ROK representative to the United Nations, Colonel Limb, had handed to General Bradley an official request that the United States arm and equip ten additional ROK divisions, to be commanded if possible by American officers. Bradley reported this to Secretary Marshall, who was interested. Syngman Rhee sent President Truman a duplicate request.

The performance of ROK units in battle up to that had been such that responsible American officers in the Far East were not eager to create additional ROK divisions. General MacArthur, shortly before his relief, had turned down a similar but more moderate request. However, when by April 1951 the JCS conceded that the problem of Korea could not be solved satisfactorily by military means alone, and an armistice appeared inevitable, it became clear to me that we should step up our efforts to prepare the Republic of Korea to take over the major share of the responsibility for its own security. On April 26, 1951, I had sent a personal message to General Ridgway requesting information on the availability of Korean manpower for military duty, the possibility of expanding training facilities to meet an expansion of

ROK forces, the requirements for American personnel to assist in training these forces, the advisability of assigning American officers to command ROK units, and other details. I concluded by asking Ridgway for his recommendation on whether Rhee's request should be granted.

Ridgway's reply was emphatically negative. Ridgway had consulted Van Fleet and agreed fully with his views. Both strongly opposed the creation of new divisions. They objected to placing Americans in command of ROK units, not only because of language difficulties but because command would require authority to administer and discipline, which the Republic of Korea, as a sovereign nation, would never agree to. Van Fleet emphasized that "the basic problems with the ROK Army at this time are training and development of leadership qualities. This is a long-range project, especially the development of an officer corps as would be true in any new army." He knew whereof he spoke, having had the experience of organizing and supervising the retraining of the officer and noncommissioned-officer corps of the outmoded Greek Army in 1950. In fact, Van Fleet's success in this basic reform in Greece was one of the factors in my recommending him to command the United Nations forces in Korea, since I had long realized the need for a comparable program there.

When it became known to President Rhee that the United States would assist in developing competent ROK units, Rhee announced that if we would only equip his "already well-trained" soldiers, American troops could be withdrawn from Korea and the United Nations job left to the ROK Army. This was not the first, nor the last, of the old patriot's misguided public claims that were to plague the United Nations commanders in the Far East. At General Ridgway's urging the State Department instructed Ambassador Muccio to convey to President Rhee "in the strongest terms" the grave concern of the United States over the continuance of such unwarranted statements.

The need for a sound program for the development of dependable ROK forces had been recognized by all responsible commanders in the Far East from General MacArthur on. A reasonably good program of training, including a set of schools for officers and noncommissioned officers patterned after the U.S. Army's system, had been established in Korea by the U.S. Korean Military Advisory Group prior to the war. However, the program had not been taken seriously by the ROK high command, and it was not until the fighting had slackened in the spring of 1951 that Ridgway and Van Fleet were able to concentrate on the task of building the ROK Army into a competent fighting force.

Colonel Arthur S. Champeny, who had been Director of National Defense under the U.S. Military Government in Korea in 1946 and had subsequently commanded the U.S. 24th Infantry Regiment in action, was placed in charge of an expanded training program. Under his able direction, and with full support of Van Fleet, Ridgway, and the U.S. Department of the Army, the ROK school system was enlarged by the fall of 1951 to handle more than 10,000 students, and replacement training centers had facilities for almost 25,000 trainees. Potential instructors were sent to Army service schools in the United States, and the Korean Military Academy was reorganized with a four-year curriculum patterned after West Point. A Command and General Staff School for majors and colonels was established. In the new training system an important element, which, as I remember, was conceived by Van Fleet, was a scheme of rotating ROK divisions from the fighting front for nine-week refresher courses in weapons and tactics at field training centers, one in each ROK corps area.

Throughout all instruction emphasis was placed on initiative and leadership and the development of a willingness to assume responsibility by officers and noncommissioned officers. This was difficult to achieve, since the ROK Army was able to pay its officers and men a mere pittance and there was little incentive for advancement. Furthermore, custom and tradition tended to suppress initiative and new methods of action on the part of younger men, on whom the future of the country would depend. Most of the Korean officers were very young. To most of them the Army offered, for the first time in their lives, an opportunity to develop their native capacity for leadership. This opportunity paid dividends in the latter stages of the war and subsequent years of peace.

If the ROK Army was to be prepared ultimately to take over the role of the U.N. Command, it would have to be increased in size as well as in quality. This would require additional logistical support from the United States, which was already heavily pledged to assist its NATO partners with ammunition and divisional equipment. My Army staff cautioned against any additional commitments. However, when in July 1952 I visited Mark W. Clark, who had succeeded General Ridgway as Commander in Chief of the United Nations Command, I agreed to support his proposal to expand the ROK Army to twelve divisions. Shortly thereafter the JCS gave our approval, including an expansion of ROK marine forces and Korean Army troops attached to United States Army units, even though this would mean that strategic reserve units in the United States would be limited to 50 percent of authorized critical supplies, and certain cuts would be made in NATO support programs. This expansion was approved by the Secretary of Defense and President Truman in October 1952.

General Clark followed up shortly thereafter with a plan, which had long been advocated by Van Fleet, to expand the ROK's to twenty divisions. Clark's program called for a gradual augmentation, to be completed by August 1953, together with the promise of releasing one American division for deployment outside Korea for every two new ROK divisions, as the latter became ready for action. If all went well, four United States divisions and two corps headquarters could be redeployed by mid-1954.

Desirable as this turnover would be, it had some drawbacks. Until additional productive capacity in the United States could be brought fully on stream, the equipment and supporting supplies for the new ROK units would have to be taken from the Far East Command's strategic reserves, which would slow the creation of Japanese paramilitary forces, which were also being planned for taking over the internal security of Japan. Additional Army appropriations would be required, augmented supply programs developed, and our plans for mutual-defense assistance to our allies adjusted.

As always in such matters, I reviewed all aspects of the twenty-division proposal with Secretary Pace and the Army staff. Pace forwarded a memorandum to Secretary Lovett on November 17, 1952, stating that the Army favored expansion of the ROK forces but that the program had ramifications beyond the purview of the Army. Lovett referred the problem to the JCS in December. Meanwhile, the election of General Eisenhower to the Presidency had taken place in November 1952. In mid-December I briefed Charles E. Wilson, the designated new Secretary of Defense, on the program. Wilson, of course, could not give even tacit approval to the program but, with the patent desire of the new Administration to end the Korean war, the JCS on January 20, 1953, told General Clark to proceed under the assumption that his plan would be approved. On January 31 Clark directed Van Fleet to go ahead with formation of two additional divisions. This was confirmed by authority from President Eisenhower for a total of fourteen divisions and six separate regiments. Progressive approvals from Washington raised the total to sixteen ROK divisions by the signing of the armistice.

Ammunition Supply

The most vexing problem that troubled me, our field commanders, and the Departments of the Army and Defense during the two years of stalemate pending an armistice in Korea was the supply of artillery ammunition.

At the end of World War II the United States Army had tremendous stocks of ammunition scattered around the world, which must have appeared inexhaustible for the shiny days of peace that seemed to lie ahead. These stocks were made up of varying quantities of the many different types, among them standard 105mm shell, 3 armor-piercing antitank, 90mm antiaircraft, 155mm howitzer, 155mm gun, 8-inch and 240mm howitzer, 57mm and 81mm mortar, 105mm shaped-charge antitank, and illuminating, phosphorous, and varicolored smoke shells, to say nothing of the hundreds of millions of rounds of small-arms ammunition. There were great quantities of some types and smaller amounts of others. In the years immediately after the war — years of economy and reduction of our war-making capacity — no Administration would have considered asking Congress for money for balancing the stocks or for even cataloguing the stockages.

The expenditures for army ammunition from the fiscal year 1947 through the fiscal year 1950, just prior to my becoming Chief of Staff, averaged less than $25 million a year. In the face of such small procurement, and the deterioration of certain types of ammunition and the utilization of others for training, our stocks were gradually being reduced.

More importantly, the lack of postwar procurement of ammunition caused most of the principal wartime manufacturers to convert their plants and machine tools to meet the surging demand for consumer goods that World War II had held in check. The prevalent belief among military planners and Administration budgeters alike, that the Korean war would be a minor one of short duration, did not warrant a sizable dislocation of the United States industrial economy.

In Chapter IV I pointed out that I and the preceding Chiefs of Staff and also our civilian Secretaries and other officials of the Administration shared the responsibility for not having recognized earlier the need for larger military appropriations, especially for ammunition.

That we did move fast after the Chinese Communists in the fall of 1950 initiated the "new war" — as General MacArthur described it — is indicated by the jump in cumulative authorized dollar expenditures for ammunition from $270 million in fiscal year 1951, to $1.7 billion in fiscal year 1952, to $6.7 billion in fiscal year 1953. However, until the President declared a national emergency on December 16, 1950, the Munitions Board had no authority to give military contracts priority over civilian requirements. With the munitions industry starting practically from scratch under "peacetime" conditions, it would require a year to a year and a half to convert to large-scale production. This meant that ammunition ordered in January 1951, when Congress approved the first large appropriation request from the Department of Defense, would not result in deliveries to troops abroad until late 1952 or early 1953.

As the military situation began to stabilize in the fall of 1951, expenditures of artillery ammunition, particularly of the heavy calibers required to root out the enemy from his deeply dug defenses, rose astronomically. For example, in the battle for Bloody Ridge during August and September of 1951 the 2d Division's artillery fired more than 153,000 rounds, and one battalion of twelve howitzers set a new record by firing 14,425 rounds of 105mm shell in twenty-four hours, whereas in World War II the average was 480 rounds at forty rounds per gun per day. Undoubtedly, much of this light-weight ammunition was used fruitlessly against heavy bunkers on Bloody Ridge and in subsequent similar situations and resulted in calls from General Van Fleet for increasing quantities of the heavier calibers, of which the Far Eastern reserve stocks were lowest.

General Ridgway called this situation to the attention of the JCS and the Department of the Army in October of 1951, but increasing production, which was just moving into high gear, could not match the mounting demands of the Eighth Army. The Department of the Army was already doing all it could to speed up production but was still encountering delays caused by reallocation of priorities for steel, tools, and facilities, common to the start-up of any mass-production program. The Under Secretary of the Army, Earl D. Johnson, who took office in May of 1952 and under whose supervision the procurement program of the war was managed, testified:

> All suppliers were by no means as responsive in bids or production as they would have been under full wartime conditions. I am sure you gentlemen all realize that we were competing in a market the capacity of which was already overtaxed. . . .
>
> Following the dynamic expansion of ammunition procurement after the entry of Communist China into the war . . . restraining forces started to become effective by the end of Fiscal Year 1951, coincident with the initiation of armistice negotiations. . . . there was a partial return to ammunition procurement and production under many of the peacetime restraints. Funds appropriated by Congress were subjected to delayed apportionment. Many of the peacetime requirements of advertised competitive bidding applied both to construction of

facilities and procurement. Rules respecting awards to small businesses and distressed areas complicated and delayed procurement actions. And it was necessary at all times to compete against generally profitable civilian business without benefit of many of the controls and driving urgencies of a wartime atmosphere.

Some of our inexperience in forecasting the duration and complexity of fighting a new type of limited war in peacetime, combined with political considerations that demanded "guns and butter," did result in shortages in depot and theater stocks in the Far East in the last two years of the war. The shortages in reserve stocks were reflected in limitations on daily expenditures of heavier calibers at the front. This did not mean that any unit under attack or engaged in any critical operation was limited in the ammunition it was permitted to shoot as required by the situation. If a unit exceeded normal allowances, its stocks at the gun positions were promptly replenished either from other units not so engaged or from local depots in the rear.

General Van Fleet, as an Army commander in the field, was justified in complaining of such shortages in Korea, though the effect of these shortages was exaggerated. However, General Clark assessed the situation in March of 1953, and he reported to me in part as follows:

There has been no shortage of small arms ammunition in the theater; stocks of other ammunition as indicated below have been less than they should have been. However, such shortages were mostly in theater stocks and the pipeline and not in forward area combat units. As far as I have been able to determine, Eighth Army has never been "out" of ammunition nor denied authority to shoot ammunition in adequate quantities when required by the tactical situation. Insofar as can be determined, no unit in Korea was refused ammunition for an essential mission.

General Clark listed the types that had been in short supply at various times and went on to state that he considered the existing levels were adequate under current conditions, provided on-hand theater stocks were maintained at the ninety-day level.

Though the problems of ammunition supply were vexing to all concerned, it is my considered judgment that any shortages, even in the more critical heavy rounds, had no substantial effect on the military situation in Korea. Whatever we may have lacked at times in artillery ammunition was more than made up for by the massive strikes of Air Force, Navy, and Marine bombers in support of our front-line ground forces. The interdiction of the combat zone was properly the responsibility of these aerial forces. But, as indicated above, not even their almost complete domination of the skies could prevent the build-up, over a period of many months, of the Communist forces defending the truce demarcation line.

An impartial military historian, Dr. Walter G. Hermes, whose history *Truce Tent to Fighting Front* is a scholarly examination of the last two years of the Korean war, has written:

> The complexity of the ammunition story made the accuracy of the shortage charges extremely difficult to evaluate. But it was doubtful whether more ammunition in the critical categories would have substantially influenced the battle situation in the last two years of the war, for the restrictions on offensive operations were not dependent upon the ammunition supply, but rather upon the political and military objectives of the United States and its UN allies at the time. As long as they preferred to settle the war at the conference table and to delimit the Korean commitment, even full stocks of ammunition could have made no real difference in the outcome.

1952: Year of Defense

Throughout the winter of 1951 to 1952 and the following spring there was little activity on the battlefield other than patrolling and some rooting out of NK guerrillas in southwestern Korea by the ROK Army. Van Fleet proposed several limited-objective attacks, but they were all turned down by General Ridgway, either because they would be too costly in casualties or would adversely affect the negotiations.

The same conditions carried over into the summer of 1952 after General Clark succeeded Ridgway as Commander in Chief, United Nations Command. Washington authorities were not disposed to change the policies established by the National Security Council, and the personnel ceilings that the JCS had to place on the Eighth Army precluded any large-scale offensive operations. The Communists were apparently similarly restricted, because they mounted no serious ground attacks and continued to afford sanctuary from bombing to Pusan and Inchon and our air and naval bases in Japan. The latter were well within range of Russian air forces in the Vladivostok area, but Russia was not interested in entering or broadening the shooting war, as long as we limited our air operations to south of the Yalu.

Communist activity picked up in the fall of 1952 in the area west of Chorwon. Fearful that the initiative was passing to the Communists and ever alert to the danger of a loss of fighting trim in his army from lack of offensive action, Van Fleet urged Clark to approve an attack by the U.S. IX Corps to seize a triangular group of hills north of Kumhwa. Our troops in the area had been suffering considerably from enemy fire, controlled by observation from the "Iron Triangle" complex. It was estimated that two battalions of the U.S. 7th Division would suffice for the attack. Although Clark, like Ridgway, had frowned on most operations of this nature, he estimated that this one, called Operation Showdown, had a good chance of achieving its objective without heavy casualties. He approved it on October 8.

Unfortunately, the Chinese were not willing to give up their advantageous position without a real fight. Well dug in, they had plenty of ammunition and covered supply routes. Two battalions of the 31st Infantry Regiment made the initial assault on October 14 without success. Additional troops were thrown in by both sides during the next six weeks, as the combat surged back and forth over the "Triangle." By November 18, when the attacks and counterattacks petered out with indecisive results, the IX Corps had employed the ROK 2d Division besides the U.S. 7th Division and had sustained more than 9000 casualties. The Chinese lost more than 19,000 men, but they still held most of the "Triangle" complex at the end and were willing to accept such disproportionate losses. The slight improvement in the U.N. Command position was not worth the cost.

As the fighting settled down into a deeper stalemate, General

Clark wrote me expressing concern that the failure to achieve an armistice was caused by a lack of military pressure on the Communists. He conceded that with the forces then available to him no decisive action by the U.N. Command was feasible. However, he had developed an outline plan that would force the enemy to seek or accept an armistice. I agreed to consider it, whereupon Clark sent three of his staff officers to Washington to explain and support it. In essence it called for a drive to the line Wonsan-Pyongyang in three stages, each to last about three weeks. It comprised enveloping attacks by Army forces, a major amphibious assault, airborne operations as opportunities might develop, and sea and air action against targets in China. A considerable increase in forces would be needed to sustain the operation. In addition to the troops already constituting the U.N. Command three U.S. or U.N. divisions (one infantry, one airborne, and one marine), two ROK divisions, two Chinese Nationalist divisions, twelve field artillery battalions, and twenty antiaircraft artillery battalions would be required. Though such an augmentation under existing conditions was most unlikely, General Clark wanted to be prepared in the event that a new administration, to be elected in November, might wish to make a major military effort to end the war.

This plan died almost aborning. President-elect Eisenhower, accompanied by designated Secretary of Defense Wilson, General Bradley, and Admiral Radford, arrived in Korea on December 2. General Eisenhower visited President Rhee, toured the front with Clark and Van Fleet, and talked to commanders of all ranks as he assayed the situation. At a press conference in Seoul at the end of his visit the President-elect admitted that he had "no panaceas," no trick solution for ending the war. Clark was somewhat dismayed that, although he was almost constantly with Eisenhower, he was never given an opportunity to present his plan and the estimate of forces required to obtain a military victory. Clark became convinced that the new President would seek an honorable armistice.

Reports from all along the front in early December indicated that the enemy was digging in for the winter. With the bleak hills of Korea in a deep freeze combat operations slowed almost to a halt. Both sides did replenish their ammunition stocks at the front and rotated personnel and units. It was during this period that an experimental small-scale attack by one infantry company on the front of the U.S. 7th Division went awry. Operation Smack had been designed to test methods of coordinating close air support, artillery, tanks, and infantry, and to take prisoners. Senior Army and Air Force officers and a number of correspondents had been invited to view this test from a convenient hilltop. Unfortunately, a malaprop "scenario" of events gave at least one newsman, newly arrived in Korea, the impression of a gladiatorial exhibition for the entertainment of the "brass." Obviously seeking a headline — which he made — he cabled home a story of this sort from Seoul without having witnessed the test himself and apparently without bothering to check with the correspondents who had observed it. The story was picked up all over the country by editorial writers frustrated at the stalemate in Korea and by genuinely disturbed critics of the war and was blown up out of proportion to the facts of the case. It was a commentary on the vexed mood of the American public and the Congress at the time that I had to spend almost a full day before a congressional committee to convince one wrathful congressman and the press at home that this action, in which the company had taken relatively heavy casualties, was a legitimate test and not intended to be a show. Fortunately, I was able to read to the committee extracts of an eyewitness account from a seasoned correspondent, Jim Robinson of National Broadcasting Company, and a *Washington News* editorial that was based on an investigation of Operation Smack made on the spot by the *News'* respected war correspondent, Jim G. Lucas, which did much to still the furor caused by the original extravagant story.

As the spring of 1953 approached, General Clark warned General Van Fleet that the Communists, who had built up their forces north of Seoul during the winter, might launch an attack to seize the capital city before the spring thaws. However, Van Fleet, who would reach the retirement age of sixty in February, was confident that his Eighth Army, of which he was justly proud, could handle any attack that the Chinese might throw against it. As February came and went without any major push by the enemy, Clark's concern was relaxed.

On February 11 General Van Fleet left for home and a richly

earned retirement. A naturally aggressive soldier, Van Fleet never fully adjusted himself to the fact that circumstances beyond his sphere of responsibility forced the Eighth Army during the last year and a half of his command to assume a defensive role, which was distasteful to him. To his credit, he never wavered in his efforts to keep up the morale and fighting spirit of the Eighth Army, which Matt Ridgway and he had done so much to fashion into one of the finest American armies ever to take the field. But Van Fleet's greatest contribution in the Korean war, in my judgment, was the transformation of the inchoate ROK Army into a fine fighting machine that stood up well under the heavy attacks of the more experienced Chinese forces just before the truce was signed. The ROK government recognized Van's outstanding service with its highest military awards. At the retirement parade, which I arranged in his honor at Fort Lesley J. McNair in Washington, he was presented with the United States' Distinguished Service Medal for his outstanding accomplishments in Korea. It was the third he had won in his long and illustrious career.

Van Fleet was succeeded in command of the Eighth Army by General Maxwell D. Taylor, who had been serving as my Deputy Chief of Staff for Operations and Administration. Max Taylor had jumped into Normandy at the head of the 101st Airborne Division on D Day in World War II and had distinguished himself in the subsequent drive across the base of the Cherbourg peninsula under my command in the VII Corps. After World War II he had served as Superintendent of West Point and as U.S. Commander in Berlin before I brought him to the Department of the Army staff as Assistant Chief of Staff, Operations, G-3, in 1951. In this capacity and later as Deputy for Operations and Administration he had closely followed the Korean war and was thoroughly familiar with its problems. I recommended to the JCS and President Eisenhower that he command the Eighth Army. Max fully maintained the fighting tradition of that army established by Walker, Ridgway, and Van Fleet before him.

But the Eighth Army was not to be tested seriously again until the Chinese initiated final operations in June of 1953 to improve their positions before the signing of the armistice. Even then the principal Chinese efforts were directed against the ROK forces. The Eighth Army was too tough a nut to crack.

XIII

ARMISTICE

Preliminary Moves

BEFORE THE STORY of the Eighth Army's operations under General
Taylor's command is continued, it is necessary to go back two
years to pick up the thread of the negotiations that began in 1951
and ultimately led to an armistice in 1953.

The United States had determined to seek an armistice when
President Truman approved the National Security Council study
of May 17, 1951.

The first indication that the Communists might consider discussing an armistice came on June 23, 1951, when Malik, the
Russian delegate to the United Nations, in a radio address in New
York suggested that a cease-fire and armistice might be arranged
on the basis of a "mutual withdrawal of forces from the 38th
parallel." This was followed up on June 27 by Deputy Foreign
Minister Andrei Gromyko, who sent a note to U.S. Ambassador
Kirk in Moscow stating that an armistice, limited to strictly military matters and avoiding any political or territorial questions,
should be negotiated by the senior military field commanders.

Meanwhile, Secretary Acheson, while appearing on June 26
before the House Military Affairs Committee, was reported in
the *New York Times* as saying that the United States' military
objectives in Korea would be satisfied if the Communists withdrew north of the 38th Parallel and gave adequate guarantees
against renewal of aggression.

After these indications, from both sides, of a willingness to negotiate, U.N. Secretary General Lie received a ruling from
the United Nations legal counsel that the United States could

legally negotiate such an armistice without further authorization from the United Nations. President Truman then instructed General Ridgway through the JCS to broadcast on June 30 the following message to the "Commander in Chief, Communist Forces in Korea":

> I am informed that you wish a meeting to discuss armistice providing for the cessation of hostilities and all acts of armed forces in Korea, with adequate guarantee for the maintenance of such armistice. Upon receipt of word that such a meeting is desired, I shall be prepared to name my representative. I would also at that time suggest a date at which he could meet with your representative. I propose that such a meeting could take place aboard a Danish Hospital ship in Wonson harbor.

On July 1 the Communists replied to General Ridgway's radio announcement in a broadcast sponsored jointly by Kim Il Sung, Commander of the North Korean Army, and Peng Teh-huai, Commander of the so-called Chinese Volunteers. They agreed to meet the U.N. Command representatives but proposed as a meeting place the old capital of Korea, Kaesong, which lay within the Communist lines northwest of Seoul. After some further exchanges it was agreed to have a meeting of three liaison officers from each side at Kaesong on July 8, who would arrange the time, place, and procedures to be followed for later meetings of the chief delegates.

General Ridgway drafted an agenda, which was submitted to the JCS along with the names of the officers he had chosen for the delegation. He had selected a distinguished group, headed by Admiral Joy, Commander of Naval Forces, Far East, and including Major General Henry I. Hodes, Deputy Chief of Staff, Eighth Army, Major General Laurence C. Craigie, Vice Commander, Far East Air Forces, Rear Admiral Arleigh Burke, Deputy Chief of Staff, Naval Forces, Far East, and Major General Paik, the able young commander of the ROK I Corps.

An incident that might have foretold the wrangling in 1968 and 1969 over the shape of the table and the seating arrangements for the Vietnam peace negotiations in Paris occurred at the first meeting of the liaison officers; it revealed a pattern of Chinese propaganda action that was to continue throughout the negotiations. The U.N. Command representatives, led by Colonel Andrew J. Kinney, U.S. Air Force, landed by helicopter near Kaesong on July 8, 1951. They were met and escorted to a nearby tea house, where the meeting was to be held. They walked in and without any ado, before the Communists could forestall them, began sitting, by chance, on the north side of the conference table. According to oriental custom, at peace negotiations the victor sits facing south and the vanquished facing north. The Communists were so flustered by this unexpected turn that their leader stammered and stuttered in replying to Colonel Kinney's opening remarks. When the main delegations met two days later, the representatives found their way barred to the north side of the table, and throughout all subsequent meetings they had no alternative but to face north.

Armed Communist guards were in evidence everywhere at the initial meetings of the delegates, menacingly herding the United Nations representatives almost as if the latter were prisoners, while Communists took reels of pictures of the unarmed "defeated" Americans. The Communist refusal to permit twenty United Nations newsmen to accompany the United Nations delegation to Kaesong, and to remove all armed guards, was finally nullified by Admiral Joy's refusal to attend any further meetings. After a few days the Communists gave in. The guards were withdrawn, and United Nations newsmen, although barred, as were the Communist pressmen, from the meeting room, were able to report freely from Kaesong.

The Communist delegation was headed nominally by General Nam Il, Chief of Staff of the North Korean Army and Vice Premier of the North Korean State. Nam was in his late thirties. He was allegedly born in Manchuria of Korean parentage and educated in Manchuria and had attended Russian military schools. He spoke Russian, Chinese, and Korean. He appeared to Admiral Joy to be dominated by the Chinese General Hsieh Fang, who wielded the real power as the senior Chinese delegate. Yet Nam was definitely the spokesman for the Communists throughout the negotiations.

Before the negotiations got under way, the JCS radioed to

General Ridgway instructions that were intended to serve as guidelines for our representatives. Neither the Joint Chiefs nor our associates in the State Department foresaw the tortuous course of the negotiations as we framed those instructions, which were destined to be changed several times.

General Ridgway was told that the chief interest of the United States was to end the fighting and to obtain assurances that it would not be renewed. Since we realized that the Communists might not want to reach a permanent political settlement in Korea, Ridgway was cautioned that it was essential to obtain a military agreement that we could live with for a long time. He was not to discuss political questions such as the disposition of Taiwan, the seating of Communist China in the United Nations, or any Communist proposal to fix the 38th Parallel as a boundary between North and South Korea.

As seems inevitable in any negotiations with Communists, ten plenary sessions were required before even an agenda was agreed upon. Haggling over agenda is not an idle Communist exercise. Whereas Americans are accustomed to regard them as simply lists of subjects to be discussed, the Communists presented an agenda phrased as conclusions. For example, if their agenda had been accepted by the United Nations delegation, it would have committed the United Nations, in advance of any actual negotiations, to the withdrawal of all foreign troops from Korea. Admiral Joy stuck to his guns in demanding a mere listing of subjects for consideration. The agenda finally adopted on July 25 read as follows:

1. Adoption of the agenda.
2. Fixing a military demarcation line between the two sides so as to establish a demilitarized zone as a basic condition for the cessation of hostilities.
3. Concrete arrangements for the realization of a cease fire, including the composition, authority, and functions of a supervisory organ for carrying out the terms of an armistice.
4. Arrangements relating to prisoners of war.
5. Recommendations to governments of countries concerned on both sides.

The inclusion of Item 5, insisted upon by the Communists at the last minute, possibly was a face-saving device to cover their agreement to delete the withdrawal of troops from the agenda.

The adoption of an agenda, instead of clearing the way for accelerated progress in substantive discussions of the various items, proved to be only the beginning of seemingly endless stops and starts.

In the Korean negotiations the normal difficulties were enhanced by the fact that the negotiators were military men, meeting in the field, without final authority to determine anything except under instructions from their senior commanders, who were located some distance away and who in turn were subject to overriding political-military guidance that came on the one hand from Peking and on the other from Washington. The United Nations delegation had a further difficulty vis-à-vis the Communists, in that they were under pressure from their government, which was responsive to an American and allied public opinion that was becoming more and more anxious to end the war. Their adversaries, habitually less concerned with time and human losses, were better equipped, both temperamentally and with instructions from their governments, to hold out for concessions.

Under the American political-military system there was more room for divergent opinions and judgments than under the monolithic Communist structure. The divergencies sometimes led to vacillating instructions and a lack of firmness, which distressed our negotiators, military men accustomed to sticking to decisions once made. I must admit that we members of the JCS occasionally had the same feeling in our consultations with the State Department and civilian leaders more directly responsible politically to the American people. Yet we had to admit that we could not guarantee the success of military courses that General Ridgway, or we ourselves, supported.

During the long period of negotiations the JCS and the State and Defense Departments, far from the tents at Panmunjom, had important roles in determining our negotiating positions. The JCS met weekly with representatives of State to prepare instructions to General Ridgway, often in answer to his queries or recommendations. The State Department's representatives changed frequently throughout the period, but they consisted usually of two or three of the following officials:

Charles E. Bohlen, Counselor
U. Alexis Johnson, Bureau of Far Eastern Affairs
H. Freeman Matthews, Under Secretary of State
　for Political Affairs
Livingston Merchant, Assistant Secretary of State
　for Far Eastern Affairs
Paul Nitze, Director, Policy Planning Staff
Dean Rusk, Assistant Secretary of State for Far
　Eastern Affairs

These were all exceptionally able men. While we did not see eye to eye with them at all times, we on the JCS had great respect for each of them, and we all worked closely together.

As Executive Agent for the JCS, I carried the responsibility with our Army staff of keeping in touch, day and night, with the situation in Korea on the battle front and at Panmunjom. In order specifically to follow developments in the armistice negotiations we set up, in agreement with the State and Defense Departments, an informal committee headed by Major General Clyde D. Eddleman, General Bolté's Deputy for Operations, G-3. The other members of this most useful group were Alexis Johnson of the State Department, Charles A. Sullivan of the Defense Department, and Lieutenant Colonel Jack B. Matthews of G-3. They met almost daily to follow up on queries or recommendations from Ridgway and to propose replies or solutions to the JCS and the State Department. General Bolté or I sometimes met with one of the State Department officials, usually Matthews or Johnson, to draft position papers or messages preliminary to State-JCS meetings.

Secretaries Acheson and Marshall, and Lovett, who succeeded General Marshall as Secretary of Defense on September 17, 1951, joined the JCS, or had us come to their offices, when matters of special importance were being considered.

Negotiations Get Under Way

No sooner had the agenda been adopted than an impasse developed over Agenda Item 2, the demarcation line. Nam Il insisted on the 38th Parallel, while Admiral Joy, following JCS instructions, proposed the actual line of contact between front-line troops. After several violations of the neutral zone near Kaesong, the Communists finally agreed to transfer the site to Panmunjom, 5 miles east of Kaesong, where both sides would assume responsibility for protecting the area. The delegates met for the first time in two months at Panmunjom the following day.

Preliminary work on Item 2 was turned over to subdelegates — Hodes and Burke for the United Nations Command and Generals Lee Sang Cho and Hsieh Fang for the Communists — who met that afternoon.

The United Nations representatives at once found themselves in a dilemma. Their instructions from the JCS called upon them to secure the line of contact as the demarcation line in order to forestall a possible Communist demand to revert to the 38th Parallel. At the same time our people were to insist on the demarcation line's being subject to revision at the time of the actual signing of the truce agreement, with a view to preventing the negotiations on other items from dragging on indefinitely. However, the ROK government demanded that Kaesong, the ancient capital of Korea, which was inside the Communist lines and south of the 38th Parallel, be returned to South Korean control.

Lee and Hsieh would not even consider relinquishing Kaesong and furthermore were adamant that whatever demarcation line was agreed upon under Item 2 would be final and not subject to later modification. Agreement by the U.N. Command to the latter point would have been tantamount to granting the Communists immunity from attack, while they might drag out negotiations on other items indefinitely.

Messages flew back and forth between Admiral Joy and General Ridgway and the JCS during the next three weeks in an effort to end the impasse on Item 2.

Accordingly, on November 14 Ridgway was instructed to press for an early settlement of Item 2 on the basis of the existing front line, with the proviso that the other items would be settled within a thirty-day period, which would expire December 27.

A United Nations proposal to this effect was submitted to the Communists. After several days of questions and argument they finally agreed, but not until they had wrung a concession that the demarcation line would not be revised until after the other agenda items were settled. The U.N. Command group agreed also to the Communist suggestion of a demilitarized zone only 4 kilometers (2.4 miles) in depth instead of the 20 miles originally suggested. There was some merit in a shallower zone, for it lessened the area in which disputed incidents might occur. Disputes continued over the exact location of the front line as it was posted on maps by staff officers from both sides. It was not until November 27, 1951, after thirty-seven sessions of the subdelegations that the demarcation line was fixed.

In thus concluding Item 2 both sides had made concessions. The United Nations delegation had succeeded in getting away from the 38th Parallel as the line of demarcation, ensuring the U.N. Command a far better military position than the indefensible Parallel. On the other hand, the Communists had obtained their goal of establishing the demarcation line as a relatively permanent cease-fire line that would be changed only slightly by subsequent fighting.

Item 3: Arrangements for Armistice

Long before the negotiators had reached Item 3, State-JCS instructions, covering the implementation and supervision of the terms of an armistice, had been sent to General Ridgway. These were keyed to only two basic points: an armistice commission should be established, with free access to all Korea, to check compliance with the armistice stipulations, and there should be no reinforcement of personnel or equipment during the armistice period.

A difference of view arose between the JCS, General Ridgway, and Admiral Joy with respect to the U.N. Command position on unlimited inspections. Ridgway had questioned the need for unlimited inspection, feeling that the Communists would never agree to inspection of areas under their control. He was also skeptical about how the enemy might exploit their right to inspect within the U.N. Command area. He was then willing to compromise by limiting inspections to selected ground, sea, and air ports of entry, whereas Joy felt that on-site checks should be made to see that there was no construction or rehabilitation of airfields in the Communist zone of North Korea.

In Washington Bolté and I, like Ridgway, were doubtful that the Communists would agree to inspections of their area, and felt that the real deterrent to a resumption of hostilities after an armistice would lie in the maintenance of sufficient allied power in the Korean area, rather than in inspections. This was to prove the case ultimately, but by late November, as a result of growing Chinese air activity over North Korea, Ridgway became convinced that inspections to prevent the construction of enemy air bases in North Korea were essential. If the enemy would not accept inspection of its areas, Ridgway favored breaking off negotiations.

However, with both domestic and foreign public opinion pressing for an end to the fighting — as they have with respect to Vietnam in 1967–1969 — political leaders in Washington were determined that any break in negotiations should come from the Communist side. Hence General Ridgway was instructed to have our delegation first hold out for inspections but then to modify its stand, if necessary, by dropping our insistence on aerial observation and photo reconnaissance.

While the State Department, the JCS, and the United Nations delegation were establishing their position on Item 3, the Communists seized the initiative by proposing a comprehensive program. Their program called for a joint military armistice commission to oversee the implementation of an armistice, stipulated that there should be no increasing of military forces, supplies, equipment, or facilities by either side after the signing of an armistice, required the withdrawal of all military forces, including guerrillas, from the territory controlled by the other side, prohibited any armed forces in the demilitarized zone except as specifically agreed by both sides, and proposed a supervisory commission, consisting of representatives of nations neutral in the Korean war, to conduct inspections of such ports of entry on both sides of the demilitarized zone as were mutually agreed upon and to report to the armistice commission the results of such inspections.

Admiral Joy suggested the appointment of a joint subdelegation to study and clarify certain aspects of the Communist proposal. The Communists accepted, appointing Generals Lee and Hsieh as their spokesmen. Admiral Joy designated General Hode and General Howard M. Turner, United States Air Force, who had replaced General Craigie.

The subdelegation met at once. It was soon made clear that under the Communist plan there would be no rotation of personnel or replacement of equipment, that reconstruction of facilities, including airfields, in North Korea, would not be interfered with, and that the neutral inspection teams would operate independently of the Military Armistice Commission.

Meanwhile the JCS and the State Department had been struggling to reconcile the various positions. By December 7 we had agreed that some concessions could be made in permitting the rehabilitation of existing airfields, the use of neutral observers, and the withdrawal of United Nations forces from coastal islands north of the demarcation line. However, it was agreed that we should stand on the question of rotation and replenishment, that the make-up of the neutral teams must be agreed to by both sides, and that these teams should operate in all respects under supervision of the Military Armistice Commission.

After approval by Secretaries Acheson and Marshall these proposals were put up to the President. Mr. Truman was loath to permit the Communists to rehabilitate the airfields, roads, and railroads that our air forces had destroyed at such high cost. But it was explained that the armistice might be the only agreement that could be reached in Korea for a long time and that it would be impossible to prevent enemy rehabilitation over a long period. On the other hand, we would wish to make extensive repairs and improvements in our zone. The President acceded to these arguments, and instructions accordingly were sent to General Ridgway on December 11, 1951.

The following day the U.N. Command delegation submitted proposals embodying the new instructions from the JCS. The Communists were told that this was a package proposal that must be accepted in total or not at all. Not unexpectedly, the Communists would not, at least immediately, buy the package.

With the approach of the thirty-day deadline on December 27 for conclusion of an armistice General Ridgway flew to Korea to discuss the situation with our delegation. In a resultant report on December 18 to the JCS he said that an extension of the time limit, unless very short, would adversely affect the morale of his troops. He deprecated the policy pursued thus far of abandoning positions, since it encouraged the Communists to become obdurate and demanding. He urged that the U.N. Command stick to its stand on airfields and rotation, neutral aerial inspection, photo reconnaissance of airfields, and free movement of neutral observer teams throughout Korea. He emphasized that the critical issue was the surveillance of airfields.

The JCS consulted the State Department, and the situation was reviewed with the President before a reply was sent the next day to General Ridgway. The President was informed that the consensus of political and military opinion in Washington was that the armistice might be the only agreement that could be reached for a long time. The best way to prevent a fresh outbreak was to convince the Communists that this would bring full retribution from the U.N. Command. To this end the State Department was working on a declaration of continuing support, to be signed by the nations participating in the Command.

With these considerations in mind the President and his advisers preferred not to adopt any firm positions at the time or to define when or under what conditions negotiations might be broken off. They did furnish General Ridgway with some further guidance. Since it would be impracticable to prevent the rehabilitation of enemy airfields for any length of time, they were willing to permit some fields, except those suitable for jet planes, to be rebuilt and maintained. Aerial surveillance, while desirable, was not essential. As long as there was no overall increase in forces, no monthly or other restrictions on the rate of rotation need be fixed. General Ridgway was authorized to stand pat on any increase of combat aircraft. He was also authorized to agree to a fifteen-day extension of the deadline for completion of negotiations, if any progress was being made by December 27.

The initial deadline passed, but during January and February of 1952 staff officers gradually narrowed the differences over Item 3. By March 15 agreement had been reached on the rotation of 35,000 men a month through five ports of entry on each side, and surprisingly the Communists agreed to retention by the U.N. Command of five groups of islands north of the demarcation line, off the west coast of Korea. This left outstanding on Item 3 only the questions of rehabilitation of airfields and Soviet participation on the U.N. Supervisory Commission.

While this whittling down of the differences over Item 3 was taking place, the importance of this item was being submerged by events in the U.N. Command prisoner of war camps and by the resultant differences over Item 4, covering the exchange of prisoners, which threatened to wreck any hope of an armistice and actually delayed it for more than a year.

Item 5: Political Discussion to Follow Armistice*

In an effort to speed up the negotiations Admiral Joy in January of 1952 suggested that Item 5 be included in preliminary discussions by staff officers. This item was to cover any political matters that might have to be settled after the armistice.

A plenary session of the Armistice Conference to consider Item 5 got under way on February 6, 1952. Nam Il at once proposed that within three months after the signing of an armistice each side designate five representatives to conduct a political conference. He listed three topics: the withdrawal of foreign troops, the peaceful settlement of the Korean question [sic], and other

* Footnote: Item 5 was settled more than a year earlier than Item 4.

questions related to peace in Korea. The United Nations delegation was pleasantly surprised with the broad vagueness of Nam's suggested topics.

Admiral Joy, with the approval of Ridgway and the JCS, at the next session suggested only minor modifications to Nam's proposals, which on February 16 were embodied essentially in a revised Communist program:

> In order to insure the peaceful settlement of the Korean question, the military commanders of both sides hereby recommend to the governments of the countries concerned on both sides that, within three (3) months after the Armistice Agreement is signed and becomes effective, a political conference of a higher level of both sides be held by representatives appointed respectively to settle through negotiation the questions of the withdrawal of all foreign forces from Korea, the peaceful settlement of the Korean question, etc.

Nam explained that by "foreign forces" he meant "non-Korean forces," and that the phrase "settlement of the Korean question, etc." had been left indefinite to meet U.N. Command objections to more specific terms.

The following day Admiral Joy stated that with the understanding that "etc." did not apply to matters outside Korea, the U.N. Command accepted the new Communist version.

Item 5 had been settled in eleven days, a record that was not again approached. The Communists apparently had had second thoughts after their initial addition of Item 5 to the agenda and, like the United States, were content to let postarmistice questions take care of themselves.

Item 4: Exchange of Prisoners of War

The United States had signed, though it had not yet ratified, the Geneva Convention of 1949 providing for the exchange of prisoners of war, and at the start of the war in 1950 the North Korean government had indicated that it would abide by the Convention. However, the drafters of the Convention had not envisioned all of the contingencies that would arise in later wars involving Communists.

After World War II the Russians had retained thousands of German and Japanese prisoners, whom they held for years in slave labor camps while repairing war damages in Russia. In an effort to prevent a recurrence of this practice the Convention provided for the quick and compulsory repatriation of all prisoners of war. Article 118 said simply: "Prisoners of war shall be released and repatriated without delay after the cessation of hostilities." Unfortunately, it took no account of the desires of those prisoners who might not wish to be repatriated.

There were now in U.N. Command prison camps many Chinese prisoners of war, former adherents of Chiang Kai-shek, and thousands of ROK soldiers who had been captured by the Communists in the early days of the war and impressed into the Communist forces. Large numbers of these men, Chinese and Koreans, had indicated that they did not desire to be returned to Communist control.

Brigadier General Robert A. McClure, U.S. Army Chief of Psychological Warfare, in July of 1951 had called this situation to my attention. He recommended that former Chinese nationalists, many of whom feared they might face prison or execution if they were turned over to Communist China, should be repatriated to Taiwan, which officially was still part of China. Aside from its humanitarian aspects, such a solution, as word of it got around, might encourage other disaffected Chinese soldiers to surrender.

This proposal appealed to me. I felt also that, if adequate safeguards could be arranged to ensure the return of all captured U.N. Command personnel, we should apply the same humanitarian principle to Korean prisoners of war who did not wish to be sent back to North Korea. I submitted a recommendation to this effect to the JCS. The Chiefs agreed, but since such a procedure transcended the military sphere, we forwarded the proposal to the Secretary of Defense with the recommendation that after consultation with the State Department it be presented for consideration to the National Security Council.

However, Secretary Lovett felt that the concept of no forcible repatriation might run counter to another basic principle already included in the instructions to General Ridgway on Item 4, that is, that prisoners should be exchanged on a one-for-one basis. Lovett feared that the Communists might insist on an all-for-all exchange, which would preclude retention by the U.N. Command of any prisoners resisting repatriation. Since Washington's primary concern was the early conclusion of an armistice, it was decided not to inject the debatable tenet of no forcible repatriation since this might unduly prolong the negotiations.

But it soon became apparent, when negotiations on Item 4 got under way on December 11, 1951, that there would be no quick and easy solution of the question. The Communists balked on any agreement and refused to discuss anything other than an all-for-all exchange. Rear Admiral Ruthven E. Libby, who had succeeded Admiral Arleigh Burke as head of the United Nations subdelegation handling Item 4, seized on the Communist insistence on forced repatriation, which was inherent in their demand for an all-for-all exchange, as being the weakest point in their position. Libby's view was somewhat in conflict with that of Secretary Lovett. The JCS, with the concurrence of the State Department, supported Libby's position, and in our instructions to General Ridgway of December 19, 1951, stated, "Any position requiring forced return of personnel must have prior approval by Washington."

Colonel Tsai, the Chinese spokesman, accused the U.N. Command of using voluntary repatriation as a subterfuge for holding on to most of the prisoners. To meet this charge the JCS suggested that a poll of the U.N. Command prisoners might be conducted under supervision of the International Red Cross. The Communists agreed to a check of prisoners of war by both sides.

By April 15, 1952, most of the 132,000 military prisoners and 37,000 civilian internees had been screened. When pressed earlier by the Communists for an approximation of the number of prisoners to be returned to Communist control, the U.N. Command had guessed it would be about 116,000. However, when the screening was over, to the amazement of the screening teams, less than 70,000 prisoners of war, of whom approximately 53,900 were

North Koreans and 5100 were Chinese, chose to be repatriated. When these figures were revealed to the usually voluble Chinese liaison officer, Colonel Tsai, he was struck speechless. The next day, his pride stung to the quick by the evident revulsion of the prisoners toward Communism, Tsai charged the U.N. Command with duplicity. Thereafter, the Communists refused to consider any type of screening and became more recalcitrant than ever on all issues.

Meanwhile, General Ridgway had secured from the JCS authority for Admiral Joy to submit at a plenary session of the armistice negotiators a U.N. Command draft of a complete truce agreement. This proposal made no mention of rehabilitation of airfields. It provided that the U.N. Supervisory Commission — on which the U.N. Command had refused to accept the Union of Soviet Socialist Republics — should consist of Switzerland, Sweden, Poland, and Czechoslovakia. The section dealing with prisoners of war provided, in effect, for the exchange of the 70,000 Communists wishing repatriation for the 12,000 U.N. Command prisoners. Though it did not say so, the Command's intent was to reclassify the nonrepatriates as displaced persons or refugees.

Any hope that the U.N. Command proposal might move the negotiations off dead center was abruptly ended when General Nam Il dismissed the package as inconsequential. He called for an indefinite recess. The meeting was not a total loss. The U.N. Command, by conceding that airfields might be rehabilitated or constructed while standing firm in refusing to accept the Soviets on the U.N. Supervisory Commission, had reduced the outstanding issues to one: the repatriation of prisoners. The differences on airfields and the Soviets were not raised again by either side in subsequent meetings.

Unfortunately, these meetings were extended for another year, largely because of disturbances created by Communist prisoners in the U.N. Command's prisoner-of-war camps on the offshore island of Kojedo and other points.

The Uprisings of Communist Prisoners on Kojedo

The problems that arose with Communist prisoners of war were totally unexpected by the State and Defense Departments and the U.N. Command. There had been a few obstreperous Filipino prisoners, captured by U.S. troops during the Philippine Insurrection of 1901, who had to be interned in Guam, but they caused no great trouble, nor had the Germans and Italians taken by American forces during World War I or II. As was to prove the case in the Communists' employment of "volunteers" in "wars of liberation" and of various forms of propaganda for psychological warfare, their deliberate utilization of prisoners of war to harass their captors and warp world public opinion in their favor was an effective new tactic, however reprehensible.

Just as the drafters of the Geneva Convention of 1949 had not foreseen the plight of the prisoners who would oppose repatriation, they had not envisaged any need for the protection of the captors against organized attacks from their prisoners. When the U.N. Command was finally driven to use force to control prisoners who were in murderous rebellion, the Communist propagandists were ready and able to picture the Command as brutally maltreating defenseless captives.

After the Inchon campaign and the U.N. Command's drive to the Yalu, in which thousands of North Koreans were captured, it became necessary to impound them on the island of Kojedo, off the south coast near Pusan. The prisoners were housed in large tents or hastily constructed buildings, grouped in compounds designed to hold about a thousand men each. The compounds were separated only by barbed-wire fences. As the war progressed and the number of prisoners mounted to over 137,000, the compounds became vastly overcrowded before additional ones could be built and before adequate numbers of trained guards could be provided by the ROK Army.

Management of the prison camps came under the jurisdiction of the Eighth Army, which delegated responsibility for the operation of the camps to the 2d Logistical Command under Brigadier

General Paul F. Yount, whose headquarters was at Pusan. Yount placed Brigadier General Francis T. Dodd in command of Kojedo. He proved to be an unfortunate choice.

There had been some bad blood between the NK prisoners and the ROK guards, but no serious trouble arose until the screening of prisoners for repatriation got under way. The hard-core Communists among the prisoners were better organized than the anti-Communists and gradually took over internal control of the camps.

The first serious outbreak occurred on February 18, 1952, when ROK teams attempted to screen some 5000 civilian internees in Compound 62, which was under *de facto* Red control. The internees refused to allow the screening parties to enter. A battalion of the U.S. 27th Infantry Regiment, which had been moved to the island in January, entered the compound with bayonets fixed. As if on signal, the Communists streamed from their barracks and attacked the troops with rocks, knives, axes, pick handles, flails, and tent poles. The soldiers were forced to use concussion grenades and, when this failed to stop the attack, the troops opened fire. In this action 77 North Koreans died, and 140 others were wounded. One United States soldier was killed, and 38 were wounded. Needless to say, General Nam and his coconspirator negotiators protested vehemently.

Subsequent bloody clashes between anti-Communist and pro-Communist groups of prisoners led General Van Fleet in April of 1952 to separate the prisoners refusing repatriation and move them to camps on the mainland, in order to protect them from the hard-line Communist prisoners. This action had merit, but it stiffened resistance among the hard-core Communists on Kojedo, who now could count on the support of all remaining prisoners of war there in their resistance to any further screening.

Answering a demand for a hearing of their grievances by the camp commander, General Dodd on May 7, without adequate security guards at hand, talked to a group of prisoners at the unlocked gate of Compound 76. Dodd foolishly allowed the prisoners to gather close to him and to Lieutenant Colonel Wilbur R. Raven, who was with him. Suddenly the prisoners leaped on the

officers and started to drag them into the compound. Colonel
Raven managed to break loose, but General Dodd was not as fortunate or as quick-witted. He was hauled behind a row of
blankets hung along an inner barbed-wire fence and then hurried
to a tent that had been prepared for him. Almost immediately
the Communist leaders triumphantly displayed a large sign announcing "We captured Dodd. As long as our demand will be
solved, his safety is secured. If there happen brutal act such as
shooting, his life is in danger."

This serious misadventure was reported at once to Generals
Yount and Van Fleet. The latter instructed Yount not to use force
to effect Dodd's release without clearance from the Eighth Army.
Brigadier General Charles F. Colson, whom Van Fleet had flown
over from the I Corps, assumed command of Kojedo, and another
battalion of infantry and a company of tanks were headed for the
island.

Unfortunately, Colson permitted the Communist leaders to
negotiate with him, while Dodd cooperated with them in trying
to arrange a bloodless settlement. Talks went on for three days
while the prisoners set up a "people's court" and had Dodd answer
to charges alleging brutality, deaths, and injuries to them. As this
bizarre performance dragged on, General Van Fleet flew into
Kojedo for a conference with Colson. He had discussed the situation with General Ridgway, who was about to leave Japan as replacement for General Eisenhower in NATO, and with General
Clark, who had just arrived in Japan as Ridgway's successor. They
wanted Colson to give every opportunity to cooperative prisoners
to surrender peaceably before employing the tanks and infantry
that now ringed the camp.

Negotiations reached a disgraceful climax on May 10 when
General Dodd, prisoner spokesmen sitting beside him, telephoned
Colson, passing on the prisoners' demands and suggesting changes
in Colson's reply as the prisoners demanded. This resulted in a
written statement from Colson assuring the prisoners that "in the
future POW's can expect humane treatment in this camp," that
there would be "no more forcible rescreening," and that a representative group or commission of prisoners of war would be estab-

lished "according to the details agreed to by Gen. Dodd and approved by me." Dodd was finally released at 9:30 P.M. on May 10, after the prisoners' leaders decided that they had wrung from the U.N. Command the last possible drop of damaging propaganda.

A board of inquiry convened by General Yount found Dodd and Colson blameless, evidently condoning their efforts to save bloodshed. General Van Fleet disagreed. He recommended administrative action or reprimand — as distinct from court martial — to both Dodd and Colson, while General Clark went further and recommended to the Department of the Army that both be reduced to the grade of colonel and that an administrative reprimand be given General Yount for his errors of omission in handling the incident. As Army Chief of Staff I concurred thoroughly with Clark's recommendation, and Secretary Pace affirmed the action.

The continued refusal of the prisoners of war to obey instructions convinced Van Fleet that they would have to be dispersed into smaller groups in more secure compounds, some on an adjacent island and some on the mainland. General Clark approved this plan. General Van Fleet sent over Brigadier General Haydon L. Boatner, a tough, able combat soldier from the 2d Infantry Division, to effect these changes. The prisoners manned trenches to combat their movement into the new compounds, but in a quick series of sharp, no-compromise moves with tanks, infantry men, and paratroopers of the 187th Airborne Regimental Combat Team, Boatner broke the Communist resistance, which ended when Colonel Lee Hak Koo, the leader of the belligerents in Compound 76, was hauled out by the seat of his pants. Recognizing force and firmness, as always, the Communists in the remaining compounds swiftly agreed to do whatever Boatner ordered.

During these final operations one United States soldier was speared to death, and 14 were injured; 75 prisoners who opposed repatriation were freed, but the bodies of 16 men, murdered by the Communists, were found; 31 prisoners were killed, and 139 were wounded. General Boatner had done the job that Dodd should have accomplished.

The Joint Chiefs of Staff had no responsibility for the camps but did have an interest in the disturbances, since they came to have a critical effect on the outcome of the armistice negotiations. As Army Chief of Staff I was deeply concerned. I had great sympathy for the officers and men who had the onerous task of controlling great numbers of recalcitrant Communist prisoners, but I had no sympathy for the general officers, beginning with Yount and including both Dodd and Colson, who let conditions in the camps get out of control in the first place and then used poor judgment in handling the worsening situation. Their failures were a blot on the record of the United States Army in Korea.

To me the most threatening aspect of the Kojedo affair was that it once again demonstrated the effectiveness of a dedicated and ruthless minority of Communists in any conflict of wills. The results of the screening of the prisoners proved conclusively that some 70,000 Chinese and North Koreans would not voluntarily return to Communist control. The amazing thing was that a decided minority of Communists, who were not under any direct pressure from their masters in either China or North Korea, were willing to risk their lives to gain domination of a majority of the prisoners for the benefit of the cause of Communism. It was only after we met their cruel use of force with equal ruthlessness that we were able to put an end to their murderous rebellion.

We have yet to master the technique of maintaining our own sense of decency, and our regard for both domestic and free-world public opinion, and still stand firm against the dastardly methods of the Communists in forcing their will on a cowed majority. Should we again become involved in such a situation, the answer probably will lie in an early decision of our own proper course of action and then an unwavering determination to maintain it.

Negotiations Reach a Deadlock

The Kojedo affair, with its attendant adverse reactions among our United Nations allies, hardened the opposition of the Communist negotiators at Panmunjom to the U.N. Command's concept of no forcible repatriation of prisoners of war.

In the middle of the uproar over Kojedo General Ridgway was transferred to Europe to succeed General Eisenhower, who had resigned as Supreme Allied Commander of NATO to run for the Presidency. Matt Ridgway had done a magnificent job in restoring the confidence and the combat efficiency of the Eighth Army after its reverse at the hands of the overwhelming Chinese armies and had ably handled his myriad duties as Commander in Chief of both the United Nations Command and the Far East. His successor, General Clark, a 1917 West Point classmate of Ridgway's and mine, with a distinguished career already behind him, was also an able administrator. He took over from Ridgway with firm, competent hands for the remainder of the Korean war.

Almost at the same time Vice Admiral Joy's tour of duty as chief negotiator for the U.N. Command was completed. Admiral Joy and his principal assistants, Admirals Burke and Libby, General Hodes of the Army, and General Turner of the U.S. Air Force, had performed admirably in the early, tough days of negotiations. Joy was succeeded by another of my classmates, Lieutenant General William K. Harrison, who had been broken in as a negotiator under Joy's tutelage. Billy Harrison was almost ideally suited for the role of final United States negotiator. He had a fine record as a staff officer and a combat commander in World War II. He was deceptively quiet and unruffled under provocation from his opposing Communist negotiators. He had a keen instinct for the weak spots in their positions and could be tough and uncompromising when he had to be, as they soon discovered.

With no sign of agreement in the offing on the one outstanding question of repatriation, General Clark, with strong support from Harrison, had obtained permission from the JCS in late July to turn over to the ROK government some 27,000 civilian internees who wished release. On June 23 Harrison notified General Nam Il that the U.N. Command intended to free these civilians in the near future. As anticipated, the Communists protested this action as unilateral. Harrison coolly told Nam that this was an internal matter, passed on to him solely for his information and not subject to debate. The Communists continued to protest but, as Harrison had predicted, took no action. Release of the internees proceeded without undue incident as rapidly as the ROK government could process and transport them to their homes in South Korea. The first step of repatriation had been taken, but the impasse on prisoners of war continued.

Clark continued to press for a solution of the repatriation problem. He and Harrison worked up a number of alternative propositions, which Clark submitted to Washington. The first provided that all prisoners be brought to the demilitarized zone and there released, without further screening or interviews, to choose for themselves to which side they wished to go. Other proposals were variations of the first, in which representatives of neutral nations determined the disposition of the nonrepatriates. The State Department representatives, meeting with the JCS, turned down all but the first of Clark's alternatives but suggested that the disposition of the nonrepatriates be postponed until after the signing of the armistice. Clark and Harrison protested this. The JCS and the Defense Department supported Clark's stand. When efforts to reconcile the State and Defense positions failed, President Truman reviewed the question, and on September 24, 1952, decided in favor of the Defense Department. The Army G-3 prepared instructions to General Clark, eliminating two of his proposals, to which the State Department agreed. The JCS and Secretary Lovett, who had succeeded General Marshall as Secretary of Defense, and the President approved the new instructions, which authorized the submission of three alternatives for the disposition of prisoners.

General Harrison presented the U.N. Command's alternatives at a plenary conference with the Communist delegates on September 28, 1952, five months after submission of the Command's April 28 package proposal. Contingent on prior acceptance of an armistice by both sides, Harrison offered the Communist negotiators a choice among three alternative proposals. They all provided for bringing the prisoners of war to the demilitarized zone. Depending on their individual wishes, the prisoners would be released from custody and turned over to representatives of the side they chose or be screened further by representatives of agreed neutral nations for final disposition. When finally released, they would assume civilian status and would not be employed in any further military action in the war.

After a ten-day recess the delegates met again on October 8. General Nam Il spoke first, rejecting the U.N. Command's proposal except to agree that after the signing of an armistice all prisoners of war would be delivered to an agreed exchange point in the demilitarized zone. Thereafter, through visits from joint Red Cross societies of both sides and under observation of inspection teams of neutral nations, the prisoners would be reclassified according to nationality and area. All captured personnel of the Chinese Peoples' Volunteers and all non-Korean prisoners of the U.N. Command would be repatriated. All captured personnel of the North Korean army whose homes were in North Korea would be repatriated; those whose homes were in South Korea would be repatriated or not, as they chose. The same procedure would be followed by captured personnel of the South Korean army.

This proposal spurned the idea of affording a choice to prisoners of war who did not wish to be returned to Communist control.

General Harrison blasted the Communists for their stand on compulsory repatriation of all Chinese "volunteers" and pointed out the falsifications and inconsistencies of the Communist propaganda efforts throughout the negotiations. He said the U.N. Command was not terminating the negotiations but was declaring a recess until the Communists were willing to accept one of the Command's three proposals or to submit in writing a constructive alternative. Meanwhile the Command's liaison officers were available for discussions. Without further ado Harrison and the Command's delegation left the conference tent.

The talking stage was over for the moment at least. Actually the recess of plenary sessions stretched out for more than five months, though the liaison officers continued to maintain contact at Panmunjom.

The Eisenhower Administration Takes Over

General Eisenhower, with perfect timing near the end of the 1952 presidential campaign, promised that, if elected, he would go to

Korea to examine personally into means of ending the Korean war, which he did.

General Eisenhower was sworn in as President on January 20, 1953. John Foster Dulles succeeded Dean Acheson as Secretary of State, and Charles E. Wilson became Secretary of Defense. The new administration had no quick and easy solution to the Korean war, and it had no intention of stepping up the military pressure on the enemy. So long as the Communists would not accept any one of the U.N. Command's proposals of October 28 nor present an acceptable alternative, there was no honorable way to end the fighting.

Operation Little Switch

General Clark came up with a suggestion in late December of 1952 that surprisingly opened the way to a break in the Communist position. By chance he saw a news release stating that the League of Red Cross Societies had adopted a resolution calling for the immediate exchange of sick and wounded prisoners of war. General Clark called this to the attention of General Eddleman, who had succeeded General Bolté as Army G-3. Clark suggested that the United Nations Command should support the resolution as a means of putting pressure on the Communists. This suggestion was reviewed by the informal State-Defense committee of Eddleman, Alex Johnson, and Charles A. Sullivan, but no action was taken until the State Department learned that the resolution might be discussed when the U.N. General Assembly met on February 24. Quick agreement was reached among the State and Defense Departments and the JCS, approved by President Truman, that General Clark propose to Generals Kim Il Sung and Peng Teh-huai an immediate exchange of sick and wounded prisoners.

More than a month went by before Kim and Peng replied. Perhaps the death of Marshal Stalin on March 5 resulted in some softening in the Communists' attitude toward the Korean war. In any event, Kim and Peng said on March 28 that they were willing to exchange the sick and wounded and added that such an exchange "should lead to the smooth settlement of the entire question of prisoners of war, thereby achieving an armistice in Korea for which people throughout the world are longing." They suggested also that plenary sessions of the chief delegates be resumed.

While this proposal was being mulled over in Panmunjom, Tokyo, and Washington, a significant break in the enemy's basic position on the whole prisoner-of-war question came when Chou En-lai, the Foreign Minister of Communist China, on April 2 issued a statement through the Chinese liaison officer at Panmunjom. Chou reviewed the negotiations, citing the agreements already reached. He then made a key proposal, urging that both sides "undertake to repatriate, immediately after the cessation of hostilities, all those prisoners of war in their custody who insist on repatriation, and to hand over the remaining ones to a neutral state so as to ensure a just solution to the question of their repatriation." Chou's proposal was seconded by Kim the following day.

An exchange of letters between Clark on one side and Kim and Peng on the other led to an agreement completing details of the exchange of sick and injured. The U.N. Command dubbed it Operation Little Switch. The actual exchange began on April 20. The number of U.N. Command personnel returned by the Communists was not as great as had been hoped. By May 3, when Little Switch terminated, the Command had received only 684 sick and wounded, of whom 94 were litter cases, in exchange for a total of 6670 Communist prisoners of war and civilian internees, of whom 357 were litter-borne.

Final Agreement on Exchange of Prisoners

While Operation Little Switch was still under way, General Harrison and Nam agreed to resume plenary sessions of the principal delegates on April 26, 1953. Little progress was made until on May 7, at the 133d meeting of the delegates, the Communists offered some major concessions. Ten additional sessions followed, each side moderating its position, until on June 4 agreement was reached essentially as follows.

Within sixty days after the effective date of an armistice each side would repatriate all prisoners of war in its custody who insisted on repatriation to the side to which they belonged at the time of capture. All prisoners of war who had not exercised their right of repatriation would be turned over in their existing camps to the custody of a Neutral Nations Repatriation Commission consisting of representatives of Czechoslovakia, Poland, Sweden, Switzerland, and India. Prison camp guards would be replaced by Indian troops.

During the next ninety days representatives of the sides to which the nonrepatriates originally belonged would be permitted to attempt to persuade them to agree to repatriation. In order to ensure that no threats or undue pressure would be used to influence the prisoners, U.N. Command observers and representatives of the U.N. Repatriation Commission would be present while ROK and Communist teams were trying to persuade prisoners who had been captured from them to choose repatriation. Those prisoners of war who still refused would then be turned over to a hazily-defined political conference for thirty days, after which those choosing to go to a neutral nation would be assisted by the U.N. Repatriation Commission and the Red Cross Society of India to do so. All others would then be brought to designated transfer points in the demilitarized zone and released to the side of their choice.

During the next two plenary sessions the negotiators reached agreement on some minor remaining issues, and on June 7, 1953, staff officers were told to work out the final terms of reference for handling the prisoners of war. Since both sides were now anxious for a settlement, they were able to complete their work the following day. After a year and a half of wearying discussion of Item 4, the document confirming the procedure for exchanging the prisoners was ready for the delegates' signatures.

The chief remaining issue for the staff officers to work out was the final location of the cease-fire line. After some give and take, and a brief Communist offensive to improve their position at one point, the agreement was reached on the demarcation line. On June 17 the plenary conference affirmed this agreement.

There were some further delays in arranging for the arrival

of the Repatriation Commission and the stationing of the inspection teams. All seemed well on the way to agreement on the terms of the armistice when Syngman Rhee, who had been objecting right along to the course of the negotiations, actively entered the game with stunning results.

Syngman Rhee Takes a Hand

From the very beginning of the armistice negotiations President Rhee had forcibly expressed his opposition to any compromise agreement with the Communists. His terms for a settlement, as stated publicly in September of 1951, were forthright and simple, but impossible of accomplishment. First the Chinese should withdraw from Korea and the North Koreans be disarmed. Then the latter would be given full representation in the National Assembly which, presumably, would settle the question of unification of Korea. If the enemy did not accept this neatly packaged proposal within a given time limit, the negotiations would be terminated. It was just as simple as that.

As it became clear to Rhee that his proposal would not be adopted, demonstrations were organized in Seoul, and students carried placards with such slogans as "No Armistice Without Unification." Such demonstrations arose "spontaneously" — whenever a truce agreement appeared imminent.

Later, as the U.N. Command and the Communists began to make progress on Item 4, doubts about ROK adherence to an armistice came to the fore. The United States, as the designated agent of the United Nations, had the legal right to negotiate an armistice, but there was no simple way to force an unwilling ROK government to abide by its terms. The United States could "walk out" of Korea, but not without great loss of prestige and an unconscionable betrayal of the men who had given their lives in this war to stop Communist aggression. On the other hand, Syngman Rhee knew that his country, which he had labored valiantly to make free, would be dependent for its freedom on military and economic assistance from the United States for years to come. The wily old patriot would have to play his cards well.

That Rhee was prepared to gamble was evidenced when the Korean National Assembly, early in April, passed a resolution urging the United States not to accept any plan that did not provide for the unification of Korea. Then, on April 24, 1953, two days before the plenary negotiations resumed, Rhee displayed his first ace in the hole. The Korean Ambassador in Washington, through the State Department, informed President Eisenhower that Rhee was preparing to withdraw the ROK forces from the U.N. Command if any armistice was signed that permitted Chinese troops to remain south of the Yalu River.

This semiultimatum drew a strong but reassuring reply from President Eisenhower. He wrote Rhee that we would continue to seek a settlement of Korea's problems but that this would be nullified if the ROK government took any action that could not be supported by the United States and other friends of Korea in the United Nations.

General Clark flew to Seoul on April 27 and was told by Rhee that he would not pull out his troops from the U.N. Command without discussing the matter personally with Clark. Clark radioed me that he felt Rhee was bluffing and would not attempt to go it alone without further careful thought. However, two weeks later, during another visit from Clark, Rhee declared that rather than let any Indian troops enter Korea, he might, on his own, release the nonrepatriates "without involving the U.N. Command."

Clark promptly reported this meeting to the JCS. He surmised that Rhee was bargaining for a security pact and increased economic aid. The State and Defense Departments were concerned about some rash action of Rhee, but the new Administration was determined to end the war, and it was too late to turn back now. On May 25, the day General Harrison was to present the U.N. Command's draft of a truce at Panmunjom, Ellis O. Briggs, who had succeeded Muccio as Ambassador to Korea, and General Clark were instructed to call on Rhee and inform him of the final terms being offered the Communists. They were to assure Rhee that the United States would continue to support the Republic of Korea militarily, economically, and politically. In addition, a "greater sanctions" statement, signed by the sixteen United Nations countries, pledging renewed support in the event hostilities were resumed by the Communists, would be issued immediately after the armistice was signed. But a bilateral security pact between the United States and Korea could not be guaranteed.

Rhee's reaction was one of emotional shock. He declared that the U.N. Command's armistice proposals were unacceptable to his people and hence he could give none of the assurances of cooperation that the United States desired. General Clark, who, while realizing the impracticability of Rhee's threats to go it alone, was genuinely sympathetic to the old man's aspirations for his country, in reporting to the JCS Rhee's reaction warned:

> . . . he may either covertly or overtly initiate action to cause the release of all Korean non-repatriates. He has the capability, and should he attempt this action, there are few effective steps that I can take to counter it.

Clark was not yet ready to believe that Rhee would continue his rash course, but he concluded, "He himself is the only one who knows how far he will go, but undoubtedly he will bluff right up to the last."

But in the dangerous poker game Rhee was playing he was not bluffing. The time had come for him to play his covered ace. Before dawn on June 18 approximately 25,000 North Korean prisoners of war broke out of four U.N. Command prisoner-of-war camps located on the mainland near Pusan and Masan. It was clear that the simultaneous outbreaks were carefully and secretly planned by the ROK government. ROK guards did little or nothing to prevent the escape. The United States personnel at the camps, limited in each case to the camp commander and a few administrative persons, exerted every effort to limit the outbreaks, but in the face of collusion between the ROK guards and the prisoners they could not prevent the escape.

As quickly as possible United States troops replaced the ROK guards who had left their posts. However, the United States was reluctant to use force against Korean nonrepatriates. Hence,

United States guards were restricted to using nontoxic gases and other nonlethal methods of control. The majority of the prisoners escaped on June 18, but large break-outs continued for some time.

In spite of Clark's warnings Rhee's action in directing the mass outbreak came as a shock to officials in Washington. Rhee readily admitted his responsibility. Replying to General Clark's protest that he had not been informed in advance, Rhee wrote, with typical oriental blandness and logic, "Under the circumstances, if I had revealed to you in advance my idea of setting them free, it would have embarrassed you. Furthermore, the plan would have been spoiled."

Rhee's solution of the nonrepatriates problem was far simpler than anything evolved at Panmunjom. His action performed a service to both the United Nations Command and the Communists. It effectively reduced the number of nonrepatriates to be handled later by the U.N. Command, and it provided a face-saving alibi to the Communists to cover their propaganda defeat when so many of their captured soldiers refused to be repatriated. They could now claim, as they did, that these men had been "kidnapped" by the ROK forces.

However, the State and Defense Departments in Washington were concerned over the ability of the U.N. Command to ensure compliance of the ROK government with the terms of the truce. Rather than rely on exchanges of communications for the cooperation of the ROK forces, President Eisenhower decided to send Assistant Secretary of State Walter S. Robertson to Korea to attempt to bring Rhee into line. I was designated to accompany and assist Robertson. I enjoyed this assignment. We hit it off well together, a fact that possibly led to my being asked later by Secretary Dulles to go to Vietnam in 1954 as Special Representative of the United States. Walter Robertson was then still in charge of Far Eastern Affairs, and we again collaborated in trying to solve some of the problems of Vietnam in the early days of President Ngo Dinh Diem's régime.

On arrival in Tokyo we met General Clark and Ambassador Briggs and Robert D. Murphy, who had been brought over to Japan to be political adviser to Clark. We all agreed that the armistice should be completed as soon as possible and that the Communists would accept it, even though the U.N. Command could not fully guarantee that Rhee would comply with all of its provisions. Clark had recommended to the JCS that, instead of turning over the Chinese nonrepatriates to a neutral state, all remaining nonrepatriates, including the Chinese, be removed to the demilitarized zone and there be transferred to the Repatriation Commission. This proposal was concurred in by the group.

After receipt in Washington of the report of this meeting President Eisenhower decided that General Clark, as the man on the spot, should be given broad authority to use his judgment and conclude the armistice, as long as he did not compromise the principle of no forced repatriation and did not imply that the U.N. Command would force the ROK government to accept the truce terms. Clark was not to make any commitment to withdraw the Command from Korea, but if he thought it would be useful in bringing Rhee around, he could let the ROK leaders think that the Command was preparing to pull out.

Clark and Robertson made an excellent team in working together in compliance with the President's wishes. Clark handled the relations with the Communist negotiators and began to put pressure on the ROK government by slowing down the movement of supplies and equipment to Korea and taking other steps to indicate preparations for withdrawal of the U.N. Command. He assured the Communist negotiators that the ROK Army was under his command, though he did not exercise control over the sovereign Republic of Korea. He reminded them that the armistice was solely an agreement between the military commanders, to be followed later by a political conference. He suggested that the chief delegates proceed at once with final truce arrangements. The Communists finally agreed on July 8 to proceed.

Secretary Robertson during his eighteen-day stay in Korea met Syngman Rhee almost daily. Robertson, a Virginia gentleman in every sense of the word, proved that he could be as tough, patient, and astute as he could be charming in handling the wily old President. Politely but firmly he pointed out the futility of any effort of the ROK people to go it alone, yet he reassured Rhee that the United States would continue its support if Rhee would cooperate and accept the armistice. Rhee drove a hard but fair bargain. He obtained five main pledges from the United States:

1. Promise of a mutual security pact.
2. Assurance of long-term economic aid, with an initial installment of $200,000,000.
3. Agreement that the U.S. and ROK governments would withdraw from the post-armistice political conference after 90 days if nothing substantial was achieved.
4. Agreement to implement the planned expansion of the ROK army to 20 divisions with modest increases in the navy and air force.
5. Agreement to hold high-level U.S.-ROK talks on joint objectives prior to the political conference.

These pledges included some important concessions, but when Robertson left Korea on July 12, he carried a letter from Syngman Rhee to President Eisenhower assuring our President that he would not obstruct in any way the implementation of the terms of the armistice.

The Communist negotiators continued to ask sharp questions of General Harrison about what the U.N. Command would do if the ROK forces violated any provisions of the armistice. In an effort to get along with the proceedings General Clark obtained Robertson's permission to inform the Communist delegates that in consequence of negotiations just completed with the ROK government we had received suitable assurances that the ROK government would work in close collaboration with the U.N. Command for our common objectives and that the Command, including the ROK forces, was prepared to carry out the armistice. Harrison made such a statement at the 153rd plenary session of the senior negotiators. General Nam Il replied that the statement was "very good and helpful" but not enough.

By now it was clear to Harrison and Clark that the Communists were stalling until the outcome of their final attack on the ROK Army south of Kumsong on the eastern front could be determined. Though he did not admit this, Nam Il proposed a recess on July 16.

The Last of the Fighting

As the negotiations at Panmunjom entered their final phase with the exchange of sick and wounded prisoners of war in April of 1953, the Communists commanders began a series of attacks to secure front-line positions they would like to occupy on a cease-fire line. The U.N. Command had already settled on the line "Kansas."

The same day, May 25, that the Command presented its final proposal on the disposition of nonrepatriates the Chinese 46th Army launched an attack to seize a group of hills called "Nevada," northeast of Panmunjom, held by the Turkish Brigade. After four days of bitter combat, in which the Turks fought gallantly and both sides suffered heavily, the outnumbered Turks were withdrawn on orders of Lieutenant General Bruce C. Clarke, then commanding the U.S. I Corps.

The Communists next turned their attention to the sectors held by ROK troops, the first area being a bulge in the Eighth Army lines northwest of Heartbreak Ridge (Map 14). Commencing June 10, elements of the CCF 60th and 68th Armies struck the ROK II Corps. By June 18 they had called off the action. They had failed to crack the ROK front but had succeeded in capturing hilltop positions east of the Pukhan River.

Limited Communist attacks to gain better observation or to straighten out lines continued throughout June and early July, chiefly against the ROK's but extending into the "Porkchop Hill" area of the U.S. 7th Division, a few miles west of Chorwon. Though these attacks were limited in scope, the Communists were willing to sacrifice thousands of casualties for modest gains. General Taylor and his corps commanders wisely gave ground that was not vital rather than match the heavy losses being taken by the enemy.

After Syngman Rhee's agreement with Ambassador Robertson to abide by the terms of an armistice it was evident that the end of hostilities was near. The Chinese apparently decided that they would have one last fling at the ROK Army, to give the ROK troops, who had shown great improvement in the recent fighting, a warning "lesson" for the future and, perhaps, to end the propaganda war with a great "victory."

On July 13, after one of their heaviest artillery and mortar barrages, elements of five Chinese armies smashed into a salient on the Kumsong front, held by the ROK 9th and Capital Divisions of the U.S. IX Corps and four divisions of the ROK II Corps. The enemy broke through the ROK positions and so disrupted the communications and control system that General Taylor ordered the Capital Division and ROK II Corps to fall back of the Kumsong River at the base of the salient.

Disturbed by this threatening development, Generals Taylor and Clark decided to fly the U.S. 187th Regimental Combat Team from Japan to bolster the front. The team relieved elements of the ROK 9th Division, and the U.S. 3d Division took over the sector of the Capital Division. By the evening of July 15 the lines had been tightened and the Communist drive blunted. The following day Taylor ordered the ROK II Corps to counterattack. Three of its divisions moved forward slowly, and by July 19 they had secured the high ground south of the Kumsong but were unable to move across the river. The Chinese were content to hold the north bank.

The Chinese loudly proclaimed a victory. They had improved their position to some extent, but the cost of this face-saving drive to cover their final accession to the armistice was extremely high. The Eighth Army estimated that more than 28,000 casualties had been inflicted upon the Chinese during this last operation. Unfortunately, the ROK losses were also high.

The Armistice Is Signed at Last

By the time the delegates resumed the meetings at Panmunjom on July 19 the last Chinese offensive was over, and Nam Il announced that the Communists were ready to go ahead with the final arrangements for the cease-fire. It was agreed that the plenary sessions would be suspended while staff officers worked out details of the four remaining points that required agreement: the revised location of the demarcation line and the demilitarized zone, the number, rate, and place of delivery of the prisoners of war, the initiation of activities of the various commissions, and the physical arrangements for the signing of the truce documents.

The staff officers, as they had throughout, did a good and prompt job. Quick agreement on the demarcation line was reached, since the recent fighting had resulted in only minor changes of location. There was some squabbling over the exact number of prisoners that would be repatriated directly, the number of nonrepatriates to be turned over to the Repatriation Commission, and the rate of delivery. As finally settled, the U.N. Command was to return 69,000 North Koreans and 5000 Chinese who desired repatriation. In addition to the 25,000 North Koreans who had broken out of the prison camps on June 18 and been granted asylum in South Korea by Rhee, 7800 North Koreans and 14,500 Chinese refused to return to Communist control and were to be turned over to the Repatriation Commission in the demilitarized zone.

The arrangements for the signing hit a snag when General Nam Il adamantly refused to agree to the presence of any official ROK representatives or any ROK or Chinese Nationalist members of the press at Panmunjom. President Rhee told General Taylor that he did not wish to have any representative at the signing, which eased that situation. The chief delegates, Harrison and Nam Il would sign at Panmunjom, Clark would sign at Munsanni, Kim Il Sung would sign for the North Koreans, and Peng Teh-huai for the Chinese, at Kaesong and Pyongyang, respectively. It was agreed that the cease-fire would be effective twelve hours after the signing. Finally, the signing ceremony was set for 10:00 A.M. on July 27, 1953.

The Communist efforts to achieve a propaganda advantage persisted to the end, as did U.N. Command's countermeasures. Two Communist "peace doves" that had been painted on the gable of the pagoda where the signing would take place were removed on the Command's demand. The Communist scheme to have the Command's delegation enter the pagoda through an only door on the north side, which would have had the delegation, as suppliants for a peace, pass through the Communist section of the building, was thwarted when General Clark insisted on another door's being made on the south side. To avoid any question who was victor or vanquished, tables for the two delegations were placed side by side on an east-west line.

An honor guard made up of members of all services and of all nations of the U.N. Command, except the Republic of Korea, lined the walk to the south entrance of the pagoda on the morning of July 27. Neatly dressed, some with white gloves and neck scarves, polished shoes, and helmets shining even under an overcast sky, they added a touch of smartness to the drab surroundings.

Authorized correspondents and cameramen, followed by the official military observers, filed into the building shortly before 10:00 A.M. In sharp contrast to the informal entrance and attitude of the U.N. Command officers, the Chinese and North Korean military marched in single file and took seats on their side of the room, sitting, as the historian Hermes has described it, "straight and rigid like students at a graduation ceremony."

In front of them on a low table were nine maroon-covered copies of the truce agreement and a small North Korean flag. On another table, in front of the U.N. Command observers, lay nine blue-bound copies and an American flag.

At 9:57 A.M. the associate delegates of both parties entered and took seats at the front. Precisely at 10:00 General Harrison and Nam Il walked briskly in from opposite ends of the pagoda and without a word of greeting or a handshake took seats at their respective tables. They began at once to sign the documents. In twelve minutes the signing was over. As Harrison and Nam Il rose, they looked one another in the eye for a moment, but, neither one bowing or speaking, turned to depart simultaneously.

General Harrison stopped for a moment to chat with the U.N. Command observers, then walked to the staff officers' tent to thank them for their fine help. He refused to comment on the truce to waiting newsmen but posed for pictures with his associate delegates. He drew a laugh from the newsmen when, in answer to a question what pen he had used, he pulled an old pen from his pocket and replied, "I used this. I've had it for eight years and it cost me five dollars!" It was the only light moment of a solemn occasion.

General Harrison and his fellow delegates left by helicopter for Munsanni with the blue-bound copies of the agreement. There at 1:00 P.M. General Clark signed the nine copies in the presence of Harrison and his senior commanders of the Army, Navy, and Air Force and more than 400 official observers and newsmen. Present also was General Choe Duk Shin, the ROK delegate who, on orders from Rhee, had boycotted the final sessions of the armistice negotiations. After the signing General Clark spoke briefly, reminding those present that the armistice was only a military agreement to cease fire and that, until a political conference, yet to follow, negotiated a permanent solution, there would be no withdrawal of the U.N. Command from Korea or relaxation of military preparedness.

As he spoke, the guns at the front, the bombers over North Korea, and the naval vessels off Wonsan continued to pound away. It was not until 10:00 P.M. on July 27, 1953, twelve hours after the ceremony at Panmunjom, that the guns fell silent and an uneasy truce settled over Korea, two years after negotiations had begun.

XIV

IN RETROSPECT

Aftermath of Negotiations

THE ARMISTICE AGREEMENT was confirmed on the morning of July 28, 1953, when General Clark, in Seoul, added his signature to the Communist-signed copies of the truce agreement. At the same time Marshal Kim Il Sung and General Peng Teh-huai signed the United Nations Command's copies at Kaesong and Pyongyang respectively.

What happened in Korea after the signing of the armistice may furnish some clues to what might develop in Vietnam, even though the two situations are not entirely similar.

The first important fact, which bears repetition, is that two long years elapsed between the beginning of negotiations in Korea and the signing of the agreement that did end the fighting.* The second is that the truce agreement was a purely military document, signed by the senior military commanders and not countersigned by any political leader on either side. It was not a peace treaty to end the war — which, officially, had no beginning, since neither side had made a declaration of war — but tacitly and morally it did commit the governments concerned to the establishment of an armistice that "will insure a complete cessation of hostilities and of all acts of armed force in Korea until a final peace settlement is achieved." The military commanders signatory to the pact did "individually, collectively, and mutually agree to accept and be bound and governed by the conditions and terms of armistice." The agreement stopped the fighting but did not solve

* For complete terms of the armistice agreement see Walter G. Hermes, *Truce Tent and Fighting Front*, Appendix C.

the basic issue of establishing an independent and united Korea. And most of the provisions of the agreement, other than ending the fighting and exchanging the prisoners of war, were never fully implemented.

In Article IV of the Korean agreement the military commanders, acting under instructions from their governments, had been deliberately vague in recommending that within three months after the signing of the truce a political conference be held "to settle through negotiation the question of the withdrawal of all foreign forces from Korea, the peaceful settlement of the Korean question, etc." The "etc." was added by the Communist negotiators — who had suggested this article early in the negotiations — with the same clarity as King Mongut in *The King and I* with his oft-repeated "Etcetera, etcetera, etcetera."

Though the three-month period was up in October, 1953, it was not until the following February that the foreign ministers of the United States, the United Kingdom, and France agreed to hold a conference at Geneva to discuss a settlement of the Korean problem.

The Republic of Korea and all the nations participating in the U.N. Command sent delegations to Geneva to meet the representatives of the Soviet Union, Communist China, and North Korea on April 26, 1954. It was quickly apparent that on the key question of the unification of Korea the two sides would never agree how this might be achieved. In the light of Russian insistence on the maintenance of a divided Germany after World War II it is doubtful that the Communists ever seriously considered unifying Korea except on their own terms. The U.N. Command proposed holding free elections under the aegis of the United Nations after Chinese forces were withdrawn. The Communists regarded the United Nations as one of the belligerents and therefore not acceptable to them as an impartial organization. They claimed to be willing to have free elections under the auspices of a body made up of an equal number of representatives of both sides, whose decisions would be made on the basis of "mutual agreement." Such a system would give each side a veto. Since experience in negotiating with Communists clearly indicated that they would agree to few, if any, compromises, this proposal indicated that elections would be long delayed, and deadlocks in agreement would be settled, if at all, on Communist terms.

The best that the delegate of the Union of Soviet Socialist Republics, Vyacheslav Molotov, could offer concerning elections was a proposal that contained four different elements, to be "the subject of further examination." How much "further" he did not say.

After two months of fruitless discussion the Geneva conference adjourned in mid-June of 1954 with the unification of Korea, the basic objective of the conference, as far away as it was when the North Koreans invaded South Korea in June of 1950.

Three commissions were established by the Military Armistice Agreement:

A Military Armistice Commission, consisting of representatives of the military commanders of the United Nations Command and the Chinese and North Korean armies, was made responsible for overall supervision of the implementation of the armistice agreement.

The Neutral Nations Supervisory Commission, consisting of four senior military officers, two appointed by General Clark, one each from Sweden and Switzerland, and two appointed by the commanders of the Communist forces, one each from Czechoslovakia and Poland. This commission was to supervise the actual implementation of the armistice by means of joint teams of observers, inspectors and investigators.

The Neutral Nations Reparations Commission of five members, one each from India, Czechoslovakia, Poland, Sweden, and Switzerland, was under the chairmanship of the Indian representative. Its function was to arrange and oversee the exchange of prisoners of war and their repatriation or other disposition.

The Neutral Nations Repatriation Commission did accomplish its task, but not without the usual Communist bickering. Between August 5 and September 6, 1953, the U.N. Command transferred directly to the Communists more than 75,000 prisoners of war who desired repatriation, and the enemy returned some 12,000 to the Command. On September 23 the Command turned over to the Repatriation Commission in the demilitarized zone more than

22,000 nonrepatriates, and the enemy delivered 350 to the Command. The Reds soon complained that the facilities afforded them to persuade their nonrepatriates to return home were inadequate. This was obviously to cover the fact that large numbers of these prisoners refused to listen to the Communist pleas. Only a few more than 600 out of the 22,000 who were importuned decided to return to the Communist side. The Repatriation Commission retained custody of those refusing repatriation until the end of the 120 days stipulated in the truce agreement and then returned them to the U.N. Command. Over the protests of the Polish and Czechoslovakian members the Indian, Swedish, and Swiss representatives adopted a resolution on February 18, 1954, to dissolve the Commission. The Korean nonrepatriates were freed by the U.N. Command and the Chinese, totaling approximately 14,066, were sent to Taiwan as their stated preference to Communist China, except for a few who chose to accompany the Indian custodial forces when they sailed for India.

The dissolution of the Repatriation Commission left intact two agencies set up under the truce agreement, agencies that are still functioning, after a fashion.

The first of these, the Military Armistice Commission, was designed to prevent either side from improving its military position during the armistice. The Commission met on July 28, 1953, and initially achieved some good results. Arrangements were made for the withdrawal of troops from the demilitarized zone, identification and checking of credentials of persons entering the zone, the removal of hazards such as mines, and other useful details. Soon these cooperative activities ceased, and in August the Communists seized upon incidents, apparently deliberately perpetrated by their Red Cross teams in the U.N. Command's prisoner-of-war camps, to renew their propaganda campaign on the issue of prisoners of war. The implementation of the terms of the armistice was obviously one-sided. Complaints of violations brought against the U.N. Command were conscientiously investigated, whereas the Communists largely ignored complaints against them. The joint observer teams set up to investigate violations of the demilitarized zone almost invariably submitted split reports.

A U.N. Command draft report on the implementation of the armistice concluded that the objective of the Armistice Commission in maintaining the equilibrium of military forces in Korea had not been achieved and the truce provisions to this end were nothing more than legalistic statements that could not be enforced. It added that any agreement that by its terms provides for inspections in Communist-controlled areas would, in all probability, be rendered ineffective by the Communists, to the detriment of the side that in good faith abided by the agreement.

This forecast has proven correct. By the fall of 1968 the duties of the Military Armistice Commission had dwindled mainly to hearing complaints of violations of the demilitarized zone by patrols from either side. Complaints have been lodged either with Joint Duty Officers located in the Joint Security Area in the demilitarized zone at Panmunjom or with the Secretaries of the Commission. The U.N. Command secretariat maintains an office at Munsanni, and the Communist secretariat is at Kaesong. Most complaints are handled by the Secretaries and usually end with an exchange of charges and countercharges, denials, and insults. The joint observation teams, designed to investigate incidents, rarely operate on a joint basis. The Military Armistice Commission has met more than 250 times since 1953, but the meetings now occur only infrequently for the purpose of hearing major charges of violations of the armistice, with no more definitive results than the meetings of the Secretaries. The U.N. Command members of the Armistice Commission are located in Seoul; the Communists, in Kaesong. The meetings are held at Panmunjom.

The second agency left intact after the dissolution of the Repatriation Commission is the Neutral Nations Supervisory Commission. Its operations have likewise been ineffective. At the start its inspection teams were stationed at ten authorized ports of entry, where replacements of military personnel and equipment entering Korea were supposed to be checked. But the inspection teams in North Korea were hampered in their duties, and the U.N. Command was soon convinced that the Communists were using other ports to bring in more men and equipment than authorized. Little or nothing could be done to prevent such violations. The inspection teams were withdrawn from the ports to the demilitarized zone near Panmunjom in 1956. Since then the Command has requested investigations a number of times, but the Poles and Czechs have usually been able to block any effective action.

The obstructive tactics of the Communist members of the supposedly neutral Supervisory Commission were duplicated in Vietnam while I was there in 1954 and 1955 as Special Representative of the United States. Investigations of charges of brutality of the Communist Viet Minh toward Vietnamese desiring to move to the south, in accordance with the Geneva Agreement of 1954, were always blocked by the Polish member of the Commission until the essential witnesses were disposed of by the Viet Minh and all evidence destroyed or removed. The same will be true of any new commission that might be established to oversee a settlement of the present Vietnamese situation, unless that commission is made up wholly of representatives of genuinely neutral states and operates under the aegis of the United Nations.

The JCS under the Unified Department of Defense

The Korean war was the first conducted under the new Department of Defense created by the 1949 Amendments to the National Security Act of 1947 and under the strategic direction of the Joint Chiefs as legally constituted under the same acts of Congress. Both organizations had to feel their way under the unprecedented conditions of fighting a war in "peacetime," not a war fought as a solely American effort but one in which the United States was acting in the unique role of executive agent of the United Nations. These conditions, combined with the depleted state of our armed forces following their headlong demobilization after World War II, presented unusual political-military-economic difficulties to the Defense Department in the procurement of men and supplies, resulted in restrictions on the operations of the U.N. Command in the field, and limited the flexibility of the JCS in providing strategic guidance to the conduct of the war.

Fortunately, the transformation of the War and Navy Departments into a single Department of Defense came along at the right time. The Defense Department was better organized to tackle the problems of defense than the old separate departments. As a division and corps commander in both the Pacific and European theaters of operation in World War II, I had observed the conflicts of interest between the two independent departments over standards and priorities for personnel and logistical support. After the war I had acted as spokesman for General Marshall in presenting to the Congress the initial proposal for a single Department of the Armed Forces, which led finally, over the determined opposition of the Navy, to the National Security Act of 1947, which created a unified National Military Establishment with three subordinate Departments of the Army, Navy, and Air Force. James V. Forrestal, who had been Secretary of the Navy during the long unification battle, became the first Secretary of Defense. Forrestal had originally opposed giving strong powers to the Defense Secretary, but after twelve somewhat frustrating months in office, during which his authority was incommensurate with his great responsibilities, he recommended to the Hoover Commission radical amendments to the National Security Act. The 1949 amendments fell short of his recommendations but did convert the National Military Establishment into the Department of Defense and greatly strengthened the authority and control of the Defense Secretary over the Army, Navy, and Air Departments and all other agencies of the Department of Defense.

Of more immediate effect so far as the JCS were concerned, the 1949 amendments created the office of Chairman of the Joint Chiefs of Staff and provided the Chiefs with an essential Joint Staff. In the outline plan for a unified department that I had presented to the Congress in 1945 there was a provision for a Chief of Staff of the Armed Forces, who would be a member of the Joint Chiefs of Staff, along with the Chiefs of the Army, Navy, and Air Force, and would be the principal military adviser and military executive for the Secretary of Defense; the Joint Chiefs as a corporate body would be advisory to the President with respect to military policy, strategy, and requirements. This suggestion was not adopted. In fact, the opponents of unification had conjured up such a fear of a Chief of Staff for the Secretary of Defense as a "man on horseback" that the 1949 amendments stipulated that the Chairman would not have a vote in the deliberations of the JCS. These amendments prescribed that "in addition to his duties as a member of the Joint Chiefs of Staff," he should preside at meetings of the JCS, provide an agenda for such meetings and assist the JCS "to prosecute their business as promptly as practicable." The Chairman was to inform the Secretary of Defense and, when appropriate, the President of issues on which JCS agreement had not been reached.

The cause of such disagreements prior to the outbreak of the Korean War was usually the inadequacy of appropriated funds for meeting the essential requirements of the services, or it dealt with the roles and missions of the Army, Navy, Air Force, and Marines. Long-drawn-out debates and much exchanging of position papers usually preceded compromise solutions that rarely satisfied anyone and sometimes failed to meet the basic elements of the problem. When compromises could not be reached, majority and minority views were presented, ultimately, in writing to the Defense Secretary. The Chairman usually did try to resolve these difficulties before an impasse was reached. But even under the 1949 amendments he had no specific duty or responsibility to do so. General Bradley, who was Chairman during my tour as Army Chief of Staff, was meticulously neutral in such cases, as was the original intent of the Congress. Once the Korean war was under way, and funds became more readily available to the Army, Navy, and Air Force, there were few "split papers" and the question of the need for definitive action by the Chairman lapsed, only to be revived again after the armistice.

I felt while I was Army Chief that the system then in vogue was wrong; that the Secretary, stipulated by law to be a civilian — and rightly so — should not be faced with the problem of resolving the divergent views of military experts without the objective recommendation of a top military man responsible directly to him. I suggested to the Nelson Rockefeller Commission, appointed by Secretary Wilson in 1953 to study a possible reorganization of the Defense Department, that in case of disagreement among the

Chiefs on any issue the Chairman should be required to present to the Secretary his own recommendations along with those of the other Chiefs. I had also suggested that the Secretary be given a senior military executive for administration, who would have the duty of assigning to one of the service departments, for study and recommendation, such military problems as did not involve strategic considerations and thus reduce the workload of the JCS. These suggestions were not adopted. However, the need of the Secretary for such professional assistance was recognized in 1954 in a directive from the Department of Defense, which assigned to the Chairman of the JCS just such responsibilities as I have outlined above. These have been continued under instructions of the Secretary of Defense and strengthened by subsequent legislation. The Chairman's authority over the Joint Staff and other supporting JCS agencies has been augmented, and the Department of Defense Reorganization Act of 1958 finally removed the stipulation that he had no vote.

On balance, from my experience as a member of the JCS and subsequent study, I believe the current system, with these added duties and authority prescribed for the Chairman, is better than having a single Chief of Staff for the Secretary of Defense, as recommended by the Army in 1945.*

One of the difficulties we encountered in the new Department of Defense had to do with its numerous Assistant Secretaries and special assistants, each with his sphere of responsibilities. I have great admiration for the men who suspend their business or professional careers to serve in governmental departments in Washington at the call of the President. Below the top secretarial level they are relatively unknown to the public and rarely receive any recognition from the public or the Congress, only criticism if something within the cognizance of the individual secretary goes wrong. The trouble we had stemmed from the fact that most of these men stay for less than two years, and few have had any military experience except in their earlier years in positions of lesser responsibility unrelated to the intricacies of Washington

* For an opposing point of view see Maxwell D. Taylor's *The Uncertain Trumpet*, pp. 175–176.

bureaucracy.* Each of them required an office staff, including at least one or more military men, ranging in rank from lieutenant colonel or commander to major general or rear admiral. The Assistant Secretaries came to rely on the advice of these officers, which did not always accord with the views of the Chief or the principal staff officers in the Army, Navy, or Air department, as the case might be. This situation resulted at times in confusion and divergent recommendations to the Secretary of Defense. In addition, the Assistant Secretaries had a tendency to send instructions directly to, or ask reports directly from, their counterparts in the subordinate departments, bypassing the offices of the Secretaries of the services and their Chiefs of Staff. The Comptroller of the Defense Department was persistent in this practice. Only vigorous protests from General Bradley and me put an end, temporarily at least, to his efforts to establish a direct chain of command to the Comptrollers of the Army, Navy, and Air Force.

The superstructure of seven Assistant Secretaries of Defense and their staffs and assistants is, in my judgment, the weakest link in the defense establishment. In the event of a major war the resulting delays in decision-making and the diffusion of responsibility would soon force a reduction and simplification of this top-heavy structure.

The Dual Role of the JCS

A feature of the JCS organization that has been the subject of criticism and debate has been the dual roles held by the Chiefs

---

* While a member of the JCS I had recommended that classes at the National War College in Washington, which operates under the direction of the JCS and is made up of members of the armed services, career representatives of State and Defense departments and other government agencies, should be augmented annually by five to ten young men direct from civil life. They would be selected from the fields of business, labor, science, law, education, and other professions. Upon graduating they would form a pool of competent men who at least had been exposed to a study of the complex political-economic-military problems that beset our government. They could be available, without any prior commitment, to the President for possible future appointments in the executive branches of the government. For a variety of reasons, most of which I thought were inconsequential, this proposal was not adopted by the JCS.

as military heads of their respective services and as members of the JCS. Two arguments have been advanced against this system. The first is that as Chiefs of Staff of the Army, Navy, and Air Force they are responsible to their service Secretaries for the morale, discipline, training, and readiness to fight of the individuals and units of their services and hence have insufficient time to devote to their duties on the JCS. The second objection has been that, as Chiefs of their individual services, they supervise under the direction of their Secretaries the establishment of military requirements of their services and then, as members of the JCS, review and pass judgment on their own handiwork. Actually, it was not until 1958, when Secretary Neil McElroy referred the budget of the Department of Defense for the fiscal year 1960 to the JCS for comment, that the Chiefs as a group had any direct say in the budget. Under Secretary Robert S. McNamara's system the JCS does participate throughout the budgetary process, so as to tie the operational programs of the budget to the requirements of the unified commands.

The usual solution proposed for the problem of the dual roles is to have a separate group of retired officers with distinguished records or of senior men on their last active-duty assignments constitute the Joint Chiefs of Staff. Such a system seems to have some theoretical merit, particularly in wartime, but it has more serious drawbacks. From my own experience I know that it is difficult for retired officers to keep abreast of new developments in tactics and weapons, and senior officers who have been passed over for selection as Chief of Staff often have biases and warped views that lessen their objectivity.

I have always felt that strategic and logistic plans should be prepared by the men with the most up-to-date knowledge of the capabilities and limitations of the commanders and of the units that will have to implement these plans, and that those who prepare such plans should have some responsibility for carrying them out. The superstructure within the Department of Defense is already too top-heavy and the responsibilities too diffused without layering on another echelon. Admittedly, the division of time and effort the Chiefs should give to each of their roles is debatable.

This is a matter of judgment, which should depend on the international situation, the importance of subjects due for imminent discussion by the JCS, and the actual conditions facing troops in the field. I disagreed with the policy — though I was not affected by it — which I understand was initiated by either Secretary Wilson or Admiral Radford, then Chairman of the JCS. This restricted the freedom of travel of the "new" Chiefs of Staff, those who succeeded us who were in office during the Korean war. The idea behind this policy — which was not put in writing — was that long trips made by the Chiefs, away from Washington, would interfere with their JCS duties.

The Chiefs are extremely busy men, but they can be spelled in their duties and relieved of many minor matters by the proper organization of their service staffs. During my tour as Army Chief I had a Vice Chief of Staff and two Deputies, one for Plans and the other for Operations and Administration, and also Assistant Chiefs, whose code numbers were G-1 for Personnel, G-2 for Intelligence, G-3 for Operations, and G-4 for Supply and Procurement. I devoted most of my time to my duties as a member of the JCS, including my responsibilities as Executive Agent for both the European and Far Eastern Theaters of Operations, while the Vice Chief (General Haislip and, after his retirement in 1951, General John E. Hull, both thoroughly competent and experienced men) supervised the day-in day-out business of the Army staff through the Deputy for Operations and Administration (General Ridgway) and the Assistant Chiefs. The Deputy for Plans kept in close touch with all JCS matters, represented me on subordinate committees of the JCS and State-Defense, briefed me and the Vice Chief before each JCS meeting, and accompanied me to these meetings. When I was away, the Vice Chief attended JCS meetings with full authority to act for me and was immediately available to the Secretary of the Army and the Secretary of Defense.

I made seven visits to the Far East during my tour as Army Chief — six during the actual fighting — and made several trips to Europe in connection with NATO and our forces stationed there and one trip to Vietnam. These visits were essential in providing first-hand information that was of great value not only to me but to the JCS, the Secretary of Defense, and the President.

I had learned in World War II that in order to keep one's mental balance under conditions of stress it is necessary to learn to relax. This is difficult to do in the Pentagon. So I not only left Washington when it was necessary to visit Army troops and installations abroad and at home, but got away from the Pentagon to our cottage on the Chesapeake Bay for weekends as often as possible. After the outbreak of war I had a direct line there from the Pentagon switchboard. One Sunday morning the telephone woke me about seven o'clock. President Truman was on the line. He inquired about some item he had just read in the morning paper. Fortunately, I knew the facts and gave them to him. Mr. Truman said, "Thank you kindly, General, that was all I wanted to know," and hung up. I doubt whether he knew where I was, but I am sure he would have applauded if he had known.

When I had to remain in Washington on weekends, I usually found solace in the great chamber-music concerts in the Coolidge Auditorium at the Library of Congress. I would lose myself in the magical playing of the Budapest String Quartet and the other artists who performed there on Friday evenings.

There was no hiatus in the work of either the JCS or the Army staff while I was away. And there was the added virtue that my absence from the office permitted many of the staff, particularly the "pick-and-shovel men," who never like to leave while the Chief is around, to get home for a respite from their long duty hours.

The JCS and the Budget

Though the 1949 amendments to the National Security Act of 1947 provided for important changes in our military structure, there was no resulting improvement in the vital area of the formulation of the military budget. Both the 1947 and 1949 acts had specified that one of the duties of the JCS was to establish unified combatant commands in strategic areas abroad. The missions of these commands and the Army, Navy, and Air forces allocated to them were to be determined by the JCS, under the Secretary of Defense and subject to approval by the President. But the JCS, as a corporate body, had no responsibility in the preparation of the annual budgets, which would really determine the effectiveness of these commands. Budgets continued to be prepared independently by the Army, Navy, and Air Force under ceilings fixed by the Secretary of Defense and the President, on recommendation of the Director of the Bureau of the Budget. The Chiefs participated individually in their capacity as Chiefs of Staff and reported to their own service Secretaries. They were not called upon to relate the service budgets to the missions of the unified commands. In fact, nowhere in the Department of Defense was this essential service performed. The resulting budget of the Department of Defense thus was based on the independent estimates of requirements of the services rather than on the integrated requirement of the unified commands.

This situation was not corrected until Secretary McNamara established his Planning-Programming-Budgeting System in 1961 which, to quote him, "permits the top management of the Defense Department, the President and the Congress to focus their attention on the tasks and missions related to our national objectives, rather than on the tasks and missions of a particular service." This is as it should be.

I know that some of the services have complained that Secretary McNamara and his efficiency experts went far beyond the realm of efficiency, as measured by statistics, and into the field of strategy and combat efficiency, neither of which is an exact science. If the complaints are valid — and I do not know whether they are — I have some sympathy for the critics. I know when, as Army Chief, I fought for the Army's participation in the development of atomic weapons for tactical use on the battlefield, opponents, chiefly in the Air Force, proved statistically that the 280mm cannon — the only weapon we had at that time that could use the minimally-sized atomic explosive package — was wasteful of plutonium and therefore inefficient. I argued that, though it might be inefficient in its use of plutonium, it and its successors could be highly efficient in terms of tactical application on the battlefield. Fortunately, I was supported by Robert Le-

Baron, then Assistant Secretary of Defense for Atomic Energy. Periodically he would tell me, "Joe, you are on the right track. Stick to your guns. It is only a matter of time before we have atomic shells that can be fired from an 8-inch howitzer." Thanks to scientific progress and Army tactical foresight, today we have a broad range of tactical nuclear weapons. Had statistical efficiency been the controlling determinant, these highly valuable weapons probably would not be available today.

Having declared my opposition to an overemphasis on the statistical measurement of tactical or strategic matters, I hasten to add that I think McNamara did a remarkably fine job as Secretary of Defense in the toughest job in Washington next to the Presidency. No Secretary of Defense worthy of his great responsibilities is ever likely to be popular with either the Chiefs of services or the military affairs committees of the Congress.

The Chiefs of Staff and the Congress

One of the unique features of our American system of government, as distinct from the European parliamentary system, is that the American Chiefs of Staff are required to appear before committees of the Congress to give an account of their military stewardship, to defend the requests for military appropriations, and to answer all manner of questions, ranging from the suitability of new weapons and tactics and the adequacy of strategic concepts and plans to matters of foreign policy. In no other country in the world that I know of are military men called upon for such testimony. On the one hand we insist, properly, on civilian control of the military; on the other, Congress demands that our military Chiefs publicly support or oppose the policies of the civilian administration, which is charged with the legal responsibility for the national security. Despite this inconsistency, and the embarrassment often caused our Chiefs of Staff, the system has merit in forcing an annual review of our military programs outside the Defense Department. In any event, in view of Congress' responsibility under the Constitution "to raise and support armies," "to provide and maintain a navy," and "to provide for the common defense" Congress will never surrender its right to hear directly from the Chiefs of

Staff their personal views on all matters affecting national security. I welcomed and usually enjoyed my many appearances before the Congress.

One drawback of this system is that it tends to put the JCS into the political maelstrom. During the "Great Debate" of 1950 to 1952 in the Senate, on the issue of sending U.S. Army troops to Europe under NATO, Senator Robert A. Taft charged that General Bradley had intervened politically to support the Truman Administration's advocacy of fulfilling our NATO commitments. Taft even went so far as to challenge Bradley's integrity. By April of 1953 the Senator was urging President Eisenhower in effect to displace the JCS by appointing a "stand-by" group of prospective appointees who, presumably, would be more amenable to the views of Taft and his Republican colleagues, and who would review all military plans and programs, including the military budget and foreign-aid program, before assuming office.

One of the ironies of Senator Taft's proposal was that the budget and foreign-aid programs had never before been referred to the JCS as a body, and to do so would tend to put the JCS into the field of politics, a role that Senator Taft had been decrying. There was some talk of requiring the "old" Chiefs of Staff to resign as a group when the new President took office, much as Cabinet members do. President Eisenhower did not entertain such an idea, which, for the first time, would have injected the JCS into partisan politics. General Vandenberg, who would have retired at the end of his tour on June 1, was critically ill and was retired for physical disability on May 7, 1953.* General Bradley's and my four-year tours would terminate the same day, August 15. Thus, three of the four "old" Chiefs would be replaced in the normal course of events. Unfortunately, the President saw fit not to reappoint Admiral William L. Fechteler, the able Chief of Naval Operations, who was serving a two-year term. I was distressed at the failure to reappoint Bill Fechteler, a failure that added some color to the rumors around the Pentagon that Senator Taft had finally had his way.

It would be most unfortunate if it should become customary for

* General Vandenberg was succeeded by General Nathan F. ("Nate") Twining, U.S. Air Force, who had had a distinguished record in World War II.

the members of the JCS to be changed with each transfer of Administrations. I have known all of the Chiefs who have held office for the past twenty-five years. Every one of them has been meticulously nonpartisan and nonpolitical in all matters pertaining to national security. It would be a sad day for the country if this should ever become otherwise. In this connection, President Eisenhower was responsible for changing the normal tours of office of the Chiefs of Staff* from four years to two, a change with which I thoroughly disagreed. As I understood the idea back of this change, it was that a newly appointed Chief would be tried out for a period of two years. If he proved satisfactory, he might be reappointed for another two years.

My objection to this procedure is threefold. It takes almost a year to become fully acquainted with the policies and procedures within the Defense Department, relations with other executive agencies and the Congress, and the many duties of a Chief of Staff. Too little time is left for effective service in a two-year tour. Secondly, under such a system there is an inevitable pressure on a Chief to conform to the policies of the Administration or the Departments, which is bound to inhibit his frank and honest military judgment of matters on which it is his duty to advise his civilian Secretaries and the President. And, finally, there is the question of continuity within a Chief's own service and, since he is a member of the JCS, in relation to the Secretary of Defense. During my four-year tour I served under three different Secretaries of the Army and four Secretaries of Defense. Naturally each of these men had somewhat different ideas of how to manage his department. The differences caused a certain loss of efficiency and morale. In the Army, at least, the Chief of Staff had furnished an essential continuity of procedure, if not of policy.

Fortunately, in 1967 Congress rewrote the law to provide for four-year terms for the Chiefs of all the services, subject to the pleasure of the President.

Not the least improvement that came out of the unification of the Defense Department was the consolidation of the Military and

---

* Chiefs of Naval Operations were normally appointed for two years, subject to reappointment.

Naval Affairs Committees of the House and Senate into single
Armed Services Committees in the Senate and House and similar
consolidations of the subcommittees on Appropriations. Under
the preunification procedures the Army (including the Army Air
Corps) and the Navy (including the Marine Corps) not only
prepared their personnel and fiscal requirements independently of
one another but submitted and defended these budgets before
separate committees of the Congress. In consequence, the Congress never looked at a balanced or integrated program based on
genuine strategic requirements. Hearing only one-sided requests
from the independent services, the congressional committees
tended to become partisans of the services with which they were
associated. This was particularly true of the House Naval Affairs
Committee, whose redoubtable Chairman, Carl Vinson of Georgia,
was most effective in securing approval of Navy requirements.
The Army never had as able an advocate as Congressman Vinson.
In tribute to Vinson, I will say that when he became Chairman of
the House Armed Services Committee he did give full and un-
biased consideration to the needs of the Army and Air Force, as
well as to the Navy, to the great benefit of all the services.

Limited Wars: Korea and Vietnam

Korea was the first "limited war" — that is, a war limited in
scope, objectives, and means employed — to be fought by the
United States in modern times. We are now engaged in another
such war in Vietnam, and we may be destined to fight others in
the future. In view of this possibility it is worth while first to
examine the similarities and differences between these two engagements and then to consider what effect our experiences in
Korea and Vietnam should have on any future limited wars in
which we might become involved.

The broad national policy under which we entered both Korea
and Vietnam was one of containing aggressive Communist expansion. This policy had been first enunciated in 1947 by George
Kennan, then head of the State Department's Policy Planning
Staff, and expressed officially later that year in the Truman

Doctrine, under which we played a decisive role in preventing a Communist take-over of Greece. The policy was confirmed when we joined NATO, the first military alliance outside the western hemisphere that the United States had ever entered in peacetime. These early actions applied to Europe and the North Atlantic area and the Near East. We had not yet given much thought to the application of containment in the Far East until the attack against South Korea by North Korea, aided and abetted by the Soviet Union and Communist China.

The United States and the United Nations had no honorable alternative to going into Korea to meet the Communist challenge. By defeating Japan in World War II — which I am convinced we could have done without any help from the Soviet Union — we were mainly responsible for establishing the independence of Korea, which had been absorbed into the Japanese empire in 1910. We were also instrumental in creating the United Nations, an organization designed to prevent just such aggression as the North Korean invasion. Though we had no commitment to come to the aid of South Korea, we did have a moral obligation to assist in maintaining its independence in the face of naked and overpowering aggression. It was essential that we move U.S. Army troops into Korea, as recommended by General MacArthur — even before the United Nations had time to act — in order to prevent the overrunning of all of Korea, which the North Koreans certainly would have done if we had not intervened at once.

Aside from our moral obligation, it was in the United States' national interest to prevent the Communists from taking over control of all of Korea, despite the earlier support that our political and military leaders in 1948 and 1949 gave to the withdrawal of American occupation forces from Korea. We had no interest in retaining a presence in the free and relatively unthreatened Korea of that period. But a Korea dominated by the Soviet Union, together with the Kurile Islands and Sakhalin to the north of Japan, acquired by the Soviets as a result of their belated participation in World War II, would pose a potential threat to Japan, the northern anchor of our position in the Western Pacific.

As I indicated in an earlier chapter, we were fortunate that the

Soviets chose for their first experiment in "justifiable wars of liberation" the only area in the world where we had forces of all military services readily available to intervene. The free world was fortunate also in that the Russian delegate to the United Nations had withdrawn temporarily from the Security Council and hence could not veto the prompt action of the United Nations in sponsoring the American action in Korea. This forthright sponsorship, including the call on all members of the United Nations to contribute to a United Nations Command under American leadership, and aside from the combat troops and medical and other supporting units furnished by twenty member countries, was of great international legal and moral value.

Vietnam Contrasted with Korea

In contrast to our abrupt and dramatic re-entry into Korea, our involvement in Vietnam developed over a period of several years. During World War II the French colony of Indo-China, consisting of Vietnam, Laos, and Cambodia, had been occupied by Japanese forces. A nationalist movement to break away from France had started in Tonkin, the northern province of Vietnam, under the Moscow-trained Communist leader, Ho Chi Minh. With aid from Russia and China the insurgents — who called themselves Viet Minh, an abbreviation of "Viet Nam Doc Lap Dong Minh Hoi," or "League for the Independence of Viet Nam" — gained control of the hinterland beyond the cities and proclaimed the self-styled Democratic Republic of Vietnam. They claimed jurisdiction over all the country, though most of their strength was in the north. Vietnamese forces loyal to the French-sponsored government of the Emperor Bao Dai controlled the cities and most of the south. For better or for worse, in order to prevent the take-over of Indo-China by the Communists, the United States decided to furnish equipment and logistical support to the French in their fighting against the Viet Minh.

During the siege of the French forces at Dienbienphu there had been some talk in Washington of our sending in U.S. Army forces to lift the siege. This had been scotched on the recommendation of

General Ridgway, who some months earlier had succeeded me as Army Chief of Staff. I had no part in this decision but had agreed with it privately.

After the fall of Dienbienphu the French agreed to withdraw from Indo-China under conditions established by the Geneva Accords of 1954. Laos and Cambodia were granted independence. An armistice and military disengagement was agreed upon between the French and Viet Minh, with a temporary demarcation line — comparable to the 38th Parallel in Korea — at the 17th parallel. The Vietnamese representative at Geneva never agreed to this arrangement, and it was later repudiated by the strongly anti-Communist patriot Ngo Dinh Diem.

Pending country-wide elections two years later, the French were to administer the region to the south of the Parallel and the Viet Minh the area to the north. Military forces were to be regrouped accordingly: the French troops and Vietnamese opposed to the Communists were to be south of a demilitarized zone centered on the 17th parallel and the Viet Minh north of it. Civilians were to be free to choose on which side of the parallel they wished to live while awaiting the elections, which were to determine whether the country would be reunited. More than 800,000 Vietnamese, assisted by the U.S. Navy, were transported south, and approximately 100,000 southerners, mostly Viet Minh insurgents, moved north of the demilitarized zone. Secret cadres of the Viet Minh, who became known as Viet Cong (Communist Vietnamese), were left behind in the south in preparation for the coming elections.

The French set up a South Vietnamese government in Saigon that was theoretically loyal to their figurehead, the former emperor of Indo-China, Bao Dai; its Premier was Ngo Dinh Diem.

Actually, Diem was opposed as much to the French and Bao Dai as he was to the Communists. What he wanted was a united Vietnam, free of domination by either the French or Communists. In late 1955 he deposed Bao Dai, who had fled to Paris, and proclaimed a republic with himself as President. As the last French troops withdrew in 1956, Diem repudiated the French agreement at Geneva to hold elections to determine the fate of the country. He declared that free elections were impossible under the Communist rule in the north.

The American public was not greatly concerned when we agreed to back the Diem government, though this meant much more than the furnishing of economic and military aid. Though it was never official United States policy, we would in fact be taking over from the French the overall political guidance of the government, which had been managed largely by French colonial civil servants and French-trained Vietnamese minor officials, who had dual French-Vietnamese citizenship and had departed for France with the French forces. We assumed the responsibility for organizing, training, equipping, and maintaining a Vietnamese Army of 200,000 men.

During his first few years in office Diem instituted a number of constructive programs and gave South Vietnam a promising degree of stability. But the autocratic methods of Diem and his brother Ngu, who wielded great power, and Diem's refusal to broaden his government to make it truly representative, gradually alienated many of the abler people in the south. The régime's influence outside the few cities waned as the Viet Cong filled the countryside with terror. By the fall of 1961 the threat to the very existence of the Diem régime caused President Kennedy to authorize a sizable increase in United States support but stopped short of committing any combat troops. American military and civilian training and advisory teams increased in 1962 to more than 11,000 men, while Viet Cong attacks on our support installations likewise increased. Though United States military personnel operated only in advisory and support roles, 42 U.S. Army soldiers were killed in 1963, and this number increased in 1964 to 118.

On November 1, 1963, a military junta overthrew Diem and he and Ngu were cruelly murdered.

There followed a succession of military governments headed by generals of little ability and less experience in politics. Taking advantage of the resulting chaotic conditions, the Viet Cong stepped up their terror campaign, and the Viet Minh increased their infiltration of the south and their combined attacks against American installations.

These attacks came to a head on August 2 and 4, 1964, when North Vietnamese patrol boats intercepted and attacked United States destroyers in the Gulf of Tonkin.* President Johnson ordered retaliatory air strikes against the patrol boats, their bases, and supporting facilities. Six days later Congress passed a joint resolution "to promote the maintenance of peace and security in Southeast Asia," which authorized the President "to take all necessary measures to repel any armed attack against the forces of the United States and to prevent further aggression." Specific authorization was included for the use of armed force to assist any member or protocol state (such as Vietnam) of the South-East Asia Treaty Organization that requested assistance.

After a Viet Cong attack on a United States compound and supply base in the central highlands south of the demilitarized zone in February of 1965 the President authorized air strikes against selected military targets in North Vietnam. These were broadened as terrorist attacks increased against United States facilities, including the American Embassy in Saigon, and as it became evident that the North Vietnamese were furnishing extensive combat and logistical support to the Viet Cong.

The fate of South Vietnam tottering in the balance, the Vietnamese government in the spring of 1965 requested direct combat support from the United States. Two battalions of Marines were landed to protect the port of Da Nang, followed shortly by the 173d Airborne Brigade, U.S. Army. They were the forerunners of a United States military command, which by mid-1968 totaled more than 538,000 men of all services.

In Vietnam the United States did not, as it did in Korea, enter the fighting under the aegis of the United Nations. But, as indicated in the congressional resolution, we did have a commitment under the Southeast Asia Collective Defense Treaty signed in 1954, one of the series of pacts negotiated by Secretary of State John Foster Dulles, designed to check the spread of Communism.

* There appears to be no doubt that on August 2, 1964, the Destroyer *Maddux* was intercepted and attacked by North Korean patrol boats. Senator Fulbright and members of the Senate Foreign Relations Committee have questioned whether an attack on th U.S. Destroyers *Maddux* and *Turner Joy* on the night of August 3–4 actually took place.

This treaty, which was ratified by a Senate vote of 85 to 1, stated, in effect, that aggression by armed forces in Southeast Asia would endanger the United States' peace and security, and in that event the United States would "act to meet the common danger in accordance with its constitutional processes."

The Southeast Asia Treaty Organization (SEATO), established under the treaty, consists of Australia, New Zealand, the Philippine Islands, Thailand, Pakistan, the United Kingdom, France, and the United States. The United States did not invoke this pact, but Australia, New Zealand, and Thailand have furnished combat troops, and the Philippines are providing a reinforced engineer construction battalion. In addition, South Korea, though not a member of SEATO, does have two divisions in Vietnam. However, the lack of a mandate from the United Nations has weakened our position in Vietnam in the eyes of much of the world, and the absence of a declaration of war by the Congress — as in the case of Korea — combined with the debatable conditions surrounding the passage of the Tonkin Gulf resolution, has led to vehement domestic opposition from some elements within and outside Congress. The resolution has not been rescinded, despite an included provision providing for such rescission by concurrent resolution of the Congress.

With regard to the military aspects of the Korean and Vietnamese wars, Korea had a number of advantages over Vietnam. Both flanks of the U.N. Command's position across the Korean peninsula were protected by the sea, which was dominated by the U.S. Navy, whereas in Vietnam the west flank is open throughout its length to infiltration via Laos and Cambodia. In addition, Cambodia affords convenient refuge to Communist troops escaping from defeat in the South, while the Ho Chi Minh Trail through Laos provides a somewhat concealed and sheltered avenue of resupply of men and supplies from the North.

Difficult as the terrain, lack of good roads and other means of communications, and the harsh climate were in Korea, these factors are all worse in Vietnam. The tropical jungles there offer better concealment to guerrillas than the more open country of North Korea, and the steaming swamps and rice paddies of the

Mekong Delta are even tougher for the heavily-laden American soldiers to fight over than the steep hills of Korea.

The greatest disadvantage we have had in Vietnam has little to do with terrain or climate. It has been the lack of a whole-hearted effort of the South Vietnamese themselves to maintain their freedom. In Korea the fiery patriot Syngman Rhee was often a thorn in the side of the U.N. Command, but he did lead his people in active opposition to the Communist aggressors from the north and provided the United Nations with valued political and military support until the armistice negotiations began. Un-fortunately, neither Diem — as devoted a patriot as Rhee — nor his military successors, at least until the elevation of General Thieu to the Presidency, have had the executive ability or the leadership to unite the divisive factions that have the greatest influence in the politics of Vietnam: the militant Buddhists, the Catholic refugees from the north, the politico-military Cao Dai and Hoa Hao religious sects, the often corrupt provincial gover-nors, and the rival officer cliques in the military services. While they squabbled, the Viet Cong flooded the countryside, gaining support from the peasants with promises of a better life or, when promises failed, applying ruthless terror to cow the villagers into submissive cooperation. Fearful for their homes, their crops, and their lives, the people have often hidden Viet Cong terrorists and have provided them with information on the movements of allied and loyal Vietnamese troops while denying comparable assistance to Americans and their allies. This has been a serious handicap.

Our troops in Vietnam do have some advantages over the Eighth Army in Korea. They are better trained and are equipped with more modern weapons. Lighter and more effective rifles, machine guns, mortars, and rockets have greatly increased their fire power, and better communications and improved techniques make close air support almost immediately available to the in-fantry. But the greatest advantage is the increased mobility pro-vided by the remarkable Army helicopters. Helicopter-borne in-fantry is the best answer yet to the Communist guerrillas, who heretofore have been able to concentrate under cover of darkness or concealment provided by the jungle, strike quickly, and then fade away before reinforcements could reach the threatened area. Thanks largely to the troop-carrying and gunfire-support helicopters and the gallant men who fly them, these Communist attacks, except the Tet offensive of 1968, have been progressively less damaging during the past two years.

A Look Forward

The principal question to come out of our limited wars in Korea and Vietnam is the effect they will have on the United States policy of containment of imperialist Communism. I deliberately use the term *imperialist* because, while the British, French, Dutch, and other European nations have been giving their colonies independence, only the Soviet Union and China have added to their satellite empires since World War II. The invasion of Czechoslovakia should have removed any doubts whether the Soviet Union would tolerate for long anything but subservience from its satellites in Eastern Europe. Once again it was demonstrated that international Communism is not a passive movement in which people may choose of their own volition whether they wish to adopt the Communist system.

There is every indication that the Soviets and the Chinese will continue to support "wars of national liberation" in the newly independent countries of the world. They will do so, as in the past, largely through indigenous troops that they have trained and equipped rather than by employing their own forces. The latter will be used only when necessary to rescue a deteriorating situation, as in Korea.

By contrast, we have had to employ great numbers of Americans far from home and sustain heavy casualties to forestall the Communist take-over of Korea and Vietnam. Consequently, there have been serious questions whether our losses are justified. Furthermore, it is characteristic of Americans to seek always for total victory, and we feel thwarted when it is not attained. Complete military victory was not achieved in Korea, though I believe firmly that we did win a definite and worthwhile victory in preventing the absorption of South Korea into the Chinese satellite empire.

This was in our national interest, and so is the safeguarding of South Vietnam, though the latter is less discernible to the American people. As the fighting there has dragged on and American casualties have mounted, our people have become disenchanted with the war and its rising cost in men, money, and materiel.

Perhaps the time has come for a re-examination of our role in world affairs. During the hundred years from the end of the War of 1812–1815 with Britain until World War I, though Britain did not consciously rule the waves for our benefit, it is true that we lived secure within the protective screen of the British Navy until marauding German submarines shocked us out of our false sense of security behind the ramparts of "Fortress America." As the British empire has contracted and British power waned, the United States has inherited Britain's leadership of the free world. We did not seek this leadership, and we have not yet accepted fully its tremendous responsibilities.

It was relatively easy for America to recognize the necessity and to accept the obligations of joining NATO, even though this action violated George Washington's admonition against "entangling alliances." Our forebears, who originally settled America, came mainly from the British Isles and Europe, bringing with them the basic concepts of our laws, our political institutions, our ideas of freedom, our very mode of life. The ties of blood and a common heritage were reinforced by trade and commercial development. It was and is clearly in our national interest to prevent Western Europe from falling under the control of imperial or Nazi Germany or of the Soviet Union. Through NATO we and our allies were able, without firing a shot, to prevent the absorption of Western Europe into the Soviet bloc.

It will be far more difficult in the future to convince the American people that it is in our national interest, and that we have some moral responsibility, to go to the aid of small nations that are threatened by Communist aggression and are not closely associated with the United States either by treaty or through geographical, historical, or vital economic interests.

In suggesting that we do have some obligation to assist weak nations threatened by Communist aggression I am not advocating that we become indiscriminately "the policeman of the world." Only when a menaced country has the whole-hearted support of its people and the will to resist to the limit of its resources should we consider an appeal for help. Even then any military participation on our part should be in conjunction with a like assistance from the United Nations or the regional neighbors of the threatened country.

At best military intervention is a stopgap measure that does not get at the root causes of the vulnerability of many countries to Communist penetration. These roots lie, first, in the indifference of the governments and wealthy ruling classes to the lot of the poverty-stricken people who constitute the mass of the population and, secondly, in the lack of financial and technical resources for developing the economic potential of the countries concerned. The first of these disabilities is difficult to overcome through outside sources, although world public opinion, education, and discreet political pressure in the form of contingent economic aid can help.

Unfortunately, our disenchantment with direct military support has extended to our programs for economic aid. Yet the second disability usually suffered by weak countries, the lack of financial and technical resources, can best be attacked through local or regional development plans, such as the Indus Basin project in India and Pakistan and the Mekong Delta plan in Southeast Asia. Without this type of help the vulnerable countries will become ever more liable to Communist subversion.

It seems to me that three things are involved in the problem of obtaining public support of our basic policy of containment of Communist aggression, if it is to be continued.

The first is to determine whether the policy is still valid. This depends on whether the threat of Communist expansion by subversion or force of arms still exists. The idea of many Europeans, that a détente with the Soviet Union had developed and lessened that threat, was shattered with the invasion of Czechoslovakia and the announced claim of the Soviets that they have the unilateral right to intervene in West Germany for the alleged purpose of suppressing a resurgence of Naziism or of reducing German influence in Eastern Europe. According to a report in the *New York*

Times of April 23, 1968, of an interview with George Kennan, the leading American authority on the Soviet Union, Kennan was quoted as saying that he had not seen any evidence of détente. Within the western hemisphere there is no sign that Castro, the Communists' Cuban ally, has abandoned his efforts to replace the governments of a number of Latin American countries with Communist régimes. And in Southeast Asia even Prince Sihanouk of Cambodia has acknowledged the continuing threat of Communist China to his country and all of Southeast Asia. There is no question in my mind that, while the immediacy of the Communist push to overthrow free governments wherever possible may fluctuate from time to time, it is still a strong and virulent menace to peace and to the American way of life.

The second essential element, if the United States is to obtain public support of any specific action we might take in the future in implementing our containment policy, is to analyze in advance the pros and cons of the contemplated action. This we did not do, at least to a sufficient extent, in the case either of Korea or of Vietnam.

We rushed into Korea with no advance planning, and we stumbled into the ground war in Vietnam with uncertain footing. In neither case did we have any fully thought-out ideas concerning our objectives or the means we would be willing to expend to attain them. As each situation arose we extemporized, unsure what the next step would be, until we were far more committed than we had expected to be. As we became more enmeshed, our public support, only lukewarm prior to Inchon in Korea and never enthusiastic since Vietnam, lessened with each setback or new commitment, until today we have widespread demands to pull out from Vietnam, almost irrespective of the consequences. There was some excuse for our precipitate action in Korea but little or none for our somewhat aimless drift into deep involvement in Vietnam. We must not let such situations develop again. We must review our commitments around the world and assess again their relative importance to our national interests and to our aim of maintaining the right of the less developed nations to determine their own fate.

The last element is the obvious one of keeping the Congress and the public informed of our objectives and, within minimal, essential security limitations, of our intentions, as specific problems arise.

Baron von Steuben, the German soldier who came to this country during the Revolutionary War to assist General Washington in organizing and training the Continental Army, quickly sensed the American trait of wanting to know the objective of any proposed action. After von Steuben had been in America only a short while, he wrote to a former comrade in the Prussian Army, explaining the nature of the American people. With remarkable perception, he said:

> In the first place the genius of this nation is not in the least to be compared with that of the Prussians, Austrians, or French. You say to your soldier, "Do this," and he doeth it. But I am obliged to say, "This is the reason why you ought to do that," and then he does it.

Americans of all walks of life still want to know the "reason why" of any proposed action and, if they find the answer reasonable, can usually be counted on for support and cooperation. This is especially true of the Congress of the United States. There may be situations arising again, as in Korea, in which the President may have to take military action under his powers as Commander in Chief, without prior consultation with the Congress and without a declaration of war. In fact, in cases of limited wars involving Communist subversion, military action without a formal declaration of war may be the rule rather than the exception in the future, by reason of the lack of a clearly recognizable enemy. But there should be no valid reason for not seeking to obtain a Senate or Joint Congressional Resolution affirming support of the action taken or proposed.

Without such congressional support, which will reflect public consensus, we should risk an exaggeration of the current mood of many Americans, particularly the young people, who tend to withdraw from involvement in world affairs except in a negative way. During the 1968 presidential campaign at least one candidate came close to saying that if he were elected there would be "no more Vietnams." It would be a sad day for America and the free-dom-loving people of the world if this attitude should ever become the official foreign policy of the United States. Such a policy would be tantamount to giving Communist China and the Union of Soviet Socialist Republics carte blanche to step up their sub-versive aggression against the poorer countries of Latin America, Asia, the Middle East, and Africa.

I do not believe this will come to pass. Despite the recent out-rageous actions of a minority of misguided students in a number of our universities, I am convinced that there is nothing basically wrong with the vast majority of the young people of America, who will be taking over the running of our country in the next few years. What they need above anything else — aside from a better example from their parents and professors — is to have more re-sponsibility placed upon them. This is attested by the magnificent performance of our young soldiers, sailors, airmen, and marines of all races, colors, and creeds in Korea and Vietnam. What they rightly demand is to know the reason for our policies and to have a part in determining what those policies should be.

BIBLIOGRAPHY

INDEX

BIBLIOGRAPHY

Acheson, Dean. *Sketches from Life.* New York: Harper and Bros., 1961.
————. *Present at the Creation.* New York: W. W. Norton, forthcoming.
American Foreign Policy, 1950–55, Vols. I and II. Department of State Document 6446, 1957.
Appleman, Roy E. *South to the Naktong, North to the Yalu, U.S. Army in Korea.* Washington, D.C.: Office of the Chief of Military History, U.S. Army, 1956.
Cagle, Malcolm W. and Manson, Frank A. *The Sea War in Korea.* Washington, D.C.: U.S. Naval Institute, 1957.
Clark, Mark Wayne. *From the Danube to the Yalu.* New York: Harper and Bros., 1954.
Dean, William F. *General Dean's Story,* as told to William Worden. New York: Viking, 1954.
Drummond and Coblenz. *Duel at the Brink.* Garden City, New York: Doubleday, 1966.
Eisenhower, Dwight D. *Mandate for Change.* Garden City, New York: Doubleday, 1965.
Field, James A. *United States Naval Operations, Korea.* Washington, D.C.: Department of the Navy, 1962.
Forrestal, James S. *The Forrestal Diaries,* edited by Walter Millis and E. F. Duffield. New York: Viking, 1951.
Futrell, Robert F. *United States Air Forces in Korea.* New York: Duell, Sloan and Pearce, 1961.
Goodrich, Leland M. *U.S. Policy in the United Nations.* New York: Council on Foreign Relations, 1956.
Gugeler, Russell A. *Combat Action in Korea.* Washington, D.C.: Combat Forces Press, 1954.
Gunther, John. *The Riddle of MacArthur.* New York: Harper and Bros., 1951.
Heinl, Robert D., Jr. *Victory at High Tide: The Inchon-Seoul Campaign.* Philadelphia: J. B. Lippincott, 1968.
Hermes, Walter G. *Truce Tent and Fighting Front, U.S. Army in the Korean War.* Washington, D.C.: Office of the Chief of Military History, U.S. Army, 1966.
Higgins, Trumbull. *Korea and the Fall of MacArthur: A Precis in Limited War.* New York: Oxford University Press, 1960.
Joy, C. Turner. *How Communists Negotiate.* New York: Macmillan, 1955.

Karig, Walter, and others. *Battle Report: War in Korea*. New York: Holt, Rinehart and Winston, 1952.

Kennan, George F. *American Diplomacy, 1900–1950*. Chicago: University of Chicago Press, 1951.

————. *Memoirs*. Boston: Little, Brown, 1967.

Kuokka, Hubard D., Montross, Lynn, and Hicks, Norman W. *U.S. Marines Operations in Korea*. Vol. IV, Historical Division, G-3, U.S.M.C. Washington, D.C.

Lichterman, Martin. *To the Yalu and Back, American Civil-Military Decisions*, edited by Harold Stein. New York: The Twentieth Century Fund, 1963.

Marshall, Samuel L. A. *Pork Chop Hill*. New York: William Morrow, 1956.

————. *The River and the Gauntlet*. New York: William Morrow, 1953.

McNamara, Robert S. *The Essence of Security*. New York: Harper & Row, 1968.

McReynolds, John A. "The Handling of Prisoners of War During the Korean Conflict," manuscript on file in the office of the Chief of Military History, Washington, D.C.

Millis, Walter. *Arms and the State: Civil-Military Elements in National Policy*. New York: The Twentieth Century Fund, 1958.

Mossman, B. C. *Ebb and Flow, U.S. Army in the Korean War*. Washington, D.C.: Office of the Chief of Military History, U.S. Army, forthcoming.

Neustadt, Richard E. *Presidential Power*. New York: John Wiley & Sons, 1969.

Osgood, R. E. *Limited War: The Challenge to American Strategy*. Chicago: University of Chicago Press, 1957.

Palmer, John McA. *Washington, Lincoln, Wilson — Three War Statesmen*. Doubleday, Doran & Co., 1930.

Phillips, Cabell. *The Truman Presidency*. New York: Macmillan, 1966.

Ridgway, Matthew B. *Soldier: The Memoirs of Matthew B. Ridgway*, as told to Harold H. Martin. New York: Harper and Bros., 1956.

————. *The Korean War*. Garden City, New York: Doubleday, 1967.

Romanov, Boris Aleksandrovitch. *Russia in Manchuria 1892–1906*, translated by Susan Wilbur Jones. New York: American Council of Learned Societies, 1952.

Rovere, Richard and Schlesinger, Arthur M. *The General and the President and the Future of American Foreign Policy*. New York: Farrar, Straus, 1951.

Sawyer, Robert K. *Military Advisors in Korea: KMAG in Peace and War*. Army Historical Series. Washington, D.C.: Office of the Chief of Military History, U.S. Army, 1962.

Schlesinger, Arthur M., Jr. *The Bitter Heritage, Vietnam and American Democracy, 1941–1966*. Boston: Houghton Mifflin, 1967.

Schnabel, James F. *Policy and Direction: The First Year, U.S. Army in the Korean War*. Washington, D.C.: Office of the Chief of Military History, U.S. Army, forthcoming.

Schilling, Warner R., Hammond, Paul Y., and Snyder, Glenn H. *Strategy,*

Politics, and Defense Budgets. New York: Columbia University Press, 1952.

Smith, Oliver P., Major General, USMC, "Log" on file with the Historical Branch, G-3, Headquarters, U.S. Marine Corps.

U.S. Congress, Senate, Committees on Foreign Relations and Armed Services, *Military Situation in the Far East: Hearings,* 66th Cong., 1st sess., 1951.

U.S. Congress, House, Subcommittee of the Committee on Appropriations. *Department of Defense Appropriations for 1951: Hearings,* 81st Cong., 2d sess., 1951.

U.S. Congress, Senate, Committee on Armed Services. *Ammunition Supplies in the Far East: Hearings,* 83d Cong., 1st sess., 1953.

U.S. Congress, House, Committee on Armed Services. *Operation SMACK: Report,* 83d Cong., 2d sess., Feb. 3, 1953.

U.S. Department of State, American Foreign Policy: Basic Documents, 1950–55. Washington, D.C., 1957.

———. The Korean Problem at the Geneva Conference, April 26–June 15, 1954. Washington, D.C., 1954.

———. The Record on Korean Unification, 1943–1960. Washington, D.C., 1960.

Whiting, Alan S. *China Crosses the Yalu: The Decision to Enter the Korean War.* New York: Macmillan, 1960.

Whitney, Courtney. *MacArthur: His Rendezvous with History.* New York: Alfred A. Knopf, 1956.

OTHER SOURCES

Records of the Department of the Army and the Department of Defense of matters with which I was personally involved during the Korean war, and the Proceedings of the Korean Military Armistice Conference which conducted the armistice negotiations. Most of these records are still classified for security reasons. For the benefit of scholars who have the requisite research clearances from the Department of Defense and the National Archives, I have filed with the National Archives in Washington, D.C., an annotated copy of my manuscript.

INDEX